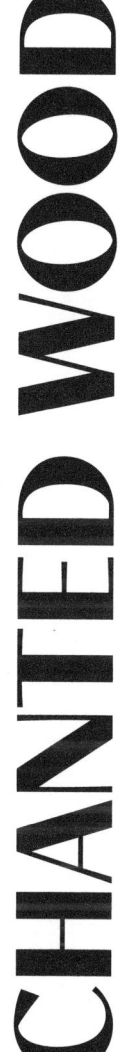

ENCHANTED WOOD

ENCHANTED WOOD

*Engraving
a Place
for Women
Artists in
Rural Britain*

**KRISTIN
BLUEMEL**

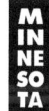

UNIVERSITY OF MINNESOTA PRESS
MINNEAPOLIS
LONDON

This work was made possible with the generous support of the Publication Grant Fund of The Leonard A. Lauder Research Center for Modern Art, The Metropolitan Museum of Art.

The University of Minnesota Press gratefully acknowledges the generous assistance provided for the publication of this book by the Margaret W. Harmon Fund.

The University of Minnesota Press gratefully acknowledges the generous assistance provided for the publication of this book by Monmouth University.

Every effort was made to obtain permission to reproduce material in this book. If any proper acknowledgment has not been included here, we encourage copyright holders to notify the publisher.

Portions of the Introduction were published in a different form in "Rural Modernity and the Wood Engraving Revival in Interwar England," *Modernist Cultures* 9, no. 2 (2014): 233–59. Portions of chapter 1 were previously published in a different form in "Windmills and Woodblocks: Agnes Miller Parker, Wood Engraving, and the Popular Press in Interwar Britain," in *Rural Modernity in Britain: A Critical Intervention*, ed. Kristin Bluemel and Michael McCluskey, 84–102 (Edinburgh University Press, 2018). Chapter 2 was previously published in a different form as "'A Happy Heritage': Children's Poetry Books and the Twentieth-Century Wood Engraving Revival," *The Lion and the Unicorn* 37, no. 3 (2013): 207–37. Portions of chapter 3 were previously published in a different form in "Clare Leighton and the Fine Art of Mass Reproduction," a blog post for *R.A.W.—Rediscovering Art by Women*, February 10, 2023, https://r-a-w.net/blog/clare-leighton-and-the-fine-art-of-mass-reproduction/; and in "Spades and Gravers: Clare Leighton, Victor Gollancz, and the Radical Countryside," in "Gardens in the Gorse: Rural Britain's Modernist Cultures," ed. Kristin Bluemel, special issue of *Modernist Cultures* 19, no. 1 (2024): 81–104. Chapter 4 was published in a different form as "The Saltire Chapbooks, Twentieth-Century Wood Engraving and 'A Vast New Public of Readers,'" *Journal of the Edinburgh Bibliography Society* 10 (2015): 158–82.

Published by the University of Minnesota Press
111 Third Avenue South, Suite 290
Minneapolis, MN 55401-2520
http://www.upress.umn.edu

ISBN 978-1-5179-1476-9 (hc)
ISBN 978-1-5179-1477-6 (pb)

A Cataloging-in-Publication record for this book is available from the Library of Congress.

Printed in the United States of America on acid-free paper

The University of Minnesota is an equal-opportunity educator and employer.

34 33 32 31 30 29 28 27 26 25   10 9 8 7 6 5 4 3 2 1

To George, Helen, and Vera Witte
and Caroline Coode

CONTENTS

Introduction

Enchanted Wood, Enchanting Words

Once upon a time, in that most magical time of all, witches and sorceresses roamed the back roads and byways of Britain, and those unfortunates who came under their power were enchanted—bewitched—to helplessness by their words and wands. In our more skeptical age, these old meanings have yielded to the figurative notions that are at play in *Enchanted Wood,* feelings of being delighted, charmed, or fascinated by something or someone. Yet even now, if the someone is a woman, the enchantment is presumed to be a sexual one; those old fears of crones and witches do not lie too far beneath the modern equivalences of enchantment with seduction and temptation (Figure 1.1).[1]

In this feminist study of women artists, rural Britain, and the twentieth-century wood engraving revival, literal and figurative enchantment are invoked in an investigation of a special kind of delightful, charming, fascinating picture, an image reproduced in reverse when an engraved and inked wooden block is pressed onto a sheet of paper. Xylography is the proper name for this art, with experts distinguishing between woodcuts, which are made with a knife carving along the grain of a soft plank of wood, and wood engravings, the subject of this study, which are made with steel engraving tools working upon the end grain of a small hardwood block.[2] In this form of relief printing, the images produced by impressing engraved and inked wood blocks upon paper typically appear as white lines shining through black ink, creating tones of gray and silver through illusions of line and light.[3] The women artists who created the wood engravings discussed and reproduced in this volume—Gwen Raverat (1885–1957),

1

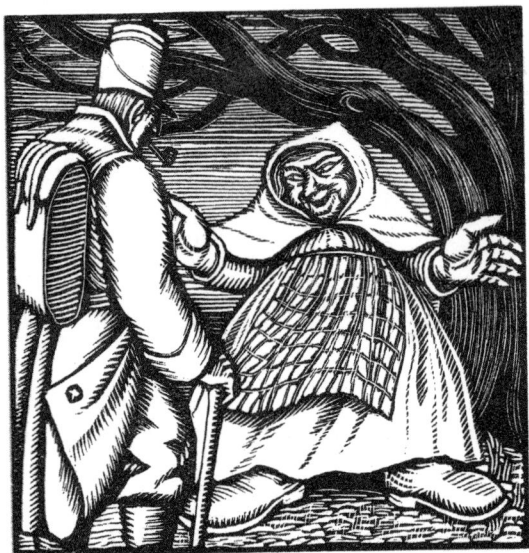

FIGURE I.1 The first and most memorable of the enchantresses reproduced in this study is Gwen Raverat's wood engraving of the witch "pointing to a tree nearby." From "The Tinder Box," in *Four Tales from Hans Andersen* (Cambridge: Cambridge University Press, 1935), 3. 2¹³⁄₁₆ × 2¹³⁄₁₆ inches. Copyright 2025 Estate of Gwen Raverat. All rights reserved. DACS/Artists Rights Society (ARS).

Agnes Miller Parker (1895–1980), Clare Leighton (1898–1989), and Joan Hassall (1906–1988)—intended these images to serve as illustrations for books of prose or poetry. They envisioned their engravings reproduced thousands of times on pages marked by lines of text, to be bound up and sold as books for children and adults who were to be delighted or charmed by their forms. In their predilection for realistic scenes of country life, as in their adoption of white-line wood engraving technique, they turned aside from the decorative wood engraving tradition associated with the nineteenth-century fine presses and popularized most successfully in Victorian Britain by William Morris, choosing instead the path laid down one hundred years earlier by the roughhewn, hardworking North Country artist, naturalist, and print innovator Thomas Bewick.[4] Like Bewick, these women engravers loved the countryside and strove to abstract its scenes into lines on wood, and like him they yearned to see these scenes printed in narratives that common readers and ordinary children could encounter in books meant for kitchen tables and window seats, not rare book rooms or collectors' libraries. Two of these women engravers, Raverat and Hassall, wrote about how Bewick exerted an immediate impact, a powerful magic, over their imaginations and artistic ambitions; all four engravers examined here testify through their art

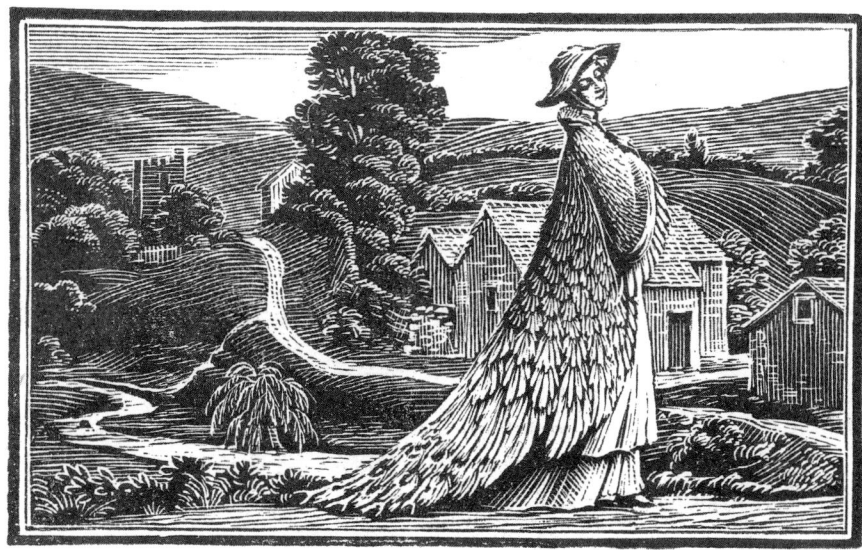

to the more ordinary magic of technical and stylistic influence that Bewick bequeathed to their wood engravings and the twentieth-century illustrated book trade (Figure I.2).[5]

Wood may be said to be enchanted when it is transformed from a natural substance into a three-dimensional art through the trained vision and laboring hand of the artist-engraver. This is of course a figural enchantment, but literal enchantments of wood should reverberate in this study's attention to popular works of fable, fairy tale, romance, and fancy that insist on the real magic of wood and woods in the Western literary tradition, from the ancient landscapes of Baba Yaga in her hut on chicken legs to the wicked witch in her gingerbread house to J. R. R. Tolkien's marching Ents and Harry Potter's wand of holly wood. In this book, the accumulated meanings and places of enchanted wood in legend and literature are associated with the prosaic materials and social relations of modern literary culture, from

FIGURE I.2   Joan Hassall, Thomas Bewick's most devoted acolyte among the four women wood engravers featured in this book, enchanted readers of all ages with this extraordinary little wood engraving of the moment "the fairy cam again, and telt her to put on the coat o' feathers o' a' the birds of the air, an' gang to the kirk." From *Rashie Coat,* Saltire Chapbook No. 12 (Edinburgh: Saltire Society, 1951), 6. 2⅞ × 1⅝ inches. Reproduced by permission of the Estate of Joan Hassall/ Simon Lawrence.

editors' and publishers' offices in London, Cambridge, Oxford, and Edinburgh to the quiet rural places of observation and residence that formed the subjects of so many of the books illustrated by Raverat, Miller Parker, Leighton, and Hassall. These women's stories and the story of their contributions to wood engraving and book publishing have been told before, most often by art and print historians, occasionally by biographers, sometimes by the wood engravers themselves.[6] However, the stories of these four women have not been told as a feminist story of collective literary and cultural achievement that touches upon the concerns of experts in diverse fields that lie immediately outside art and print history. Here, Raverat, Miller Parker, Leighton, and Hassall, their wood engravings, and the books in which their wood engravings appear are presented for the first time as important cultural figures and forms for scholars working in fields of twentieth-century literature, children's literature, modernist and middlebrow studies, and rural history and geography, in addition to those who might already be familiar with them through their studies in art, book, and print history (Figure 1.3).[7]

Recognizing Raverat's, Miller Parker's, Leighton's, and Hassall's contributions to early twentieth-century book and literary culture as the stuff of modern history, the materials of a modern story, this study pursues a claim made by print historian and wood engraving authority Joanna Selborne:

> As a rediscovered medium wood-engraving [of the 1920s and 1930s] was highly experimental. . . . The medium *itself* was the message; the engravers' understanding of the inherent aesthetic qualities peculiar to wood determined their modernness, not necessarily the images *per se*.[8]

Adopting Selborne's media-based definition of the experimental "modernness" of twentieth-century wood engraving, *Enchanted Wood* aims to engage readers in technical details of the medium in order to illuminate its meaning for literary, cultural, and historical scholars who care about British books. These details, and the beautiful black-and-white, often miniature forms they compose, explain how a group of women artists achieved unprecedented critical success in the field of book illustration and how their art and success led to their thoroughly modern, independent lives as professional women in conditions of depression and world war. This study maintains that only a woman born around the beginning of the

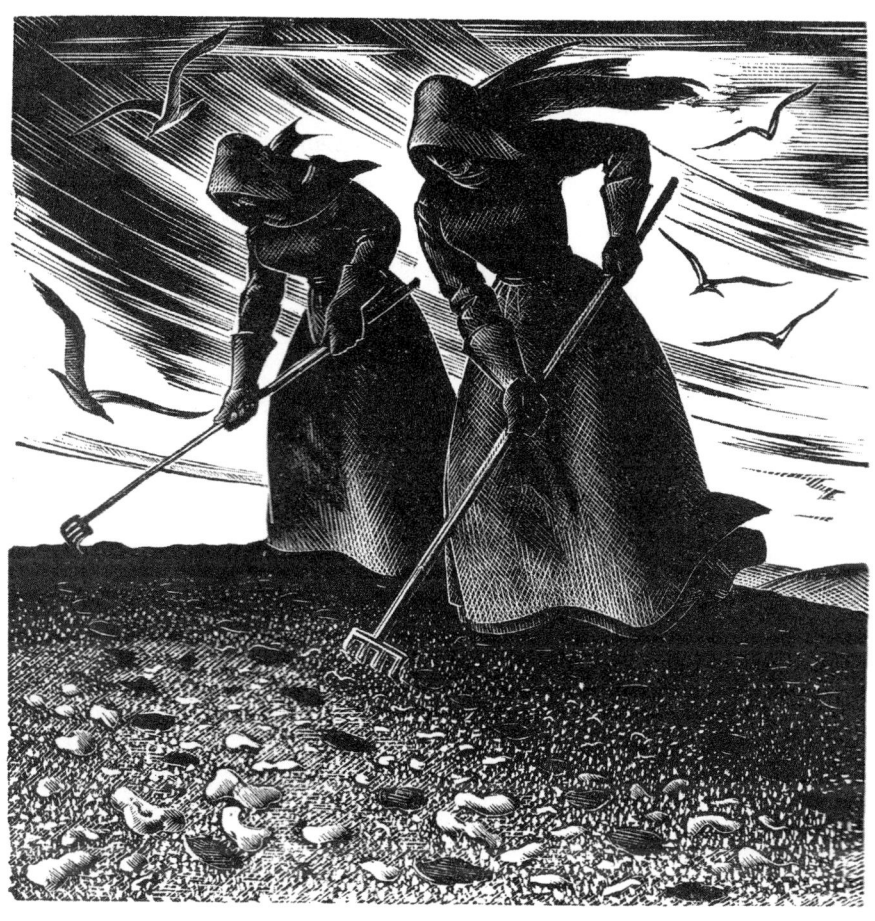

FIGURE 1.3 Agnes Miller Parker's story is probably the least well known of the four women wood engravers studied here. Her illustration of Thomas Hardy's "pure woman," Tess, in Hessian "wropper" (a sleeved brown pinafore) "hacking" in the hundred-acre swede field of Flintcomb-Ash farm, is too beautiful to reside in the archives. From Thomas Hardy, *Tess of the D'Urbervilles* (New York: Limited Editions Club, 1956), 320. 3¾ × 3¾ inches. Reproduced by permission of the Estate of Agnes Miller Parker.

twentieth century, with access to arts education, the ability to put that education to use in the literary marketplace, and the freedom to travel wherever her art and interest demanded, could assume the heroic persona of "the female Bewick." No longer confined to the traditional role of artful woman as object, fascinating viewers through male artists' representations of her sexual performance or display, these modern-day enchantresses helped transform British books, literature, and culture by delighting readers of all sexes and ages with the work of their hands, the ink traces of their authoritative acts of engraving pictures on wood.[9]

This book argues that the allegiance of these female Bewicks to the materials and techniques of an old-fashioned illustrative art popularized in books of the late eighteenth century, coupled with their apparent lack of attention to contemporary artistic trends and coteries, was instrumental to their collective success as book illustrators. In the same years that modernist writers and artists were redefining Victorian and Edwardian aesthetic conventions and cultural expectations, Raverat, Miller Parker, Leighton, and Hassall turned away from avant-garde movements recognized as modernist, providing British readers with alternative genres and media for understanding the challenges, comforts, and contradictions of modernity.[10] They also provide feminist scholars with alternative models of twentieth-century women's artistic and literary achievement.[11] Like others of their generation, they suffered terrible losses of friends, family, and security during a period defined by two world wars.[12] However, as middle-class women they thrived, confronting personal necessity while pursuing professional opportunities that few British women of any class had ever before encountered.[13] This study assumes that their stories are more powerful and more meaningful when joined together and told as one, as it is in this arrangement that we can see patterns emerging around gender, age, marriage, and motherhood that might otherwise appear ancillary to the wood engravers' efforts to make beautiful images for quiet books in times of deprivation, darkness, and death. As book illustrators who cared about the whole process of bookmaking and book reading, from the subjects they illustrated to the multiplying relations and meanings of pictures and words of the books in which those subjects appeared, Raverat, Miller Parker, Leighton, and Hassall emerge here as important literary characters fully engaged with their modern worlds, representing larger social and cultural movements to redraw the boundaries of women's living.[14] It

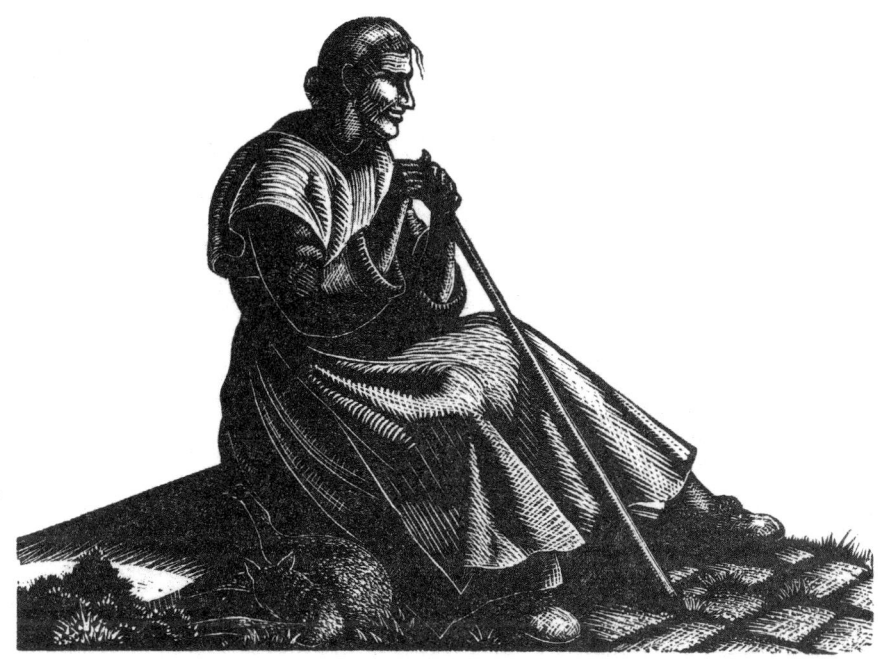

is the challenge of this book to reveal how and why wood engraving facilitated this transformation in women's living in rural and urban places, and why women wood engravers who took up the materials and techniques used by Bewick and his male descendants were able to achieve professional stature, public affirmation, and personal independence. They formed no collaborative workshop or feminist community, they did not study with the same teachers or develop the same style, and they were not all working self-consciously or deliberately in Bewick's tradition. Rather, in adopting and adapting Bewick's techniques and rural subjects, they took up his role as the people's wood engravers, heroically shaping their modern women's lives according to their separate visions of beauty and their unique interpretations of its ideal forms (Figure 1.4).

FIGURE 1.4 Clare Leighton, an artist, writer, teacher, and traveler who forged a life on two continents as a single professional woman, looks back at *The Village Witch,* Bessie Domoney, "old, bent, wizened and ugly." From Clare Leighton, *Country Matters* (London: Gollancz, 1937), 25. 3⁹⁄₁₆ × 2⁹⁄₁₆ inches. Copyright 2025 Estate of Clare Leighton. All rights reserved. DACS/ Artists Rights Society (ARS).

CONJURING MRS. BEWICK

In 1952 Gwen Raverat published *Period Piece*, a memoir of her Cambridge childhood as the granddaughter of Charles Darwin and daughter of the astronomer Sir George Darwin and the American Philadelphia belle Maud Du Puy. It enchanted critics and common readers alike, and has remained continuously in print for over seventy years. Upon first publication, the *Times Literary Supplement* reviewer described it as "delightful" and "endearing"; Rose Macaulay, also writing in the *TLS*, described it as "practically perfect."[15] Nowadays, Faber and Faber's cover copy describes *Period Piece* as a "classic," although Raverat in her day described her memoir in more modest terms as "a circular book," writing in her preface:

> It does not begin at the beginning and go on to the end; it is all going on at the same time, sticking out like the spokes of a wheel from the hub, which is me. So it does not matter which chapter is read first or last.

The best illustration in *Period Piece* of Raverat's remembered self as a revolving center with spokes sticking out is an image from the chapter titled "Education." Captioned *The Génie. Of course this is not what school was really like, but it is what it felt like to me* (71), it depicts the awkward, bespectacled, miserable sixteen-year-old Gwen Darwin surrounded by schoolgirls whose nickname for her, "The Génie," hurt her deeply (Figure 1.5).

The most important thing to note about this picture is not its gentle self-mockery or even its communication of the adolescent Gwen's acute alienation from her peers. Rather, it is the fact that it is an ink drawing, not a wood engraving. Raverat began writing and illustrating *Period Piece* after she had suffered a stroke and could no longer endure the rigors of engraving the hard end grain of the boxwood blocks that functioned as the material basis of her art. As a cartoon, this illustration, like all the others in *Period Piece*, cannot represent the medium that Selborne tells us is the message of interwar wood engraving nor the subject of this book. Instead, it operates on another narrative level, one that is familiar to critics of children's books like *Doctor Dolittle* (1920) or *Mary Poppins* (1934), in which visual line and verbal caption work together to extend and

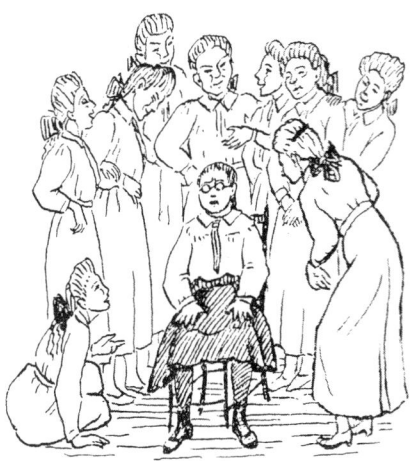

The Génie. Of course this is not what school was really like,
but it is what it felt like to me.

FIGURE I.5 Gwen Raverat's pen-and-
ink doodle of herself, *The Génie*, a
perfect rendering of adolescent misery.
From Gwen Raverat, *Period Piece*
(London: Faber and Faber, 1952), 71.
2¼ × 2⅜ inches. Copyright 2025 Estate
of Gwen Raverat. All rights reserved.
DACS/Artists Rights Society (ARS).

change the feeling and humor of the surrounding narrative. Read in a circular
fashion, whether before or after chapters titled "Ladies," "Propriety," "Religion,"
or "Clothes," *Period Piece*'s cartoon of "The Génie" translates into social terms the
mathematical idea that a center is always at angles and odds with its spokes, separate from the thing to which it gives shape.

Looking back on her younger self, Raverat reflects that "The Génie" was "a
hybrid term, neither The Genius, nor yet *le Génie*" (72). Ostensibly assigned by
the schoolgirls to the newcomer Darwin because she had been "put into rather
high classes on her first arrival," it was actually chosen "because they thought
me queer" (72). One was queer if, as a girl in a small private boarding school at
the turn of the twentieth century, one was "interested in anything whatever except horses, or things like hat-pin-knobbing; or, of course, games or gossip" (71).
It might have been a new and modern century, but its upper-middle-class girls
were still gripped by Victorian norms of feminine beauty and idiocy.

If we choose to follow Raverat's instructions, reading *Period Piece* in a queer
and circular way, neglecting its first chapters in order to start with her description of "The Génie," we understand that the quality that most obviously marked
her out as different, the quality that defined her girlish queerness, was her com-
pulsion to draw "everything [she] saw" (64). Raverat dispassionately describes

the drawings that filled her youthful sketchbooks as "bad," interpreting her failure as a consequence of trying to copy reality, her conformity to the contemporary notion that "pictures ought to be photographically like reality" (64). It took her "a long time to find . . . out for [herself]" that "drawing is not copying" (64), but in the meantime she took hope from imaginings or visions that, while not approaching anything as elevated as genius, could in retrospect be seen as evidence of a simultaneously painful and saving difference, an unladylike "keenness" strong enough to defy the constraints of stultifying convention and inherited gendered fashions:

> Every now and then I would suddenly see a picture in my head—usually a vision of a landscape, not a remembered scene—and when I drew it, I did realize that it turned out better than the landscapes I copied so laboriously from nature. But I did not realize why this was. I am sure that no one would have picked me out from the [drawing] class as a promising artist; . . . there was nothing to notice about me, except my keenness. (64)

The keenness that Raverat recalls as the only sign of her artistic promise is another form of the passion she records several chapters (or spokes) later when describing her life-changing discovery of Thomas Bewick.[16] This story is told in a chapter titled "Aunt Etty" in honor of her father's elder sister Henrietta. We learn from the first sentences of the chapter that Aunt Etty was "most emphatically" a Lady, a person who did not do things for herself. Only one generation older than Raverat, this adored and doting female relative could say at age eighty-six that "she had never made a pot of tea in her life; and that she had never in all her days been out in the dark alone, not even in a cab" (119). This is a vivid, almost surreal reminder of the gendered and classed privileges that imposed nearly immovable constraints upon the bodies and imaginations of upper-middle-class Victorian girls, constraints that they were urged to copy through their elders' loving examples and their peers' vindictive social policing. Raverat's description of Aunt Etty's queenly captivity at 31 Kensington Square, London, emphasizes the virtual impossibility for girls of her generation to imagine themselves as great artists. Lying on Aunt Etty's sofa amid Morris wallpapers and peacock-blue serge curtains, the young Gwen finds herself enraptured, enchanted, by Bewick's vignettes,

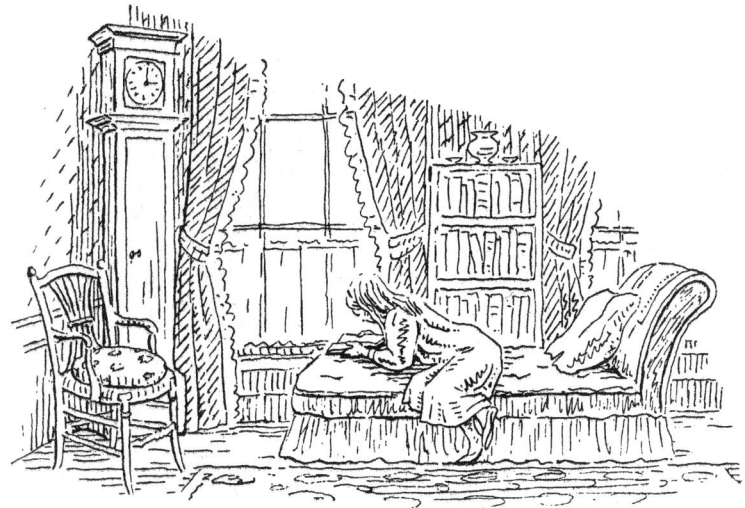

Mrs. Bewick.

wishing "passionately" that she could have been "Mrs. Bewick" (Figure I.6):[17]

> Surely, I thought, if I cooked his roast beef beautifully and mended his clothes and minded the children— surely he would, just sometimes, let me draw and engrave a little tailpiece for him. I wouldn't want to be known, I wouldn't sign it. Only just to be allowed to invent a little picture sometimes. O happy, happy Mrs. Bewick! thought I, as I kicked my heels on the blue sofa. (129)

FIGURE I.6 Gwen Raverat's pen-and-ink rendering of herself as Mrs. Bewick, lounging on Aunt Etty's blue sofa at 31 Kensington Square, London. From Gwen Raverat, *Period Piece* (London: Faber and Faber, 1952), 128. 4 × 2⁹⁄₁₆ inches. Copyright 2025 Estate of Gwen Raverat. All rights reserved. DACS/Artists Rights Society (ARS).

The most important word in this tender, funny passage is "allowed," Raverat's only half tongue-in-cheek acknowledgment that someone else would determine even the fortunate and humble Mrs. Bewick's access to block and scorper. As the wife of a working man, Mrs. Bewick was no Lady and certainly had more freedom than Aunt Etty to move in the dark or fix herself tea, yet her daylight hours inevitably were dominated by women's work. This vision of housework

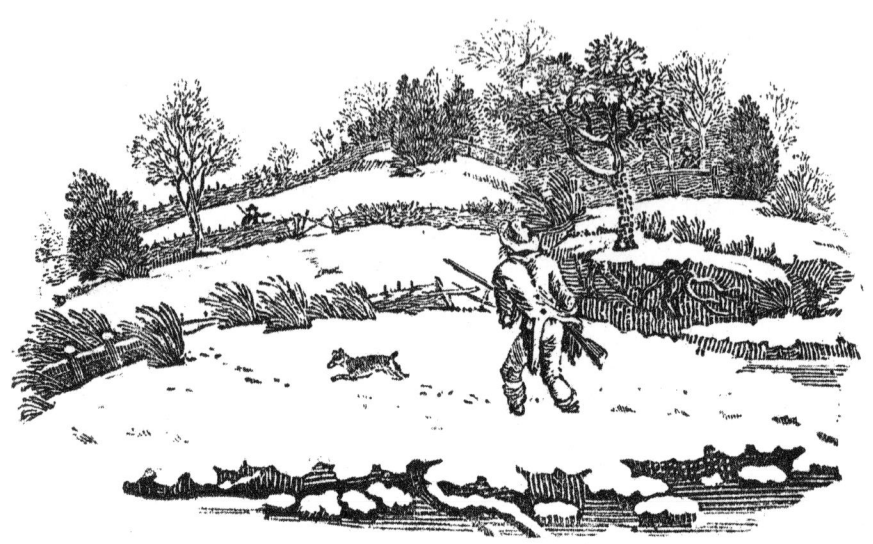

and dependence is the height of artistic ambition for the young Gwen. To imagine herself as Mrs. Rembrandt "seemed too tremendous even to imagine" (129); more tremendous altogether is the fantasy of being a boy, any boy, and thus able to grow into a man and painter. This desire, what Gwen Darwin wanted "more than anything in the world," was so deeply, essentially, despairingly impossible "that I did not dare to think about it at all" (129). Instead, she projects her impassioned response to Bewick's

FIGURE I.7 Which of Bewick's miniature rural scenes inspired Gwen Darwin's impassioned desire to "draw and engrave a little tailpiece"? Thomas Bewick, wood engraved tailpiece of hunter and hounds. Who is that waiting at the gate? From Thomas Bewick, *A History of British Birds*, vol. 1, *Land Birds* (1797, 1826), 72. 3⅛ ×1¾ inches.

art and her similarly impassioned identification with Bewick's masculine space in art history onto an imaginary Mrs. Bewick. Readers, delighted by the doodle of the restless, desiring Gwen on the blue sofa, may discount the second Mrs. Bewick, conjured by Raverat's words. This feminine figure, surrounded by her tasty beef, scoured saucepans, thread, needle, and children, pays with housewifely labor for her privilege to "only just . . . be allowed" to draw and engrave a little picture—a little picture that *Period Piece* cannot represent (Figure I.7). These are the visual-verbal conundrums of a modern woman's "classic," one that documents comic desire and domestic tragedy: the ordinary, everyday tragedy of artistic women's reduction to happy, happy anonymity.[18] Raverat reminds us that this status awaited most woman artists working in Bewick's day and virtually any day prior to that on which she and her female contemporaries decided to pick up the engraver's tools and give themselves permission to draw and engrave "a little picture."

We embrace Raverat as Mrs. Bewick, married with children, and as the adolescent and awkward "The Génie." These characters are endearing, enchanting abstractions in patterns of dark and light of the artist as an outsider woman among men or outsider girl among girls, both set apart from their social worlds and gendered destinies. Raverat does not here, nor elsewhere in *Period Piece* or in this book, represent the mainstream of anything—not the mainstream of art history, book illustration, children's literature, or modernism. Rather, she is the paradoxically eccentric center, the outsider who teaches us differently about the insider's world of British literary and book culture. That Raverat was aware of and even terrified by this difference from the youngest age is apparent from a memory recorded at the end of the *Period Piece* chapter titled "Propriety." Describing an epiphanic moment formative of her character and identity, Raverat says it "has nothing to do with the rest of this chapter," although it is associated in her memory with the Victorian courtships whose propriety she guaranteed as a child chaperone (Figure 1.8).

At age six, "it" happened, Raverat's first experience of the "terrifying and lonely" conviction, felt with the intensity of an otherworldly visitation, that "seemed to point to the contrast between ME and all those other friendly people" (118). She describes how she had walked away from older adults, ladies and gentlemen, sitting comfortably and flirtatiously on the Little Island amid the Cam to the familiar interior comforts of the night nursery of Newnham Grange. Looking out of the big end window, catching glimpses of sunshine on the dresses of the ladies, hearing the voices of the men "in a pattern of light and dark," she was suddenly aware of rain falling down upon the sunny scene:

> Not much, but a few big drops falling splash, splash, on the green lilac leaves. And suddenly the world stood still. It simply stopped, and I was quiet alone and *outside*. I did not belong, I was separate, just looking on; *outside*. (117)

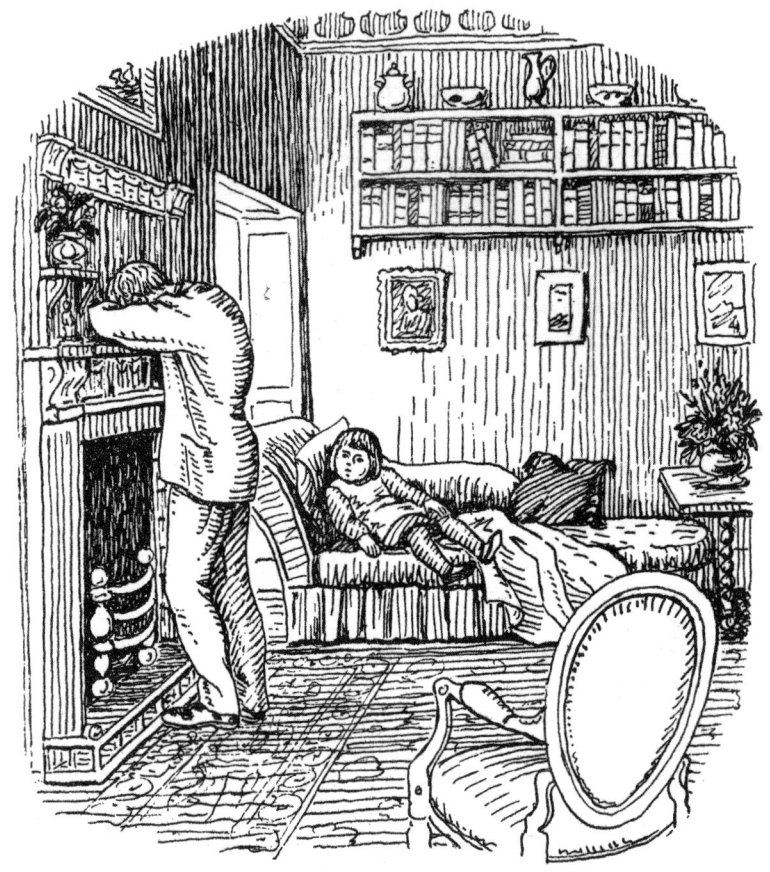

Love. How ridiculous.

Although she is inside the nursery, watching and waiting for the remote, mysterious knowledge and sexual self-consciousness of those elegant others outside, she is transported to a position outside everything, all time, all society, all humanity. This feeling of separation for one so young and the remembering of its significance by one so old is at once unique to Raverat and representative of the group of women wood engravers examined in *Enchanted Wood*. Raverat's, Miller Parker's, Leighton's, and Hassall's outsiderness, their eccentricity and that of their art, is in large part the source of our interest in them, of our enchantment by them. Paradoxically, it is also the source of their collective claim to a position at the center of this book.

THE 1930S WOOD ENGRAVING REVIVAL

Women constituted a significant portion of those active in the British wood engraving revival of the 1920s and 1930s in part because, even as members of an undereducated, underfunded class, they could afford to enter the field, which required little capital investment.[19] Tools, sandbag, ink, water-filled globe, and wood blocks were within the means of most practitioners, professional instruction was optional, and the work could be done in small domestic spaces. In her 1932 book for The Studio's How to Do It series, *Wood-Engraving and Woodcuts*, Leighton attributes the "enormous rush of wood-engravings produced nowadays" to two factors: improved education and reduced incomes. More widespread and better education had created "a vast new public of readers," but this public, embracing a "widening of the circle of good taste," was "not wealthy" (94).[20] Leighton reassures her tasteful, cash-strapped readers:

> Fortunately, the boxwood block, unlike the copper plate, will yield an almost indefinite number of perfect prints. A large edition of a wood-engraving at a low price is therefore the ideal thing to satisfy the modern public in the modern home. (94)

The modest art of wood engraving that Leighton recommends for the modern home was at its cheapest and most accessible in mass-produced illustrated books like her own popular volumes of the mid-1930s published by Victor Gollancz. The sheer number of books on wood engraving in the interwar period, with their reproductions of country scenes, rural workers, and minutely realized studies of Britain's flora and fauna, gesture toward the cultural phenomenon of the interwar cult of the countryside that was inflamed by what historian John Lowerson refers to as a "flood" or "powerful current of 'countryside literature.'"[21] Malcolm Chase asserts that "the opening-up of the publishing market mirrored the opening-up of the countryside itself," while Howard Newby blames a "plethora" of books, pamphlets, and magazines for creating a rural population that enjoyed the countryside as a "cultural and aesthetic matter" rather than through direct personal experience.[22] Lowerson, Chase, and Newby are joined by more contemporary historians Alun Howkins, Paul Brassley, Jeremy Burchardt, Lynne Thompson, and Trevor Wild in documenting the ways a post–World War I "rash of books, pamphlets and articles" on England's rural spaces and conditions persuaded British readers of all classes and regional affiliations to endorse Sir Stanley Baldwin's sentiment that "England is the country, and the country is England."[23] The prime minister first articulated this simple and powerful idea, with its reduction of nation, heritage, and patriotism to images of "wild anemones in the woods in April, the last load at night being drawn down a lane as the twilight comes on," in a 1924 speech to the Royal Society of St. George.[24] By 1926, when Baldwin's speech was published as a book and circulated throughout the country, "there [could] be no doubt that culturally the countryside had become absolutely central."[25]

The 1930s wood engraving revival had as one of its roots the English countryside fantasy that Baldwin so poignantly described. Yet once labeled as such, this revival was tainted, as all revivals are, by its proximity to death and corruption, to the idea that something that has approached the end of its natural life or relevance has been brought back to a presumably brief life through some extraordinary intervention.[26] Georgina Boyes, for example, argues that the turn-of-the-century English folk music revival signaled a "fundamental change" in English national character, a turn toward a newly imagined consensus around rural, nostalgic, antimodernist, and conservative values.[27] Contributing to what became known as the Englishness thesis, Boyes contends that such rural-nostalgic values were adopted by the dominant classes "in order to tame or thwart the tendencies of their day toward modernism, urbanism and democracy."[28] Englishness critic Peter Mandler agrees with Boyes and the "Englishness" scholars that after World War I, "a much larger social constituency now discovered the England of the Arts and Crafts movement," but he emphasizes that "the countryside became a playground and an imaginative space in which urban society could reconstruct itself *on new lines.*"[29]

Enchanted Wood inserts itself into the breach between Mandler and "Englishness" scholars such as Boyes because its rural subjects invite study and endorsement by an "Englishness" school of cultural scholars, while its debts to metropolitan communities of publishers and readers and industrialized processes of reproduction place it within the orbit of modernizing forces that the "Englishness" thesis opposes. Seen within these material, social, and economic contexts, the "new lines" of the wood engraved illustrations and books by Raverat, Miller Parker, Leighton, and Hassall resist the idea of a 1930s wood engraving revival in part because wood engraving as an autonomous art extended well beyond the 1930s and in part because of the dangers of dualism latent within the "Janus-faced concept of revival itself."[30] While adopting for the sake of convention the pithy term "wood engraving revival," this book argues that the wood engravings of Raverat, Miller Parker, Leighton, and Hassall are not attempts to return to the past and reincorporate that past in contemporary living culture, but rather are dynamically, beautifully, and simultaneously rural and modern arts. Wood engraved books about rural life could satisfy conservative nationalist pastoralists like Prime Minister Baldwin, but they could also satisfy people whose enthusiasm for the countryside was "unrelated to pre-war romanticism and, in fact, not very nostalgic."[31]

THE CULT OF THE COUNTRYSIDE

Writers and artists circulated ideas about and images of an ideal or disappearing rural modernity that differed from those of the late Victorians who hearkened to John Ruskin's warning that English art was threatened by young artists' attraction to European and Asiatic influences.[32] The founding of the Slade in 1871 was an expression of an imperial cultural crisis manifesting as "anxieties about the Englishness of English art and the reshaping of art institutions," both of which "were inextricably bound together by the late 1880s."[33] By the 1920s and 1930s, poets, writers, and artists trained in these art institutions, dismayed by the emergencies of urban modernity and a very different kind of looming European-Asiatic threat, turned from city scenes to the countryside for solutions to and relief from industrial and metropolitan problems.[34] Writers and editors, with able contributions from illustrators and photographers, exhorted members of the new reading public to head out into the countryside, if not to a villa, then to a garden suburb or weekend retreat.[35] The working classes were encouraged

to retire to vast new rural developments like Peacehaven, while the more afflu-
ent were encouraged to take up hiking, cycling, golf, and tennis—all were seen
as rejuvenating individuals and, implicitly, "the" race.[36] But it was not primarily rural people who needed to seek out these countryside activities. Those who,
like farmer-writer A. G. Street, had survived the crises of agriculture brought
on by new patterns of global imports were getting plenty of exercise attending
to their cows.[37] The people described by historians and sociologists as resettling
the country lands in the interwar years were urban workers leaving the cities.
Whether clerks, councillors, or their wives, these new rural residents might have
wielded a trowel, but they did not follow the plow. However, they were very interested in reading about those who did.[38] Lowerson describes their reading as
having no uniform "direction, structure or quality," and as often "submerged
in a lowest common denominator of popular books" that "fostered a bitty and
soft-centred approach to rural life, as distinct from living."[39] Echoing in feeling
and reason a literary distaste that Virginia Woolf and other interwar defenders
of literature for elites associated with the middlebrow, Lowerson's language suggests why the work of the period's white-line women wood engravers occupies an
ambiguous position within studies of a national literary and arts culture.[40] On
the one hand, the women wood engravers' metropolitan training in their nation's
finest art schools represents the privilege of well-connected, well-educated families. Unlike working-class youth and many rural middle-class girls, these women
could take advantage of expanding opportunities for women's professionalism in
urban arts institutions founded or shaped by Victorian crises of national identity. To this extent, they were culturally and economically central, allied, as
Raverat was socially, with cosmopolitan intellectual and artistic elites. On the
other hand, their "reduction" to commercial printing, their willing "submission"
of their wood engravings to the constraints of literary texts and technologies of
book illustration, appears to diminish their claim to modernist stature in histories of modern art and modernist literature. Too low or commercial to earn
treatment as elite modernists, they were at least high enough in stature to avoid
association with any "debased school of photographic landscape pictorialism,"
which Lowerson and other historians of rural Britain associate with problematic
"surface images" that denied the "hardness of agricultural economics."[41]

The origins of wood engraving in the end grain of wood blocks ensures encounters with "hardness" and guarantees the reader's contemplation of depth

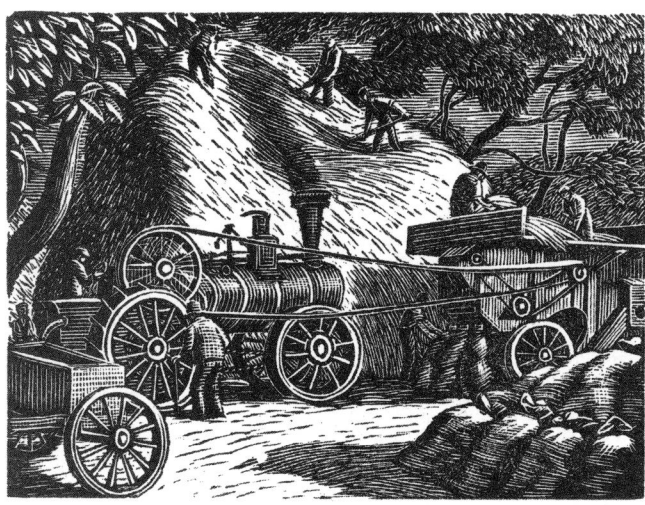

relations carved out between artist and wood, wood and paper, paper and pressmen, pressmen and publishers, publishers and writers, writers and artists. Depending on the interaction of visual and verbal media within books illustrated with wood engravings, the depth relations of the medium may indeed illuminate the depth relations of contemporary agricultural economics as they always also illuminate the economics of contemporary publishing and art production (Figure I.9).

Among the wood engravers examined in this volume, Leighton was the most explicit about her leftist politics and socialist sympathies; no one who has viewed her pictures of flowers and reapers in relation to their surrounding texts or biographical

FIGURE I.9 We can easily find invitation to trace depth relations of contemporary agricultural economics in a wood engraved headpiece or "decoration" by Gwen Raverat. This one illustrates the agricultural laborer, "very capable with machinery," during the pre–World War I "spacious days" of English tenant farming. From A. G. Street's memoir, *Farmer's Glory,* 1934 (London: Faber and Faber, 1956), 67. 3½ × 2½ inches. Copyright 2025 Estate of Gwen Raverat. All rights reserved. DACS/Artists Rights Society (ARS).

and publishing contexts would assume that their natural, rural subject matter communicates the notorious conservativism of magazines such as *Country Life* and *Yorkshire Dalesman,* let alone the Green Fascism of a Henry Williamson.[42] Leighton's example should serve as a caution to readers about judging on the basis of rural subject or traditional medium the political, ideological impacts of any wood engraver's country scenes reproduced in imaginative literary texts. Literary scholars do not assume that the politics of classic novels by Jane Austen, the Brontës, and Thomas Hardy align simply because the books share village or rural contents, and we should not assume that these novels share a uniform politics once they are published with wood engravings by women artists working in Bewick's tradition.[43] Analysis of children's and middlebrow books illustrated with wood engravings asserts the larger point that wood engraving brings no inherent stability to readers nostalgic for a golden age of lost time or place. The value of these books as advertisement for any one political or ideological view on the countryside, on nature, or on a nation fixated in the interwar period on both collapses upon careful examination of all the forms and processes that make up a book and all those that make it available for reification in our criticism and histories as art or literature.

Feminist art and literary historical interpretive approaches reveal ambiguous progressive intents and effects of illustrated and middlebrow books and the implicitly sexist values that make both seem "easy" or "soft," well suited to women readers and teenage girls.[44] These could be the same readers who, with the encouragement of Leighton's How to Do It manual, might take up scorper and burin and attempt their own wood engraved kitchen art (Figure 1.10). Their methods would be virtually the same as Bewick's, right up to the moment of printing. First, they would draft on paper the image they wanted to engrave. Then they would draw that image in reverse on paper. Next, they would transfer that reversed design to the wood block, typically by blackening the back of the paper and pressing the lines through. Only then would they use their steel engraving tools to carve in three dimensions the incisions that would eventually appear as two-dimensional white-line pictures after they had inked the block, laid it on paper, and pressed both paper and wood with the back of a spoon. Even for those few women who chose to become professional wood engravers, there was only one way to earn a living by the art, and that was, in the words of James Hamilton, "by mixing book illustration with commercial work for advertising and, ironically enough, as a teacher of wood engraving."[45] That particular modern and modernist irony is latent within the numerous wood engraving guidebooks and instruction manuals published in the early twentieth century. Thomas Balston could list in his *English Wood-Engraving 1900–1950* twenty-two studies

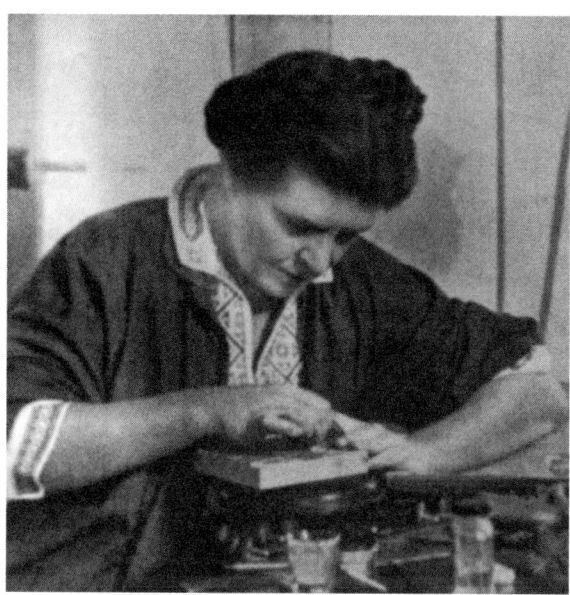

FIGURE I.10 Mere kitchen art? Clare Leighton's *The Artist at Work,* with sandbag, tools, and a "hard Arkansas stone" for sharpening. From Leighton's book on wood engraving in the How to Do It series, *Wood-Engraving and Woodcuts,* 1932 (London: The Studio Publications, 1948), 9. Copyright 2025 Estate of Clare Leighton. All rights reserved. DACS/Artists Rights Society (ARS).

about English wood engraving that had been published since 1919 by mainstream publishers, including Edward Gordon Craig's *Woodcuts and Some Words* (1924), Douglas Cleverdon's *The Engravings of Eric Gill* (1934), and George Mackley's *Wood-Engraving* (1948).

METHODOLOGY

Enchanted Wood is a work of feminist recovery that begins with the observation that while Raverat and other women artists have rarely been included in critical accounts of the prestige arts of avant-garde modernism, publishers, authors, and readers believed that their wood engravings elevated every book in which they appeared.[46] If not high art, these works communicated, through their delicate, miniature forms, the higher and "artier" aims of whatever pieces of writing they decorated.

Why did this women's art, virtually alone among women's arts, manage to escape cultural degradation—of art's diminishment to craft—by association with a woman's hand? Was it merely national nostalgia overwhelming gender bias in an age of international aggression? Certainly the nation's cultural enthusiasm

for books illustrated with scenes of rural life promoted these women wood engravers' pursuit of an everyday, everyman's art in the rural and urban places
where they made their homes. What else, if anything, did the hunger for books
about the countryside and for books with wood engravings have to do with these
women's refusals of the cultural mandate to make home and husband the exclusive basis of their identities and livelihood? This book answers these questions
through a story about midcentury British women's lives and national imaginings,
demonstrating how a seemingly obscure illustration practice of the interwar and
war years can direct scholars to the most lively areas of humanistic inquiry, at
the crossroads of modern art, literary studies, book history, and gender studies.

The cultural context that brings together the following chapters on literature,
book illustration, and an idealized British life imagined in rural scenes includes
the publishing and printing industries located in London, Oxford, Cambridge,
Glasgow, and Edinburgh. Drawing on publishers' archives and the work of social historians, sociologists, and cultural geographers who have since the 1980s
documented the relations among the cult of the countryside, modern transformations of rural social and economic life, and an upsurge in publications about
rural and natural Britain, this study analyzes scenes and experiences of rural
modernity captured in and mediated by the wood engravers' books. The materials of these books, the affordances of specific print media—everything from the
density of the wood block to the type of tool to the ink and paper, to the proofs
and presses—invite discussion as they contribute to the special status of these
cheap but beautiful books in the literary economies and amid the dire political
threats of interwar and wartime Britain.[47] The books themselves point us in two
directions: from city to country and from country to city. The close and contextual readings of their images and surrounding words presented here suggest
that we can see and make sense of the women wood engravers' lives, work, and
impacts on British literature and British books only when we read one kind of
cultural travel in terms of the other, locating ourselves at the intersection of a
busy byway that admits interdisciplinary traffic across the boundaries separating fine art from popular art, modernism from middlebrow, pictures from words,
conservative from progressive, criticism from history.[48]

Indebted to an interdisciplinary scholarship built on the research and meth-
odologies of modernist and middlebrow literary critics and social, art, and
print historians, this book is also indebted to scholarship on modern children's

who had come to pay a visit and was sitting on the sofa. He never could bear the student and always got cross when he saw him cutting out those comic figures which were so amusing —sometimes it was a man hanging from a gibbet, with a heart in his hand because he was a stealer of hearts; sometimes an old witch riding on a broomstick, with her husband perched on the bridge of her nose. The Councillor couldn't bear that sort of thing, and he always used to say just what he said now: "What rubbish to put into a child's head! All stuff and nonsense!"

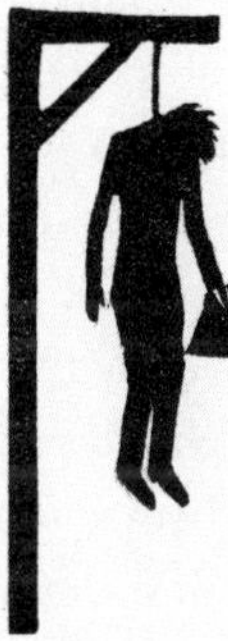

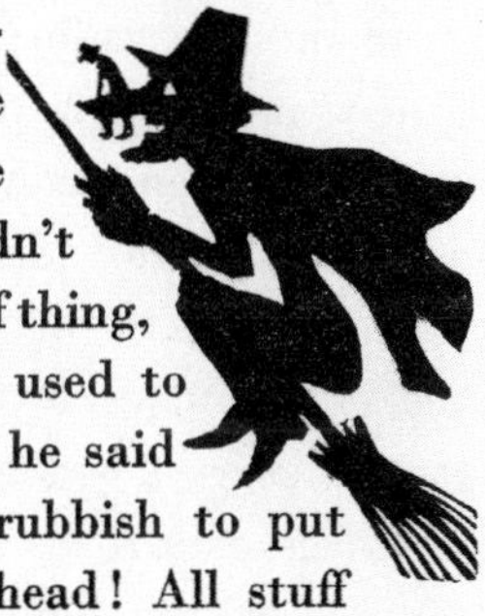

But little Ida was most amused at what the student had said about her flowers, and she thought about it for a long time. The flowers drooped their heads because they were tired out from dancing all night. No mistake about it, they were ill. So she took them along to her other playthings, which stood on a nice

FIGURE I.11 Gwen Raverat's text-integrated wood engravings of comic silhouettes cut out by Hans Christian Andersen's Danish student make obvious what is latent in any illustrated text: the demands for multimodal interdisciplinary reading. From "Little Ida's Flowers," in *Four Tales from Hans Andersen* (Cambridge: Cambridge University Press, 1935), 65. *The Hanged Man*, ⅝ × 1⅝ inches; *The Witch*, 1⅜ × 1⁹⁄₁₆ inches. Copyright 2025 Estate of Gwen Raverat. All rights reserved. DACS/Artists Rights Society (ARS).

literature that has only recently begun to influence these other fields.[49] Bridging adults' and children's literature, it models a new way of situating scholarship on modernity in relation to related but divided fields. It seeks to more fully incorporate children's literature scholars who are at the forefront of word–image and book historical studies into studies and networks of modernism. It also bids scholars of modernist literature and art to consider the immense impact of book illustration on twentieth-century habits of reading, the impact of children's literature on modernity, the impact of illustrated books on visual culture studies, and the robust body of social historical and geographical studies of mid-twentieth-century rural Britain.[50]

Enchanted Wood makes its argument visually and verbally, treating words and pictures, type and line, as forms demanding a multimodal interdisciplinary reading of the women engravers' texts and lives (Figure I.11). Five chapters illustrated with the wood engravings and drawings of Raverat, Miller Parker, Leighton, and Hassall range widely over the women's work and artwork of decades, moving from the post–World War I years of the early 1920s to the post–World War II years of the 1940s, 1950s, and 1960s. Each chapter raises questions about the impacts of sex and gender on the artists' embodied, envisioned, and historical experiences, as it reads their texts in relation to interwar and wartime media ecologies, cultural hierarchies, the artists' interpretations of nature in rural environments, their technical handling of diverse forms, materials, and genres, and their regional or national allegiances. The chapters are framed by this Introduction and an appendix containing brief biographical sketches of a selection of midcentury women wood engravers. In addition, reproductions of tailpieces ("tale-pieces") from Bewick's two-volume *History of British Birds* introduce five brief "vignettes" (miniature chapters) into the discussion of the book's focal female characters. Together, the chapters and vignettes suggest that no matter how invested any individual British woman wood engraver might have been in rural life, literature, art, printing, or book economies, a "female Bewick" was destined to emerge—and could only emerge—at precisely the moment Gwen Raverat, Agnes Miller Parker, Clare Leighton, and Joan Hassall took up their scorpers, spitstickers, and gravers.

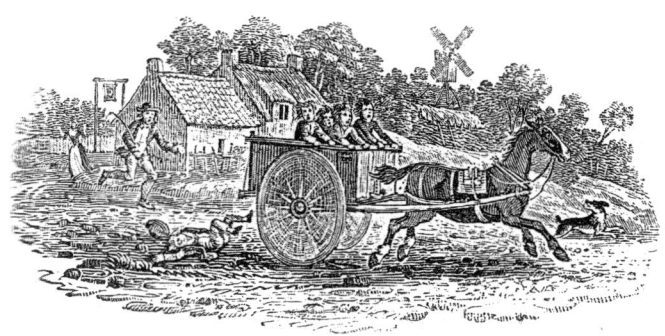

"TRUTH is to bend to nothing, but all to her."

Thomas Bewick's vignettes, his small tailpieces, or what he cheerfully called "tale-pieces," inserted into the spare white spaces at the ends of chapters, sent critics into encomiums when they first discovered his miniature wood engravings of animals and Tyne Valley country folk in *A General History of Quadrupeds*. Bewick authority Nigel Tattersfield records one critic's affirmation of "many little elegant vignettes," while another enthused over the vignettes' "peculiar spirit and fancy." Still another praised "the degree of novelty in the design and neatness of the execution."[1] Encouraged, Bewick included more and more ambitious vignettes in his two volumes of *A History of British Birds*. The tailpiece *The Runaway Cart* is a great favorite from volume 1, *Land Birds* (1797), earning attention from critics who find its comic narrative and moral commentary enchanting. It tells an ordinary story of country life, of five boys who steal a horse and cart to play a prank on the carter, who has been drinking inside the local public house. Choosing to illustrate the moment most likely to combine moral instruction of youth with their amusement, Bewick shows us a fallen prankster, a frightened

Thomas Bewick, *A History of British Birds,* vol. 1, *Land Birds* (1797, 1826), 47. 3 × 1½ inches.

horse, frightened boys, an alarmed carter, and a distressed publican's wife or perhaps distraught mother, all against the backdrop of a quiet country landscape. At the bottom of the page facing Bewick's header for "The Stone Falcon," and following a staid paragraph about debates between naturalists regarding the integrity of the stone falcon species, this illustration does indeed fulfill Bewick's aim, stated in his preface to the sixth edition of *A History of British Birds,* to intersperse "*Tale*-pieces of gaiety and humour" among paragraphs advancing "more serious studies" (iii).

In the same preface, Bewick tells us that he was motivated in his "labours in Natural History" by a desire to "lead the minds of youth to the study of that delightful pursuit" (iii). These studying youths are always imagined as male, presumed to share the sex and gender identity of the boys featured in many vignettes, even as we know that girls as well as boys read Bewick's books and delighted in his tailpieces. *The Runaway Cart* is typical of his vignettes in its focus on vigorous and social outdoor boyhood pursuits. While girls do enter an occasional *British Birds* vignette, they are never seen with other girls, are rarely set in motion, and, as one would expect, are constrained by decorous caps and ankle-length skirts, with never an inclination to naughtiness, mischief, or pranks. To anyone who might say that this sexual difference makes no difference to either natural history or art, that Bewick's commitment to children's learning and amusement transcends sex, one might reply that every vignette from *A History of British Birds* appears in a book that is structurally, thematically, and epistemologically founded on a belief in the essential difference of sex as an organizing category of life. The first thing we read about the sparrowhawk in the chapter preceding "The Stone Falcon" is that the "length of the male [is] twelve inches; the female fifteen" (44); we learn in the following chapter that the merlin "differs from the Falcons, and all the rapacious kind, in the male and female being of the same size" (49). To urge close observation of the sex of animals in nature and the sex of humans in Bewick's vignettes is consistent with the Enlightenment values that Bewick endorsed: "It has been an undeviating principle with me that TRUTH is to bend to nothing, but all to her" (preface, v). The truth is that in Bewick's world, boys have more fun. They also have more space, more attention, more reality. They are preferred subjects of art, even an ordinary workman's art of wood engraving, and by association the preferred subjects and readers of the literature and scholarly studies that surround that art. Their landscapes, their texts, become masculine territories and, by extension, the genres of natural history and the media of wood engraving become masculine genres and media.

Why does this matter for study of the art, lives, and impacts of women wood engravers working in Bewick's tradition one hundred fifty years later, in a modern world that had extended the vote to women, was extending opportunities for higher and better education to girls, was beginning to tolerate women working outside the home as artists, writers, and professionals? Gender matters because it reminds us with every turn of a yellowing page in a Bewick volume, with every bewitched examination of his pictures of birds in chapter headers or vignettes at chapter ends, of the "TRUTH" of historical and ideological barriers encountered by eighteenth-century *and* twentieth-century girls. These are the girls who, like their brothers, might have wanted to traipse about the countryside, go fishing or tree climbing, or dare to steal a drunken carter's horse or have yearned to go out into the world, learn a trade, and become an artist. For the vast majority of these girls, such activities and ambitions could only be imagined in an ideal world, not pursued in the real one rife with sexual barriers and dangers. Bewick did not consciously promote sexist views of girls; a man who genuinely loved children, he inspired devotion in his own daughters, Jane, Isabella, and Elizabeth. In adulthood, Jane and Isabella were caretakers not only of his reputation but also of the many, many documents, letters, ledgers, proofs, and publications that have been vital to Bewick scholars and collectors. Girls, in Bewick's lived world, are good. Once we leave the field of biography for literary, cultural, or art criticism, however, Bewick's good girls pose a problem for studies of his vignettes and of wood engraving more generally. Bewick's vignettes inevitably create an ideal as well as real rural modernity, one in which boys are entitled to a range of human experiences while girls are largely excluded, located just beyond in an unreal, uncomplicated, unnatural world. Bewick's rural modernity, no less than that created by twentieth-century wood engravers who adopted his techniques and style, brings nostalgia and idealism to realistic representations of rural Britain. This contradictory rural vision is in itself interesting, an invitation to critical exploration and explication. Problems emerge, however, when we dismiss women artists for the very qualities of nostalgia, charm, or idealism that in Bewick's work highlight and ensure, through the logic of opposition, the steely, earthy, vigorous,

"real" masculine qualities critics traditionally value as signs of artistic original-
ity and strength.

Bewick's vignettes teach us many things about rural Britain and his experience of natural life through their exceptional artistry, technical merit, social
vision, and warm embrace of ordinary human frailty and dignity. They also
teach readers that there is no nature that can be apprehended without sex and
gender ideologies determining how we get into it, what we see and experience
once we are there, and how we interpret it once we get out into a supposedly separate cultured world of books and reading. Feminist analysis of Bewick's volumes
of *British Birds* reminds us that natural history is an engagement with an ideal
modernity, a discipline whose historical processes of construction are implied by
the very prints that freeze Bewick's images on pages, put ink in place of roots,
feathers, skin, and fur. It is a gendered discipline that came of age in the Enlightenment, propelled by good men like Bewick who hoped to overwhelm "opinions,
begotten by superstition, or fostered by credulity" through objective, scientific
observations of nature. These observations would "revere and promote" the laws
of "the Author of Truth" (preface, v). It does not take much sustained study of
Bewick or his critics to determine that omission from Bewick's world is also ex-
clusion from the call to do God's work on earth. Bewick might claim that girls,
akin to angels, are protected from and thus above earthly concerns, but contemporary art, literature, and cultural critics are wise to seek out girls and women in
the pages of men's and women's nature books, where, as in the illustrative work of
Gwen Raverat, Agnes Miller Parker, Clare Leighton, and Joan Hassall, they can
themselves do the work of revising what we think we know about women's social
history, women's art, and children's literature.

ONE

Green Worlds in Black and White

Women Artists, Rural Lives, Urban Publishers

In 1909, a twenty-four-year-old Gwen Raverat wrote to her sister Margaret, "I have found happiness this summer—I can't tell you the inexpressible joy woodcuts have been to me . . . I now know that I am fit to live alone on my own happiness."[1] She had taught herself wood engraving while enrolled at the Slade School of Art, which she entered joyfully on October 5, 1908. With some informal tutoring from Elinor "Eily" Monsell, an artist and adored mentor who had become part of Raverat's family when Eily married Bernard Darwin, Raverat was ready to exhibit. In 1910, ten of her wood engravings and a painting were included in one of Vanessa Bell's Friday Club shows.[2] Biographer Frances Spalding reports that critical recognition of Raverat's talents as a wood engraver was immediate, with the London *Times* reviewer noting, "The little woodcuts by Miss G. Darwin, throwing back to the days of Bewick and Blake, are quite excellent."[3]

The first born and most thoroughly Victorian of the wood engravers examined in this study, Raverat begins the biographical stories condensed within this chapter. Well educated and well connected, Raverat was an avid child reader of poetry and prose who benefited from the libraries and conversations of her Darwin relations in Cambridge and at her grandfather Charles Darwin's summer home of Down, and, starting in late adolescence, from the friendship of Julia and Leslie Stephen's children, Vanessa, Thoby, Virginia, and Adrian. She met her husband, the Cambridge mathematician and painter Jacques Raverat, through association with the Neo-Pagans, a group of creative, ambitious undergraduates gathered around the charismatic figure of Rupert Brooke.[4] She lived for several years in France near Jacques Raverat's family, giving birth to two daughters, Elisabeth and Sophie (Figure 1.1). Raverat's sketching, painting, and engraving of this period were undertaken while she was caring for her children and Jacques, the latter suffering from multiple sclerosis. She returned to England in 1925, bewildered and exhausted after nursing Jacques through his long final illness and agonizing death. As a young widow and single mother, she made new homes for herself among old friends, first in Bloomsbury, then in Harlton, near Cambridge.[5] Rather than undertaking limited edition engravings based on direct observation as she had in France in the 1920s, she fulfilled commissions from commercial publishers for illustrations of fables, romances, and rhymes.[6] This change of media and motive initiated the most critically productive and rewarding years of her career as an artist-engraver: Critics raved, readers purchased, and children benefited. Most surprising of all, Raverat was able to live independently as a woman and wood engraver in the years darkened by the Great Depression and world war.

Joan Hassall, the youngest of the wood engravers examined in this book, also benefited educationally and professionally from her family connections. Her father, John Hassall, was the famous "poster king" of late nineteenth-century London, whose bold, flat, colorful designs defined a generation of outdoor advertising and indoor children's books.[7] As late as 1960, Ruari McLean could report that Joan Hassall's studio and printing office, which she inherited from her father along with his house at 88 Kensington Park Road, contained generations of art and oddities, including "English transfer-printed pottery, books, and glass oil-lamps . . . Valentines, miscellaneous printed ephemera . . . family Victoriana, and a large collection of early printed children's books."[8] This material manifestation of family history and eccentric individuality seems a miniature and private expression of the spirit that animated the Victoria and Albert Museum, so near to Hassall's home. Yet in a brief memoir, Hassall recalls with a sense of belated incredulity that she was in her early twenties before she discovered the museum (Figure 1.2). With this,

whole worlds of enchantment opened to my view. And yet every Sunday of my life we had been a few yards from it, for we used to walk across Kensington Gardens to the Natural History Museum once a week, but never set foot in the building across the road.[9]

Yes, my darling, well I know
How the bitter wind doth blow;
And the winter's snow and rain
Patter on the window-pane:
But they cannot come in here,
To my little baby dear.

For the window shutteth fast,
Till the stormy night is past;
And the curtains warm are spread
Round about her cradle-bed:
So till morning shineth bright
Little baby dear, good night!

ANN AND JANE TAYLOR

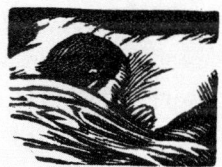

FIGURE 1.2 Joan Hassall's title page wood engraving of animals of field and stream exploring a naturalist's notebook and binoculars. From Bernard Gooch, *The Strange World of Nature* (New York: Thomas Y. Crowell, 1950). 2½ × 3 inches. Reproduced by permission of the Estate of Joan Hassall/Simon Lawrence.

This anecdote about Hassall's encounters with London's public Victorian institutions of imperial collecting and display captures the two great and sometimes competing forces within her art. It hints at the complexity of relations, including gendered relations, between natural history and art and design. It helps us understand how Hassall came to be the artist who could inspire McLean to declare that we would be in her debt "if all she had ever done was to engrave, as exquisitely as only she and Bewick can, a few of the smaller things in Nature like fieldmice and finches' wings" (Figure 1.3).[10]

Hassall's first formal art training was in the London School of Art, of which her father was principal; Hassall senior's intense desire that his daughter become an artist gave direction and strength to Joan's otherwise gentle and uncertain adolescent self. Joan Hassall studied drawing and painting at the Royal Academy Schools as a probationary student in 1927 and full student in 1928. Her first encounter with wood engraving took place at London's School of Photo-Engraving, at a night class given by R. J. Beedham.[11] Looking back at this class at a distance of five decades, she recalled experiencing

a strange moment of enlightenment for, as I looked at [Beedham's] block, a feeling of absolute certainty more like remembering, came to me that I too could engrave like that. I knew how to achieve those precise lines and deep clean clearing of the background though as yet I had only produced one unstable capital "D."[12]

Shortly after Hassall experienced this "strange moment" of vocational enlightenment, she encountered her first Bewick vignette in a Royal Academy lecture.[13] Startled, delighted, she bought a used and illustrated copy of Bewick's *Memoir*, "thus initiating one of the great admirations and pleasures of [her] life."[14] Beyond the influences of her father, her teachers, and her "master" instructor, Bewick, Hassall learned from classic writers whom she describes as "old friends": "Shakespeare, Dickens, the Brontës, Jane Austen, Maria Edgeworth, Flora Thompson, Fanny Burney, and some isolated books such as Gosse's *Father and Son*."[15] In what could be taken as instructions on how to recognize middlebrow books such as those she would later illustrate, she recalls reading "again and again the same loved books," seeking in the classics not excitement of the new but rather the "most perfect and enjoyable relaxation" of the old and familiar.[16]

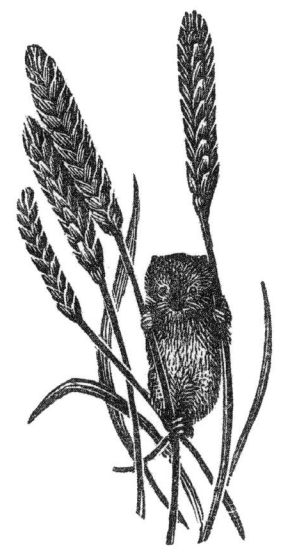

FIGURE 1.3 Joan Hassall's wood engraved tailpiece of "the lowly people of the grass," illustrating "Harvest Song." From Mary Webb, *Fifty-One Poems* (London: Jonathan Cape, 1946), 31. ⅞ × 1⅝ inches. Reproduced by permission of the Estate of Joan Hassall/Simon Lawrence.

Clare Leighton, like Raverat and Hassall, described her vocation as an artist as a kind of destiny determined by otherworldly forces. In an unpublished essay titled "The Growth and Shaping of an Artist," she wrote:

It isn't a matter of deciding, as though one were planning for a career as a doctor or a lawyer, the decision is already made and one has been stamped by it from the earliest moments—even before one could formulate what was happening.[17]

Her nephew and literary executor David Leighton comments on this passage, describing Leighton's decision to be an artist as a matter of "predestination." He also attributes Leighton's artistic ambition to childhood circumstances, above all "the almost obsessive enthusiasm for creative work in the Leighton household."[18] Clare Leighton was to describe these domestic enthusiasms in her memoir of her St. John's Wood childhood, *Tempestuous Petticoat,* providing a vivid portrait of her mother, the prolific romance novelist Marie Connor Leighton, and her father, Robert Leighton, an amateur painter and successful author of adventure novels. Although her father's deafness seems to have kept his daughter at a remove, he brought into her life valuable influences, including her Uncle Jack Leighton, a painter who led her on sketching tours of Europe during her teenage years, and her Aunt Sarah Leighton, a spinster with whom Leighton became close as a young adult (Figure 1.4).[19] Clare was to write of the latter:

> There was such power in this frail little woman; the power to produce in another those things she had not been able to produce herself. She was the first person to show me love. . . . In me she placed the hope that I might create those things that she had not been able to do.[20]

Leighton's belief that she was able to inherit creative power through the love of an older woman who, owing to Victorian restrictions on girls' bodies and minds, had been unable to pursue a creative career herself, goes to the heart of this study's argument. The magic of artistic talent will manifest as an artistic career only if forces of real time and material circumstance allow. Leighton lived out what was denied to her Aunt Sarah and so many other women of creative potential because she was born into a creative and middle-class family just late enough in the nineteenth century to be allowed to pursue an excellent formal arts education at Brighton College of Art and the Slade.[21] Seeking a means of earning her living through her art, Leighton, like Hassall, was able to afford additional instruction in illustration, in her case at the Central School of Arts and Crafts. Her teacher was Noel Rooke, a man famous among print historians for moving wood engraving away from the black-line tradition of William Morris and Charles Ricketts and from the pictorial tradition of William Blake and Edward Calvert, to the white-line "literary, book-bound tradition" of Bewick.[22] Rooke's commitment and that of his students to Bewick's illustrative tradition led members of the more avant-garde school of wood engraving led by Leon

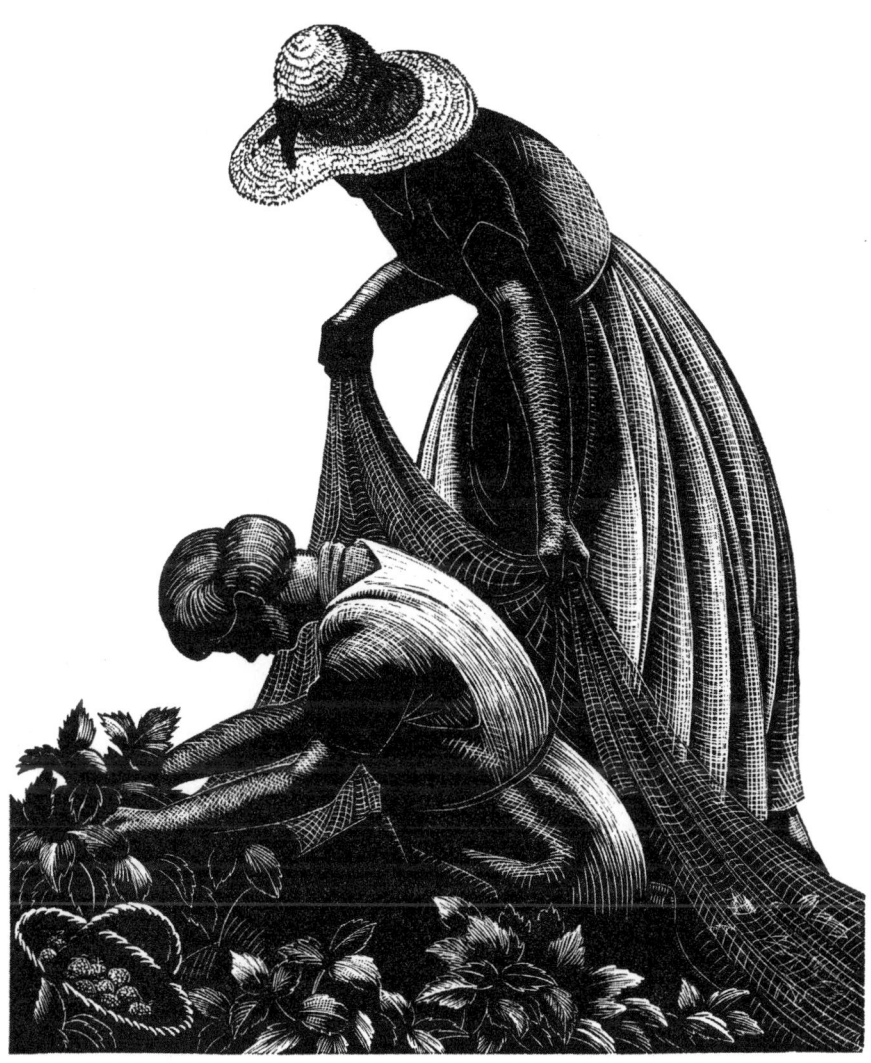

FIGURE 1.4 Clare Leighton's wood engraving *Picking Strawberries,* depicting herself working with Annie, the village woman who provides domestic help. Which is the mistress, which the maid? From Clare Leighton, *Four Hedges: A Gardener's Chronicle* (London: Gollancz, 1935), 49. 4¹⁄₁₆ × 4¾ inches. Copyright 2025 Estate of Clare Leighton. All rights reserved. DACS/Artists Rights Society (ARS).

Underwood—which in the 1920s informally included Agnes Miller Parker—to refer slightly contemptuously to "the Rookery."[23] Certainly Rooke's instruction served Leighton well; print authority James Hamilton describes her consistent style as "a wood engraved form of the Slade School manner of drawing, formal, erudite and controlled," praising her "shaplier lines" for their "joyous swing" while distinguishing her style from the "visionary richness developed by pupils of Leon Underwood."[24]

More so than any of the other women wood engravers examined in this study, Leighton pursued a dual career, enriching literature as a writer and illustrator.[25] In addition to authoring the autobiographical texts for her popular wood engraved countryside books of the 1930s, *The Farmer's Year: A Calendar of English Husbandry* (1933), *Four Hedges: A Gardener's Chronicle* (1935), and *Country Matters* (1937), she was the first woman to write a how-to book on wood engraving, *Wood-Engraving and Woodcuts* (1932). Yet it is the peculiar *Sometime—Never* (1939) that provides significant context for her thinking about history and gender at the end of the 1930s. Neither quite memoir nor fiction, illustrated with lithographs rather than wood engravings, this stream of consciousness meditation or dream prose takes place on board a transatlantic steamer that brings Leighton's first-person alter ego, with its "cargo of seven hundred Jewish refugees," to a neverland or no time of memory and desire (3). Set among images of embittered American veterans of the Spanish Civil War, of World War I soldiers, of bewildered Jewish refugees of what would be known ten years later as the Holocaust, is a memory of her first ride on a horse-drawn omnibus as it makes its way through the London streets to Kensington Gardens on her seventh birthday. Looking down on the horses from a seat near the driver, the adult narrator revisits the child's imaginative encounter with "the magic steeds in all the fairy tales that were ever written" (53). This inspires the adult's regretful exclamation, "Oh, lost enchantment, oh, irrevocable disillusion," a cry that captures in all its ambiguous regret the acquisition of real knowledge of plodding horses at the cost of "phantom horses" of fantasy (53). Leighton's life's work, both her writings and her wood engravings, the latter with their distinctive, sinuous fidelity to the realities of plant and human form, can be seen as an effort to recover the child's belief in enchantment through imaginative reproduction of real scenes as mundane as a ride on an omnibus. Her people's art and illustration resonated with readers who had been trained by William Morris to venerate common people doing ordinary work in beautiful ways, by Thomas Bewick to associate that ordinary work with white-line wood engravings of rural landscapes, and by popular literature of the interwar period to read contemporary wood engravings as part of a broader media-inspired cult of the countryside.[26]

Leighton immigrated to America in 1939, fleeing a broken, more than decade-long love affair with socialist journalist H. N. (Henry Noel) Brailsford. Irritated, too, by Agnes Miller Parker's assumption of the role of Gollancz's favored wood engraver, she sought professional renewal in American scenes of southern heat and northern cold.[27] Johanna Selborne cites Leighton's rather desperate comment to Gollancz, "I have a feeling that I want to break off from doing books & run away somewhere," as evidence that her immigration to America was motivated at least in part by the Gollancz–Miller Parker "fracas."[28] There, in her new homeland as in her old, she lived as a single, childless woman, earning an independent living through her art. Like the other women artists examined in this study, she founded no workshop and established no school, although she did travel, teach, and lecture widely (Figure 1.5).[29]

Agnes Miller Parker shared with Clare Leighton a girlhood defined by Edwardian sexual proprieties and a womanhood transformed by modern gender opportunities. She was born in Irvine, North Ayrshire, the oldest of eight children of a middle-class couple with standard bourgeois Victorian expectations for their daughter.[30] While they supported her formal art education at the Glasgow School of Art, they were only brought to tolerate, not approve of, her marriage in 1918 to fellow artist and conscientious objector William McCance. Mac, as he was called, figures large in histories of British wood engraving and typography, and he exerted a defining influence on Miller Parker's career.[31] The couple left their teaching jobs at their alma mater in Glasgow and settled near Hammersmith, the site long associated with Morris's Kelmscott Press and still in the interwar period a byword for artistic community.[32] Referred to in a 1925 *Daily Chronicle* article on "the Chiswick Group" as "the clever couple from Scotland who believe in cubist methods," the McCances depended on Miller Parker's teaching for any regular income.[33] At this time she received advice on wood engraving from her friend Gertrude Hermes, who, like her husband, Blair Hughes-Stanton, was active in the Underwood school.[34] When Miller Parker and McCance moved to rural Wales to work

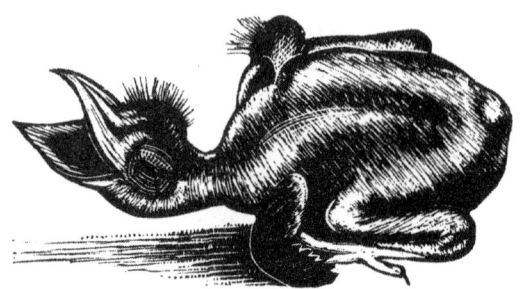

FIGURE 1.5 Clare Leighton's wood engraved tailpiece *Blackbird Fledgling,* a fearless, "grotesque object," for her chapter "May." From Clare Leighton, *Four Hedges: A Gardener's Chronicle* (London: Gollancz, 1935), 40. 3¼ × 2⅛ inches. Copyright 2025 Estate of Clare Leighton. All rights reserved. DACS/Artists Rights Society (ARS).

with Hermes and Hughes-Stanton for the private Gregynog Press, Miller Parker changed her style of wood engraving (Figure 1.6). Her cubist wood engravings of the 1920s, with their abstract designs and heavy blacks, gave way to her delicate, silvery, more naturalistic and romantic illustrations of the 1930s (Plate 1).

Miller Parker as illustrator and McCance as controller were together responsible for one of the most beautiful limited editions of the twentieth-century wood engraving revival, *The Fables of Esope,* published by Gregynog in 1931. The equally elegant *XXI Welsh Gypsy Folk-Tales* came next in 1933. With all their debts to Bewick for subject matter, technique, and tradition, and all their debts to fine press publishing for their ambitious design, sumptuous materials, and prohibitive pricing, these Gregynog books rightfully preoccupy print historians, but it is Miller Parker's first mass-distributed, unlimited edition, *Through the Woods: The English Woodland—April to April* (1936), written by H. E. Bates and published by the enterprising Victor Gollancz, that allies her most clearly with the decade's broader social commitments to ordinary people and their art. Here she brought her "deep interest in natural history and a special talent for illustrating animal life" to a much larger audience, earning critical accolades and further commissions, including one for a companion Bates volume, *Down the River* (1937) (Figure 1.7).[35] Unfortunately, neither praise nor profits brought her either riches or happiness.

Miller Parker is the only one of the four women studied here who remained married into late middle age and the only one to have suffered abuse at the hands of her husband, the very man whose professional collaboration with her has led Rogerson to describe the Gregynog *Esope* as "the result of the true marriage of two minds."[36] Reading her wood engravings of natural and rural Britain against the evidence of her suffering at the hands of her husband in their pastoral homes exposes the simultaneously liberating and cruel ironies of rural modernity as it was experienced by a woman artist. The awful, hidden story of spousal anger and dominance cannot be found in the texts or footnotes of specialized scholarly studies on Miller Parker or wood engraving, but only in the archived letters of friends, including William and Dorothy Bell, Jessica Knish, Lavinia Derwent, Bernard Chambers, Peggy Grieves, and Celandine Kennington. These documents tell a tale that is different from the fables and fairy tales

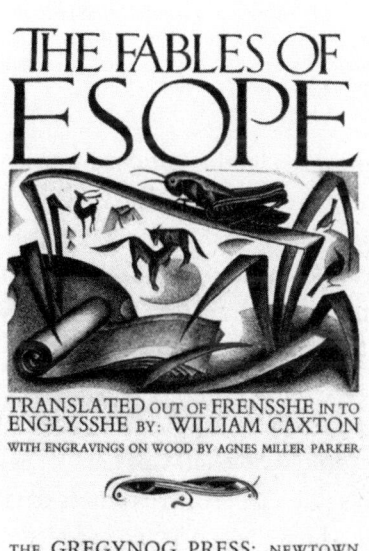

FIGURE 1.6 Agnes Miller Parker's celebrated title page illustration for *The Fables of Esope* (Newtown, Montgomeryshire: Gregynog Press, 1931). $4^{15}/_{16} \times 3$ inches. Reproduced by permission of the Estate of Agnes Miller Parker.

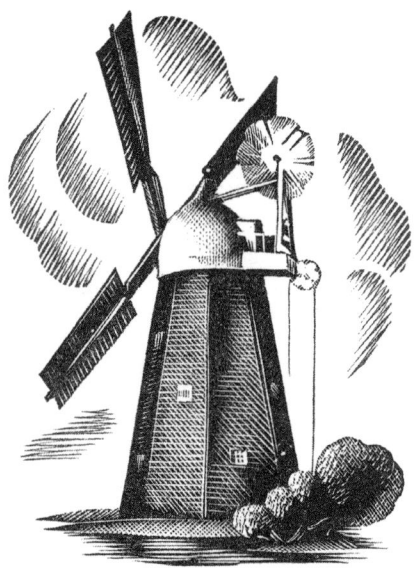

FIGURE 1.7 Agnes Miller Parker's wood
engraved tailpiece *Wind-Mill.* Miller Parker
and McCance lived in an abandoned windmill
along with resident doves when she received her
crucial first commission from Victor Gollancz
for *Through the Woods.* From H. E. Bates,
Down the River (London: Gollancz, 1937), 115.
1½ × 2 inches. Reproduced by permission of the
Estate of Agnes Miller Parker.

that Miller Parker illustrated. Stored next to clippings of wood engravings and boxes of inky blocks that testify to the source of some of the century's most discreet and delicate illustrative compositions are private communications that chill the heart—one friend describes Miller Parker's escape from her husband as "the best thing" that she had ever done, and another declares her past "a waste." What must Miller Parker have had to endure for a friend to write off as "a waste" her lifetime of extraordinary artistic production? We can only imagine what strengths of mind and character were required of the petite Miller Parker to design and produce the dozens of beautiful wood engravings of bluebells, kingfishers, and catkins while waiting, tools in hand, for her brothers to sweep her away from the goblin in prince's guise to whom she had bound herself.[37]

In 1955 Miller Parker finally left McCance, initially finding safety with family in Glasgow. A 1958 article in *The Bulletin* newspaper quotes Miller Parker from Riddrie as saying, "I am looking for a house in the country, or by the sea. . . . I'd like to live on an island best of all."[38] She eventually found her island, Arran in the Firth of Clyde. With it, she found happiness as a single woman, working, fishing, sailing, and swimming.[39] Wood engraving allowed her to accomplish what relatively few women in human history have been able to achieve: independent life as a professional artist. It also allowed her to turn the grim tale of women's gendered fear and domestic oppression into what might seem a fairy-tale ending of tranquility and beauty in rural Britain. We can detect in this story two kinds of strong magic that animate all of Miller Parker's books, both the binding magic of Victorian and Edwardian women's devotion to husband and marriage amid literally unutterable shame and pain, and the liberating magic of modern women's rebellion from convention, habit, and expectation amid unprecedented opportunities for gendered self-re-creation offered by a postwar world. This is part of the story of the wood engraving revival in Britain that this book attempts to tell for the first time.

"THE ROAD TO ARCADIA"

Raverat, the most thoroughly Victorian of the four women wood engravers treated here, was also the one most committed to illustrating children's books. Her career as an illustrator was launched by a 1932 Cambridge University Press children's poetry book, discussed in chapter 2, but as other chapters will attest, all four women artists were transformed by acceptance and completion of illustrative commissions for children's books.[40] Valuing these women's material and social contributions to twentieth-century children's books has the potential to transform the way we recognize and read modern literature by ranging freely over the divides separating the study of literary biography and literary criticism, histories of books and literature, and analyses of twentieth-century children's and adults' literature. In allying interdisciplinary critical practice with modernist studies, this and subsequent chapters reverse standard literary values that begin and end with words in the mind rather than ink on the page.[41] Renaming literature as "adults' literature" is part of this revisionary effort. The term "adults' literature" is uncommon and awkward, seemingly redundant.[42] In practice, only children's literature scholars need qualify their field with a term that gestures toward the age of an intended readership, rather than descriptors of nation, period, style, or identity that define other specialties of literary study (e.g., British literature, eighteenth-century literature, modernist literature, women's, rural, or queer literature).[43] The term "adults' literature," deployed throughout this text, will have done its critical work if it persuades scholars in traditional literary fields to perceive as arbitrary and ideological a divide between children's and adults' literatures. This divide is treated by most scholars as so essential, sensible, and natural that it need not be examined or even named. Literature is adults' literature—that goes without saying. This book's peculiar passions, its feminist pursuit of knowledge about modern British women's lives, art, books, and reading through study of mid-twentieth-century wood engraved illustration, affirms a path into the literary past whose largely unknown course is illuminated by the simple idea that we cannot read literature without reading books. In other words, it returns to Peter Hunt's motivating questions, posed in his *Criticism, Theory and Children's Literature* (1991): "What does the book look and feel like? What does the reader look and feel like?"[44]

Hunt's questions about books and readers are just as alive, just as intriguing, to scholars working today on word–image relations and on children's canons and classics as they were at the end of the twentieth century when William Moebius's landmark essay, "Introduction to Picturebook Codes" (1986) was first published. Moebius's work, along with that of other scholars of word–image relations in children's books, scholars of children's classics and the Golden Age of children's literature, and print and art historians studying Bewick's life and art and the history of wood engraving, provides the critical theoretical framework for this chapter and thus the basis for valuing women wood engravers as *modern* artists whose work and lives matter for those who love literature as well as those who love wood engraving.[45]

Joyce Irene Whalley and Tessa Rose Chester contend that in the interwar years "there was very little experiment with new illustrative ideas apart from one or two notable exceptions. In fact, one of the main features was a revival of 19th-century techniques, particularly that of white-line wood-engraving." They name Gwen Raverat, Joan Hassall, and Agnes Miller Parker as three of the "most prominent engravers in this revival" (Plate 2).[46] From a perspective informed by knowledge of the economic, social, and political contexts that produced the Spartan volumes of children's illustrated books during the war and in the immediate postwar years, Whalley and Chester regard Raverat, Hassall, and Miller Parker as uniquely innovative women artists, sensitive and exciting experimenters who accomplished for mass-marketed children's books what their more avant-garde peers accomplished for adults and their limited editions (Figure 1.8).[47] These art historians emphasize

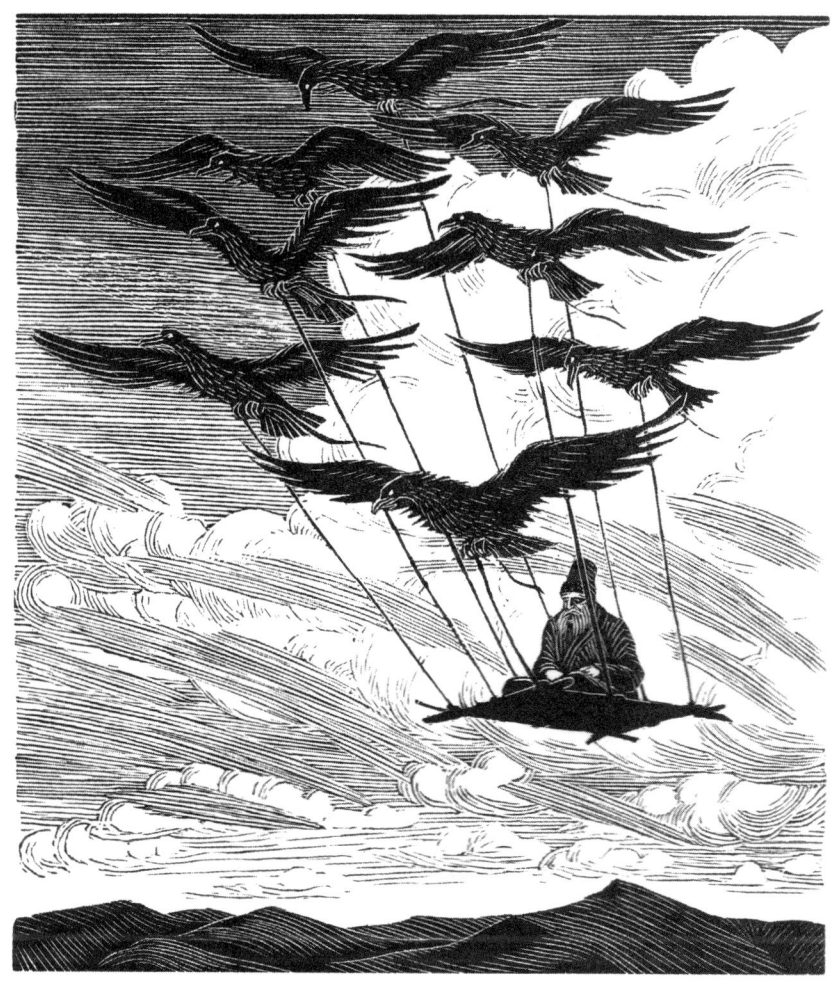

FIGURE 1.8 Gwen Raverat's wood engraving *The Magician's Chariot*, which depicts the old king, grandfather to the heroine princess, returning to home and rule on a "wonderful flying seat." From Henry Allen Wedgwood, *The Bird Talisman: An Eastern Tale* (London: Faber and Faber, 1939), 69. 4⅜ × 5 inches. Copyright 2025 Estate of Gwen Raverat. All rights reserved.

that Raverat's white-line engravings draw "obvious inspiration" from Bewick, although they represent her work for children with a reproduction of a rare colored wood engraving, *A Tiger! A Tiger! Awake! Awake!* from *The Bird Talisman.* Claiming that she "mainly worked in the adult field," they refer scholars of children's book illustration to Raverat's "different, but equally attractive" *Four Tales from Hans Andersen* (1935), discussed here in chapter 5.[48]

Agnes Miller Parker, who contributed linocut, not wood engraved, illustrations to only one children's book, earns from Whalley and Chester the most illustrative space. They reproduce her picture *The Coocooburrah* from the first chapter of Rhoda Power's *How It Happened* (1930).[49] In Power's book, *The Coocooburrah* embellishes the Australian tale "How the Sun Was Made," its bold, minimalist strokes inviting comparison to sixteenth-century English woodcuts or late nineteenth-century John Hassall illustrations more so than to Bewick's white-line wood engravings. Displaying none of the subtle textures or silvery tones for which Miller Parker's wood engravings are famous, the linocut illustrations in *How It Happened* seem more likely to attract adults with modernist tastes, eager to expose their children to cubist abstractions and flat surface pleasures, rather than to share with child readers the Bewickian delights of miniature white-line realism, visual-depth storytelling, and illustrative humor. Bewick's influence, to the extent that it registers at all in *How It Happened,* is relayed through the book's natural historical contents and fable and folktale generic forms. Miller Parker honors with full-page illustrations what Bewick's devoted readers would call quadrupeds, folktale heroes ranging from the monkey to cow and caribou, hare, hippos, and fox. These mammals illustrate stories translated from native peoples of the Philippines, Germany, Nigeria, and Brazil, but it is Miller Parker's full pages of birds that reveal most surely her Bewickian bias: In addition to *The Coocooburrah,* her illustrations include *The Hawk and the Hen, The Raven and the Goose, The Peacock,* more hens in "How the Speckled Hen Got Her Speckles," and, best of all, *The Wagtail and the Wren* (Figure 1.9).[50] The story in which this last linocut appears, "Why the Wagtail Wags Its Tail," described as "Roumanian," begins irresistibly: "Once upon a time, the birds lived together in a world of their own. They had a very pleasant life and on the whole they were happy though, of course, awkward things do happen just as awkward things happen in our world."[51] Its feathered characters invite child readers to

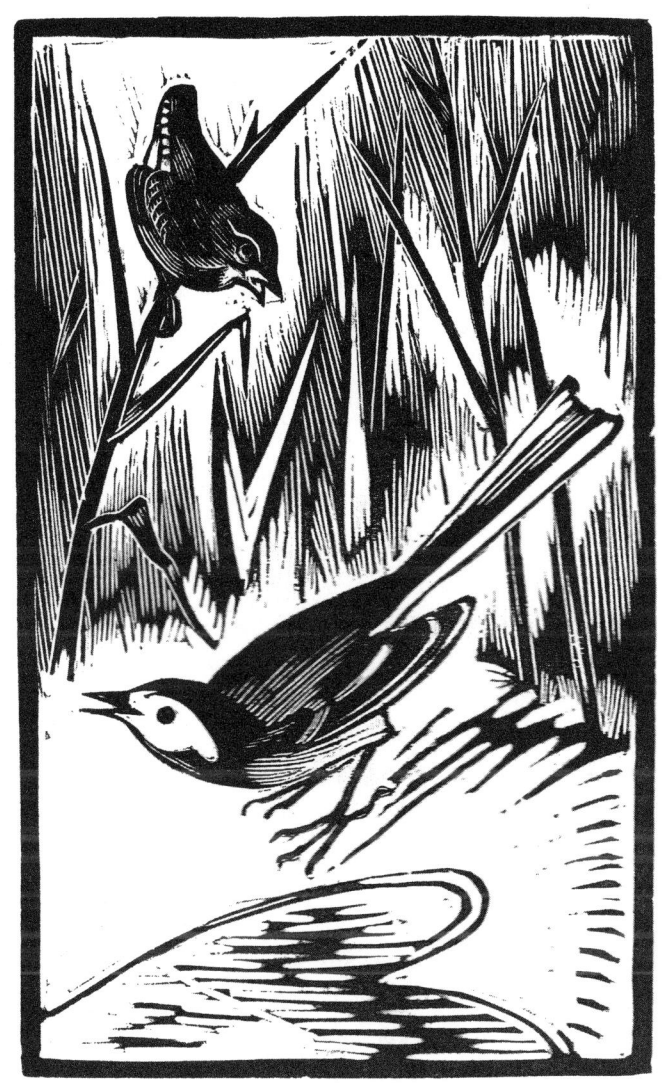

The Wagtail and the Wren

FIGURE 1.9 Agnes Miller Parker's linocut *The Wagtail and the Wren*. From Rhoda Power, *How It Happened* (Cambridge: Cambridge University Press, 1930), 169. 3⅞ × 6⅛ inches. Reproduced by permission of the Estate of Agnes Miller Parker.

judge their too-human foibles of vanity, foolishness, and stupidity, even as Miller Parker's illustration *The Wagtail and the Wren* reduces the contentious avian chorus into a beautiful postcard defined and quieted by a solid black frame. We must look to Miller Parker's adult books of the mid-1930s for evidence of her formal engagements with Bewick's illustrative tradition.

THROUGH THE WOODS

Children's literature is generally assumed to be literature written for children, but it also encompasses literature read by children, the latter including adults' literature like Bewick's *A History of British Birds,* which, no matter the complexities of the text, enchants children with its illustrations.[52] If Agnes Miller Parker's books belong in the annals of British children's literature, it is primarily in this second sense, the sense modeled by Bewick's *British Birds.* In the challenging economic climate of the Great Depression, those responsible for marketing and distributing her first mass-produced books, *Through the Woods* and *Down the River,* commissioned by Victor Gollancz, hoped that her wood engravings would appeal to both children and adults. Henry Holt's American edition of *Down the River,* for example, was wrapped in a dust jacket bearing the promise that the attractive volume "will be cherished by young and old alike."

Ian Rogerson, Agnes Miller Parker's most astute scholarly interpreter, advises, "Those wishing to study Agnes Miller Parker's art at its very peak of perfection can do no better than turn to the Gollancz books of the 1930s."[53] With seventy-three wood engravings in *Through the Woods* and eighty-one in *Down the River,* these books brought ordinary readers miniature, mobile, accessible, affordable collections of Miller Parker's most beautiful work. They appeared at the height of the so-called cult of the countryside and at the same time that Gollancz was publishing Clare Leighton's wood engraved countryside books. Chapter 3 discusses Leighton's reaction to what she perceived as Gollancz's defection and Miller Parker's competition;[54] this first chapter reads Miller Parker's Gollancz book illustrations in terms of her earlier work for children in *How It Happened* and her later work for adult readers of classics published by the Limited Editions Club and the Heritage Press.

Gollancz was responsible for creating what was to be the most fruitful collaboration between Miller Parker and any living writer when he persuaded H. E. Bates, best known in the mid-1930s as the "Country Life" columnist of the *Spectator,* to write essays to accompany Miller Parker's illustrations.[55] In March 1936 Miller Parker first mentioned Bates in her correspondence with her friend and patron Philip "Gibby" Gibbons, noting that Bates "wants spotted toadstools." She continued, "I'm doing some odd things until Bates produces some words."[56] Later, as she piled up her finished blocks, she confided to Gibbons:

> I'm slogging away but Bates has been very naughty. I imagine it was the money he was being advanced that he's used to have 2 months alterations done on his house. He says he has not been able to do any work on the book, but that I'm not to worry that he'll do it alright. I'm doing animals, birds and waterfowl so he'll have to write round my illustrations if he doesn't hurry up.[57]

Yet she had nothing but praise for Bates when *Through the Woods* and, later, *Down the River* came out. After publication of her second Gollancz volume she wrote Gibbons, "I'm so glad you like Bates' writing so much too. He didn't get his fair share of appreciation last year but I think he will walk off with the laurels this year." She directed Gibbons to what she called "very good notes" that appeared in the *Observer* and *John O'London's Weekly,* but, contemplating other reviewers' criticism, concluded somewhat stoically, "As long as some folks like yourself, like the book as a complete whole as you do I am happy."[58]

Woven throughout Miller Parker's letters to Gibbons are detailed descriptions of wild and domestic plants that serve as both inspiration for and distraction from her artwork. In October 1936, satisfied by though weary from her labors producing *Through the Woods,* she told Gibbons, "I'd like to do something away from books but the ideas won't come yet. . . . I just keep looking at things for themselves."[59] These "things for themselves" were the natural things in her garden and in the countryside around her new home in Pheasant's Hill, Hambledon, located near the River Thames. We know that by February 1937 Miller Parker was back at work on her next Gollancz book as she mentioned in a letter to Gibbons a "good fishing chapter" by Bates (presumably "Fish and Fishermen"). More compelling than news about Bates, however, was "the excitement" in her garden, where bulbs were sprouting, hazel catkins showing off in "grand display," and "wild plum blossom . . . snowdrops and plum roses were popping up all over the place."[60] Her ability to translate her passionate responses to "things for themselves" into designs of line and light that also communicate her collaborator-author's narrative visions is one of the reasons her small wood engravings with close-up views of tree buds, birds, and beasts in her Gollancz books and elsewhere are among her most accomplished. The swooping lines of *March Hares* in *Down the River,* for example, move us joyously through the white space of the page, giving form to our imaginings of what Bates describes as the "inexplicable lunacy" and "strange beauty" of hares gathered together at the springtime riverside (Figure 1.10).[61]

Miller Parker's full-page wood engravings of human figures rarely achieve the sense of visual intimacy or felt reality communicated by her small animal engravings or her beguiling scenes of distant rural landscapes (Figure 1.11). Rogerson is right to worry that Miller Parker's portraits of rural people disguise the signs and smells of poverty and dirt that her laboring characters experience in their verbal worlds.[62] He identifies Miller Parker's gamekeeper in *Through the Woods* as a fortunate, ferocious exception to her preference for clean scenes of gentle human activity, citing Bates's comment, "very good, just like him [Bates's gatekeeper] . . . my work is not up to the standard of your pictures" (Plate 3).[63] Every line of Miller Parker's austere, imposing gamekeeper communicates Bates's "good, simple, hot-blooded hatred" of keepers who embody the latent violence of a state hostile to common walkers seeking access to beautiful grounds.[64] In part this is due to her gamekeeper's location within a wood, typically the most striking and emotionally ambiguous of Miller Parker's rural landscapes. He dominates the foreground of *The Villain and His Dog* and, like all of Miller Parker's most dramatically rendered subjects, is seen from below. His shadowed body is framed by vertical tree trunks that evoke on the one hand claustrophobic prison bars and on the other vaunting columned temples. The reader's only possible escape from this gothic scene is a gleaming white path that stretches in a winding diagonal from the upper left to the lower right corner of the engraving. It leads out of the picture, out of the woods that the reader has come to love and hopes to pass through. To go forward, to turn the page, is to face the gamekeeper's gun, the precise white lines of its steel barrel reflecting as they mock the gentle whites of the woodland footpath. Here as in so many other Miller Parker illustrations, trees on the page, pressed from engraved wooden blocks, convey the darker, more

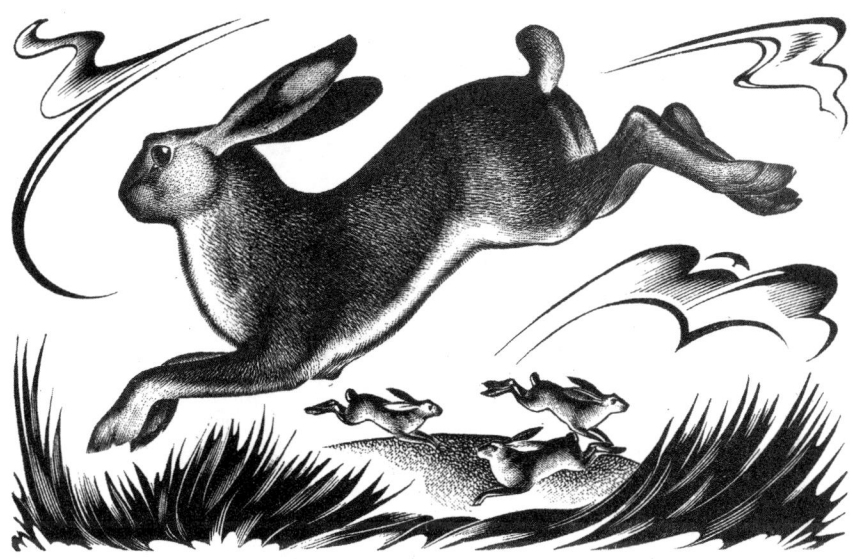

conflicted feelings of human relations worked out in a rural scene.

The gamekeeper is Miller Parker's embodiment of the cruel violence of an invisible squire and anonymous state. He is also her version of a witch in the woods. The woodland fears of Hansel and Gretel, Snow White, and Little Red Riding Hood haunt Bates's account of this "evil spirit" (*Through the Woods*, 21) who is most threatening when he appears at the twilight hour, when the trees themselves give

FIGURE 1.10   Agnes Miller Parker's wood engraved *March Hares*, framed by modernist abstractions of scudding clouds and waving grasses that elegantly repeat the natural curves of the leaping creatures. From H. E. Bates, *Down the River* (London: Gollancz, 1937), 95. 4¾ × 3 inches. Reproduced by permission of the Estate of Agnes Miller Parker.

the woods a "powerful quality of darkness, some awful intimidating blackness" (42). Bates, who came of proud Northamptonshire poaching stock, tells us that his irrational twilight terror of trees, the trespasser's inheritance, "flourishes on littleness and confinement" (43). It is a reaction to the "spell" cast by woods that makes itself felt in "the strange silence of a small and confined world" (15). Unable to precisely define the source of this woodland mystery, Bates unwittingly chooses imagery that could just as aptly describe the qualities that give Miller

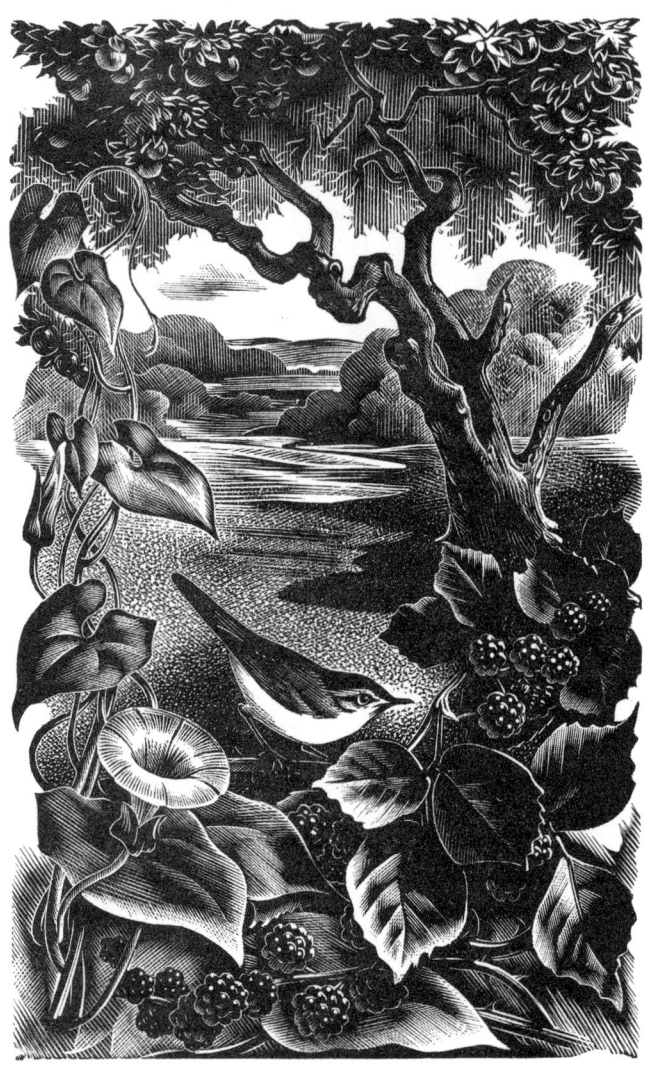

AUTUMN

FIGURE 1.11 Agnes Miller Parker's wood engraving *Autumn*, a perfect pastoral scene. From Eiluned Lewis's forgotten *Honey Pots and Brandy Bottles* (London: Country Life, 1954), 63. 3¾ × 6 inches. Reproduced by permission of the Estate of Agnes Miller Parker.

Parker's wood engravings their interpretive power: darkness, awful blackness, littleness, and confinement. *Fox Cubs* (43), *Passage of Tiny Feet* (27), and *Keeper's Victims* (20) are perfect small, dark worlds that lead us to conclude with Rogerson that "the lines of an engraving could also evoke such magic" (66) (Figure 1.12).

GEORGE MACY AND THE LIMITED EDITIONS CLUB

Miller Parker, who had complained in a 1935 letter to Gibbons about the "slap dash style of [Jonathan Cape's] mass production," became with Gollancz reconciled to the paradoxical condition of being a fine artist, expert in the slow and painstaking engraving of boxwood blocks, who was dependent on the speedy technologies of mass reproduction for print exhibition and income.[65] The American publisher George Macy replaced Gollancz as the businessman-innovator-mentor whose commissions of book illustrations introduced her wood engravings to an even wider public. His Limited Editions Club, or LEC, brought 1,500 subscribers new semifine, semilimited illustrated editions each month, advancing his Depression-era aims of publishing "the best work that could be done at a moderate cost with the finest book people available."[66] "The finest book people available" meant, for Macy, not only the finest authors, both classic and modern, but the finest illustrators, designers, printers, and binders. To his credit and profit, he did not honor the industrial and academic difference between good literature and good books. When he died in 1956, his wife, Helen Macy, took over the LEC and its unlimited partner enterprise, the Heritage Press, extending Macy's values, Miller Parker's influence, and the twentieth-century wood engraving revival into the late 1960s. In the words of Rogerson, the LEC "provided an absolutely indispensable outlet for creative wood engravers."[67]

We have no evidence that Miller Parker perceived her LEC-commissioned illustrations as children's book illustrations, but if we treat them as part of Whalley and Chester's story of 1930s women's art and accomplishment begun with Power's *How It Happened,* we can make better literary sense of this woman wood engraver's total life and work. Reading from Miller Parker's children's to adults' books with wood engraved illustrations and then reading adults' books as children's literature tests the integrity of multiple critical divides: between fine books and good literature, between British literature and American publishers, and between the wood engraving of the 1930s revival and that of the 1940s, 1950s, and

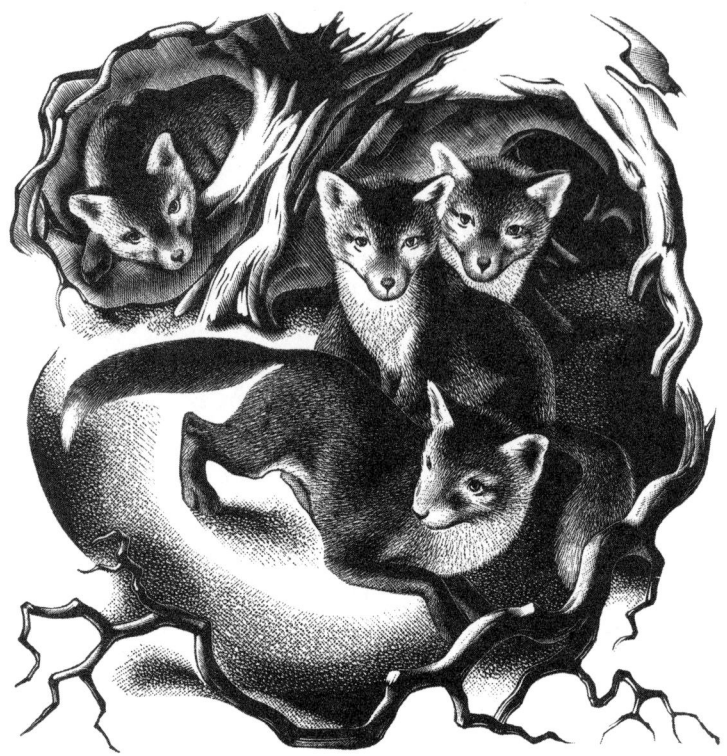

1960s, when, in the words of LEC historian Carol Porter Grossman, "most of [Agnes Miller Parker's] best work was done for either George or Helen Macy for the Heritage Press or the LEC."[68]

In *The Making of Middlebrow Culture,* Joan Shelly Rubin reminds us that in these post–World War II decades, "Americans created an unprecedented range of activities aimed at making literature and other forms of 'high' culture available to a wide reading public. Beginning with the Book-of-the-Month Club . . . book clubs provided subscribers with recently published works chosen by expert judges."[69] Rubin does not mention George Macy, but her groundbreaking history provides a context for understanding Macy's Limited Editions Club as part of the

FIGURE 1.12 Agnes Miller Parker's *Fox Cubs,* depicting the creatures whose "endlessly fascinating . . . devilries" on the riverbank bewitch the narrator. From H. E. Bates, *Through the Woods* (London: Gollancz, 1936), 43. 4⅝ × 4⅞ inches. Reproduced by permission of the Estate of Agnes Miller Parker.

larger movement to bring "high" culture into ordinary Americans' living rooms through subscription-based book clubs. Macy loved good books, fine papers, fine design and illustration, and he wanted anyone and everyone to be able to share this love. His Limited Editions Club combined a great books ideology of access with a fine books ideology of refined cultural consumption, and, in books illustrated by Agnes Miller Parker, white-line wood engraving was the guarantor of these seemingly contradictory cultural aims. Whether these wood engravings and aims were packaged up in books for children or adults made no difference; in the LEC program there literally was no difference.

Grossman tells us that "[Miller] Parker was one of George's favorite artists, and also one of his best."[70] By October 1937, she was well on her way to completing her first commissioned project for him, writing to Gibbons that she had "accepted this job as a change," putting Gollancz on hold until the next year in order to do "this more precious stuff."[71] Macy had launched the LEC less than ten years earlier, in 1929, entering a market dominated by expensive fine book imports from English private presses like Nonesuch, Golden Cockerel, and Doves, and overpriced "shoddy" American books that he told his club members were "conceived in commercialism and untouched by the thirst for beauty."[72] Many in the book industry were skeptical of Macy's enterprise when he first announced it. On the one hand, he was criticized by some New York publishers who were threatened by potential erosion of their profits on imported fine press books. On the other hand, some fine printers were suspicious of this newcomer's capacity to pull off this popularizing venture.[73] We know from Macy's defense of his project in his July 1929 *Monthly Letter* that still others in the literary world criticized his lack of focus on "literature itself." In response to an attack of this kind published in the *Saturday Review,* Macy protested:

> The Saturday Review's gentleman horrified us by saying that we were under-emphasizing the literature itself. The first words in our announcement are "Your favorite books . . ."; the first words in the statement of our purpose are: "To furnish to lovers of beautiful books, unexcelled editions of their favorite works."[74]

Macy's determination to publish "your favorite books" is archivally recorded but practically useless as a measure of understanding his literary criteria for publication. Favorite for whom and upon what basis? His motto, printed on the masthead of the *Sandglass* newsletter that accompanied subscribers' monthly book deliveries, was "The classics which are our heritage from the past, in Editions which will be the heritage of the future." Reviewing the entirety of Macy's LEC editions from 1929 through 1956, Grossman concludes that Macy organized his publishing programs around the vague and powerful (and powerful because vague) idea of a classic, publishing "Western classics [and] important works from other cultures," and "a contemporary book touted to become a classic."[75] Into this last category, "a contemporary book touted to become a classic," we may insert as a prime example Macy's edition of Joyce's *Ulysses* (1935), with six commissioned illustrations by Henri Matisse, from the LEC's sixth series of 1934–35. Yet in contrast to Agnes Miller Parker's highly celebrated LEC volumes of established classics by Shakespeare, Spenser, Gray, and Hardy, Macy's *Ulysses* was considered a failure as measured by club member return rates. Even with an introduction by Stuart Gilbert, Joyce's first scholarly interpreter, there are virtually no mentions of the book in modernist or any other kind of book or literary history.[76] This book arrived in the mailboxes of book club subscribers within months of LEC editions of Lewis Carroll's *Through the Looking-Glass,* illustrated with copies of John Tenniel's original engravings; O. Henry's *The Voice of the City,* illustrated by George Grosz; and *Slovenly Peter,* Mark Twain's translation of the nineteenth-century German children's picture book *Der Struwwelpeter.* Conveying more confidence in the quality of Macy's *Slovenly Peter* than his *Ulysses,* Grossman writes, "[*Slovenly Peter*] would be the perfect publication for the Club—a charming first edition of an unknown Twain manuscript issued in the centennial year of his birth."[77] "Charming" and children—these words suggest aesthetic values that are powerful enough to elevate an illustrated *Struwwelpeter* above an illustrated *Ulysses* or a Miller Parker illustration above a Matisse print.

The disappointments of LEC readers with Macy's illustrated *Ulysses* help us understand Miller Parker as an artist whose wood engravings in LEC and Heritage Press books take us into conversations that matter to scholars of modern and modernist art and literature. If we entertain Macy's belief that new methods of bookmaking and distribution make old works modern, Miller Parker's LEC and Heritage Press volumes, through the peculiar affordances of wood blocks, gravers, and ink and through Macy's professional mediations, become part of Rozsika

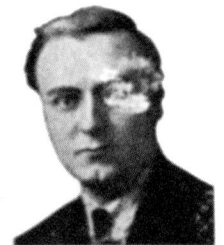

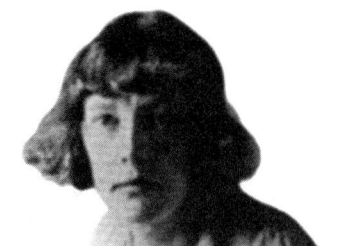

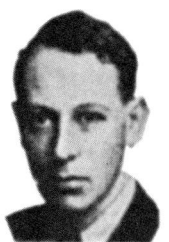

D. W. BROGAN   AGNES MILLER PARKER   ALEXANDER WERTH

Parker and Griselda Pollock's feminist story of women's right to restoration within Western art history (Figure 1.13).[78]

Academia has institutionalized through stratified and often competing departments and fields the difference between adults' and children's art and literature that Macy was content to ignore. Late in the twentieth century, structuralism and semiotics helped bring children's and adults' literatures back together again, with Moebius positioning children's picture books at the forefront of studies of what we now call multimodality.[79] Moebius argued that children's picture books demand our close reading in relation to their surrounding words and white spaces, and that together the visual and verbal create meaning for readers. Writing at about the same time as Moebius, children's literature scholar Perry Nodelman observed in his full-length study *Words About Pictures* (1988) that "the words of the texts so permeate our experience of the pictures that the two seem to mirror each other. But they do not in fact do so—as becomes obvious as soon as we separate them from each other."[80] For Nodelman, pictures are not irrelevant or distracting marginalia, posing more or less of a threat to the meaning of a central text. Rather, "pictures actually change the meanings of texts in the process of supporting them."[81] Nodelman's argument reversed the logic of John Berger's 1972 BBC TV series and partner book, *Ways of Seeing,* in which Berger argued that technologies of visual reproduction force paintings to surrender their "original independent

FIGURE 1.13 The only photograph of Agnes Miller Parker surviving in the public sphere? Miller Parker's intense gaze draws our eyes to her image situated between two other contributor photographs in the forgotten first pages of *The 1943 Saturday Book,* edited by Leonard Russell (London: Hutchinson, 1943). 1¾ × 1⅜ inches. Reproduced by permission of the Estate of Agnes Miller Parker.

meaning" to words. Berger believed that in reproduced texts like illustrated books, "the meaning of an image is changed according to what one sees immediately beside it or what comes immediately after it."[82] A narrative, a caption, any words whatsoever, can take over the power of the reproduced painting.

Miller Parker's wood engravings, as unique, three-dimensional sculptures engraved on wooden blocks, are subject to the same kinds of evacuations of meaning by words as the paintings Berger discusses. However, wood engravings as two-dimensional prints whose designs anticipate their ends as multiplying illustrations in a book achieve the power attributed by Nodelman to images in children's picture books; they "actually change the meanings of texts in the process of supporting them." While Macy might have assumed that Miller Parker's wood engraved illustrations, with their Bewick associations, would hold time still while holding up a canon of English classics, in fact their literary meanings and effects are destabilizing and ambiguous. Wood engraving in the LEC volumes could signify mobility and modernity as well as conservation, turning a familiar classic into something different: something dynamic, uncertain, and yearned for rather than fully known and previously realized.

Perhaps the best example of Miller Parker's destabilizing effects on an LEC classic is her *Tess of the D'Urbervilles* (1956), the second of five Hardy novels that she illustrated for Macy and her first major commission after her traumatic rupture with McCance. Rogerson assures us that when Miller Parker and McCance "[went] their separate ways . . . much of her best work was still to come," with *Tess* representing "a new beginning in Agnes Miller Parker's illustration."[83] Certainly *Tess* marked a new beginning in Miller Parker's personal life, a time of anguish, liberation, and self-reinvention. It matters for women's history and art history that during the months that Miller Parker had planned and then executed her escape from McCance, she was reading and illustrating a novel whose heroine is trapped and then destroyed by men's social power and the law's sexual hypocrisy. The success of Miller Parker's *Tess* does not lie in its experiments with full-page colored landscape wood engravings or its black-and-white figural illustrations, but rather in the mere fact of its existence.[84] A modern visual object and print commodity, it testifies to Miller Parker's creation of a happy Scottish ending for her English story, one lived in defiance of inherited tragic plots that defined and ruined many women's lives in the decades between suffrage and sexual revolution.

ABIDING WITH TESS

Miller Parker learned from Bewick more than tricks of tone and design; her full- and half-page illustrations in *Tess* adopt the undefined, unframed edges of Bewick's small vignettes, capturing not charm but some kind of darker magic (Figure 1.14). Tom Lubbock, attempting to identify the source of magic in Bewick's vignettes, resorts to metaphors; Bewick's vignettes are "contained environment[s]" from which "there is no exit"; they are like "a desert island or a snow-dome," a "kind of secret," creating the illusion that "you'd put your eye to a glass or your ear to a shell."[85] Lubbock explains that in contrast to a figure in a frame, which we view as though through a window, with the figure free to pass into the scene beyond our gaze, a figure in a Bewick vignette is trapped. When this figure "meets its irregular edge it can't go farther. It would start to dematerialize or break up. It must stay inside, on pain of destruction."[86] This is the threat that confronts Miller Parker's Tess, who lives inside unframed wood engravings that keep her alive but whose shifting, shimmering borders threaten her with self-destruction if she attempts to walk outside them.

Miller Parker's wood engravings of Tess dissolve more thoroughly than any kind of framed or color picture in what W. J. T. Mitchell would identify as the unobtrusive, invisible frontier of the white page separating verbal and visual, the sayable and the seeable.[87] This has the effect of bringing the pastness of Hardy's words into the presentness of the wood engraving through integration of the white of the image and the white of the paper. Meanwhile, the black lines of Miller Parker's wood engravings speak back to the black lines of Hardy's typeset text, changing it and, through the vehicle of LEC distribution, sending it into the futures of unknown readers. If those readers should happen to be children, girls even, they might say as Jane Eyre did about Bewick's vignettes, "Each picture told a story: mysterious often to my undeveloped understanding and imperfect feelings, yet ever profoundly interesting."[88] Inviting us to read from picture to picture, just as often turning pages from back to front as front to back, Miller Parker's *Tess* turns Hardy's *Tess* into a book that modern girls can bear to dwell in.[89] This book, this world, is one in which the heroine organizes the rural landscape around her illustrated self, challenging Hardy's conviction that the rural landscape will tragically disorganize the too-modern girl who walks through it

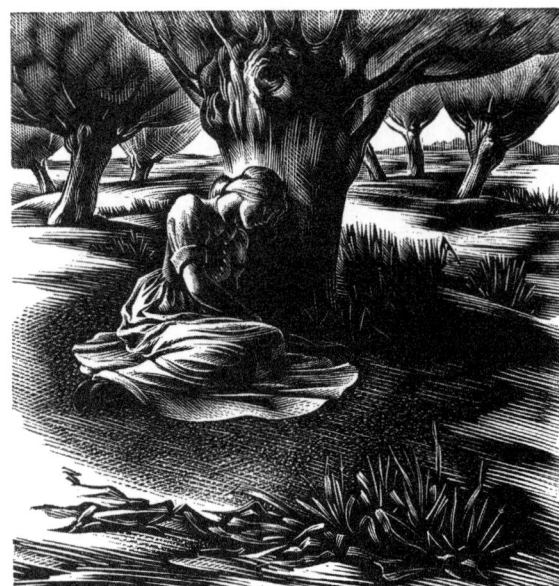

FIGURE 1.14 Agnes Miller Parker's Tess, sorrowing among the pollard willows. From Thomas Hardy, *Tess of the D'Urbervilles* (New York: Limited Editions Club, 1956), 203. 3¾ × 3¾ inches. Reproduced by permission of the Estate of Agnes Miller Parker.

alone. *Tess*, and every other Hardy novel that Miller Parker illustrated for the Macys, escapes the verbal demands of narrative progression, re-creating with each reproduction of a white-line wood engraving the secret story of Miller Parker's escape from punishing masculine control. Even the tragic Tess may speak of the possibility for women's freedom, independence, and happiness in the rural places of modern Britain.

More so than Gwen Raverat, Miller Parker "mainly worked in the adult field," her linocuts for Rhoda Power's *How It Happened* proving the exception to her rule of accepting commissions for wood engraved illustrations that would appear in books for adults. Yet as her illustrations for Gollancz and for George and Helen Macy suggest, and as this book argues more broadly, something magical, something transformative, happens to our disciplinary assumptions about the people, places, and media of modernity if we begin our literary studies of modern books with their wood engravings. Children's literature scholars like Moebius, Nodelman, and Hunt and art historians like Hamilton, Selborne, and Whalley and Chester can model for scholars in other disciplines how to perform adult readings of children's literature, teaching us how to value culturally

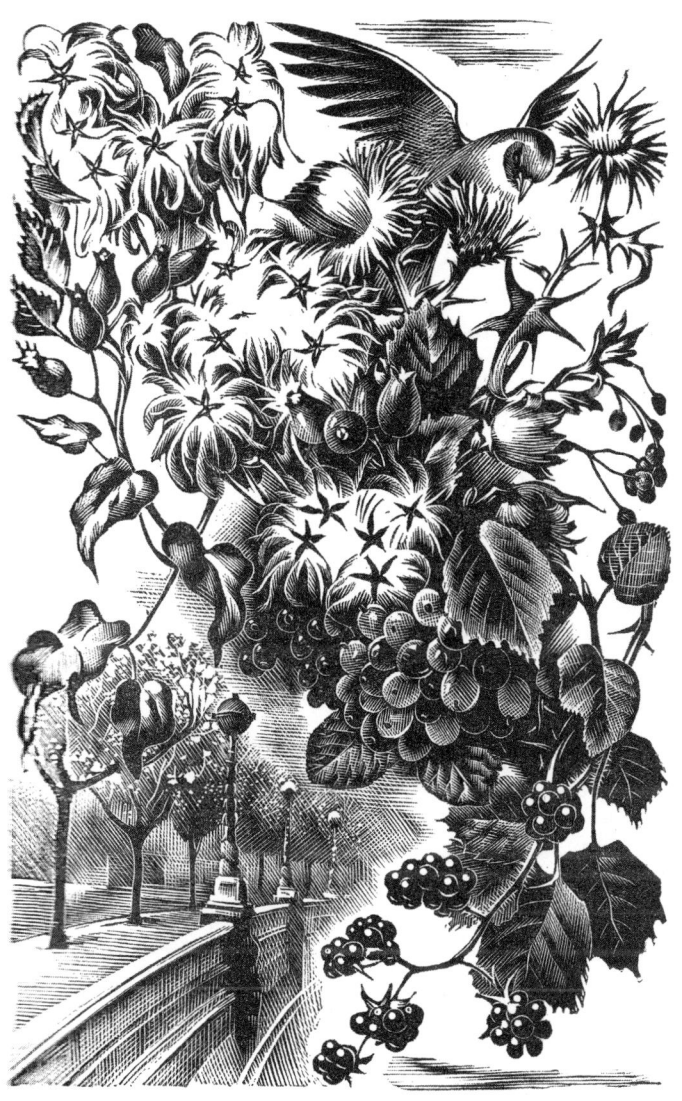

FIGURE 1.15 Agnes Miller Parker's wood engraving of an effusion of native trees, plants, and birds superimposed on a staid image of London plane trees is a fanciful realization of a late Victorian city freed from nonnative species. From Richard Jeffries, "Trees in and around London," in *"The Old House at Coate" and Other Hitherto Unpublished Essays* (London: Lutterworth Press, 1948), 125. 3½ × 5½ inches. Reproduced by permission of the Estate of Agnes Miller Parker.

diminished literary forms. The chapters in this volume adopt these scholars' cultural values and disciplinary practices for modernist studies while also reversing them to suit feminist purposes, performing childlike—or what Hunt once called child*ist*—readings of literature published in books for adults.[90] This means approaching complex, multimodal texts illustrated with wood engravings the way a child might encounter Bewick's *Quadrupeds* or *British Birds*: with wonder, open to enchantment, moving from image to image, often back to front, little to big, from artist to author and from book to literature. Such revisions of method are both products of and inspirations for radical questionings of disciplinary boundaries, confounding as they cross divisions between picture and literature, art and illustration, child and adult in order to recover British women's art for a more capacious and inclusive modern literary and book history (Figure 1.15).

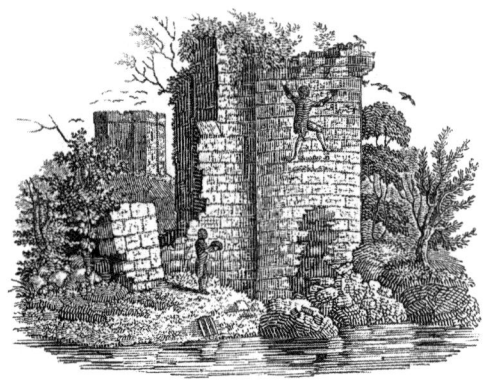

"figures delineated with all the fidelity and animation I was able to impart"

In the mid-eighteenth century when children's books were introduced into British markets, increasing numbers of middle-class parents were able to buy in town shops and stalls child-sized pages of moral, mathematical, or alphabetical instruction bound between handsome covers. Yet many would find to their disappointment that their children preferred cheap chapbooks hidden in wandering peddlers' packs, seeking delight in tales about Jack the Giant Killer, Guy of Warwick, or Robin Hood. Children's literature scholar Humphrey Carpenter reassures us that "the young themselves loved such [peddled] stuff; Boswell, Wordsworth and Lamb were among those who looked back at it nostalgically when they were grown men."[1]

Thomas Bewick was less easily impressed. Some of his earliest wood engraved book illustrations, completed when he was still apprenticed to the Newcastle silver engraver Ralph Beilby, his future business partner and coauthor, appeared in ephemeral children's books that took the place of just this kind of peddler's

Thomas Bewick, *A History of British Birds,* vol. 1, *Land Birds* (1797, 1826), 182. 2⅞ × 2¼ inches.

chapbook. Bewick records in his *Memoir* that as a "school Boy" in the early 1760s he had been "displeased with most of the [wood]cuts in children's books, & particularly with those of the 'Three Hundred Animals'" (105). This book of animals, Thomas Boreman's *Description of Three Hundred Animals,* "served as a natural history primer for generations of eighteenth-century schoolchildren."[2] And for as many generations of children who suffered like Bewick with its conventional illustrations, just so many generations of printers and booksellers increased their profits by recycling old woodcuts instead of commissioning new illustrations in their children's books. Their old blocks produced images that were so simple and smudged that Bewick knew, even as a boy doodler, that he was capable of better illustrative art. He vowed then and there, so the story goes, to create children's books illustrated with animals that, in their fidelity to nature, would register his "extreme interest . . . in the hope of administering to the pleasures & amusement of youth" (*Memoir,* 105).

For Bewick, knowledge of natural history and pleasure in illustrated children's books were inseparable and essential.[3] We know this in part because he tells us so many times, and for the last time in 1826 when as an old man still working at his engraver's bench, he began his preface to the sixth edition of *A History of British Birds* with these words:

> When I first undertook my labours in Natural History, my strongest motive was to lead the minds of youth to the study of that delightful pursuit, the surest foundation on which Religion and Morality can efficiently be implanted in the heart, as being the unerring and unalterable book of the Deity. My writings were intended chiefly for youth; and the more readily to allure their pliable, though discursive, attention to the Great Truths of Creation, I illustrated them by figures delineated with all the fidelity and animation I was able to impart to mere woodcuts without colour. (iii)[4]

In this statement, we see Bewick's characteristic Enlightenment faith in education, application, and devotion to nature as a path to the "unalterable book of the Deity." Adopting John Locke's ideal, expressed in *Some Thoughts Concerning Education* (1693), of providing beginning readers with "some easy pleasant book" suited to the young person's capacity, Bewick also insists on youth's entitlement to "delight" through education or what he elsewhere describes as "instruction" with "constant cheerfulness" (preface, iii). Animals had been regarded as enticing subjects for beginning readers since the fifteenth century, when William Caxton first translated Aesop's fables into English from French. Locke preferred Aesop to the Bible, ignoring altogether contemporary children's books, and Bewick published multiple versions of Aesop, the last one in 1818.[5] By this time, Bewick was famous. He kept busy in his workshop, happily preparing revised editions of *Quadrupeds* and *British Birds,* receiving visitors, and drafting his memoir.[6]

In 1827 Bewick's status as national celebrity was confirmed by a visit from John Audubon, the renowned American ornithologist and bird portraitist, who recorded his impressions of the aging artist.[7] The account is, as Iain Bain notes, "a most engaging portrait of the man and his hearthside":[8]

At length we reached the dwelling of the Engraver, and I was at once shewn his workshop. There I met the old man, who, coming towards me, welcomed me with a hearty shake of the hand, and for a moment took off a cotton night-cap, somewhat soiled by the smoke of the place. He was a tall stout man, with a large head, and with eyes placed farther apart than those of any man that I have ever seen:—a perfect old Englishman, full of life, although seventy-four years of age, active and prompt in his labours. . . . The old gentleman and I stuck to each other, he talking of my drawings, I of his wood cuts.[9]

After Bewick's death in November 1828, praises from other prominent Victorian artists and scholars cemented his reputation as one of England's most original and talented artists. Thomas Carlyle, William Wordsworth, and Alfred Lord Tennyson all paid him tribute.[10] John Ruskin urged his students to read Bewick's *Memoir* and study his vignettes in order to understand both his "utmost strength and utmost rudeness." He was especially taken with Bewick's vignette *The Frog and the Stork* in *Aesop's Fables,* urging his students to study how Bewick's "perfectly good woodcutting" had expressed the "essential frogginess of mind—the marsh temper." Only then could they realize the "magnificent artistic power, the flawless virtue, veracity, tenderness,—the infinite humour of the man."[11] Elsewhere Ruskin claimed Bewick as one of the most English of English artists, an engraver whose treatments of rustic life helped the "very amiable and worthy" English people resist the "disease" of Italian and French taste for art of the demimonde.[12] Before our eyes, we see a man becoming a myth. As with Audubon's "perfect old Englishman," Ruskin helped to transform Bewick from a human artist, embedded in vibrant and diverse rural and urban cultural contexts that shaped his mind and informed his art, into a northern icon of nature and nation.[13] For Ruskin, Bewick *is* England, and Englishness explains "why Hunt can paint a flower but not a cloud; why Turner can paint a cloud but not a flower; why Bewick a pig, but not a girl; and Miss Greenaway a girl, but not a pig."[14]

Bewick, the mythic hero, is big, bold, strong, friendly, naturally keen and acute while also a bit naive and unpolished, utterly at home in his hearty, thoroughly English masculinity. He is a delightful, irresistible fiction assembled over time out of the words of admirers who were busy interpreting and reshaping for new generations of readers the words of his *Memoir* and the pictures of his books.

TWO

A Happy Heritage

Children's Poetry Books and Prestige Publishing

In 1936 Gwen Raverat testified in the preface to her wood engraved edition of Elizabeth Anna Hart's *The Runaway* (1872) to the girlhood happiness she had found in Victorian children's books. Here, in a little-known piece of writing, Raverat describes how she delighted to climb into a "great, curtained bed [like Miss Simmonds's bed in the picture in Figure 2.1]" and hear a sick aunt read aloud Hart's "Victorian Story for the Young." A similar testimony to the impact of favorite children's books on family reading and identity introduces Raverat's 1939 wood engraved edition of *The Bird Talisman*, a "Fairy Tale" written in 1852 by her great-uncle Henry Allen Wedgwood and passed down to generations of young Darwins and Wedgwoods. Though fearing she commits some kind of "sacrilege" in "tampering with a sacred work," she defends her version of the tale as improving the "arid" appearance of the original work, whose pen-and-ink illustrations were too few and too small. The illustrations she created are some of the most striking and complex wood engravings she ever produced, in or out of a book (Plate 2; Figure 1.8).

More familiar to adults than either *The Bird Talisman* or *The Runaway* is *Period Piece*. As discussed in the Introduction, it is here that Raverat publicly reveals her love affair with Thomas Bewick and, in conjunction with her pen-and-ink "sillier sort of drawings," records her gendered awakening to her vocation as wood engraver.[1] This vocation brought her many commissions to illustrate children's books; the story of Raverat's and other women wood engravers' contributions to children's fiction—fables, fairy tales, stories, and novels—is

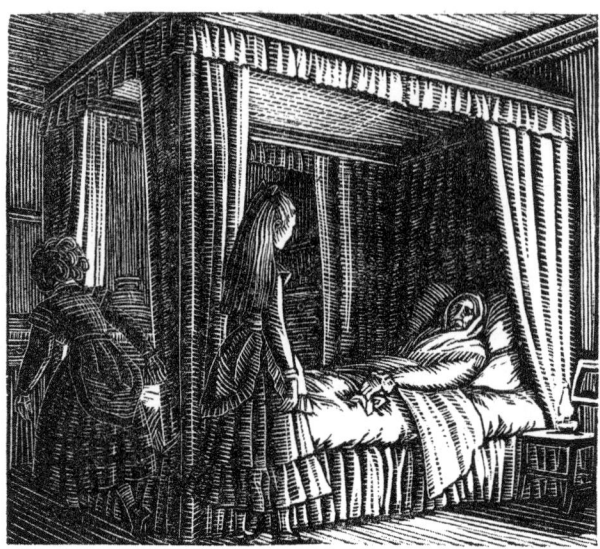

important enough to earn its own extended treatment in chapter 5. This chapter is devoted to analysis
of Raverat's and Joan Hassall's contributions to children's books of poetry.

In *Period Piece,* Raverat adopts the convention,
made familiar by Humphrey Carpenter in *Secret
Gardens,* of nestling the child characters in an ordinary Arcadia that is accessible right through the
looking glass, or, in Raverat's case, window glass.
No sooner does Raverat introduce herself into the
family story—"Here at the Grange I was born in
the summer of 1885, and here I and my brothers and sister spent all our youth"
(42)—than she inserts a pastoral scene. Visible through the big night nursery
window of her father's new home along the Cam is "the slow green river," its boats
and islands, weir and footpath "where I always thought the Lord walked when
he led his flock to lie down in green pastures" (42). Next we are directed to look
at the scene out the children's day nursery window, "across the road to the grass
bank and the lime trees opposite; and over Queens' Green to the great elms of

FIGURE 2.1 Gwen Raverat's wood engraved illustration of the unimaginative Miss Simmonds, ill in bed, with impudent Olga hiding and Clarice providing cover. From Elizabeth Anna Hart, *The Runaway: A Victorian Story for the Young* (London: Faber and Faber, 1936), 157. 3³⁄₁₆ × 2¾ inches. Copyright 2025 Estate of Gwen Raverat. All rights reserved. DACS/ Artists Rights Society (ARS).

the Backs" (42). Again, memories of childhood are composed of pastoral images, of "horses graz[ing] on the smooth ancient turf, which can only be made by
hundreds of years of pasturing animals" (42). This scene is the "original place"
Raverat says she associated with the poem she then thought so lovely, Mary
Howitt's "Buttercups and Daisies":

> Buttercups and daisies—
> O the pretty flowers!
> Coming ere the spring-time,
> To tell of sunny hours. (42)

Readers familiar with Raverat's children's books will recall Raverat's engraving for this same poem in *The Cambridge Book of Poetry for Children* (Figure 2.2).
Reissued in 1932 with fifty-four of Raverat's wood engraved illustrations, this
children's poetry anthology was the first publication to bring her to the attention of a general public that was instructed by enthusiastic critics to regard her
as one of England's leading wood engravers and artists.[2] Biographers are quick
to explain the significance of this commission for Raverat's career and for popular perceptions of the importance of white-line wood engraving as a revived
illustration technique.[3] Less common is the kind of critical work undertaken in
this chapter, which seeks to explain the *literary* significance of Raverat's contributions to children's literature, children's book illustration, and contemporary
visions of an enchanted and enchanting English childhood.

Reading *The Cambridge Book of Poetry for Children* as an object that speaks
to us in multimodal ways, we see how its pictures and poems associate images of
childhood with feelings of nostalgia and a belief in an eternal, ahistorical nature.
But we should also see in these same pictures and poems modern possibilities
that endorse contemporary art and childhood's modern freedoms. We can trace
this complex dynamic of regressive and progressive symbol and feeling if we
read all the verses of "Buttercups and Daisies" against Raverat's accompanying
wood engraving. Howitt's poem is still popular with teachers, presumably because its soothing rhymes and predictable meters reinforce ideas about a stable,
unchanging world, symbolized by the predictable, recurring signs of spring. The
last four lines of the poem's first stanza read:

BUTTERCUPS AND DAISIES

Buttercups and daisies—
O the pretty flowers!
Coming ere the spring-time,
    To tell of sunny hours.
When the trees are leafless;
    When the fields are bare;
Buttercups and daisies
    Spring up here and there.

Welcome, yellow buttercups!
Welcome, daisies white!
Ye are in my spirit
    Vision'd, a delight!
Coming ere the spring-time,
    Of sunny hours to tell—
Speaking to our hearts of Him
    Who doeth all things well.

MARY HOWITT

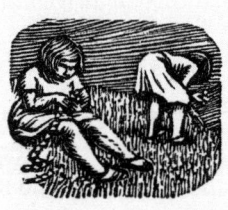

When the trees are leafless;
When the fields are bare;
Buttercups and daisies
Spring up here and there.[4]

Raverat's illustration in the white space at the end of this poem responds to the verbal images of Howitt's verse. She populates Howitt's fields with two children, one creating a daisy chain, the other bending, looking for additional flowers to add to her companion's garland. This image may strike some readers as quaint or old-fashioned, but it is also modern. Its children are girls in the open air, unsupervised, free to roam. They wear the bobbed hair of Raverat's period, not the bound hair of Howitt's. Their dresses are short, ending at the girls' knees, a phenomenon of twentieth-century girlhood. These details exert the pressure of contemporary culture on the image, complicating the poem's endorsement of a conservative vision of rural life that promises endless cycles of buttercups and daisies existing outside human history, an analogue for God's timelessness. If we then read this modern illustration against Raverat's testimony in *Period Piece,* we realize that Howitt's pretty promises of reliably unchanging natural cycles are qualified by Raverat's childhood memories. Raverat's citation of the first four lines of "Buttercups and Daisies" in *Period Piece* leads to this reflection:

> Then the Town Council decided that the level of the Green must be raised; and for a long time—two or three years—it was in a most repulsive mess, while cart after cart dumped refuse there. . . . At last the grass grew on the Green again; but the old, old turf was gone and most of the daisies, too; and it has never been so beautiful since the level was raised. (43)[5]

Raverat's chapter of origins in *Period Piece,* a sort of Darwin's Genesis, buys progress at the expense of pastoral beauty; aesthetic sin has entered paradise.

FIGURE 2.2 Gwen Raverat's wood engraving for Mary Howitt's "Buttercups and Daisies." From *The Cambridge Book of Poetry for Children* (Cambridge: Cambridge University Press, 1932; New York: G. P. Putnam's Sons, 1933), 27. 1⅛ × ⅞ inches. Copyright 2025 Estate of Gwen Raverat. All rights reserved. DACS/Artists Rights Society (ARS).

Like the majority of poems in Raverat's interwar edition of *The Cambridge Book of Poetry for Children,* "Buttercups and Daisies" had been selected for inclusion in the first edition of the Cambridge volume published with illustrations by Maud Fuller in 1916. This date is significant; we can imagine the first edition of *The Cambridge Book of Poetry for Children* appearing in a bookshop window next to 1916 numbers of Harriet Monroe's modernist little magazine *Poetry,* which in February featured poems by W. B. Yeats and in September poems by Ezra Pound.[6] We can also imagine a recruiting poster for the British army hanging on a nearby wall. Recalling these literary, commercial, and political contexts helps us understand how illustrated books and especially illustrated books for children, just as much as poems by Yeats or Pound, offer complex challenges to scholars of twentieth-century modernism and modernity. In the case of the children's poetry anthologies that are the subject of this chapter, wood engraved illustrations embellish or decorate the more authoritative or primary poems, initiating an internal and unpredictable dialogue between the poets and their illustrators and between the illustrators and anthology editors. Illustrations also speak back to previous visual models; we see Raverat "listening" to Bewick and addressing him as surely as she does Howitt. This doubled synchronic-diachronic conversation between forms and media is doubled once again if we recall, as children's literature scholars always do, that children's books are written for two implied readerships: child readers and adult readers who will mediate children's access to the book and the text. Such reflections raise a number of questions: What did the old-fashioned book illustration method of wood engraving mean for elite publishers and ordinary buyers in the context of Depression-era and wartime publishing? What does the work of women wood engravers for children's books in these commercial contexts tell us about wood engraving's role in defining or redefining cultural hierarchies? What difference did the sex of these artists make for their art and its reception? Interesting answers to these questions reside at the intersection of modernist and middlebrow studies, yet it is the field of book history, and specifically the cheery history of Noel Carrington's Puffin Picture Books, that begins this chapter's investigation into the contributions of children's poetry books with wood engravings to a national iconography, a national myth or fable of childhood attachments to rural England and English rurality.[7]

NOEL CARRINGTON, ALLEN LANE, AND PUFFIN PICTURE BOOKS

As a young father in the 1930s, London editor Noel Carrington saw a need for children's books that were "simply written and well illustrated . . . in which children could find for themselves what they wanted to know; to have them in their nursery or at bedtime, and the books so cheap that they could easily be replaced."[8] He concentrated on "home education" for children who were curious about "the how, why and wherefore of what they observed," rather than the "great staples of popular tradition: nursery rhymes, fables, fairy stories."[9] He was equally focused on the business considerations of producing these books as cheaply as possible. Carrington later recalled how he found his answer to his problems in a commercial booklet on aviation that had been produced by Jack Beddington, advertising manager of the Shell Oil Company. Beddington had engaged an artist to illustrate "autolithography," in which the artist him- or herself drew in reverse directly onto stone or zinc plates, thus "doing their own colour separations directly."[10] This avoided complex and expensive camera work, and, in the words of Ian Rogerson, book historian and author of a 1992 exhibition catalog on Noel Carrington and Puffin Picture Books, "cheap books printed in colour became a reality."[11]

Such innovation appealed to the publishing genius of Allen Lane, famed instigator of the paperback revolution sprung in 1935 upon the British public.[12] Lane supported Carrington's idea of a cheap children's series, telling Carrington before he dashed off on a trip to India, "If you can show me that you can produce such books in colour and which can be sold at sixpence, it's on."[13] "That was in August 1939," recalls Carrington. "By the time he returned the Second World War had been declared." Carrington figured war meant the end of his dream, but Lane arranged a meeting and declared, "The worst has happened but evacuated children are going to need books more than ever, especially your kind on farming and natural history."[14] They agreed reluctantly that conditions required initial titles to be geared toward war, so that the first book issued in the series was James Holland's *War on Land,* followed, predictably, by *War at Sea* and *War in the Air* (all 1940).[15] But within a year they had published Clarke Hutton's *15 Nursery Rhymes,* with copy on the inside front cover listing twenty-one Puffin Picture Books, all edited by Noel Carrington. Although Hutton's book shared a subject with Raverat's and Hassall's children's poetry books, it turned the illustration of traditional nursery rhymes into an opportunity for visual experiment rather than visual confirmation of an idealized rural past.

15 Nursery Rhymes is more fanciful than exemplary Puffin Picture Books like *Trees in Britain,* by S. R. Badmin (1943), or *The Magic of Coal,* by Peggy M. Hart (1945), but in other ways is typical of the series' publications. With a simple stitched binding, it boasts four-color images, with double-page spreads of eighteen inches, alternating with black-and-white spreads. Turning the colorful pages of text and illustration for "Old King Cole," for example, brings the reader to the black-and-white two-page spread for "The Lion and the Unicorn." There are no deep blacks anywhere on these pages, and the line art looks gray, as though done in pencil. There are quick, energetic strokes of pen or brush, which keep one turning pages, in motion, but this contributes to an impression that the book is so ephemeral and casual as to be disposable. Disposable—or, more accurately, "replaceable"—is exactly what Carrington had in mind. Nowadays this Clarke Hutton Puffin Picture Book symbolizes the confusion of cultural categories that is one of the subjects of this chapter because it is simultaneously a popular and invisible book—the latter because it is so delicate as to be almost impossible to locate, read, and reproduce.[16] Certainly the book is not charming, nostalgic, or collectible; on the level of production, there are no signs of the aspiration toward permanence or "classic" significance evident in the poetry anthologies illustrated with women artists' wood engravings.[17]

In the context of the 1930s development of color lithography and new technologies of reproduction, it is not surprising that children's books with wood engravings struck readers as old-fashioned, elite, or "classic." However, just like the more celebrated adults' books with illustrations by women wood engravers—books like Agnes Miller Parker's *Esope's Fables,* Clare Leighton's *Four Hedges,* and Hassall's *Portrait of a Village*—children's poetry books illustrated with wood engravings depended on modern industrial processes of mechanical reproduction, mass distribution, and international marketing. Our understanding of Raverat's and other women engravers' accomplishments expands if we emphasize the relations between Bewickian techniques of woodblock engraving and the equally important techniques of modern printing, or the relations between Bewickian inspiration and contemporary gendered publishing, social, and economic contexts. We also gain appreciation of the significance of these women's achievements once we understand the relations between the pastoral subjects associated with Bewick's eighteenth-century books of natural history and twentieth-century engravers' human, social, and occasionally metropolitan subjects. This study's feminist engagement with twentieth-century women's book art reads Raverat's celebrated *Cambridge Book of Poetry for Children* within a wider trend of aspirational, *higher*brow publishing for children, a cultural pattern also supported by publication of Joan Hassall's wood engravings in three volumes of poetry for children, including *A Child's Garden of Verses* (1947), *All Day Long: An Anthology of Poetry for Children* (1954), and *The Oxford Nursery Rhyme Book* (1955).

GWEN RAVERAT AND THE MAKING OF CLASSIC CHILDREN'S POETRY ANTHOLOGIES

The poems in *The Cambridge Book of Poetry for Children* were selected by Kenneth Grahame, best known for publication of the classic children's text of rural retreat, *The Wind in the Willows* (1908). They range from nursery rhymes (e.g., "Curly Locks") and lyrics written for children (e.g., William Roscoe's "The Butterfly's Ball") to lyrics written for adults (e.g., William Wordsworth's "Daffodils") and long narrative poems (e.g., Lord Macaulay's "Horatius"). Raverat's wood engravings in the Cambridge anthology are small, ranging from 1⅛-by-1-inch tailpieces such as that accompanying the Taylor sisters' "Good Night!" (17) (Figure 1.1) to the 3-by-4-inch full-page illustration heading the section titled "Nature, Country, and the Open Air" (114), which appears opposite Robert Bridges's "London Snow" (115–16) (Figure 2.3). Most of her engravings feature children, and all feature animals or elements of the natural world. They are simultaneously delicate and heavy, with stark whites and deep blacks. For example, the engraving opposite "London Snow" ingeniously uses patterns of lines to represent the clean whites drifts of new-fallen snow, the buildings of London, including St. Paul's dome, and a silent city street, with immobilized cars attracting men with shovels while small white specks amid the horizontal black and white lines of night sky perfectly represent the slow, heavy flakes that continue to silence the city. The visual contrasts of the engraving encourage us to notice in the first lines of the poem the verbal contrasts of moving snow and still men, white flakes and brown city, hush and traffic:

> When men were all asleep the snow came flying
> In large white flakes falling on the city brown,
> Stealthily perpetually settling and loosely lying
> Hushing the latest traffic of the drowsy town. (115)

Both the hushed traffic in the poem and the quiet white cars in the accompanying wood engraving refer child readers to a city street scene. It represents an urban nation quieted, tamed, by a benevolent Nature whose weather disguises signs of its metropolitan modernity. Yet critics who praise Raverat's contributions to 1930s children's books revert to language that suggests the modern *contents* of some of her illustrations must give way to the antique black-and-white *forms* of the engraving. The Cambridge University Press *Book of Poetry for Children,* so richly illustrated with wood engravings, seems to mount a deliberate appeal to nationalist nostalgia even as the readers for whom the book is destined are themselves too young to understand nation or nostalgia. The volume depends on more sophisticated buyers or readers to generate nostalgia out of the forms of Raverat's wood engravings, to discover in their black-and-white designs a visual code signaling a past *time* of childhood rather than its present *places.* To the extent that these adults then assign to Raverat their own nostalgic refusals of modernity, Raverat and the other women wood engravers examined in this study might seem supportive of conservative nationalist idealizing, particularly in the context of twentieth-century printing innovations, which, as Noel Carrington discovered, could bring books with large print runs into the budget of a child. The competing literary values in a stressed Depression-era literary marketplace meant that during the very decade Allen Lane was establishing the Penguin paperback empire, editors at elite and specialized presses chose to publish a culturally devalued form of poetry—children's poetry—while simultaneously attempting to signal its "elevated" status within children's book publishing through the use of the old, labor-intensive art of wood engraving.[18]

This chapter argues that white-line wood engraving emerges as a significant component in a complex verbal-visual signifying system within midcentury

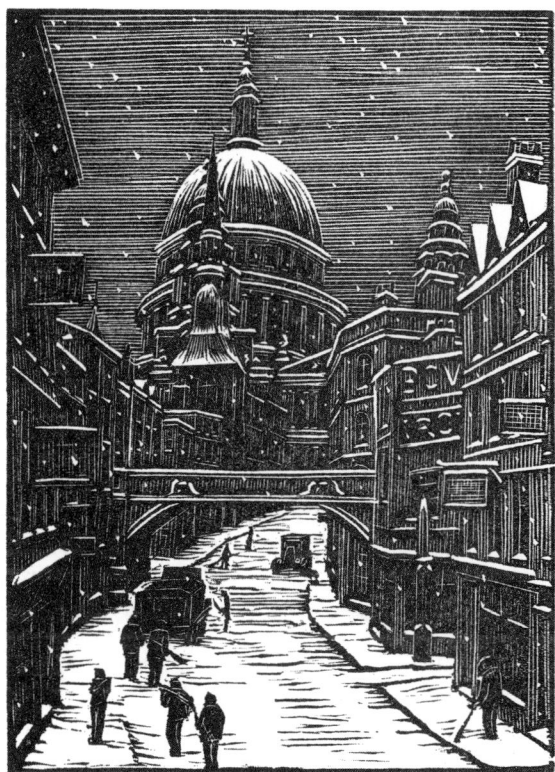

FIGURE 2.3 Gwen Raverat's wood engraving of the quiet metropolis submitting to weather, illustrating Robert Bridges's "London Snow." From *The Cambridge Book of Poetry for Children* (Cambridge: Cambridge University Press, 1932; New York: G. P. Putnam's Sons, 1933), 115. 3 × 4 inches. Copyright 2025 Estate of Gwen Raverat. All rights reserved. DACS/Artists Rights Society (ARS).

children's publishing once Raverat's Cambridge anthology is examined alongside Joan Hassall's contributions to the odd subgenre of wood engraved poetry books for children. The 1932 Raverat volume comes closest in structure, theme, and editorial intent to Hassall's illustrated volume *All Day Long: An Anthology of Poetry for Children,* compiled by Pamela Whitlock and published by Oxford University Press in 1954. The later Oxford volume lacks the sheer number of petite engravings woven throughout Raverat's Cambridge volume, but it has the same general format: more than two hundred pages of poems organized by divisions into numbered parts that are themselves subdivided by sections that are organized thematically. Typically, these subsections are defined by pastoral subtitles such as "Snowflake and Fall," "The Sea! The Sea!," "Flowers and Trees," and "The Singing Wind," or more romantic subtitles like "Travellers" or "Splendid Ships" or "Battles Long Ago."[19] Hassall's full-page wood engravings in two colors announce the beginning of each major section—in order: *The Early Hours, Morning Glory, Afternoon's Amazement,* and *Evening*—and smaller black-and-white tailpieces announce the ends of sections (Plate 4).

Few poems appear in both the Oxford and earlier Cambridge volumes, although Whitlock chose several unique poems by authors also represented in the Grahame anthology (e.g., William Blake, Robert Louis Stevenson, Walter de la Mare).[20] In general, Grahame's tastes led him to choose more nursery rhymes and poems for the very young and Whitlock's led her to choose more nonsense and contemporary poems and more poems by women. While these observations might seem to argue for Whitlock's independence from the Cambridge model and suggest that British children's publishing was starting to adopt American-style postwar innovations, it is more likely that the editors and publishers of both volumes were signaling their shared claims to serious children's literature through the apparatus standard to adult poetry anthologies: a robust table of contents, an editor's preface, an index of author names (Cambridge) or biographical notes on authors (Oxford), an index of first lines, and an index of titles (Oxford only), not to mention a title page with a wood engraving of a child with eyes downcast, reading, and the imprint of an esteemed university press (Figure 2.4). Above all, the illustration form of wood engraving, associated as it was with Bewick and his scenes of North Country life and with his treasured books of natural history, confirms both volumes' aspiration for that designation, "children's classic."[21] The publishers trusted readers to arrive at this "classic" designation upon making other associations—among them, "treasured," "charming," "nostalgic," "beautiful," and "enchanting"—between eighteenth-century wood engravings, the anthologies' contemporary wood engravings, the individual poems printed between the engravings, and the books themselves as paper-and-ink objects.

Aspirational meanings are not necessarily achieved meanings, of course. The Hassall–Whitlock volume, a book apparently designed to evoke all these associations, seems as likely to win classic status as any Raverat volume published two decades previously during the height of the wood engraving revival. However, it is the Opies' *Oxford Nursery Rhyme Book,* published in 1955 with wood engravings by Hassall, that has become famous among children's literature scholars.

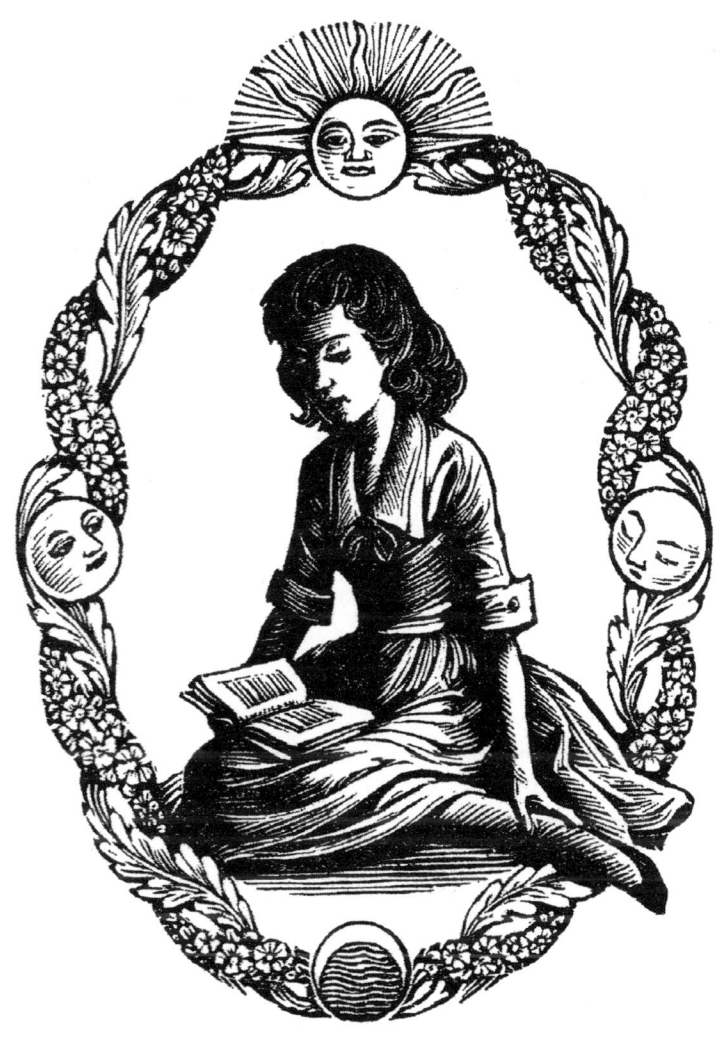

FIGURE 2.4 Joan Hassall's wood engraving of a child reading. Title page art for Pamela Whitlock's postwar collection of poems *All Day Long: An Anthology of Poetry for Children* (Oxford: Oxford University Press, 1954). Reproduced by permission of the Estate of Joan Hassall/Simon Lawrence.

The title page of the Oxford book tells us that it was "assembled" by Iona and Peter Opie and published "with additional illustrations" by Joan Hassall.[22] Such curious language on the title page reflects the novelty of the challenge the Opies presented to Hassall. In a book that was intended to capture "the happy heritage of oral tradition" (v), the editor-assemblers explain in their preface that they did not want Hassall to create engravings that appeared to be original or modern, but rather engravings that, when reproduced in the anthology, would be indistinguishable from reproductions of old woodcuts and engravings.[23] Choosing to convey in visual form an oral (and aural) heritage, they selected illustrations from chapbooks and toy books of the eighteenth and early nineteenth centuries, a period when, they inform readers, "wood engraving was brought to its zenith in the work of Thomas Bewick" (x). They promise readers that they will recognize in the anthology's pages several of Bewick's engravings, as well as some by his brother John (x). Pleased to include illustrations that accompanied traditional rhymes when they first appeared in print, the Opies were equally pleased to boast of the accomplishments of Hassall, whose initial task it was to "illustrate those rhymes which never appeared in the early juvenile literature or of which no satisfactory woodcut impression remains" (x). The final engraving of the volume is Hassall's group portrait of herself with Iona and Peter Opie (Figure 2.5).

In the only footnote attached to their preface that mentions illustration, the Opies emphasize the technical challenges Hassall confronted as she tackled a commission that expanded over the course of two years to include enough engravings for eighty pages:

> For instance, in the illustration of "Old Mother Hubbard" three chapbook cuts were lacking, and Joan Hassall was given a commission similar to the one Ruskin gave Kate Greenaway when he induced her to illustrate additional verses to *Dame Wiggins of Lee*. Joan Hassall's skill in making good the 120-year-old deficiency may be measured on pp. 28–30. (xi)

Here we see the editors placing Hassall in a visual arts tradition that ordinary readers would recognize, associating her with Britain's most famous nineteenth-century art critic and most famous nineteenth-century female illustrator. While Kate Greenaway is not considered highbrow, Ruskin surely may be; combined

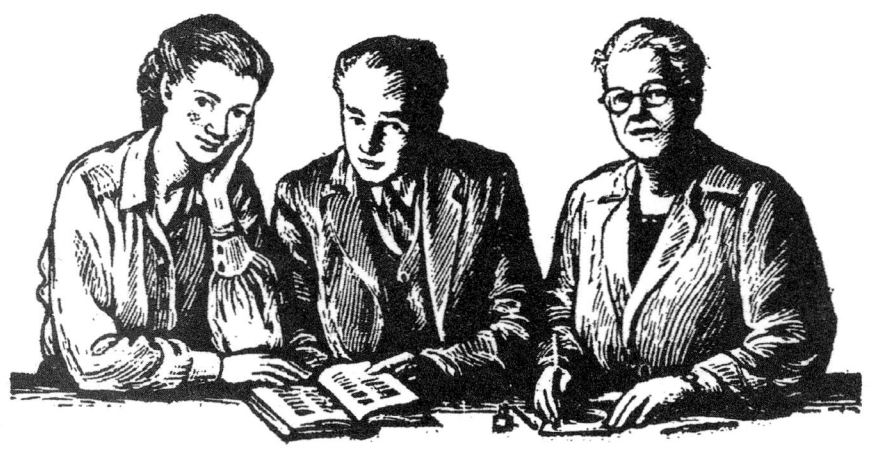

with the preface and footnotes, this brief genealogy has the effect of elevating Hassall within dominant cultural hierarchies and, by association, elevating the humble "800 rhymes and ditties" that surround and support her art. The Opies unapologetically describe the book's contents as "infant jingles, riddles, catches, tongue-trippers, baby games, toe names, maxims, alphabets, counting rhymes, prayers, and lullabies, with which generation after generation of mothers and nurses have attempted to please the youngest, and have, somehow, usually succeeded" (v). Their subject is, in other words, the lowest forms of poetry, those that popular custom associates with some of the most feminized and devalued spaces of the nation—nurseries—and least discerning consumers of literature—babies, toddlers, and small children. How odd, and yet how gratifying, that the Opies had as a publisher Oxford University Press.[24]

FIGURE 2.5 Joan Hassall's affectionate portrait of children's literature collectors, compilers, curators, and interpreters Iona and Peter Opie, with her bespeckled, wood engraved self cautiously joining in their fun. The final and only obviously modern wood engraving from *The Oxford Nursery Rhyme Book,* edited by Iona and Peter Opie (Oxford: Oxford University Press, 1955), 210. 2⅜ × 1⅛ inches. Reproduced by permission of the Estate of Joan Hassall/Simon Lawrence.

It seems likely that Oxford University Press was attempting with Hassall's two postwar poetry anthologies to duplicate and even surpass the success of Cambridge University Press's Raverat–Grahame poetry anthology. The nature of this success may be gauged by the fact that the 1932 Cambridge University Press book with Raverat's wood engravings was a new edition of an earlier publication; as mentioned above, the first edition of Grahame's anthology appeared in the midst of World War I, in 1916, and a second imprint appeared in 1919, immediately after the war. Thus the Cambridge book, in its multiple editions, was a wartime, postwar, and interwar publication, its essentially constant verbal contents belying the radically different social and economic conditions lying just outside the nursery windows of successive generations of middle-class British child readers.

Even with the expanding literacy rates in the first decades of the twentieth century, the parents of poorer children would not have been able to afford any of these competing "classic" poetry volumes. And despite the folk heritage of chapbook woodcuts, twentieth-century wood engraving was a specialized illustration form, appearing most often in books priced for middle-class buyers or upper-class collectors. The gap between folk or popular associations and middle-to-upper-class consumption is just as evident in the children's poetry anthologies examined here. Despite being published in different decades, Raverat's and Hassall's poetry anthologies have a shared class bias, the nature of which can be understood in part through comparative analysis of the iconography of Raverat's Depression-era Cambridge University Press anthology and Hassall's edition of Robert Louis Stevenson's *A Child's Garden of Verses,* published by the small Hopetoun Press in Stevenson's hometown of Edinburgh.

JOAN HASSALL, BRITISH HERITAGE, AND AUSTERITY PUBLISHING

Hassall was, like Bewick, an English artist with emotional and geographical ties to Scotland. Chapter 4 focuses on her experience in Edinburgh during the war, particularly her contributions to the publications of the newly formed Saltire Society.[25] This chapter focuses on her partnership with another Edinburgh publisher, the small Hopetoun Press, which brought out an edition of *A Child's Garden of Verses* with forty-four original Hassall wood engravings in 1947, when Britain was victorious but in ruins and on rations. This children's poetry volume, like Raverat's Cambridge University Press anthology published fifteen years previously, was produced for children by a specialized press, in a time of economic austerity and cultural depression, using an illustration style and technology that readers typically associated with the eighteenth century. Also like Raverat's anthology, it is demonstrably a work of love and labor, with Hassall's delicate, small, detailed wood engravings appearing on virtually every page, most representing children, all representing animals or elements of nature. At a time when the more democratic Puffin Picture Books were still going strong, with dozens of titles in print, including two more titles on poetry,[26] and at a time when few other children's book illustrators or publishers achieved anything of particular note,[27] Hassall was just beginning what would prove to be a remarkable thirteen-year stint of illustrating poetry books for children.

The year that marks the beginning of Hassall's contributions to children's poetry books, 1947, is the same year Mass-Observation undertook a survey for Penguin designed to test the market for a new Puffin series of quality children's books. As McAleer notes, the survey's authors found "that the tuppenny blood trade militated against the sale of books in general, not to mention well-produced ones."[28] They concluded:

> Puffins obviously try and attract by quality, but the effects of quality production on children are unknown and virtually unexamined. For decades children have been reading with enthusiasm badly produced magazines, badly printed on bad paper, and it seems as things are, the rival to the Puffin is not primarily the cloth bound book at all but the paper magazine.[29]

This must have come as fairly sobering news for Puffin's editors, let alone anyone at Oxford or Cambridge University Press who might have happened upon it. Similarly sobering would have been *The Bookseller*'s account in 1935 of the reading habits of one Matilda, a "normal" fourteen-year-old girl, who "had read fifty-eight books over the past year, eleven by her favourite author, 'Sapper,'" and the remainder by P. G. Wodehouse, Sir Arthur Conan Doyle, Ian Hay, and Dennis Wheatley, all "with a traditionally male (and adult) appeal."[30] Both the Mass-Observation survey and this anecdote from *The Bookseller* highlight the cultural and market conditions that mark out as Promethean the efforts of Hassall, Raverat, and their reputable publishers to sell expensive, clothbound, "classic" wood engraved children's poetry books during the interwar, wartime, and postwar years. We are justified in asking, What were these publishers thinking?

The striking similarities revealed by even a casual comparison of pages from Hassall's postwar and Raverat's interwar children's poetry books point to some possible answers. General readers—parents shopping for a birthday present, for example—who train their gaze first on the spare page designs and wood engravings, with their dramatic use of black ink and white line, will find they are unable to tell artists, engravings, or books apart. Positioned above Stevenson's "The Hayloft" and functioning as a visual introduction to it, Hassall's wood engraving depicts a boy high in a hayloft staring dreamily out the window at the tree and sky beyond. Raverat's more boisterous, though tiny, figure playing atop a huge wagon of hay in her engraving for Walter de la Mare's "Bunches of Grapes" (37) might just as easily be used to illustrate Stevenson's poem (Figure 2.6). Here we see the sunlight, the meadow-side, the wagon, even the shining scythe described in Stevenson's first stanzas. Yet this pastoral farm scene, which appears not at the head of "Bunches of Grapes" but at its tail, refers us to only one line of the twelve-line poem, which is not really about hay or fields but about children's fantasies of ownership. We read about Timothy's desire for exotic "bunches of grapes," then Elaine's for "pomegranates pink," and Jane's simple desire for the very English things "a junket of cream and a cranberry tart." Jane is the heroine of the poem, whose wishes for homegrown or homemade things become increasingly attractive when opposed to the grandiose wants of her companions. It is Jane's last wish for "a bumpity ride in a wagon of hay" that Raverat chooses to celebrate with her engraving, showcasing similarities between Hassall's and Raverat's illustrative imaginations and styles in two otherwise very different poetry books for children.

More striking even than the similarities between the two engravers' illustrations of children in hay are those between their illustrations of children with cows (Figure 2.7). As with the engravings of hay, most general readers would not be able to tell which engraver made which illustration. And children would not be able to distinguish Stevenson's poem "The Cow" from the Taylors' work of the same title. Both poems idealize the cow, describing her as "friendly" (Stevenson), "pretty" (Taylors), generous with her milk, and enjoying in her placid way the pastoral delights of "meadow grass" (Stevenson) or "grass" that is "fresh and fine" (Taylors). Similar design elements—such as location on the page, spatial relation between image and poem, breaks in the black framing to create a

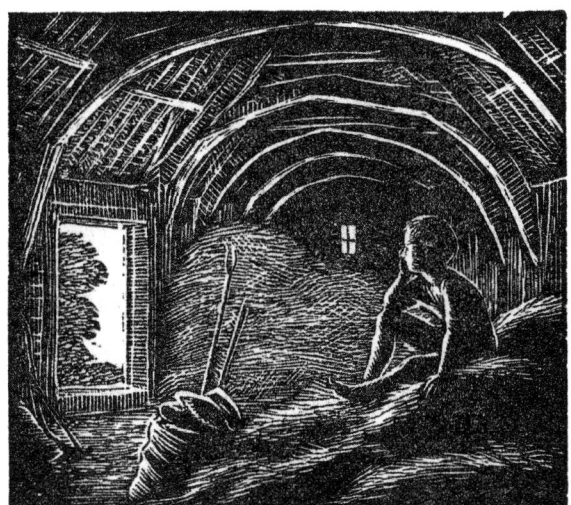

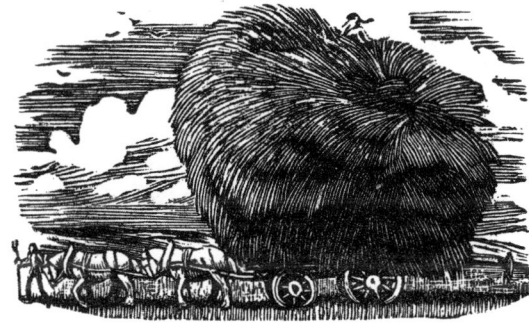

FIGURE 2.6 Which is which, whose is whose? These wood engravings could be switched from one volume of poetry to another. *Above:* Joan Hassall's wood engraving for "The Hayloft," by Robert Louis Stevenson. From *A Child's Garden of Verses* (Edinburgh: Hopetoun Press, 1947), 45. 2 × 2 inches. Reproduced by permission of the Estate of Joan Hassall/Simon Lawrence. *Below:* Gwen Raverat's wood engraving for "Bunches of Grapes," by Walter de la Mare. From *The Cambridge Book of Poetry for Children* (Cambridge: Cambridge University Press, 1932), 37. 2⅞ × 1⅝ inches. Copyright 2025 Estate of Gwen Raverat. All rights reserved. DACS/Artists Rights Society (ARS).

time-space continuum with the reader—further emphasize the shared meanings of the two poetry volumes.[31]

Finally, comparison of Hassall's wood engraving for "Windy Nights" to Raverat's wood engraving for "The Wind in a Frolic" suggests how both engravers' representations of nature in its unpredictable and dangerous moods seem intended to strengthen the alliance between children on the page and children holding the book (Figure 2.8). Hassall manages the sense of panic riding just beneath the surface of Stevenson's famous lines by enclosing her manic adult rider

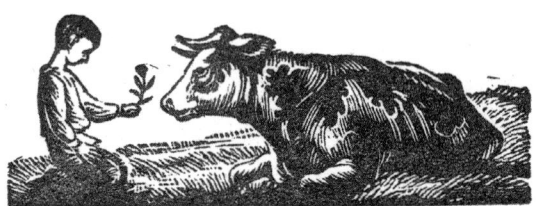
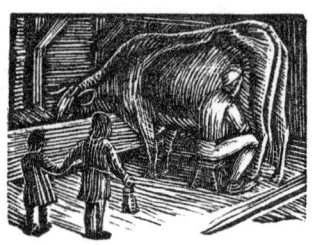

within a double frame of trees waving wildly in the dark gusts. For Howitt's less menacing poem about a wind that is "Laughing to think, in its fearful fun, / How little of mischief it had done" (24), Raverat depicts two boys in short pants flying kites. One boy's kite is outside the frame of the engraving, flying high in the air, while the other boy's kite is close by his side, awaiting a launch. Unlike the schoolboy in Howitt's accompanying poem, who, touched by the wind, finds "his hat in a pool and his shoe in the mud" (24), the boys in Raverat's engraving still have hats and shoes on, their ability to turn the wind's energy to pleasure modifying while alluding to the threat of the unruly verbal "monster" in the poem (23).

FIGURE 2.7 Again, which is which? Whose is whose? *Left:* Joan Hassall's wood engraving for "The Cow," by Robert Louis Stevenson. From *A Child's Garden of Verses* (Edinburgh: Hopetoun Press, 1947), 31. 2 × ¹¹⁄₁₆ inches. Reproduced by permission of the Estate of Joan Hassall/Simon Lawrence. *Right:* Gwen Raverat's wood engraving for "The Cow," by Ann and Jane Taylor. From *The Cambridge Book of Poetry for Children* (Cambridge: Cambridge University Press, 1932), 77. 1⅝ × 1³⁄₁₆ inches. Copyright 2025 Estate of Gwen Raverat. All rights reserved. DACS/Artists Rights Society (ARS).

Raverat's engraving for "The Wind in a Frolic," like her engraving for "The Cow," invites child readers into its miniature world through the white space at its bottom, coextensive with the viewer. In contrast, Hassall's rider, fearsomely heading Stevenson's poem, needs to be closed up in a box, separated from the child readers who are encouraged to join their voices to that of the anxious child speaker, who asks, "Why does he gallop and gallop about?"

The subtle differences of interpretation and design noted in the three examples above establish the independence of the postwar engravings of Joan Hassall from the interwar engravings of Gwen Raverat but cannot disguise a larger ideological-aesthetic regime that upholds common assumptions about the function of illustrations in poetry anthologies: that they should serve the

poems to which they are attached, attracting attention to salient images or figures and thickening
meanings that are communicated by a verbal text
that is thought to remain untouched by anything the
image might say or do.[32] As a result, Raverat's and
Hassall's engravings, while existing in dynamic relation with the words and white space around them,
end up confirming dominant beliefs that children
enjoy poems about nature in its cultivated, domesti-
cated, and wild forms; that this natural life may be
encountered in equally enriching ways whether in
outdoor or interior spaces; that it will improve children's characters no matter if it leads to adventure
or contemplation; and that adults (mowers, dairy-
men, the poets) may mediate children's access to
the objects, values, or experiences called up by the
natural life described in a poem, but truth is not reserved for them. Rather, it is revealed in apparently
simple terms, to children trailing clouds of glory
who are supposed to recognize in the accompanying
images an ideal world that aspires to the stability of
simple oppositions, of white and black, of line and
space, all achieved through steel on wood. Any nation that raises its young on such stuff must enjoy, in
the Opies' words, a "happy heritage"; any nation that
defines itself in terms of such stuff must be a happy
nation. And what better time to convince young and
old alike that they can hold the simple materials of
national happiness in their hands than when stocks,
bombs, or buildings have fallen all around? Perhaps

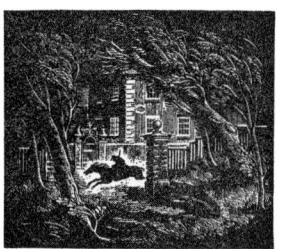

FIGURE 2.8 What a difference
a frame makes. *Above:* Joan
Hassall's wood engraving for
"Windy Nights," by Robert
Louis Stevenson. From *A
Child's Garden of Verses*
(Edinburgh: Hopetoun Press,
1947), 19. 2¹⁄₁₆ × 1¾ inches.
Reproduced by permission
of the Estate of Joan Hassall/
Simon Lawrence. *Below:* Gwen
Raverat's wood engraving for
"The Wind in a Frolic," by
William Howitt. From *The
Cambridge Book of Poetry
for Children* (Cambridge:
Cambridge University Press,
1932), 24. 1¹⁄₁₆ × ⅞ inches.
Copyright 2025 Estate of
Gwen Raverat. All rights
reserved. DACS/Artists Rights
Society (ARS).

this is what Hassall's Edinburgh publishers were thinking when they decided to
publish *A Child's Garden of Verses* with wood engravings in 1947 and what Raverat's publishers were thinking when they decided to publish Grahame's poetry
anthology with wood engravings in 1932. It is also likely that this is what Hassall's

Oxford publishers were thinking when they commissioned her work for *All Day Long* and *The Oxford Book of Children's Nursery Rhymes* in the early 1950s.

IDEOLOGIES OF ILLUSTRATION

Morag Styles bemoans the canon-building tendency of "influential editors" who establish a tradition where "adult poetry by the so-called 'great' poets is considered preferable to writing directed at children."[33] *The Wind in the Willows* notwithstanding, Kenneth Grahame is no better than the other stuffy, self-serving editors that Styles cites, intent on defending canons rather than providing pleasure. In his October 1915 preface to the first edition of the *Cambridge Book of Poetry for Children,* reprinted in the 1932 edition, Grahame writes about the "disheartening" difficulties of selecting poetry for children:

> For he [the editor] has to remember that his task is not to provide simple examples of the whole range of English poetry, but to set up a wicketgate giving attractive admission to that wide domain, with its woodland glades, its pasture and arable, its walled and scented gardens here and there, and so to its sunlit, and sometimes misty mountain tops—all to be explored more fully later by those who are tempted on by the first glimpse. (xiii)

Hardly prose to persuade the prospective buyer to purchase, these words are interesting for their deployment of pastoral metaphors, their overdetermined references to cultural sorting, and their investment in a conservative ideology of reading and childhood. As the poems become substitutes for outdoor environments, children, metaphorically, become the domestic or wild animals invited within pasture or garden. The editor controls the pastoral terrain, setting up a "wicketgate" before the verbal Eden or Arcadia enclosed within. This "gate" metaphor swings two ways, however, as it provides child readers access—or, in Grahame's words, "attractive admission"—to a wide domain of English poetry while simultaneously limiting the domain to something less than "the whole range of English poetry." The acutely self-conscious work of cultural discrimination going on here suggests an anxiety about the activity of sorting, the materials being sorted, and the quality of the potential readers sorted into the garden. The high ideological stakes of deciding what kind of poetry is suitable for what kinds of children—is it too limited, too lofty, too sunny, too misty?—are linked at the end of Grahame's winding sentence to the ideological stakes of deciding why children should read poetry in the first place. Grahame suggests, obliquely, that the whole point of his selections and the volume itself is to provide children with a "first glimpse" of something they will "explore more fully later." Grahame's "later" is the least stable of the many unstable elements of his sentence, as it withholds fulfillment of the promise of the volume's poetry to a future moment while extending into that same future anxieties about the volume's purpose and contents. Grahame's language symbolizes the unstable, anxiety-inducing cultural location of poetry volumes published for Britain's least experienced and least influential readers, its child readers. It seems that editors at elite presses hoped to stabilize and elevate children's poetry volumes within cultural hierarchies with the addition of redeeming and nostalgic wood engraved illustrations indebted to the beloved figure of Thomas Bewick, himself always imagined as thoroughly rustic and thoroughly English. On the surface of the pages rather than in the depth of their processes, the wood engravings in these modern, twentieth-century poetry volumes, in opposition to the quick and democratic illustrations of Clarke Hutton's Puffin book 15 Nursery Rhymes, invoke with their tiny black-and-white worlds the comforting myths of land, folk, and national heritage that mechanized warfare had threatened to snuff out.

It appears that Raverat and Hassall paid for their professional, "manly" experiments in self-sufficient living with the enchanting (mystifying, soothing, idealizing) subjects and forms of their illustrations. Their pastoral illustrations in children's poetry anthologies provided a kind of Bewickian disguise that enabled them to do what few men and even fewer women attempted: to live by their hands, practicing an art that, contrary to the rules of feminine subservience and decorum, projected both women to the top of their profession. Reputable and university presses endorsed each woman's art and ambition, while simultaneously taming that art's potential to disrupt traditional gender ideologies through the presses' associations with generally child- and woman-free national and institutional traditions.[34] The publishing houses themselves appeared unchanged by their investment in children's publishing, suffering no diminishment in status, even as publication of children's books for a trade market contradicted just about everything in their missions, frontlists, and backlists. As David McKitterick emphasizes in his *History of Cambridge University Press,* the principal business of CUP lay in "monographs, textbooks, scholarly editions and journals."[35] From the late nineteenth through the mid-twentieth centuries, CUP devoted a considerable portion of its business to educational publishing, at both school and university level, with the educational market critical to the press's success.[36] However, best-selling educational texts like Godfrey and Siddons's mathematics textbooks were not at all the same thing as illustrated children's poetry anthologies. In McKitterick's bald statement, "The popular and the academic markets were not the same."[37] Scholars of British children's literature, presumably accustomed to seeing the Oxford and Cambridge University Press colophons, may be blind to the incongruity of scholarly presses with leading titles such as *Problems of Philosophy, Elements of English Law,* and *Metabolism of Living Tissues* publishing children's literature in the first place, no matter how good that literature is assumed to be. Peter Sutcliffe mentions in his history of Oxford University Press that after World War II, OUP refurbished its juvenile list, selling off the popular Biggles series to Hodder & Stoughton. He comments, "Oxford children's books then came to epitomize 'good taste,' and won many prizes."[38] Such shifting commitments to academic and children's publishing by the staid Oxford and Cambridge University Presses is why it is important to measure Raverat's and Hassall's children's poetry books against Noel Carrington's contemporary Puffin Picture Books, in particular Clarke Hutton's *15 Nursery Rhymes.* Judged by its surface content, Hutton's book was just as committed as Raverat's and Hassall's to nurturing future generations on cultural staples—nursery rhymes—that were perceived as being as old as England itself. However, judged by its forms and materials, Hutton's book is both more experimental and more democratic than anything Raverat or Hassall produced. Perhaps it is for this reason, the development of a cheap, disposable children's book, that Raverat and Hassall stuck with expensive, hardcover books from reputable elite and university presses. It is possible that they could not risk the freedom and fortune history had so recently given their sex, allowing them to prosper outside constraining feminine ideologies, mere upstarts in the twentieth-century art world, by investing their time and energy in an equally upstart enterprise: inexpensive, ephemeral, paperback Puffin Picture Books.

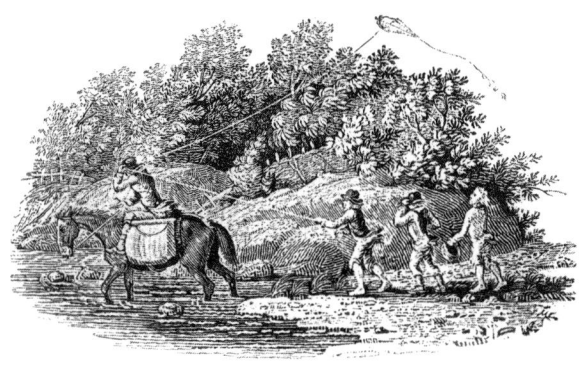

"the overflowings of an active, wild disposition"

Thomas Bewick never singled out rural children as his intended or preferred audience, but he did assume as a basis of judging his child readers' capacity for visual narrative delight his own remembered childhood feelings and experiences. These he captured most adroitly in the vignettes that illustrate the pleasures of fishing, hunting, climbing, and many other kinds of mischief in the river, woods, and fields that a boy of his "active wild disposition" could pursue (*Memoir,* 11). In a vignette from the second of Bewick's natural history volumes on British birds, we see three boys flying a kite whose string has wrapped around the hat of a passing horseman. The traveler looks straight ahead, leaning into the wind, ignoring the exuberant and perhaps mocking boys. He looks beleaguered, isolated in his responsible adulthood, as he attempts to preserve his hat and make his heavily laden way across the river to some distant destination. The background against which this miniature drama plays out is full of movement, the trees cast in gray tones that convey depth of shadow and light, their branches bending and leaves blowing in the sunshine. The kite waves from the

Thomas Bewick, *A History of British Birds,* vol. 2, *Water Birds* (1804, 1826), 309. 3 × 1⅝ inches.

upper right corner of the vignette, its tail framing the happily ragged country boys who appear on the riverbank barefoot, in pursuit of the kite and the rider who is ensnared in its string. Bewick attends to each minute detail of Northumbrian natural life and human interactions with it. His devotion to an exacting realism is evident in every white line that reveals the path of his engraving tool, even as he believed, as he states in the preface to the 1804 edition of volume 2 of *A History of British Birds,* that his "every attempt to depicture nature must fall short of the original" (v).

In this perfectly designed and executed vignette, the dark water beneath the adult directs our eye inward, to the boys, but also symbolically announces the rider's dark way forward. The lead boy faces the same obstacles of wind and current as the adult, but his toy mediates his passage through the natural environment. His kite is precious enough that he clutches its string with two hands, careless of whether or not he loses his hat, even as the white string in the image defines an arrow pointing left, toward the rider and his adult troubles. The second boy, eyes downcast, clutches his hat in a gesture that mirrors the rider's, also suggesting, like the white arrow formed by the kite string, that he and his companions must follow the rider into the work and worries of adulthood. Yet as our eye moves rightward to the third boy, such worries fade in the gleaming paper white of his face, hair, and body. He is the brightest and lightest of the four figures, the last but least encumbered, preserving the possibilities of playful youth in his upward gaze at the kite as he retains his hat firmly in hand.

Populated by boys, Bewick's scenes of rural England contain toys, play, and joy, but they fascinate in part because they also depict nature's volatility, violence, and danger, mirroring though not necessarily causing or explaining the kinds of violent human behavior that so disturbed Thomas Bewick.[1] As we know, Bewick sought in his vignettes to "illustrate some truth, or point some moral," an impulse we see clearly in his scenes of daring or error, such as the previously discussed vignette from *Land Birds* of four boys absconding with a runaway cart ("Preface to the Sixth Edition," iii).[2] In contrast to the children in the greenery investigated by scholars of later classic children's literature—the gardens and woods of Alice, Peter Rabbit, Peter Pan, Mary Lennox, Winnie-the-Pooh, even Jim Hawkins—Bewick offers us a more realistic visual history of childhood. We could say that he offers us natural histories of boys within his natural histories of birds.

Girls appear more often in children's books with illustrations attributed to Thomas Bewick than they do in his books of natural history. We glimpse them here and there, noticing Bewick's illustration in *Cottage Tales* of "the sly child," who had "a trick of pocking down her head so low" it rested upon her stays (15), or his illustration prepared as a frontispiece for *Mother Goose's Melody* of one girl holding a doll while another reads near her in mannered and managed domestic safety.[3] Possibly these girls share the "gaiety and humour" that Bewick hoped to communicate through his tailpieces. They smile and play, and while they socialize, are never cruel. They read books with the same enthusiasm as their brothers, though usually indoors.

Analysis of Bewick's vignettes suggests that for Bewick there is no Mother Nature, but rather boys' nature. This is a masculine, vigorous, unpredictable, exciting kind of nature, one constructed out of Bewick's memories of the Tyne Valley during his youthful explorations. It is enhanced and enlivened by things: the toys and objects, purchased or homemade, that boys bring to the rivers and woods when they play. In effect, Bewick gives us nature mediated by manufacture, teaching us in image after image that there is no firm separation between countryside and marketplace. Rods, hats, trumpets, and guns in the hands of his rural boys throw into question the binary divisions between nature and industry, country and city, innocence and knowledge that often organize our thinking about children's and pastoral literatures. Yet Bewick, too, had his binary biases, dividing nature and childhood by sex. Bewick's girls, imagined in worlds of play that preserve them from boys' violence, are typically removed from nature itself.[4]

Bewick's boys are in nature in two senses: They are in vignettes that represent them in natural environments, and these vignettes are printed in books of natural history.[5] With a turn of the page, we see boys creating a snowman in unsupervised winter play or boys collecting razorbill eggs from seaside cliffs. All these boys communicate what Bewick reports of his own childhood: pure joy in the wild, untutored play available to a healthy, strong boy who roamed the countryside in defiance of adult constraints, no matter the price to be paid. Bewick recalls in his *Memoir* that he was "constantly engaged in some mischievous prank or other" and wonders at the miracle of his survival even as we sense no real regret as he looks back over his youthful pursuit of outdoor adventures (11). Bewick's books of natural history insist on the constant change of fate and fortune that boys experience in natural environments. And in subtle ways they teach us to see those natural environments as never purely natural. The Fall has always already taken place no matter how determined later readers might be to find unsullied Eden in their images. The miniature boys in his vignettes, engraved by hand on a wooden block and mechanically reproduced innumerable times on paper, reflect real mid-eighteenth-century imperatives to prepare youth for uncertain futures in which they will need to transition between country and city, nature and manufacture, rural and industrial economies. Such social and geographical mobility, understood as expressions and consequences of rural modernity, is represented by Bewick's vignettes of natural youth gripping manufactured or homemade toys. Suspended and held as singular characters in Bewick's wooden blocks, multiplying into the future through mechanical means, they are always ready for new generations of readers who may adopt their gendered ideals about boys' ownership of English nature at the dawning of the Industrial Revolution.

THREE

The Fine Art of Mass Reproduction

Clare Leighton, Victor Gollancz, and the Radical Countryside

Clare Leighton's striking black-and-white wood engraving of lovers dallying in the sheaves of harvest corn captures in its miniature two-by-three-inch dimensions some of the most complex, contradictory elements of modern wood engravings depicting rural Britain (Figure 3.1). Appearing for the first time on the title page of Leighton's 1937 book *Country Matters,* it seems to conflate modern love with ancient patterns of agricultural life, promising reproduction of human and natural worlds in what might be regarded as timeless cycles of generation, reproduction, and regeneration. On the other hand, working against such appeals to comforting fantasies of unchanging rural life, its austere black and white, its linear design and forms, suggest modernist ideals of abstraction, purity, and refinement. Also complicating the wood engraving's rural romanticism is its status as an illustration in a commercial trade book published by the London house of Victor Gollancz. Gollancz's career as a trendsetting London editor and publisher was distinguished by his canny capitalist business acumen and passionate commitment to radical politics. He is best known today for launching the Left Book Club in 1936; the 1937 publication of George Orwell's work of urban industrial discovery and documentary, *The Road to Wigan Pier,* was one his most important commissions. Rarely is Gollancz remembered as a publisher of middlebrow women's books, art books, or countryside books, but it is exactly in this capacity that he enters the present study and contributes to the happy endings of its women artists' stories.

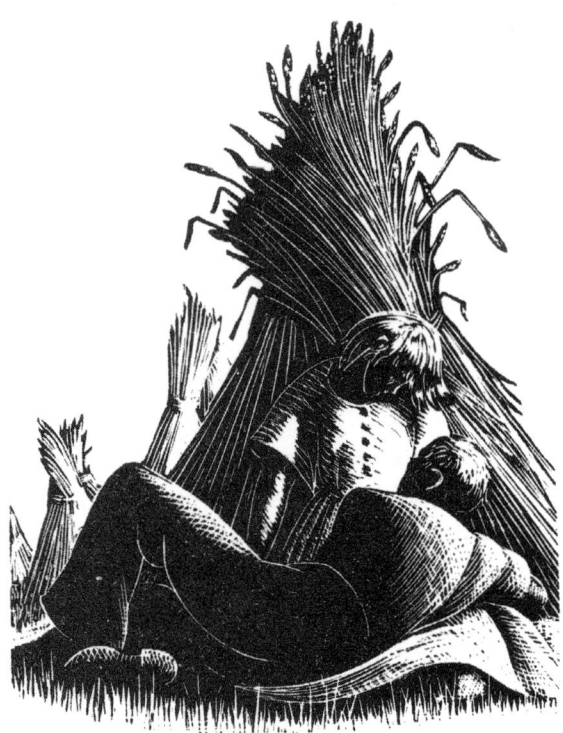

FIGURE 3.1 Clare Leighton's untitled title page wood engraving of modern lovers in the sheaves. From Clare Leighton, *Country Matters* (London: Victor Gollancz, 1937; New York: Macmillan, 1937). 2 1/16 × 2 1/2 inches. Copyright 2025 Estate of Clare Leighton. All rights reserved. DACS/Artists Rights Society (ARS).

Gollancz was the literary entrepreneur whose ceaseless energies and wide-ranging interests brought him first to Leighton and then to Agnes Miller Parker, initiating their respective careers as trade book illustrators. An illustrative impresario despite himself, Gollancz is the wizard or magician who turned British wood engraving from an illustrative practice largely associated with limited fine press editions into the stuff of common books for common readers. According to Joanna Selborne, Gollancz was "largely responsible for popularizing wood-engraved nature illustration" during the 1930s, beginning with his edition of Leighton's 1935 countryside book *Four Hedges: A Gardener's Chronicle*.[1] James Hamilton notes with tones of wonder *Four Hedges*'s achievement of four impressions within three months of first publication. This affirms for him Leighton's status as "the people's wood engraver, the artist who was seen to have most effectively taken wood engraving away from the private presses and, with no loss of

craftsmanship or quality, into the wide public domain."[2] Gollancz certainly recognized that with *Four Hedges* he had stumbled upon a profitable kind of book
that in the depressed book markets of the mid-1930s rewarded his readers' desires for countryside literature. Immediately after its publication, he requested
from Leighton "another book . . . in the same format."[3] Leighton worked hard
through 1936 and 1937, writing, designing, and illustrating *Country Matters.* Little
did she know that at the same time, wood engraver Miller Parker was working at
Gollancz's behest on seventy-two illustrations for *Through the Woods,* the illustrated countryside book by H. E. Bates discussed in chapter 1. Published in 1936,
Through the Woods led Miller Parker and Bates to a second volume "in the same
format," *Down the River,* published in 1937, the year *Country Matters* came out.

Two years later, in 1939, Leighton left England for America, seeking a new life
across the Atlantic. Stunned and bewildered by Europe's descent into a second
world war, and devastated by her lover Henry Noel Brailsford's abandonment of
her at the very moment his wife's death freed them to marry, Leighton seems to
have experienced Gollancz's acquisition and publication of books illustrated by
Miller Parker as yet another abandonment. This chapter regards these personal,
human joys and griefs among the many contexts that inform our understanding of the meanings and methods of Leighton's Gollancz books and their impacts
on the 1930s wood engraving revival. It also looks to a broader literary context
that Gollancz's activities bring into focus, the leftist pursuit of truth and protest
against poverty and hunger through the 1930s documentary movement. While
the origins of the documentary movement are typically assigned to cinema, and
particularly to John Grierson's films and cinematic statements, the movement's
fullest impact on public reading was achieved through Mass-Observation publications organized by Tom Harrison, Charles Madge, and Humphrey Jennings
and socially conscious reportage published by writers like John Sommerfield,
J. B. Priestley, W. H. Auden, and Graham Greene.[4] John Baxendale and Christopher Pawling explain that "the Thirties is the decade of realism in literature
and the arts in general, producing documentary film, reportage, the *Living Newspaper,* proletarian fiction, workers' newsreels, the 'pylon poets' and a myriad
of responses to the growing crisis."[5] With this broad gesture to "a myriad of responses," Baxendale and Pawling make room for Leighton as a key contributor
and fabricator of the documentary thirties:

It is the moment, then, when the "ordinary people" start to invade the spheres of politics and culture, partly as the objects of concern for a liberal, reforming middle class, but also as the subject of a new discourse, documentary realism, which articulates a new attitude to popular culture.[6]

With diverse motives and politics, many writers contributing to this "new discourse" committed to recording the "real lives" of "ordinary people" turned with stern eye to scenes of depressed urban life. The Worktown project famously associated with Mass-Observation's origins recorded everyday life in the depressed Lancashire town of Bolton. It was launched in 1937, the same year that Gollancz published the iconic documentary *The Road to Wigan Pier*, by George Orwell. This and other similar volumes of masculine reportage would soon overwhelm Leighton's and Miller Parker's gentler stories, bending the literary historical memory of the 1930s toward muscular work and urban geographies.[7] This chapter focuses on Leighton, locating both her and Miller Parker's Gollancz books in this story of documentary realism, seeking to expand it with analysis of women's art and words about the countryside.[8] Rather than upholding the differences of gender and genre that separate out and then submerge women wood engravers from the masculine record of leftist thirties reporting and recording, this chapter argues that Leighton's wood engraved countryside books and Orwell's urban industrial reportage were different forms of media that contributed equally to Gollancz's leftist, socialist cultural project and commercial ventures.[9] This may seem an unlikely alliance, as at first glance Leighton's books may appear to conform to and extend the quietist countryside beloved by conservative commentators like Sir Stanley Baldwin and Henry Williamson, not the rebel Orwell. However, this chapter maintains that once Leighton is read in terms of her 1930s editorial and publishing contexts, her texts and the illustrations of plants and animals within them become part of England's largely forgotten radical countryside.

Leighton's countryside books have been relegated to the literary historical margins of a notoriously red decade in part because literary critics tend to see wood engraving as a traditional art form disengaged from the genres of modernity (Figure 3.2). As noted in the Introduction, print historians and wood engraving experts see the same images as cutting-edge, unique expressions of a modern imagination working in a visual medium defined by the most advanced

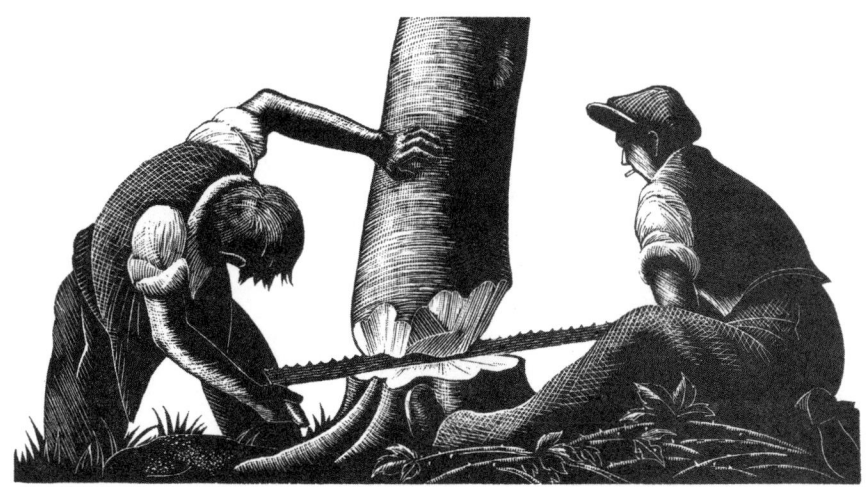

mass-reproductive print technologies. Hamilton, for example, describes wood engraving of the late 1920s as "in the avant-garde . . . the catalyst of a new language for art," while Selborne subtitles her authoritative volume on British wood engraved book illustration of the period *A Break with Tradition.*[10] Selborne argues that artist-engravers or autonomous wood engravers like Leighton and Miller Parker, those who created every element of design and image on a wood block and the relief print that emerged from its ink traces, were at the forefront of the early twentieth-century's

FIGURE 3.2 Clare Leighton's inset wood engraving *Sawing a Tree,* depicting woodmen at the foot of a great beech. From Clare Leighton, *Country Matters* (London: Victor Gollancz, 1937; New York: Macmillan, 1937), 147. 4¹³⁄₁₆ × 2¹⁄₁₆ inches. Copyright 2025 Estate of Clare Leighton. All rights reserved. DACS/ Artists Rights Society (ARS).

modern arts. In Selborne's account, Leighton and the other artist-engravers who drove the 1930s wood engraving revival were "pioneers" who "produced some of the most exciting and innovative prints of the period."[11] Selborne admires wood engravers like Paul Nash, Robert Gibbings, Gertrude Hermes, and Blair Hughes-Stanton, whose work displayed "modernist tendencies," but she assumes other nonmodernist wood engravers of the 1930s revival were also committed to artistic experiment and engaged with modernity.[12] It bears repeating that what matters for those who seek to understand modern wood engraving's relation to

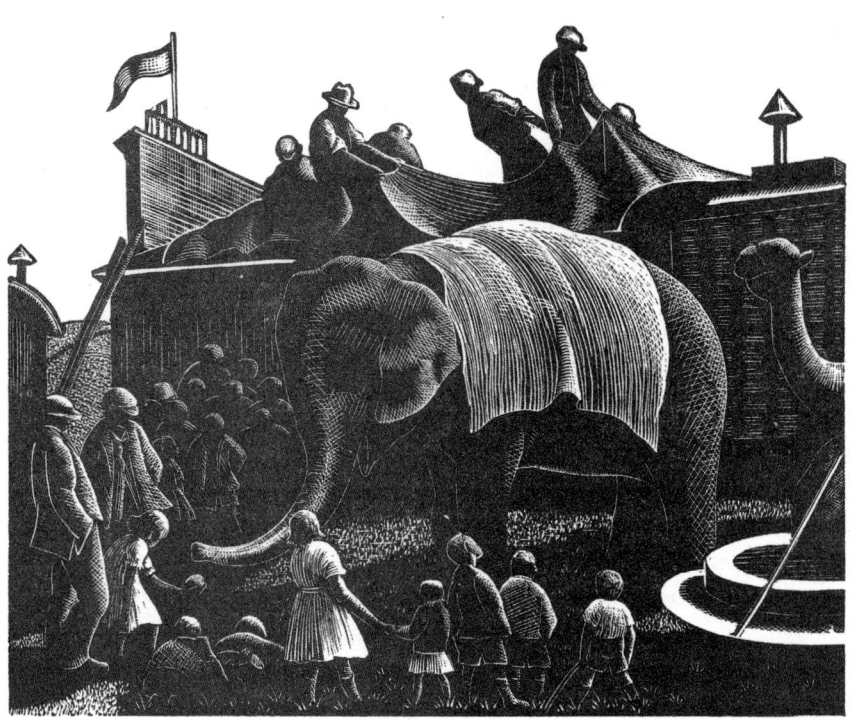

Britain's literary culture is that an artist's "understanding of the inherent aesthetic qualities peculiar to wood determined their modernness, not necessarily the images per se."[13] In other words, even if the rural subjects of Leighton's books and their wood engraved illustrations strike readers as quaint and old-fashioned, the cutting-edge commercial technologies and economies that produced these books, while invisible and unimportant to the casual reader, actually determined the illustrator's creative methods and cultural status.[14] Selborne warns against any essentialist association of conservative, regressive ruralist attitudes with the traditional natural subjects and apparently

FIGURE 3.3 Clare Leighton's wood engraving of children agog and men at work, *Unpacking the Fair.* From Clare Leighton, *Country Matters* (London: Victor Gollancz, 1937; New York: Macmillan, 1937), 47. 4¾ × 3¾ inches. Copyright 2025 Estate of Clare Leighton. All rights reserved. DACS/Artists Rights Society (ARS).

conventional shapes of twentieth-century white-line wood engraving.[15] For her, the meaning of any given wood engraved illustration is determined by the materials and methods adopted by the wood engraver and reproduced and circulated by the printer and publisher. When we look back at this history and see that the wood engraver is a woman, the conditions of production that we consider must include the materials of her art and the social contexts of her practice, including the immaterial effects of the everyday sexism this woman artist would have encountered no matter where she lived or worked.

In what follows, *Country Matters* and Leighton's two earlier books, *The Farmer's Year* of 1933 and, most famously, her *Four Hedges: A Gardener's Chronicle* of 1935, are read as modern, progressive texts whose leftist politics emerge when we examine relations between the books' dual verbal-visual forms, these forms and the social effects of Gollancz's mediations, and relations between all these forms and effects and the stylized values of the literary genre of 1930s documentary exemplified by Orwell's *Road to Wigan Pier.* Leighton's Gollancz books can be seen as progressive, even propagandistic, texts, imagining for others the socialist ideal of a radical countryside (Figure 3.3). Her countryside is feminine and feminized, its gendered rurality constructed in part by the peculiar affordances of the wood engraved countryside trade book that Gollancz invented. Restored to our sight by recent critical attention to the history, literature, and visual cultures of rural Britain, Leighton's 1930s countryside books for popular readers contest the gendered terms of Orwell's and many other male artists' heroic urban and industrial documentaries. In part because of this gendered contest, they represent what they are themselves: instances of rural modernity in Britain.

VICTOR GOLLANCZ IN THE HEDGES

In 1933, when Leighton published her first mass-produced, self-authored and illustrated country book *The Farmer's Year* with the trade publisher Collins, she was known already as a leader of the decade's wood engraving revival (Figure 3.4). Her *Wood-Engraving and Woodcuts* had appeared in 1932 in The Studio's How to Do It series, and her *Wood Engraving of the 1930s,* also with The Studio, followed in 1936. Patricia Jaffé celebrates the first of these studies as "herald[ing] the total liberation of wood-engraving from the professionals," noting approvingly that the How to Do It series "aimed to make the practice of various art forms accessible to every man and every woman."[16] Her interpretation of wood engraving as a popular art, suited to democratizing impulses of a red decade, pursues implications of Leighton's conclusion that "the growth of a vast new public of readers has brought an immense stimulus to wood-engraving."[17] A series of education acts in the late nineteenth century, including in 1891 the Free Education Act and in 1897 the Voluntary Schools Act, had made education compulsory for elementary-aged children and led to state-funded schools. These and other social changes dramatically increased the nation's literacy rates and, two generations later, produced Leighton's "vast new public of readers"—a public that in its democratic origins, state-funded means, and Depression-era economy was interested in Gollancz's 1930s mass-produced books with wood engravings, unable to afford the gorgeous limited editions associated with the excesses of the previous decade.

Honoring the distinct social, economic, and political pressures exerted on British publishing during the years when the cult of the countryside was at its peak in the 1930s illuminates the radical possibilities this chapter discovers within Leighton's countryside books (Figure 3.5). By way of contrast, we can look back at the art Miller Parker and her colleagues Gertrude Hermes, William McCance, and Blair Hughes-Stanton produced for the Gregynog Press. Gathered in Wales at a time when young wood engravers "could indulge in enthusiastic internecine strife over the proper way to use a graver, and pore in quasi-religious ecstasy over the tiny wood engravings of Bewick, Blake and Calvert," Miller Parker and the Gregynog artists were contributing to Britain's culture of rural modernity, but to the extent that none of their Gregynog book arts advanced British popular culture, none could be regarded as advancing the radical countryside of Leighton's socialist imagination.[18]

An admirer of Leighton's writing as well as her wood engraving, Hamilton credits the high quality of Leighton's illustrations in Gollancz's books with "keeping appreciation and practice of the art [of wood engraving] alive in the late 1930s."[19] *Four Hedges* brings eighty-eight wood engravings together with fourteen first-person documentary chapter-essays to form a distinct kind of visual-verbal narrative that remakes the conservative clichés of the period's countryside books and its socialist urban documentaries. In black and white, the shades of truth, clarity, and fair dealing, Leighton's essays and wood engravings

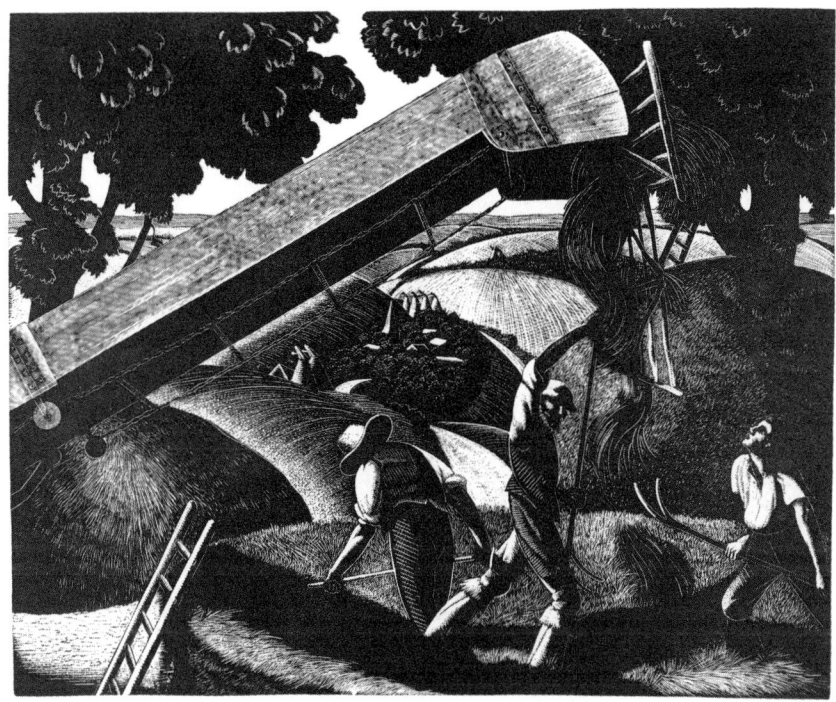

provide a multimedia representation of the artist's transformation of a quadrangle of Buckinghamshire pastureland into a garden (Figure 3.6).[20]

Heading the November chapter of *Four Hedges* is a wood engraving titled *Transplanting Walnut Tree.* It represents the physical work of creating a garden and then re-creating it through art. We see two men moving from right to left, bending away from the blasts of November winds. The image communicates through the taut curves of both men's backs their equality in shared labor. We recognize the figure pushing the wheelbarrow as the hired gardener, Alf. The man before him gripping the young tree is Noel, Leighton's constant "Companion within the Four

FIGURE 3.4 Clare Leighton's first mass-reproduced book of illustrated essays captured in full-page wood engravings many readers' yearnings for a bountiful rural landscape, responding to peaceful human labor amid the agricultural and industrial conflicts of the Great Depression. *June— Haymaking,* from Clare Leighton, *The Farmer's Year: A Calendar of English Husbandry* (London: Collins, 1933), 28. 10 × 8 inches. Copyright 2025 Estate of Clare Leighton. All rights reserved. DACS/Artists Rights Society (ARS).

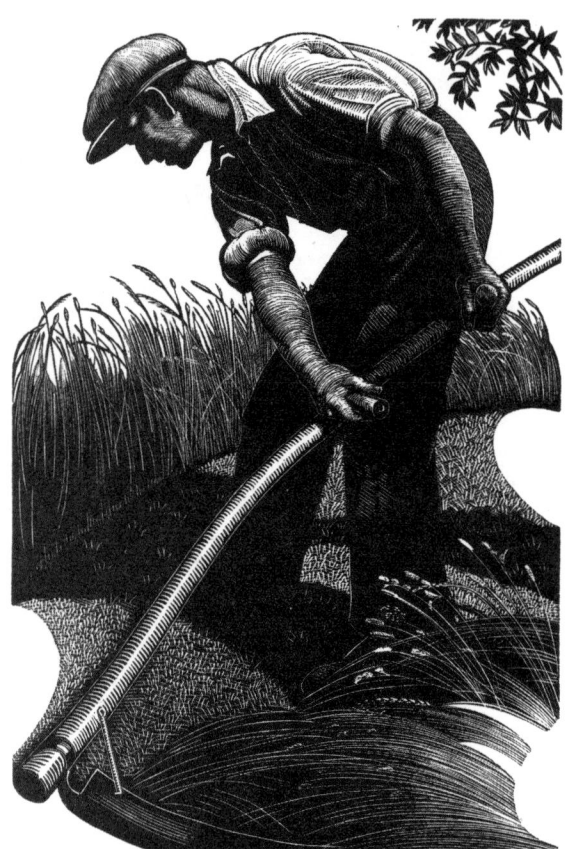

FIGURE 3.5 Clare Leighton's full-page wood engraving *Scything,* showing difficult work that appears "most beautiful" in the hands of an experienced reaper. From Clare Leighton, *Four Hedges: A Gardener's Chronicle* (London: Victor Gollancz, 1935; New York: Macmillan, 1935), 59. 4¾ × 7 inches. Copyright 2025 Estate of Clare Leighton. All rights reserved. DACS/Artists Rights Society (ARS).

Hedges" to whom she dedicates her book. In 1935, when Gollancz published *Four Hedges,* only those readers in left-wing literary and artistic circles would have known that Noel was socialist journalist H. N. or Henry Noel Brailsford, a man with a wife in Scotland. Born in 1873, Brailsford had married in 1898 the Scottish suffrage activist Jane Edson Mallocha, who was his student at the University of Glasgow. This was the same year that Leighton was born. Brailsford and Mallocha made each other miserable and lived apart almost from the beginning of their marriage, with Mallocha refusing to grant Brailsford a divorce.

Readers of *Four Hedges* would never guess that such conflicted domestic relations defined the lives of the happy socialists gardening in its pages. They might

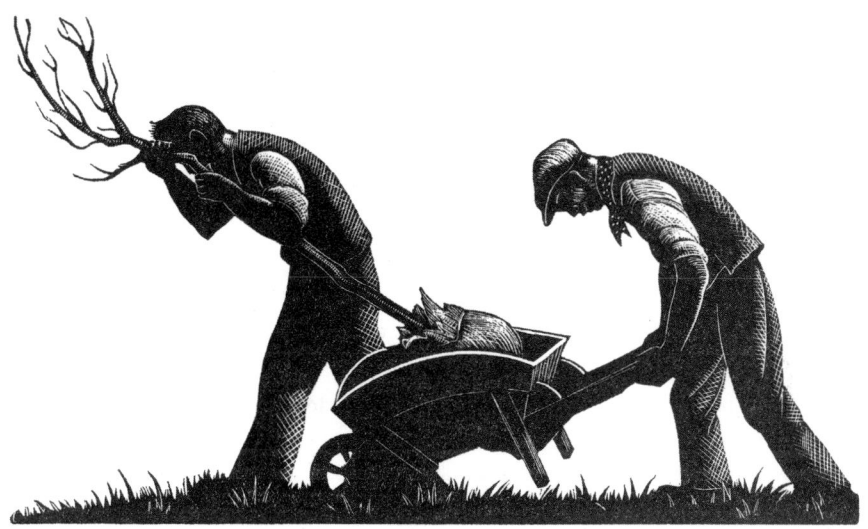

not even guess that these gardeners were socialists. Other than wind and frost-killed plants, the only "disaster" that seems to darken their lives is the departure of their beloved gardener Darville (91). The Depression and Leighton's socialism are minor, not major, influences on her garden story, her leftist politics felt primarily in her representations of manual labor and laborers. Admittedly, even with her caring portrayals of rural workers in the garden, there are signs of Leighton's bourgeois assumptions. Yet unlike the "ever-present (and almost untouchable)" 1930s

FIGURE 3.6 Clare Leighton's evocative, windy, wood engraved header for "November," *Transplanting Walnut Tree,* showing Alf and Noel at work. From Clare Leighton, *Four Hedges: A Gardener's Chronicle* (London: Gollancz, 1935; New York: Macmillan, 1935), 108. 4⅞ × 2¹³⁄₁₆ inches. Copyright 2025 Estate of Clare Leighton. All rights reserved. DACS/ Artists Rights Society (ARS).

author George Orwell, who recorded his youthful belief that *"The lower classes smell"* in *The Road to Wigan Pier* (127), Leighton never expresses sweeping class biases.[21] Naive rather than hostile, her worst error is her confession that she dismisses one of the hired men because he does not love the garden but rather regards it as something "that earns him money for bread." Worse yet, he lacks the "earthy look" (91). Alf, the workingman pushing the wheelbarrow in the wood engraving, is a "woodman" whom Leighton describes approvingly as being "at one with" the earth, "himself as rough as the ground he digs" (92). She writes:

> We dig the holes for the new trees. . . . Alf digs with us, a rhythmic figure as he sways and moves in his pink and blue striped shirt and loose brown corduroy trousers. His massive boots have iron tips to them. He reminds me of an upright brown hairy caterpillar. . . . The solid chalk below the earth is so hard that we have to break it up with an iron bar. (109–10)

Composed of and compared to the materials of the garden—his boot tips made of the same stuff as the tools the gardeners depend upon, his upright shape recalling brown hairy caterpillars that presumably inhabit the garden's soils and stems—Alf belongs in the beloved garden as guide, expert, and employee. Despite the hints of middle-class condescension, this passage testifies to Leighton's love for Alf, one that aims for what Baxendale and Pawling would recognize as "a more *inclusive* notion of citizenship," an egalitarian community of three workers in this lovers' paradise.[22] Eden has its Adam and Eve but also its Alf. The intimate "we" of the narrative invites us inside the four hedges, including us in Leighton's modern Eden even as or because it admits workers, but not family or friends. We meet only lovers and locals and thus feel ourselves to be at one with both.

As a figure in an illustration, Alf exists as a reversed imprint of an engraved and inked wooden block upon cream-colored paper, part of an illustration that would have taken Leighton hours to design and execute with gravers and spitstickers, and modern printing presses just seconds to reproduce. The striking darks and sinuous curves of the print of Alf and Noel in the header image for "November" communicate the two men's equality in shared labor. Meanwhile, the top of the young tree that Alf pushes in the wheelbarrow alludes to future and past physical labors, the planting yet to come in holes already dug. Leighton's female form is not in the picture, even as her narrative indicates she was working alongside the men, right there in the garden, breaking up chalk with an iron bar (116). Her visual absence, felt against her dominant narrative presence, reminds us that her book, even with its depictions of men's gardening, depends on the

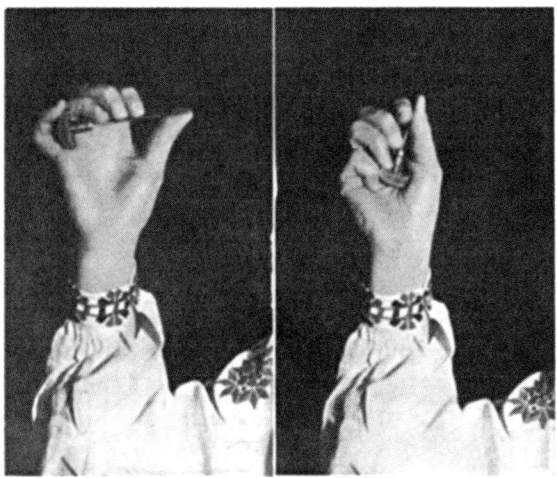

FIGURE 3.7 Photographs of Clare Leighton's hands holding steel tools for wood engraving in "the right way," in her How to Do It series book. From Clare Leighton, *Wood-Engraving and Woodcuts* (London: The Studio Publications, 1932), 11. Copyright 2025 Estate of Clare Leighton. All rights reserved. DACS/Artists Rights Society (ARS).

paradoxically invisible and visible work of the woman artist. For no matter how pristine and apparently empty the backgrounds of Leighton's wood engravings of snapdragons or blackbirds or blossoms may be, somewhere there is the artist, observing, sketching, working with pencil and paper in preparation for her work of engraving on wood.

WORKING CLASS AND WORKING HANDS

Alf and other working-class characters in *Four Hedges* use the work of their hands to earn money to buy bread, just as Leighton, a middle-class professional artist, depends on the work of her hands to earn money to buy bread. Our attention is drawn to those hands in an early scene in the book that emphasizes bodily pleasure and spiritual renewal through a woman's work in the garden. Leighton describes her "need" to "do things in the garden myself," by which she means she needs to garden without gloves. She writes: "Throwing them off, and with them the restraints and respectabilities of my recent existence, I am at last one with my garden, and I am happy" (16). Here, without men, sin, or seduction, Leighton provides a radically different kind of representation of women's consummation in the garden. The bare hands that we imagine dirtied by the gray chalky Chiltern soil are the same hands dirtied by the black ink of her proofs (Figure 3.7).

For Leighton, wood engraving, like gardening, was a protofeminist activity, building the radical countryside out of a woman's work with graver, ink, and paper as well as chalk, iron bar, and spade.[23]

Leighton supplemented her earnings from publishers' commissions for wood engravings with fees from lecturing and teaching, both in England and the United States. During one of her lectures she told her listeners:

> It is not the person who escapes from the fullness of life into his little ivory tower of preciousness who writes or paints the best. It is he who lives and who mixes with his ordinary fellows. For it is he who knows life. But never forget that it is work, work and yet again work.[24]

These words were delivered to an audience in 1949, ten years after Leighton had immigrated to America with a broken heart, her decade-long relationship with Brailsford ended by his guilt over the death of the wife he had ignored. But the words "work, work and yet again work" bring us back to England, to ideas popularized by Leighton's Gollancz books of the mid-1930s: that art is not escape but engagement with life; that the best artists are those who mix with "ordinary fellows"; and that art itself is labor.

We see all these values—of the artist's engaged work with the everyday world—when we look at the full-page wood engraving of Noel and Alf titled *Planting Trees* (Plate 5). The picture's subject, a tree, plus its architectural design and tonal contrasts, suggests alliances between the work of the gardeners with a living tree and the simultaneously visible and invisible work of the wood engraver who represents them on dead wood. There is an even more direct call to connect male work with trees with the female artist's work upon wood in Leighton's header illustration for "January" in *Four Hedges* (133) (Figure 3.8). This wood engraving titled *Axe and Block* gestures self-referentially toward the artist's engraving tools and wood block. It also anticipates Leighton's arresting tree pictures in her later volume, *Country Matters*, in the chapter "Chair Bodgers."

The solitary, wandering, autobiographical "I" narrating *Country Matters*, upon hearing chopping and sawing when she enters a Buckinghamshire beech wood, tells us that she is delighted to find a small hut "shaped like two playing-cards that had been placed against each other" (66). Illustrating Leighton's

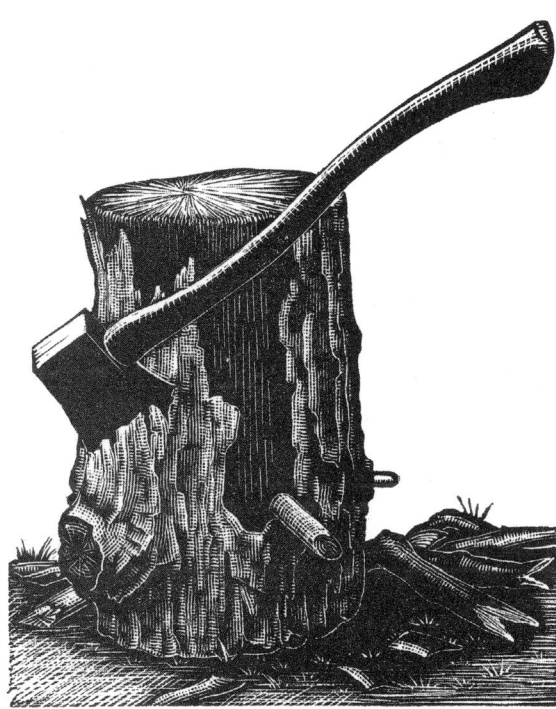

FIGURE 3.8 Clare Leighton's wood engraved header *Axe and Block*, which invites us to find allusions to the tools of her indoor art—steel and wood—in this outdoor winter scene. From Clare Leighton, *Four Hedges: A Gardener's Chronicle* (London: Victor Gollancz, 1935; New York: Macmillan, 1935), 133. 2½ × 3 inches. Copyright 2025 Estate of Clare Leighton. All rights reserved. DACS/Artists Rights Society (ARS).

encounter with chair bodging, which should, by all logic, be a dead craft in an age of mechanical production, is a full-page wood engraving, one of Leighton's most accomplished (Plate 6). In *Chair Bodgers* we see Leighton's modern art achieving stunning reality effects, even though all wood engraving is abstract, a reversed image printed out of light lines on black background creating illusions of tone, shape, and perspective. The narrator does not comment on her own wooden art, which should by all logic *also* be a dead craft in an age of mechanical reproduction, but rather remarks:

> As I reached the hut I felt that I was looking at a museum piece. It seemed impossible that here and now, in the nineteen thirties, a mere six miles from one of the biggest centres of the furniture trade, this primitive craft could hold its own against

the factory-made goods of the town. For here, in the shelter of a thatched hut, with a pole lathe that each generation had repeated through many centuries, two men sat from half past seven in the morning until half past seven in the evening, turning chair legs, three dozen to the hour. (69–70)

Watching an old and young chair bodger at work at their traditional, exacting, exhausting craft, Leighton wonders aloud, "Was this, then, the way to live and work? Did the beauty of the woods around them, and the sense of direct crafts-manship, balance the long hours at their trade? And how long can they survive?" (70). While Leighton's attention to chair bodgers may play into rural nostalgia, Leighton herself is keenly aware of the difference between the sense of direct craftsmanship she enjoys when engraving lines on wood and that of the laboring chair bodgers she discovers in the beech woods. Out of respect for their "ritual-ism," their impoverished and threatened difference from her artist's relation to the "magical wood" (65), she refrains from taking a seat at the third tree stump the bodgers have prepared for the stranger who might arrive for tea, as she tells herself and her listening readers: "It isn't all as romantic as you might think. . . . It is not always a morning in May" (71).

Other chapters invite and yet diminish her own and her readers' romanti-cism in similar ways. Chapter titles including "Picking Primroses," "The Village Smithy," and "The Village Witch" seem to feed what Alexandra Harris calls "the dream of the 1930s," the "conjured village of the mind's eye [that] was a substitute for real experience, aimed at a largely urban and suburban audience."[25] Leigh-ton's wood engravings of flowers in baskets, the smith at his horse or anvil, the witch in her doorway, if taken out of context—perhaps cut out of a book, framed, and hung in a city flat—might seem to preserve insular and exclusive narratives of rural Englishness. Yet the essays and illustrations of *Country Matters* contain and constrain hints of magic and romance with black type that materially and metaphorically insists on the exigencies of contemporary rural realities. There is in each chapter of *Country Matters* an image of modern rural Britain making its claim upon our visual and political imagination. The primroses are sweet, but they are enclosed with their pheasants behind barbed wire (40); the smithy is congenial, but motorcars are louder (18); the witch is feared, but her successor is unable to cast a spell (29). While her characters may regret these changes, the effects of the press of modernity upon their lives, Leighton does not join in nostalgic mourning because it is the conditions of modernity, her real present, not England's imagined past, that have brought her, the wandering woman artist, alone and safe into these rural places to sketch and eventually engrave and print the truth of her impassioned social and geographical witnessing.

The most exuberantly modern and feminist of Leighton's *Country Matters* chapter-essays is "The Village Fair," whose observing narrator ranges as freely as any omniscient novelist through the characters' solitary minds. This is 1930s documentary with a difference, one whose fictions contest as they testify to the artist's ability to capture in black and white the confusing, contradictory truths of rural modernity. We read about the secret yearnings of the elderly, unloved spinster Miss Emily Stacey, whose discovery of "what a woman should look like" in the curves of a cheap fairground prize of a white plaster Venus speaks to the gendered denials and repressions upholding village life. We overhear Miss Stacey's most private thoughts, witness her hidden, secret movements:

> This, then, was what a woman should look like. Those were the curves that lay hidden from sight under the cotton frocks of the village girls. . . . Nervously Miss Stacey felt down her own side, touching the bones of her body with distaste. She must have that statuette to look at always. No matter what the village thought, she yet must have it. She hesitated for one moment as she wondered what the rector would say. (53)

Forbidden by the rector's code to enjoy sexual feeling outside of marriage, including desire for her own or other women's bodies, Miss Stacey runs her fingers "down her own side," reminding us of other fingers, other hands in Leighton's 1930s country books that determine access to and expression of female pleasure. The tragicomic destruction of Miss Stacey's Venus in the rush of a fairgrounds crowd electrified into movement by an evening storm and the day's misrule leaves "a heap of crushed white plaster" in the middle of the village street, pathetic and public proof that Miss Stacey's private passion "was lost for ever" with her Venus (63).

The image of the crushed Venus seems to offer itself up as a stale metaphor of the sacrifice of art and beauty to country convention, to "what the village thought." Yet such a metaphor makes sense only if the Venus of Leighton's essay and illustration endorses the autonomy traditionally assigned to unique and perishable artworks.[26] Instead, Miss Stacey's Venus, like Miss Leighton's wood engravings, is a product of commercial mass reproduction. There is no singular, irreplaceable white plaster fairground Venus, just as there is no singular, irreplaceable print of Leighton's wood engraving of the Venus. Instead, there are multiple identical copies of plaster Venuses and black-ink wood engravings circulating through both country and city of 1930s Britain. Leighton's fine art of mass reproduction provides readers hope where Miss Stacey finds despair. The ending of "The Village Fair" may seem to deny Miss Stacey her statuette and its metonymic associations of art, beauty, divinity, and naked women "to look at always" in her village home, but it puts in its place other images and other modern art forms that offer to rural people, in addition to urban and suburban people, possible consolation for rural loss and transformative, liberating opportunities for rural futures. Instead of plaster, we get ink; instead of Venus, we get a circus.

One of the most beautiful wood engravings to enchant our gaze in *Country Matters* is the full-page illustration titled *Storm at the Fair* (Figure 3.9). A patterned scene dominated by the curves of tent tops and white engraved slashes of lightning bolts and driving rain, its dramatic clashes and pristine curves are positively biblical in their gathering of animals, angry clouds, and massed crowds within the illustration's strict rectangular borders. This wood engraving endorses in a recognizably modernist idiom the mass tastes of all the Miss Staceys of the English countryside, honoring their simultaneously democratic and discriminating loves. Published at nearly the same time as F. R. Leavis's and Q. D. Leavis's famous ivory-tower defenses against highbrow cultural decay and the decline of civilization, *Country Matters,* in its contents, verbal-visual forms, and mass media circulations, situates the powerful, unspoken desires of women "in the very middle of the village" (63) in order to represent rural change as not only frightening or saddening but also potentially redemptive.[27]

RURAL IMPRESSIONS, CRITICAL REFLECTIONS

Very different effects and associations are conveyed by Leighton's 1931 wood engraving *Chalfont St Giles,* which appears in the middle of the title page of a scholarly book published at the end of the twentieth century, Christopher Shaw

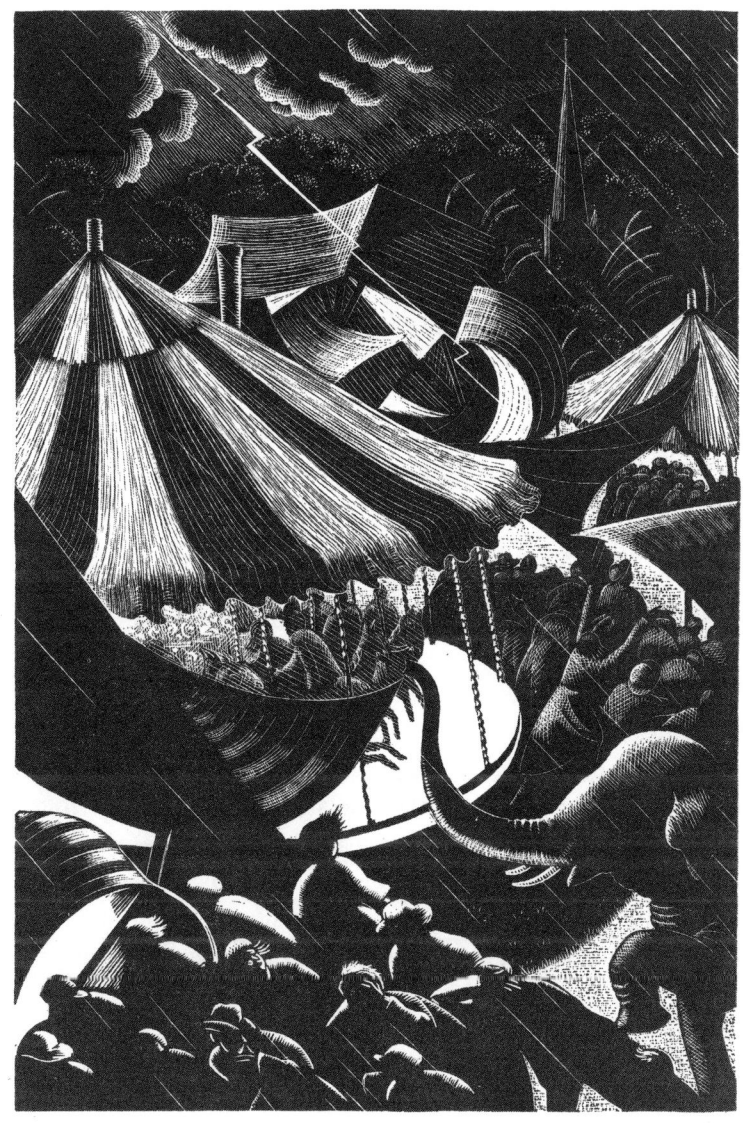

FIGURE 3.9 Clare Leighton's full-page wood engraving *Storm at the Fair,* conveying modernist tempos in lightning bolts. From Clare Leighton, *Country Matters* (London: Gollancz, 1937; New York: Macmillan, 1937), 59. 4¾ × 7 inches. Copyright 2025 Estate of Clare Leighton. All rights reserved. DACS/Artists Rights Society (ARS).

and Malcolm Chase's *The Imagined Past: History and Nostalgia* (1989). The wood engraving's black and white contrasts represent a quiet Norman church behind two-story buildings of antique design, all foregrounded by a village green with no signs of life aside from several ducks and a single elderly man walking with the aid of a cane. *Chalfont St Giles* seems to indulge in the kind of rural fantasizing that Harris associates with the "conjured village of the mind's eye." Weighed down by the heavy type of the book's title, the words "History and Nostalgia" framing its top, Leighton's wood engraving does not communicate her "real experience" of being in Chalfont St Giles on July 13, 1931, the date inscribed below the picture in her handwriting, but rather some lost "dream of roses around the door."[28] By book design, if not authorial intent, Leighton's wood engraving, extracted from its 1930s contexts of production and consumption, bears in *The Imagined Past* the burden of representing the worst kind of nostalgia, the kind that all scholars love to hate: nostalgia as evil enchantment, as falsification of the past by the present.[29]

Shaw and Chase's 1989 reproduction of a 1930s Leighton wood engraving represents a pattern of cultural thinking that has casually conflated rural landscapes and social geographies with modern nostalgia and Bewickian white-line wood engraving.[30] The problem with such conflation is that it reinforces essentialized ideas about the "nature" of the connection between these separate subjects—landscape, society, nostalgia, and wood engraving. We need look no further than the first paragraphs of Chase and Shaw's introduction for "documentary evidence from the history of ideas" that encourages multiple ways of looking at nostalgia and thus multiple ways of looking at wood engravings.[31] Chase and Shaw foreground David Lowenthal's efforts to historicize twentieth-century reactions to nostalgia in order to show how nostalgia is not inevitably "reactionary, regressive, ridiculous" but may also be a source of compassion and sympathy, a "special way of being involved in the past."[32] Chase and Shaw write, "Such variations of meaning and emphasis were evidence that nostalgia was not a one-dimensional concept with clean-cut edges."[33] The same could be said of efforts to realign wood engraving within 1930s modernist cultures: Such variations of meaning and emphasis were evidence that wood engraving was not a one-dimensional art with clean-cut edges. While Chase and Shaw's title page inclusion of Leighton's wood engraving risks reinforcing one-dimensional notions that white-line wood engraving is singularly representative of history and nostalgia, the evidence and arguments within their volume contest this very assumption.

Chase asserts from the outset of his chapter "This Is No Claptrap: This Is Our Heritage," that "writing about rural England, and seeing in it all the essential qualities of Englishness, arguably reached a climax in the years 1930–45."[34] This claim establishes a cultural framework that helps us align the interwar climax of rural writing with the interwar climax of wood engraving in causal and historical rather than casual and essentialized ways.[35] While Chase marshals print evidence to demonstrate that "the widely-circulated non-fictional rural writing of the 1930s and 1940s" represented and produced "the emotional geography of inter-war rural England . . . ultra-conservative in its implications, and profoundly reactionary in its social philosophy," he also acknowledges economic conditions that paved the way for progressive women like Leighton to gain leadership positions in British publishing, arts, and literary culture:

> To a considerable extent the continued success of rural writing in this period reflected market demand, and the increasing capability of printers and publishers to issue attractive books at reasonable prices. The opening-up of the publishing market mirrored the opening-up of the countryside itself.[36]

The historical reflection or mirroring that Chase notes between the demand for books about rural Britain and a commercial book industry's entirely modern capacity to produce those books at low cost finds Leighton at its center, right where Selborne, the wood engraving expert cited earlier, places her.

Decades after Chase and Shaw attended to vexed relations between the realities of interwar rural modernity and the unrealities of nostalgic yearning, scholars are turning again to the landscapes of rural England in their search for understanding of modern and modernist English artistic values and national life.[37] Of the newest studies, Stuart Sillars's *Picturing England Between the Wars: Word and Image 1918–1940* devotes the most space to discussion of wood engraving.[38] It includes reproductions of wood engravings by Leighton, Joan Hassall, and Helen Binyon, discusses rural-themed wood engravings of Gwen Raverat, and credits Charles Tunnicliffe's wood engravings for turning Henry

Williamson's *Tarka the Otter* into a best-selling countryside book in 1932. Adopting a "middling focus" on illustrated books of the 1920s and 1930s, Sillars argues that "the years between the two world wars are unique in the presentation of identities through texts that unite word and image, in a manner not seen in precisely the same way before or later" (3). Concerns about rural England and its everyday realities propel Sillars's argument, as he, like rural historians before him, connects interwar "idealizations of the countryside" to countryside images in mass-produced books for adults printed and bound with new technologies and distributed along efficient networks (3). Also like earlier rural historians, Sillars regards these illustrated texts as both symptoms of and contributors to the disorienting social and economic changes that altered the appearance and population of the countryside as well as the urban and suburban areas proximate to them. He writes in his first chapter, "Some Versions of Arcady":

> [In] their new forms, the books present a double, and to most readers an invented, nostalgia: first, for the places described and illustrated, by then much changed, and then for the books themselves, in the visual and literary styles that together have the leisure tone of an earlier age lacking the anxiety of loss. (12)

Sillars suggests that invented nostalgia is at once a product of a sense of loss for a once known and loved rural place, now changed by the usual "culprits" of the car, the arterial road, and the speculative builder, and a product of a sense of loss for a once known and loved kind of *book* about this rural place.[39] When we get to Sillars's chapter "Moving Towards Truths," the first chapter to examine 1930s wood engraved illustrations, he suggests that the nostalgia effects produced by interwar texts about the countryside may be as various and unpredictable as their sources.

Sillars draws our attention to volumes that "challenged and undermined the idyllic presentation of the country in word and picture" (53), citing Francis Brett Young's 1938 *Portrait of a Village,* with wood engravings by Joan Hassall, for our special admiration (Figure 3.10). But even here, the white-line wood engravings of the woman artist who illustrated Brett Young's movements toward rural truth are suspected of indulging in nostalgia. They are placed "firmly within the tradition of rural imaging dating back to the eighteenth-century wood-engraver

Thomas Bewick" (55), and as a result are "uneasily matched" (55) and again "quite unmatched" (57) to Brett Young's "greater concern for contemporary actuality" (58). Sillars distrusts his own discomfort, neglecting to connect the inevitable mismatch between word and image in any book, of any genre and any style, with the "tension between word and image" that he says makes interwar books with Bewick-style white-line wood engravings "so intriguing to the later reader" (58). In the case of *Portrait of a Village,* Sillars regards this word–image tension as confusing, "deceptive," the book's readers "seduced" with the "too easy" attractions of its white-line wood engraving style presumably guilty of producing invented nostalgia (58). On the other hand, Sillars praises Leighton's *Farmer's Year* for its "more critically aware" approach to "familiar countryside images" (139) materialized in its "more distanced" designs guaranteeing its "firmer hold on the actuality of farming" (140) (Figure 3.4).[40] When the artist and writer of an interwar illustrated book are the same person, Sillars happily notes that the aesthetic and ideological effects are "of a special kind" (9), more unified, more harmonized, the link between the two forms nicely "tauten[ed]" (140).

With Sillars's approach to interwar illustrated books, no matter whether the books are written by the artist, whether they are illustrated by wood engraving or another kind of medium, or whether they are about the country, city, or suburb, we risk losing sight of the differences of materials, media, and circumstances that determine the ways differently gendered, classed, and raced artists produced their art—the different ways they got their hands dirty in the real and metaphorical gardens of rural Britain. We also risk losing sight of the social reality of art, those networks among agents, writers, editors, publishers, and printers that are required to turn an individual artist's picture into a book illustration. This chapter's inclusion of Victor Gollancz and his colleagues in our pictures of interwar Britain builds a more complete understanding of interwar print culture and what Sillars might call the "truths" or "actualities" of rural modernity.

THROUGH THE WOODS AGAIN

In what must be one of the most unlikely coincidences of 1930s literary life, another one of Gollancz's authors was wandering around the beech woods of Buckinghamshire in the early 1930s, seeking not chair bodgers but sex. Eric Blair, bored by his job teaching schoolboys in Hayes, Middlesex, would invite his

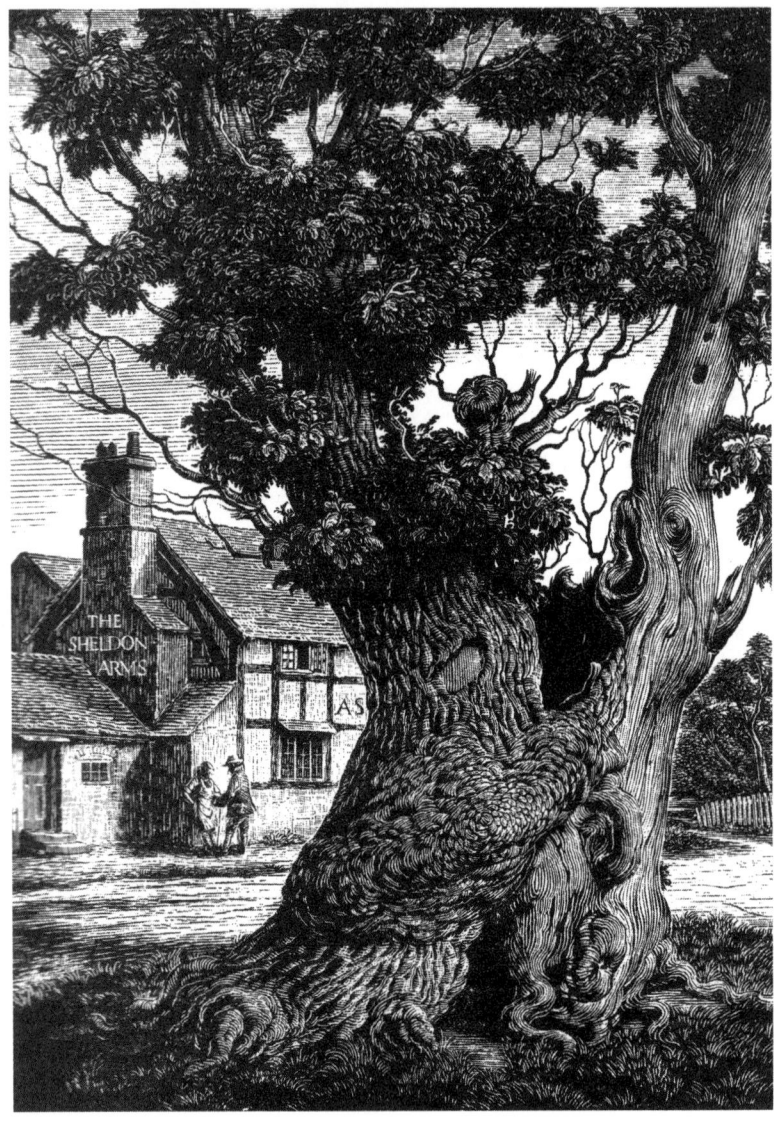

FIGURE 3.10 Joan Hassall's first major book illustration project was a triumph of artistic imagination and execution. This is her wood engraved frontispiece *Stricken Oak*. From Francis Brett Young, *Portrait of a Village* (London: Heinemann, 1937; New York: Reynal and Hitchcock, 1938). 4¼ × 6 inches. Reproduced by permission of the Estate of Joan Hassall/Simon Lawrence.

girlfriends for country walks to Burnham Beeches. According to his biographer Gordon Bowker, Blair "saw the countryside as his sexual stamping ground—a place to take women in both senses of the word."[41] Interrupting Blair's adventures in seduction was a letter from Victor Gollancz expressing interest in publishing his first documentary travel book, *Down and Out in Paris and London.* Gollancz scheduled this book for publication in 1933, the year Leighton published her first mass-reproduced wood engraving trade book *The Farmer's Year* with Gollancz's rival, Collins. By January 1936, with Leighton and Miller Parker contracted for additional illustrated countryside books, Gollancz advanced enough money to his new author, now known as George Orwell, to travel to the urban north and write a book about mass unemployment.[42] The result, as everyone knows, is *The Road to Wigan Pier,* the autobiographical travel narrative that established Orwell as a "major socialist writer."[43] Leighton's *Country Matters,* coming out in the very same year from the very same publisher, is also an autobiographical travel narrative set in the "here and now, in the nineteen thirties," but in down-and-out rural rather than industrial England.

Orwell's conflicts with Gollancz over *Wigan Pier* are legendary, but there is no denying the social impact of his documentary's chapters on middle-class readers who for the first time felt what it might be like to be an unemployed miner in a slum of a depressed northern town.[44] Orwell's realism is not Leighton's, his passion for exacting detail conveyed through statistics on wages, unemployment benefits, and square footage of deplorable housing rather than lines in wood, describing lives of plants. Yet like Leighton, Orwell conveys, in black-and-white prose, the colors of life in the Great Depression. For example, a passage that begins by describing an area in Wigan as "a world from which vegetation had been banished," leaving only "smoke, shale, ice, mud, ashes and foul water" for apprehension by horrified readers, ends with a description of Sheffield that by comparison, we are told, makes Wigan "beautiful":

A frightful patch of waste ground (somehow, up there, a patch of waste ground attains a squalor that would be impossible even in London) trampled bare of grass and littered with newspapers and old saucepans. To the right an isolated row of gaunt four-roomed houses, dark red, blackened by smoke. To the left an interminable vista of factory chimneys, chimney beyond chimney, fading away into a dim blackish haze. Behind me a railway embankment made of the slag of furnaces. In front across the patch of waste ground, a cubical building of red and yellow brick, with the sign "Thomas Crocock, Haulage Contractor." (107)

Hellish reds, yellows, and blacks fill this vision, which is no more or less realistic, no more or less documentary, than any one of Leighton's gentle black-and-white scenes of Depression-era Buckinghamshire. Yet the masculine confrontation with "dark" slum life is the one that has come to represent modernity in the 1930s, despite the diversity of scenes and what Orwell elsewhere calls the "uproar of voices" that women and men writers and artists were documenting at that time in their prose and pictures.[45] Given the dominance of Orwell and the invisibility of Leighton in literary critical accounts of the decade, one would never guess that they were embarked on similar artistic journeys, each measuring social and documentary value through aesthetic criteria ("beautiful," "the ugliest"; 106). Nor would one guess that their 1937 Gollancz books arose from the same love of rural living that is violently excluded from the patch of waste ground that represents for Orwell the worst abandonments of England and its workers by its privileged middle and upper classes.[46]

Literary critics' stories about British 1930s documentary will tell deeper truths about both rural and urban life if they open themselves up to the vocabularies and values of book historians and feminist critics who bring women artists and writers like Clare Leighton into interdisciplinary conversations about modern literature and print culture. Leighton is at her best as a rural documentarist in *Four Hedges,* her intimate portraits of plants and people communicating her joy in gardening, writing, and engraving. The book is a brave, beautiful, scandalously public love letter from Leighton to Brailsford, testifying to the possibilities of equality in work and art in an English garden composed of black and white in an age of Depression and darkness. Revealing the artist's curiosity about the work and lives of all rural people, male and female, young and old, with or without families, wealth, or education, Leighton's wood engravings are meditations on the impacts of geography, landscape, and culture on modern feeling. Such feeling cannot be understood apart from the material and social conditions that shape all testaments of personal and political life, including in her case the materials of her art of wood engraving, the materials of her rural life, Victor Gollancz's

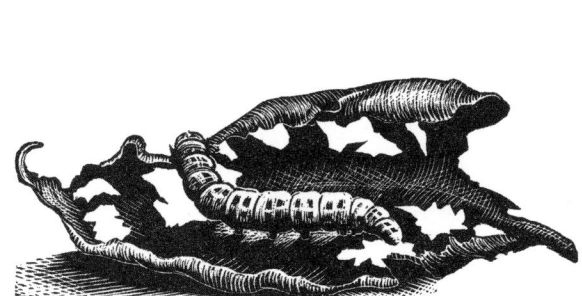

FIGURE 3.11 Clare Leighton's wood engraved portraits such as *Mullein Caterpillar* testify to her respect for even the lowliest of creatures as they, like the artist, leave traces on the page of the hard work of reproduction. From Clare Leighton, *Four Hedges: A Gardener's Chronicle* (London: Victor Gollancz, 1935; New York: Macmillan, 1935), 53. 3¼ × 1¼ inches. Copyright 2025 Estate of Clare Leighton. All rights reserved. DACS/Artists Rights Society (ARS).

bookmaking materials that brought her art into readers' lives, and the material, bodily woman's life that Leighton joined to the married Brailsford's, risking immaterial, emotional loss of all that love made possible within four hedges on a windy hillside in Buckinghamshire (Figure 3.11).

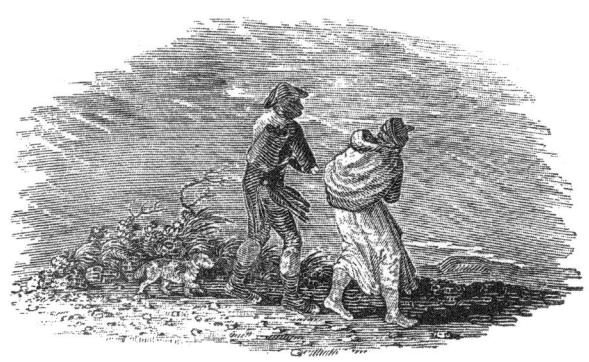

"my Wild Goose chase"

In *Nature's Engraver*, Jenny Uglow describes Bewick's vignettes as "lyrics without words, songs on wood."[1] When we look at Bewick's *The Runaway Cart* (see this volume's first "Vignette") or *Making Up the Difference* (in the final "Vignette"), Uglow's words seem exactly right, appearing as they do amid her discussion of Bewick's love of Northumbrian piping and ballad singing. But when we look at Bewick's vignette of a ragged, wandering couple and their dejected dog, the visual lyrics seem cruel and the song more akin to a sigh. With a gray, monotonous background that suggests relentless fog and unattainable destinations, this small illustration seems to gather into itself the felt reality of its stooping figures' miserable hunger and cold. Their feelings and our identifications attain more power when they are condensed into or projected onto miniature characters. We see no faces, but we feel we know this man and this woman. They are brave outcasts, venturing forth with bare necessities—a coat and hat for him, an apron and cap for her. The large sack the woman hauls on her back arouses our keenest hopes

Thomas Bewick, *A History of British Birds*, vol. 2, *Water Birds* (1804, 1826), 115. 3 × 1⅝ inches.

and worries. Does it contain all their worldly goods? It must be heavy because she leans farther forward than her partner with his basket. Perhaps she carries some crusts of bread, a bit of cheese, maybe an extra shawl, a spoon, a pot—but no extra boots or shoes, for if those existed, they would certainly be on the feet of the sorry woman crossing the vignette's stony ground.

The more we look, the more desperate the scene becomes. There is no tree for our wanderers to shelter under, but only a nude twig to point the featureless way. We look again at the woman and wonder and worry anew: What if there is a baby in the improvised carryall? Is that a small head behind the woman's own? What are they to do? Where to go? We find no answers in the obscured view, even as we feel called upon to provide not only answers but also aid. For this vignette, like all of Bewick's vignettes, implies a "one-to-one confidentiality with the reader," and with that confidentiality comes a sense of responsibility that persists in urgency and intimacy no matter how small the image.[2]

Diana Donald tells us that *A Glossary of North Country Words* (1829) "listed some nine different Northumbrian dialect words for such itinerants, denoting varying occupations and degrees of disreputability." These included "Faw-gang," a "general name for 'all sorts of wandering people, who go about in companies,'" and "Trampers," "mendicants who traverse extensive tracts of country . . . finding subsistence and lodgings where they may."[3] For Donald, the wood engraved vignette of the wandering couple with their small dog and dim path is "typical" of Bewick's compassionate renderings of "wayfarers [who] easily became symbols of all social breakdown and injustice."[4] Contrasting Bewick's wayfarers in his *British Birds* of 1804, first published during the wars with France, to romantic portrayals of winsome peddlers or Gypsy families painted by contemporaries like W. H. Pyne or Julius Caesar Ibbetson, Donald comments that in Bewick's work, "the men's solitariness is striking." Alone, lost, or abandoned, "Bewick's lonely men" invite our identification as we imagine their thoughts and sensations in a landscape that may or may not fulfill the promise of home.[5]

Bewick's reflections in his *Memoir* on his own solitary wanderings in 1776 across the borders to Edinburgh and Glasgow, and through the Scottish Highlands, provide another kind of picture that contrasts with his vignettes of strikingly lonely men. A vigorous, curious, fearless twenty-two-year-old traveling by foot, he met with welcome and kindness everywhere, but valued this reception most when he

> bent my way in many a zig zag direction through the interior of part of the Highlands—by the sides of its Lakes & its mountains—the beauty & serenity of the former & the grandeur or terrific aspect of the latter I gazed upon with wonder & with both, was charmed to extacy. (63)

Bewick records how, falling in with "herds or drovers," he was directed to "some Farmers or Graziers House," where he "took up my abode and often by the pressing solicitation of my host or hostess was prevailed upon to remain with them for a day or two" (63). No evil befell the ecstatic artist, no desperate search for food or lodging. Agog with nature's beauties, Bewick occasionally slept outdoors, roughing it, having spent so much time during the day "in admiration of the varied prospects" that he "was benighted and was obliged to take shelter under some rockey projection, or to lay myself down among the heather 'till day light" (64).

This picture of a young Bewick sheltering contentedly under a rock invites another contrast, another picture of a rural wanderer sleeping among the heather. Jane Eyre, years after retreating into Bewick's *Birds* while hiding behind the scarlet draperies of the Reeds' breakfast room, finds herself alone and "absolutely destitute" on an unpopulated moorland while night approaches (Brontë, *Jane Eyre,* 317). Plagued by the "intolerable questions," "What was I to do? Where to go?," Jane takes council with herself and determines, "I have no relative but the universal mother, nature: I will seek her breast and ask repose" (318). Initially, mother nature is benevolent:

> I struck straight into the heath; I held on to a hollow I saw deeply furrowing the brown moorside; I waded, knee-deep, in its dark growth; I turned with its turnings, and finding a moss-blackened granite crag in a hidden angle, I sat down under it. High banks of moor were about me; the crag protected my head: the sky was over that....
>
> Beside the crag, the heath was very deep: when I lay down my feet were buried in it; rising high on each side, it left only a narrow space for the night air to invade. I

folded my shawl double, and spread it over me for a coverlet; a low, mossy swell was my pillow. (318–19)

After a night untroubled by man or beast, Jane seeks human aid only to find herself spurned by the house- and shopkeepers who equate her lonely mobility with immorality and criminality. As with Bewick's lonely men, the blind musicians, beggar boys, and tramps who traverse his tailpieces, she invites our identification as we share her thoughts and sensations in a landscape that fails to fulfill the promise of home.

Jane's misadventures in heath and bog recall Bewick's narrative of his Scottish ramble as well as his tailpiece engravings of "'sublime' and melancholy scenes" that Donald tells us "permanently affected [the Brontë children's] mature writing."[6] Charlotte, Branwell, Emily, and Anne Brontë join Jane Eyre as child readers of Bewick's vignettes, but they cannot affirm the small engravings' cheerful status as "songs on wood." As we know, the fictional Jane prefers Bewick's solitary and fearful scenes, finding in them inspiration for childhood rebellion. This experience predicts or at least prepares us for her later impulsive, dangerous solitary flight into the wild north-midland rains and crags. Jane's difference from the young Bewick as we imagine both sleeping among the heather is defined not only by her sex and class but also by Bewick's and Brontë's differences of literary generation, aesthetic values, and dramatic temperament. Jane Eyre and Charlotte Brontë may admire but cannot fully share or extend into their own Victorian literary worlds Bewick's "sublime" feeling because his sublime is not theirs. His art never flies entirely free of the mundane knowledge derived from a childhood and youth spent living among the rural poor. Because Bewick recognized rural country people as his own, because he had grown up as one of them and because he loved them, his representations of them are not romantic, idealizing, or gothic, but knowledgeable, realistic, and embracing. In the age of enclosure, rapid industrialization, and devastations of village economies and traditions, Bewick recorded both the pleasures and the labors of England's displaced peasantry. Rather than communicating sympathy, the quality Nigel Tattersfield associates with the vignettes' depictions of "the trials and tribulations of ordinary country folk," they extend the more radical quality of empathy. And this is true whether they illustrate a pathetic scene of rural homelessness, a peaceful scene of rural leisure, or a scene of rural vulgarity, foolhardiness, or vice.[7]

Bewick's only vignette of a solitary woman wanderer is among the smallest in *British Birds*. At a mere 1⅛ by ¹¹⁄₁₆ inches, this vignette arrests our gaze, a song on wood calling us to look again and linger in contemplation of this minuscule walker. We are lured into her scene, compelled to wonder what will become of her as she, with hitched skirts and solid calf, strides away from us, burdened but stalwart and upright. If she is heading north, as Bewick did on his walking tour of the Scottish Highlands, the day is old, the sun is setting behind a distant hill, and the woman's long shadow on the ground warns of real, not gothic, dangers in the encroaching dark. If on the other hand she is heading south, the sun is rising, and our woman traveler has made an early start, moving with strength and freedom into a new and cloudless day. Either way, the solitary female walker at dusk or dawn makes an anxious visual ending for Bewick's chapter "The Grey Phalarope." Bewick's verbal ending for this chapter informs us that while the grey phalarope is "seldom met with in any part of the British Isles," one Capt. Sabine, in his "Memoir of the Birds of Greenland," reported seeing "a flock of these birds . . . swimming in the open sea amongst some icebergs" (148). Happy birds, to have such company on their chilly migrations. Not so Bewick's woman in the vignette, a tiny human among the birds, held apart by type on the page while striding purposefully through our imaginations to who knows what end.

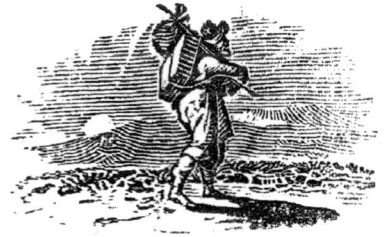

Thomas Bewick, *A History of British Birds,* vol. 2, *Water Birds* (1804, 1826), 148. 1⅛ × ¹¹⁄₁₆ inches.

FOUR

Joan Hassall's Saltire Chapbooks

Discovering "A Vast New Public of Readers"
in Wartime Scotland

In 1945, the most popular of Joan Hassall's Saltire Chapbooks, *The Marriage of Robin Redbreast and the Wren,* was published in Edinburgh by the Saltire Society (Plate 7). Illustrated with nine unique wood engravings, it was promoted to members of the Saltire Society and the Scottish reading public as the perfect Christmas gift, with illustrations that would inspire reflection and amusement, enchanting old and young alike. Hassall had come to Edinburgh from wartime London to teach printing and composition at the Edinburgh College of Art. She was thirty-nine at the time, young enough to be willing to try a new life in a new city and old enough to have established a reputation as one of Britain's most original and skilled wood engravers working in Bewick's white-line tradition.[1] The cover design of *The Marriage of Robin Redbreast and the Wren* communicates the technical, formal, and tonal qualities that earned Hassall such comparisons. The extraordinary control and detail, the subtle sense of humor, the allusions to the decorative elements of eighteenth-century wood engraved vignettes—all these are apparent upon initial examination. The delicate double borders that frame the chapbook's front combine rigid linear patterns with graceful curves and arcs, all directing our eyes to the central image of wee Robin and his wife, themselves encircled by the graceful petals of a flowered wreath that is knotted with a bow.

The pleasing symmetry of the cover of *The Marriage of Robin Redbreast and the Wren,* so suitable for a book that ends with a happy marriage, is typical of Hassall's Saltire Chapbooks, the last of which, *Rashie Coat,* was published in 1951.[2]

This was six years after Hassall had returned to England and long after critics had declared the end of the wood engraving revival. Aside from the colored borders that decorate the covers, the chapbooks tell their tales in words and pictures worked out in black type and black image on white page: Words and pictures are equal in this regard, furthering the chapbooks' commitment to values of balance, harmony, and equilibrium.[3] Each is very small—a mere 3½ by 5¼ inches. According to print and design historian Rosemary Addison, the World War II–period Saltire Chapbooks were intended to recall not just the size but also the contents and functions of eighteenth-century Scottish chapbooks that were filled with subversive stories or Jacobite songs and verses and were sold by peddlers through the backwaters of the land.[4] The Saltire Chapbooks, though more elegantly designed than their eighteenth-century models, were equally ephemeral.[5] Miniature and fragile, compliant with wartime economy restrictions on paper, they were sold at the affordable price of one shilling. They announced themselves as lightweight paper books for the people: small, inexpensive, short, and presumably short-lived. In the words of print and wood engraving scholar David Chambers, "Slight pamphlets though these all were, they yet contain a great deal of [Hassall's] most pleasing, and finely engraved, work."[6] Readers recognized the beauty of Hassall's Saltire Chapbooks upon the publication of her first, *Four Scottish Poems of the Sixteenth Century*, in 1943. The chapbooks' delicate wood engravings share through their forms the idea that the public deserves fine books—not necessarily fine editions, but books with fine design, appreciated for their fine illustrations, produced and distributed with a fine sense of purpose (Figure 4.1).

Cheap and beautiful: It is this unusual combination of qualities that in Scotland, in the mid-1940s, made the Saltire Society's edition of *The Marriage of Robin Redbreast* so popular with readers (Figures 4.2 and 4.3).[7] It is also this combination of qualities that brings Hassall into the same trade book markets as those Victor Gollancz targeted for his countryside books illustrated by Agnes Miller Parker and Clare Leighton. Apart from George Bruce's account of the first fifty years of the Saltire Society and specialized studies of Joan Hassall's career and influence, the chapbooks are mentioned rarely by historians and usually only in connection with twentieth-century wood engraving.[8] As a result, the chapbooks are lost to multiple constituencies who would delight in their petite forms: scholars of modernist art, middlebrow and children's literatures, and

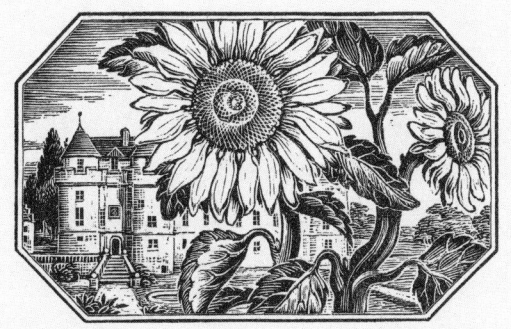

THE SOLSEQUIUM
(THE SUNFLOWER)

Lyk as the dumb solsequium, with cair ourcome
   And sorrow, when the sun goes out of sicht,
Hings doun his head, and droops as dead,
             and will not spread,
   Bot locks his leavis throu languor of the nicht,
      Till foolish Phaeton ryse
        With whip in hand,
      To cleir the crystal skyis
      And licht the land :
Birds in thair bour luikis for that hour
   And to thair prince ane glaid good-morrow givis ;
Fra then, that flour list not till lour,
   Bot laughis on Phoebus lousing out his leavis.

2

FIGURE 4.1 Joan Hassall's wood engraving for "The Solsequium (The Sunflower)." From *Four Scottish Poems of the Sixteenth Century,* Saltire Chapbook No. 1 (Edinburgh: Saltire Society, 1943), 2. 2½ × 1½ inches. Reproduced by permission of the Estate of Joan Hassall/Simon Lawrence.

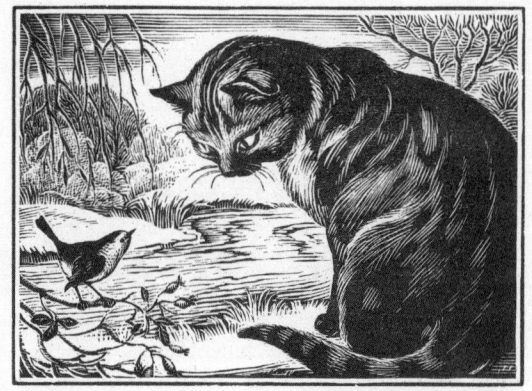

THERE was an auld gray Poussie Baudrons, and she gaed awa' down by a water-side, and there she saw wee Robin Redbreast happin' on a brier; and Poussie Baudrons says: 'Where's tu gaun, wee Robin?' And wee Robin says: 'I'm gaun awa' to the king to sing him a sang this guid Yule morning.' And Poussie Baudrons says: 'Come here, wee Robin, and I'll let you see a bonny white ring round my neck.' But wee Robin says: 'Na, na! gray Poussie Baudrons; na, na! Ye worry't the wee mousie; but ye'se no worry me.'

2

FIGURE 4.2 Joan Hassall's wood engraving of wee Robin Redbreast and the scheming "auld gray Poussie Baudrons." From *The Marriage of Robin Redbreast and the Wren,* Saltire Chapbook No. 4 (Edinburgh: Saltire Society, 1945), 2. 2⅝ × 1⅞ inches. Reproduced by permission of the Estate of Joan Hassall/Simon Lawrence.

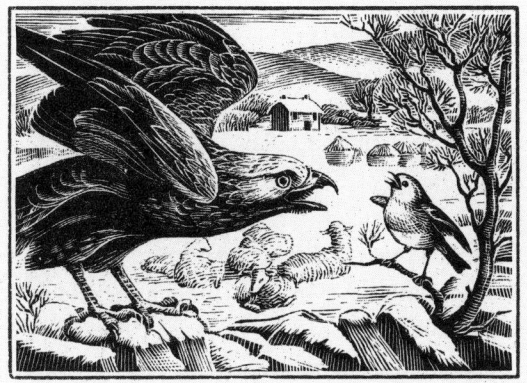

So wee Robin flew awa' till he came to a fail fauld-dike, and there he saw a gray greedy gled sitting. And gray greedy gled says : 'Where's tu gaun, wee Robin ?' And wee Robin says : 'I'm gaun awa' to the king to sing him a sang this guid Yule morning.' And gray greedy gled says: 'Come here, wee Robin, and I'll let ye see a bonny feather in my wing.' But wee Robin says: 'Na, na! gray greedy gled ; na, na ! Ye pookit a' the wee lintie ; but ye'se no pook me.'

3

FIGURE 4.3 Joan Hassall's wood engraving of wee Robin and the mendacious "gray greedy gled." From *The Marriage of Robin Redbreast and the Wren,* Saltire Chapbook No. 4 (Edinburgh: Saltire Society, 1945), 3. 2⅝ × 1⅞ inches. Reproduced by permission of the Estate of Joan Hassall/ Simon Lawrence.

Scottish and British book history, and anyone intrigued by the forms and fantasies of British rural modernity.

This chapter argues that scholars of modern art, literature, and print cultures should regard the Saltire Chapbooks' illustrations, the enchanting wood engravings that, separated out from their texts and contexts, seem to ensure their historical significance, in relation to and as expressions of contemporary, everyday, popular *literary* contents and contexts. The people, and more specifically the Scottish people, as real collaborators and creators of the chapbooks and as an imagined market of ready readers and book consumers, shape every stage of the Saltire Chapbooks' publication. Yet as we approach the one hundredth birthday of the Saltire Society's publication of *The Marriage of Robin Redbreast,* the people and publics that contributed to the chapbooks are largely forgotten. Instead, only one lonely person, the artist Joan Hassall, is celebrated for her contributions to the chapbooks, which are seen as Scottish objects marking a transformative moment in her otherwise English career. This kind of narrative limits Hassall's significance along with the significance of the Saltire Chapbooks; it is too quiet and too obscure to inspire an evolving understanding of the chapbooks' place in midcentury modernity or twentieth-century women's art (Figure 4.4).

For a series of books undertaken with the intent of recalling a revolutionary Scottish textual history, how could such forgetfulness, such textual invisibility, set in? It is beyond the scope of this chapter to answer this question fully, but it is worth observing that celebration of an artist as a solitary print heroine, divorced from the institutions and publics that supported her, furthers a highly specialized, formalist art history at the expense of social and cultural history. To create a more dynamic and authoritative place for Joan Hassall and the Saltire Chapbooks in British literary criticism and book history, this chapter asks: How did notions of and commitments to the people, and especially to Clare Leighton's "vast new public of readers," influence the chapbooks' inspiration, design, contents, and production? How did this new public affect the chapbooks' marketing, consumption, and critical reception? Answering these questions leads to a different kind of scholarly narrative, one that is shared between the people—in all their imagined solidarity and real diversity—and the individual wood engraver and illustrator. This broader, louder story, involving more makers and players, more readers and places, advances Hassall's reputation as a creator of modern

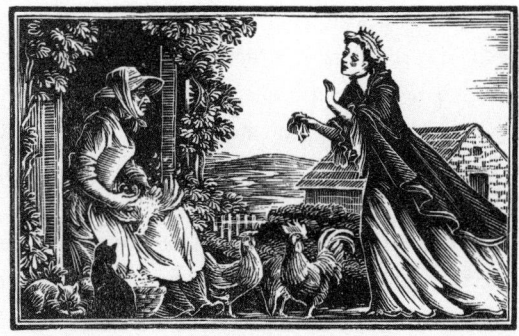

RASHIE-COAT was a king's daughter, and her
father wanted her to be married ; but she
didna like the man. Her father said she had
to tak him ; and she didna ken what to do.
Sae she gaed awa' to the hen-wife to speer
what she should do. And the hen-wife said :
' Say ye winna tak him unless they gie ye a
coat o' the beaten gowd.' Weel, they ga'e
her a coat o' the beaten gowd ; but she
didna want to tak him for a' that. Sae she
gaed to the hen-wife again, and the hen-wife
said : ' Say ye winna tak him unless they
gie ye a coat made o' the feathers o' a' the
birds o' the air.' Sae the king sent a man

1

FIGURE 4.4 Joan Hassall's wood engraving of the king's daughter seeking advice from the
sympathetic hen-wife, who will help her escape marriage to a man "she didna like." From *Rashie
Coat,* Saltire Chapbook No. 12 (Edinburgh: Saltire Society, 1951), 2. 2⅝ × 1⅝ inches. Reproduced by
permission of the Estate of Joan Hassall/Simon Lawrence.

art more than any number of previous tributes constructing a narrow tale of a singular figure's technical and design acumen. Joan Hassall may have been un-married and unpartnered, working as an independent, self-employed woman who practiced a "revived" art that was threatened, as are all revivals, by fears of extinction or irrelevance, but she was never alone. She and her wood engraving grew out of and responded to many of the most acute crises of the twentieth century, including the prolonged crisis of modern sexism, with the support of many other people from all over the British Isles.

The social narrative this chapter tells about the Saltire Chapbooks emerges in part through study of the wartime Edinburgh background apparent in biographical and critical studies of Hassall's career and in part through study of the 1940s general correspondence, annual reports, and minutes of the Saltire Society Publications Committee.[9] It attempts to bring members of the Publications Committee, including John W. Oliver, Agnes Mure McKenzie, George Scott-Moncrieff, Alison Cairns, and Robert Hurd, out from the shadows of the archives so they appear as collaborators in the Saltire Chapbook project. This group of people, small and devoted, constitutes one of the publics that, if integrated into the story of the Saltire Chapbooks, can strengthen the chapbooks' position in literary and book history. Scottish readers constitute another group of people to consider, as they are the audience for whom Saltire Society leaders published the chapbooks and in whom they hoped to instill a greater sense of national identity and continuity. Larger still is the abstract group of British readers and consumers that art critics addressed through articles in popular publications destined for "the modern public." This modern public was not construed as a body of specialists or connoisseurs but, in the words of art critics Sir Edward Marsh, Barnett Freedman, and W. E. Williams, as a body of "ordinary," "everyday," or "plain" readers who were interested in discovering and creating an art for the people.[10] They composed a generation of do-it-yourselfers, some of whom took up the wood engraver's tools and contributed to the popularity of white-line wood engraving in twentieth-century Britain. They were also the people who bought wood engraved books and prints, thereby creating a market for wood engraving that was strong enough to support Joan Hassall's career as teacher and artist in Scotland in the 1940s. These publics—both Scottish and British—were integral to the chapbooks' success. Hassall's story is told here as one of private accomplishment made possible through the contributions of the people and publics that surrounded her. It is a quiet story of a shy woman's enduring love for Bewick's art, English books, and Scottish people, suggesting that Hassall's wood engravings and designs are best understood in social terms, as part of a collaborative book art (Figure 4.5).

A STUDENT AMONG TEACHERS

Joan Hassall was born in 1906 at 88 Kensington Park Road in Notting Hill, London, to John Hassall and his second wife, Constance Maud Webb. The historical record tells us little about the influence of Joan's mother on her development, but it has preserved many details about her father, who was also her first art teacher.[11] We get a glimpse of the family dynamic in a letter from the young Joan Hassall, then a student at the London School of Art, where her father was principal, to her brother, the poet and dramatist Christopher Hassall. The letter is addressed to "Topher," Joan's nickname for her beloved brother, and though undated, has been identified by the editor of her letters, Brian North Lee, as written in 1927.

> As you know, I am getting on rather well with Art, and the School is running smoothly and well, etc., etc. At the end of next term Mums says I must leave, and go and find a teaching post. Not only do I dislike teaching, but I am far better at Art, and stand a fair chance of doing something at it. Also I think the social difference between "Artist" and "Teacher" is immense, although that doesn't matter much. Also there seems some chance of making a name at art, whereas there is no future for a teacher unless one is marvelous at it, which I am not, and even then I would rather be a great Artist than a great Teacher, it seems so much more universal. The final thing is that Dads so much wants me to take up Art. I simply don't know what to do. I don't want a battle royal over my prostrate body, so to speak, but I have determined not to teach if I can possibly help it. I am dreading the inevitable moment when the thing will have to be fought out. After all, I am twenty-one, and ought to be allowed to choose my own life, but the habit of obedience is strong, and I am terrified that I will not have sufficient willpower to stick up for myself.[12]

Torn by loyalties to parents with different professional visions for their talented daughter, Hassall conveys a third, equally strong loyalty and debt: that to her brother, the confidant to whom she proclaims in this same letter: "I AM NOT

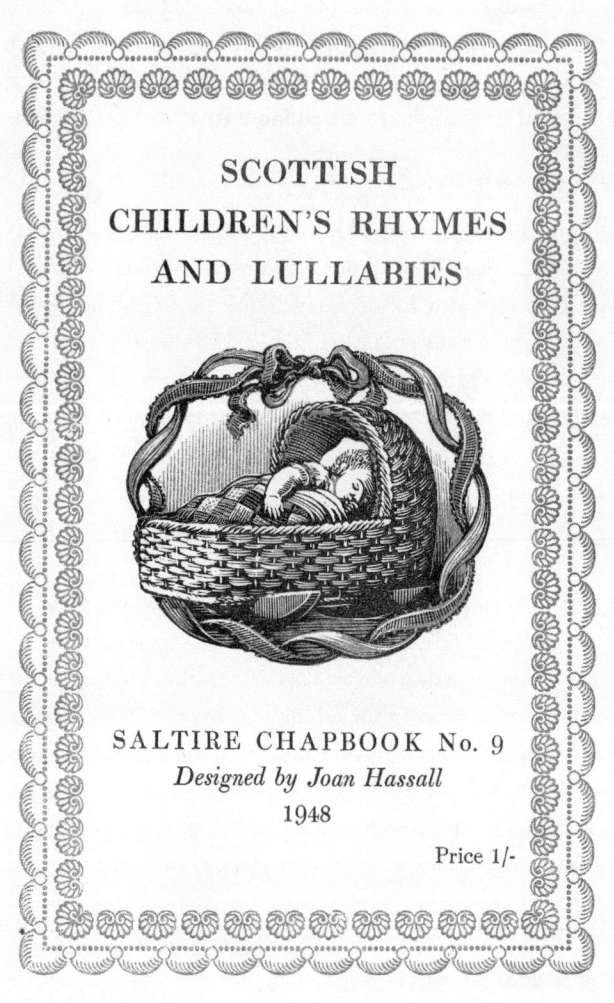

FIGURE 4.5 Joan Hassall's wood engraving and designed cover, with black and blue ink, for *Scottish Children's Rhymes and Lullabies*, Saltire Chapbook No. 9 (Edinburgh: Saltire Society, 1948). 3½ × 5¼ inches. Reproduced by permission of the Estate of Joan Hassall/Simon Lawrence.

GOING TO TEACH, SO THERE! I shall feel an awful brute, sticking up for myself, but it must be done."[13] Joan Hassall's declaration to her brother, a solitary witness of her artistic ambition who also functions as her earliest collaborator and public, is followed by a sentence that signals the emotional cost of her refusal, her sense of being "an awful brute." We can feel her anguish over her act of self-assertion, over her sense of betrayal of her mother and what readers today would see as her sense of betrayal of a gender code that demanded of middle-class girls obedience and self-abnegation.

Reading Joan Hassall's 1927 declaration of freedom from her mother's expectations is, to some extent, to encounter evidence of her father's influence. John Hassall has been described as "a man of strong personality" and as "one of the last of the Bohemians—impecunious even when he was successful, convivial, a reckless spender."[14] The Hassall father had been destined for a bold career. His parents raised him to be a military officer, but instead of Sandhurst he went in 1888 to work on a ranch in Manitoba for two years, returning to Europe for artistic training. In 1895 he began what turned into a fifty-year career with the London advertising agency David Allen & Sons, during which his posters such as the iconic "Jolly Fisherman" of 1908 and "Kodak Girl" of 1910 became part of the designed landscape of England.[15] Joan Hassall followed in her father's footsteps to the extent that she acquired a formal art education in the Royal Academy Schools from 1927 to 1933. Also like her father, Joan Hassall pursued a career in the commercial rather than the fine arts. However, her discovery in 1931 of the miniature art of wood engraving during a night course sponsored by the London County Council School of Photo-Engraving and Lithography and her devotion to what many regard as the most conservative, nostalgic strand of this illustrative art seem to be deliberate acts of defiance in the face of her father's oversize personality, exuberant public art, and bold illustrative forms.[16] When John Hassall died in 1948, Joan took over his Kensington Park house and studio. That same year she was elected a fellow of the Royal Society of Painter-Etchers and Engravers and was made a fellow of the Society of Industrial Artists and Designers.[17] Although she had made significant progress toward artistic and emotional independence while in Edinburgh, only after her father's death does she seem to have come out fully from under his shadow, achieving and accepting public recognition for her unique contributions to British art.

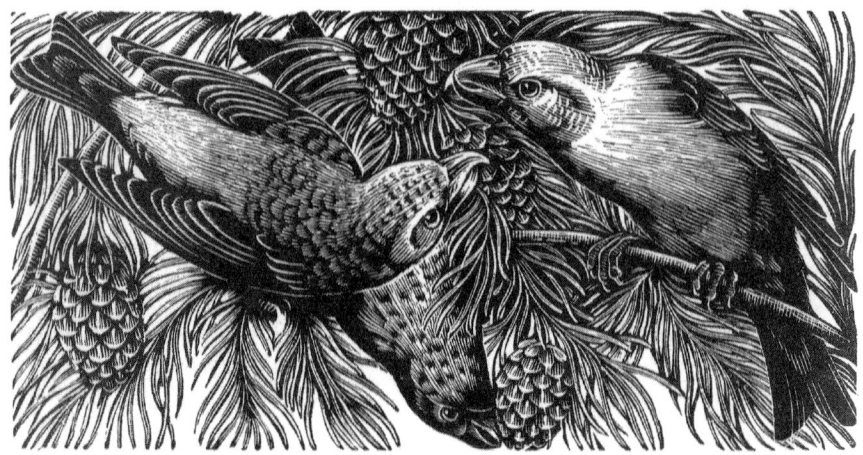

FIGURE 4.6 Joan Hassall's wood engraved chapter header for "The Use of Tools," recalling in its avian subjects and scientific exactitude the headers of Bewick's *British Birds*. From Bernard Gooch, *The Strange World of Nature* (New York: Thomas Y. Crowell, 1950), 104. 4 × 2 inches. Reproduced by permission of the Estate of Joan Hassall/Simon Lawrence.

From the early 1930s until she had to give up wood engraving because of arthritis, Hassall's devotion to Bewick and wood engraving was complete. In the words of McLean, a foremost scholar of Hassall's work, Bewick was an "an intoxicating and vital influence" on her art and life; arguably, he was her most important teacher, an imagined, idealized public.[18] Critics have since validated the results of that intoxicated instruction, Chambers for example asserting that of all the brilliant English wood engravers who made the "nineteen-thirties and forties as important as the early eighteen-hundreds" for achievements in wood engraving, Hassall, "in her quiet way, most nearly matched the delicacy, the humour and the fine workmanship of Bewick's vignettes."[19]

Bewick recorded in his memoir his close contact with the wild creatures and countryside scenes that informed his art during his childhood and his postapprenticeship ramble, or what he fondly called "my *Wild Goose chase*" of more than three hundred miles around Scotland.[20] Hassall, the daughter of a middle-class London artist, could not in 1930s England have duplicated this wandering life in rural Britain, with all its advantages of natural observation, because it would have been too dangerous for a solitary woman to do so.

The soger frae the wars returns,
  The sailor frae the main,
But I hae parted frae my love
  Never to meet again, my dear—
    Never to meet again.

When day is gane, and night is come,
  And a' folk bound to sleep,
I think on him that's far awa,
  The lee-lang night and weep, my dear—
    The lee-lang night and weep.

ROBERT BURNS (*Scots Musical Museum*, 1796)

2

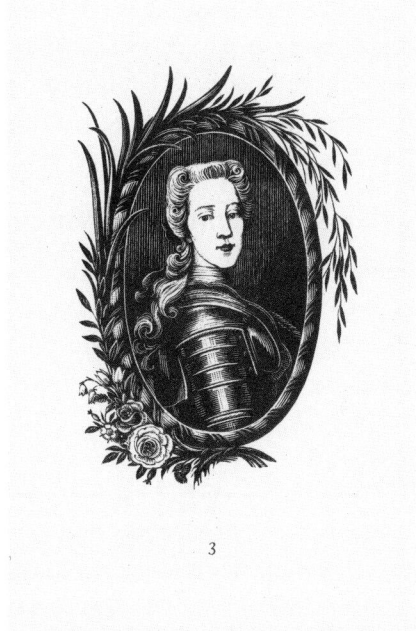

3

FIGURE 4.7 Joan Hassall's tiny wood engraved tailpiece illustrating "It was a' for our righfu' King." From *Songs of the '45*, Saltire Chapbook No. 5 (Edinburgh: Saltire Society, 1945), 2. ⅞ × 1⅝ inches. Reproduced by permission of the Estate of Joan Hassall/Simon Lawrence.

FIGURE 4.8 Joan Hassall's wood engraved illustration of Bonnie Prince Charlie, with roses and thistles. From *Songs of the '45*, Saltire Chapbook No. 5 (Edinburgh: Saltire Society, 1945), 3. 2⁷⁄₁₆ × 3½ inches. Reproduced by permission of the Estate of Joan Hassall/Simon Lawrence.

Her accomplishments as an illustrator of nature, despite the limitations on her motion and thought imposed by her sex, are in some ways even more marvelous than Bewick's. Her detailed, realistic representations of animal and plant life in the 1950 edition of Bernard Gooch's *The Strange World of Nature,* for example, enlarge and pull to the foreground natural subjects that are, in her Saltire Chapbook illustrations, largely relegated to background (Figure 4.6). But creatures, plants, and landscape are integral to all Hassall's chapbook illustrations, no matter how urban or urbane the figures represented. In Saltire Chapbook No. 5, *Songs of the '45* (1945), the subjects are primarily human and regal. But

even a vignette illustration of the contested crown has a singing bird upon it, and
Bonnie Prince Charlie's portrait is enwreathed with roses, grasses, and a thistle
(Figures 4.7 and 4.8). In Chapbook No. 12, *Rashie Coat* (1951), the princess heroine may draw our eye, but it is her exquisitely carved and reproduced leafy or
feathered surroundings, relegated to backdrop, that insist that the natural world
is always just outside the cottage or castle door (Figure 4.9).

WARTIME EDINBURGH AND THE SALTIRE SOCIETY

Edinburgh had castles to spare and enough nature to satisfy the most romantic
of personalities. Hassall arrived at this gusty northern city in 1940 or early 1941,
about ten years after her introduction to wood engraving.[21] In a letter to McLean
dated August 25, 1950, she describes the conditions that initially soured her feelings about her new home:

> You will be horrified to know how deeply I felt the exile from the South when I was
> in Edinburgh. I realize now that my unhappiness was bred by the irksomeness
> and exhaustion of teaching and also by a very definite hostility which I was quite
> unprepared for from some "Scotland for the Scottish" people who resented my ap-
> pointment. It took me quite three years to discover any Scots I really liked, but of
> course by the end of my time there I had made many loving and faithful friends,
> and had laid the foundation for that "feeling for Edinburgh" which I do not deny
> that I have.[22]

McLean extends the implications of this statement, claiming that Edinburgh
itself "gave her commissions—and inspiration—for some of her best work."[23]
Hassall recorded another source of inspiration: children's books. In an undated
letter written during the war to her friend the publisher John Guest, she notes
that she has set up in her private rooms "what 'The Trade' would call a 'Cock
Robin Shop'" and that she hopes one day to "produce a small but steady stream of
elegant ephemera."[24] Teaching, the very thing that brought her to Edinburgh, is
what keeps her from achieving this ambition:

> The College work is going well and they spent £500 on a new room & fresh equip-
> ment so that it is quite an important affair now but I long to be done with it. I was

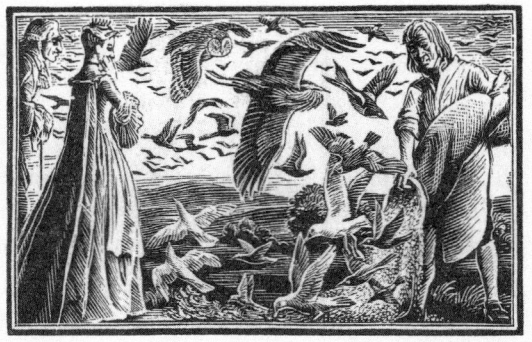

wi' a great heap o' corn ; and the man cried
to a' the birds o' the air : ' Ilka bird tak up
a pea and put down a feather ; ilka bird
tak up a pea and put down a feather.' Sae
ilka bird took up a pea and put down a
feather and they took a' the feathers and
made a coat o' them, and ga'e it to Rashie-
coat ; but she didna want to tak him for a'
that. Weel, she gaed to the hen-wife again,
and speered what she should do ; and the
hen-wife said : ' Say ye winna tak him
unless they gie ye a coat o' rashes and a pair
o' slippers.' Weel, they ga'e her a coat o'
rashes and a pair o' slippers ; but she didna

2

FIGURE 4.9 Joan Hassall's wood engraved headpiece of the moment when "ilka bird took up a pea
and put down a feather." From *Rashie Coat*, Saltire Chapbook No. 12 (Edinburgh: Saltire Society,
1951), 2. 2⅝ × 1⅝ inches. Reproduced by permission of the Estate of Joan Hassall/Simon Lawrence.

horrid ill most of last term and much was said about my giving it up, but I am now in such robust health that that excuse is no longer of any value. . . . My only other acquisition is a fair collection of early Childrens *[sic]* books that I have picked up here and there or been given, and I find them quite enchanting. These [Saltire] Chapbook's format was very much inspired by some of them.[25]

Edinburgh offered enchanting children's books, a well-stocked print room at the college, and, as we learn from another letter from Hassall to McLean written after the war, two ideal publishers, the Saltire Society and Hopetoun Press, both of which offered her "the only jobs I have ever done [the Saltire Chapbooks and *A Child's Garden of Verses*] where I had complete control."[26] Although Mc-Lean singles out the Saltire Chapbooks as evidence of Hassall's maturation as an artist and designer during her sojourn in Edinburgh, the Saltire Society itself does not play much of a role in his account.[27] This chapter tries to convey the shared vision and energy of a small group of people on the society's Publications Committee who nurtured Hassall's talent, helped with virtually all aspects of book production, and, through publication and promotion of the Saltire Chapbooks, facilitated her contact with a larger reading public than she had known in the past.[28]

The minutes and annual reports of the Saltire Society Publications Committee suggest the degree of cooperation required of many generous figures to achieve the publication of each Saltire Chapbook.[29] Joan Hassall's name appears frequently in the minutes and reports of the early 1940s, while the chapbooks themselves earn a line-item entry in each of the Publications Committee minutes up to 1949. Just one of many publication initiatives of the war and tough postwar years, these little books clearly preoccupied the members of the committee, who oversaw their production, distribution, sales, and profits (Figure 4.10).

The minutes in the files of the first years of the Publications Committee, circa 1944–49, lack complete dates, but those dated August 31 with penciled-in year of 1944 (but probably taken in 1943) record the first key moments when chapbooks rather than broadsheets were agreed upon as the format of Hassall's Saltire art. Once the committee accepted the proposal to adopt "the form of a Chapbook," it went on to "discuss with Miss Hassall the format of the Chapbook and the estimates submitted by [Edinburgh printers] Mrssrs. R&R Clark and Oliver and

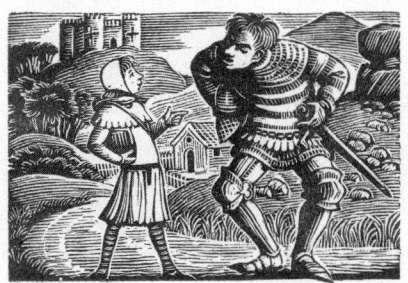

THE FAUSE KNICHT AN THE
WEE BOY

" O, whaur are ye gaun ? "
Quo the fause knicht upon the road ;
" I'm gaun tae the schule."
Quo the wee boy, an still he stude.

" Whit is that upon yer back ? "
Quo the fause knicht upon the road ;
" Atweel it's my bukes,"
Quo the wee boy, an still he stude.

" Whit's that ye've got in yer airm ? "
Quo the fause knicht upon the road ;
" Atweel it's ma peat,"
Quo the wee boy, an still he stude.

" Wha's aucht thae sheep ? "
Quo the fause knicht upon the road ;
" They're mine an ma mither's,"
Quo the wee boy, an still he stude.

1

FIGURE 4.10 Joan Hassall's wood engraved header of the defiant wee boy upon the road. From "The Fause Knicht an the Wee Boy," in *The Fause Knicht and Other Fancies,* Saltire Chapbook No. 10 (Edinburgh: Saltire Society, 1950), 1. 2 × 1⅜ inches. Reproduced by permission of the Estate of Joan Hassall/Simon Lawrence.

Boyd. . . . Dr. Oliver agreed to compile a selection of Scottish verse suitable for the Chapbook, and Mr. Hurd, Miss Hassall and Miss Cairns were asked to form a consultative group on the production of the Chapbook" (Figure 4.11).[30]

Minutes of a meeting of the Publications Committee held at Gladstone's Land on September 25 (presumably 1944) record "plans for new chapbooks."[31] At the center of these plans is Dr. John Oliver, who was busy collecting possible textual materials, and George Scott-Moncrieff, who brought to the committee the idea for what proved to be the society's most popular chapbook, none other than *The Marriage of Robin Redbreast and the Wren,* which was attributed to Robert Burns. The committee secretary notes that "Miss Hassall's 'dummies' for the proposed Chapbooks were handed round and warmly approved."[32] These words are a testament to the committee members' appreciation of Hassall's artistry, but also to their collective investment in solving not only questions of chapbook contents but questions of art and design as well. Actions taken during a meeting held on May 17, 1945, and recorded in the minutes of the committee continue the pattern of group "authorship" of the chapbooks.[33] In that year, which saw publication of *Robin Redbreast,* Dr. Oliver proposed the selection of songs for a "Jacobite Chapbook," for which "Miss Hassall had agreed to undertake illustration and general design, while Mr. Hurd, Dr. Oliver, and Miss Cairns were asked to consult with Miss Hassall as to the final selection."[34] The process of composition for what would become Chapbook No. 5, *Songs of the '45,* was another collaborative effort. Every chapbook earned from committee members' consultation, collective input, and sustained, coordinated, and imaginative contributions. Recognizing the signs of a dynamic process recorded in otherwise dry minutes of Saltire committee meetings encourages us to regard Joan Hassall as an integral member of the Publications Committee that created the chapbooks; she is important but not isolated, single but not alone. Indeed, the minutes of the committee prove more than anything else her position at the center of an arts community that she enchanted into love for her art of wood engraving (Figure 4.12).

George Bruce has done the most to preserve and publicize the history of the remarkable organization to which these committee members devoted themselves. In his volume on the Saltire Society's first fifty years, he cites archival documents such as the society's first annual report of 1936, which functions as the society's founding manifesto. In this report, Saltire Society Secretary

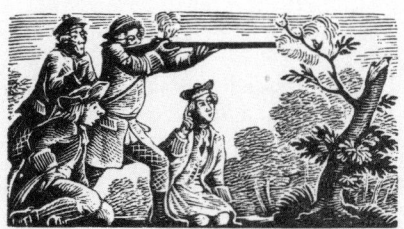

THE HUNTING OF THE WREN

" Will ye go to the wood ? " quo Fozie Mozie ;
" Will ye go to the wood ? " quo Johnie Rednosie ;
" Will ye go to the wood ? " quo Foslin e'en ;
" Will ye go to the wood ? " quo brither and kin.

" What to do there ? " quo Fozie Mozie ;
" What to do there ? " quo Johnie Rednosie ;
" What to do there ? " quo Fozlin e'en ;
" What to do there ? " quo brither and kin.

" To slay the wren," quo Fozie Mozie ;
" To slay the wren," quo Johnie Rednosie ;
" To slay the wren," quo Fozlin e'en ;
" To slay the wren," quo brither and kin.

" What way will ye get her hame ? " quo Fozie
    Mozie ;
" What way will ye get her hame ? " quo Johnie
    Rednosie ;
" What way will ye get her hame ? " quo Foslin
    e'en ;
" What way will ye get her hame ? " quo brither
    and kin.

9

FIGURE 4.11 Joan Hassall's wood engraved header of Fozie Mozie, Johnie Rednosie, and Foslin. From "The Hunting of the Wren," in *The Fause Knicht and Other Fancies,* Saltire Chapbook No. 10 (Edinburgh: Saltire Society, 1950), 9. 2 × 1⅟₁₆ inches. Reproduced by permission of the Estate of Joan Hassall/Simon Lawrence.

" We'll hire carts and horse," quo Fozie Mozie ;
" We'll hire carts and horse," quo Johnie Red-
    nosie ;
" We'll hire carts and horse," quo Foslin e'en ;
" We'll hire carts and horse," quo brother and
    kin.

" What way will ye get her in ? " quo Fozie
    Mozie ;
" What way will ye get her in ? " quo Johnie
    Rednosie ;
" What way will ye get her in ? " quo Foslin e'en ;
" What way will ye get her in ? " quo brither
    and kin.

" We'll drive down the doorcheeks," quo Fozie
    Mozie ;
" We'll drive down the doorcheeks," quo Johnie
    Rednosie ;
" We'll drive down the doorcheeks," quo Foslin
    e'en ;
" We'll drive down the doorcheeks," quo brither
    and kin.

" I'll hae a wing," quo Fozie Mozie,
" I'll hae anither," quo Johnie Rednosie ;
" I'll hae a leg," quo Foslin e'en ;
" And I'll hae anither," quo brither and kin.

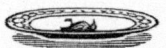

Published by THE SALTIRE SOCIETY
Gladstone's Land, Lawnmarket, Edinburgh
Printed by R. & R. Clark, Ltd, of Edinburgh

FIGURE 4.12 Joan Hassall's wood engraved tailpiece of the main course in "The Hunting of the Wren." From *The Fause Knicht and Other Fancies,* Saltire Chapbook No. 10 (Edinburgh: Saltire Society, 1950), 10. ¾ × ⅜ inches. Reproduced by permission of the Estate of Joan Hassall/Simon Lawrence.

Mrs. Alison Bonfield describes the society's purpose as "restoring Scotland to its proper position as a cultural unit" through making "Scots conscious of their heritage."[35] Looking back in order to "move forward," the society from its beginnings saw the encouragement of Scottish arts and education as central to its modern mission. While it may seem odd that an explicitly nationalist cultural organization adopted as a founding principle the goal of being "entirely non political," Bonfield states that its aim is "to be inclusive and not exclusive—all that was asked of members was to be friends of Scotland."[36] Hassall, a Londoner who came to think of herself as a friend of Scotland, would have found this formulation congenial. A self-described perfectionist, she would also have found congenial the fifth and last principle of Bonfield's Saltire manifesto: "Rejection of the second rate."[37] Though not directly associated with the early twentieth-century Scottish Renaissance, the Saltire Society drew from the ideals of the modernist aesthetic endorsed by Renaissance writers Hugh MacDiarmid, Edwin Muir, Eric Linklater, Catherine Carswell, and others in refusing to acclaim "inferior work . . . simply because it was Scottish."[38]

In Saltire Society Publications Committee annual reports and minutes of the 1940s and 1950s, the society's nationalist and aesthetic aims seem to be taken for granted, left unspoken, as editorial decisions are typically explained in commercial terms. For example, an archived carbon copy of a letter dated November 3, 1944, preserves the words of "R.H." (presumably Robert Hurd, president of the Saltire Society from 1943 to 1948) to Sir Robert M'Vittie Grant, a potential donor:

> As a Society we do not seek to become a major publishing concern, but we are anxious to be in a position to publish from time to time books and pamphlets which it would be a public benefit to issue, but which the average Scottish publisher, at any rate, would not be prepared to sponsor as a commercial proposition.[39]

With less restraint, he elaborates in a subsequent paragraph: "Our main object is to facilitate the production of books which ought to come out, but which the commercial publisher will not touch. Sometimes, of course, he proves wrong in his caution. . . . Our little chapbook of Scottish verse issued last Christmas at 1/- [Hassall's *Four Scottish Poems of the Sixteenth Century*, 1943] made a handsome profit."[40] Here we see the assumption of the comfortable, underlying purpose of the Saltire Society: to publish for "public benefit." Despite emphasis on the society's interest in noncommercial ventures, validation of the chapbooks and other society publications comes to be measured in terms of profits, not aesthetics or politics.[41]

At approximately the same time that Hurd was writing his letter to Sir Robert M'Vittie Grant, there is reference in the 1944 annual report of the Saltire Society Publications Committee to the market and financial values that prompted continued chapbook publication. The report describes *Four Scottish Poems of the Sixteenth Century,* the first chapbook, published in 1943, as a success that has motivated the committee to commission two chapbooks for Christmas 1944:

> Once again the selections were made by Dr. John Oliver and the design and illustrations by Miss Hassall. Mally Lee proved the more popular in sales to the general public through the shops, but in direct sales to members she was neck and neck with William Dunbar, and we should like to congratulate our membership on their discrimination. Only a few copies of each chapbook remain, and our profits on the two came to £26.15.6. . . .
>
> Our publications are of course designed for the general public, but we do count very strongly indeed on support from our members.[42]

Two publics for the chapbooks are mentioned here: the "general public" of readers that preferred Chapbook No. 2, *Mally Lee and Three Folk Songs,* and the Saltire Society members who, through joining the organization and subscribing to its publications, prove their superior sensibilities, their "discrimination," by purchasing Chapbook No. 3, William Dunbar's *Seasonal Poems* (Figure 4.13). The relation of both general and specialist publics to the success of the society's publication program is clearly articulated: Popularity with the general public is a primary and determining factor in the Publications Committee's editorial decisions, but this public cannot be counted on to fully endorse the society's nationalist and aesthetic aims of "stimulating a greater awareness and appreciation of the arts in Scotland." Thus the body of member-readers bears a disproportionate responsibility for building up a "strong publications Fund, so that we may be in a position to issue books and pamphlets in line with the Society's aims, which we feel should be published, even if they are from the financial point of

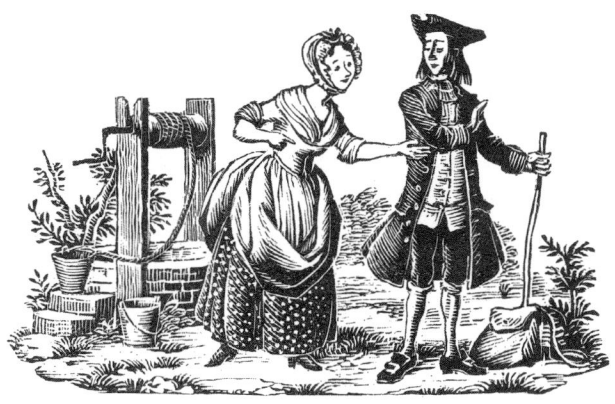

view, unremunerative."[43] That larger and larger numbers of readers from the general public joined the
smaller group of Saltire Society member-readers
is clear from records of society membership during
the war years. In 1941, early in Hassall's Edinburgh
stay, the society had 420 members; five years later, in
1946, it had more than quadrupled in size, claiming
1,725 members.[44]

FIGURE 4.13 Joan Hassall's
wood engraved header for
"My Jo Janet." From *Mally Lee
and Three Folk Songs*, Saltire
Chapbook No. 2 (Edinburgh:
Saltire Society, 1944), 6.
2⅜ × 1½ inches. Reproduced
by permission of the Estate of
Joan Hassall/Simon Lawrence.

THE SALTIRE CHAPBOOKS: CHILDREN'S BOOKS FOR ADULTS

In George Bruce's view, Saltire Society members were buying with the Saltire
publications a folk culture that was a heritage of "the playground."[45] This implies
another public for the chapbooks, more unruly than Saltire Society members
and more Scottish than the general British book-buying public: children in
Scotland who themselves or whose parents or older siblings had bought the
chapbooks. Not a market, not even necessarily readers, children still constitute
an important popular audience to consider if the chapbooks are to find a more
prominent and enduring place in Scottish and British literary and book history. Bruce speculates that Scottish speech, songs, dances, tales, and historical
folk knowledge were kept alive longer in schoolyards than elsewhere, precisely

because they were "disregarded or devalued in school."[46] The ambiguity of the chapbooks' purpose—preservation and re-creation—is felt in the peculiar relations between their words and pictures. In most instances, the words are supposed to represent the unprofessional, spoken voice of a lost and plebeian Scotland, yet the pictures represent the entirely professional, visual imagination of the Englishwoman Joan Hassall (Figure 4.14).

For example, Chapbook No. 6, *Whuppity Stoorie,* is a comic folktale meant to be read by an adult to a child. It concerns a young and lovely wife who outwits her wealthy husband's cruel demand that she not only learn to spin before he returns from a business trip, "but to have spun a hundred hanks o' thread" (2). Finding under a rock "six wee ladies in green gowns" singing as they spin on a little wheel, she is reassured by them that they will cure her husband forever of his demand for a spinning wife. Their solution to the problem of masculine tyranny lies in their mouths, which are permanently hitched up to one side, an effect best realized through Hassall's cover design. Invited to dinner by the young wife on the evening of her husband's return, the six wee ladies prompt him to ask, in English, "Ladies, if it be not an uncivil question, I should like to know how it happens that all your mouths are turned away to one side?" (7). We read, "'Oh,' said ilk ane at ance, 'It's with our constant SPIN-SPIN-SPINNING'" (7) (Figure 4.15).

The joy of the tale is communicated partly by Hassall's illustrations and partly by editor John Oliver's text, adapted from Robert Chambers's 1826 collection *Popular Rhymes of Scotland.* Saltire Society historian Bruce calls Oliver a "transmitter," drawing attention to the way generations of Scottish readers had depended on professional intermediaries to transmit Scottish children's culture.[47] The imposition of modern print on ancestral oral culture is most blatantly conceded in *Whuppity Stoorie* upon a page turn where we read, in English, in italics, and in square brackets, "*[Here speak with the mouth turned to one side, in imitation of the ladies.]*" (8) (Figure 4.16). This instruction to parents or teachers shows more explicitly than any other aspect of the chapbooks how *Whuppity Stoorie,* a text that aims to convey an oral history, gets caught in the associations and limitations of modern print culture. Hassall's wood engraved illustrations do not and perhaps cannot teach Scottish children about their heritage speech or oral culture. If anything, they teach them about a visual and print culture associated with an eighteenth-century Newcastle artist and businessman, Thomas Bewick.

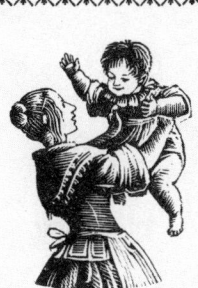

Dance to your daddie,
My bonnie laddie,
Dance to your daddie, my bonnie lamb;
And ye'll get a fishie—
In a little dishie—
Ye'll get a fishie
when the boat comes hame.

Dance to your daddie,
My bonnie laddie,
Dance to your daddie, my bonnie lamb;
And ye'll get a coatie
And a pair o' breekies—
Ye'll get a whippie and a supple Tam.

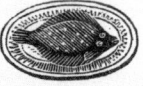

FIGURE 4.14 Joan Hassall's wood engraved headpiece, tailpiece, and border illustrating "Dance to your daddie." From *Scottish Children's Rhymes and Lullabies,* Saltire Chapbook No. 9 (Edinburgh: Saltire Society, 1948), 2. 5¼ × 3½ inches. Reproduced by permission of the Estate of Joan Hassall/ Simon Lawrence.

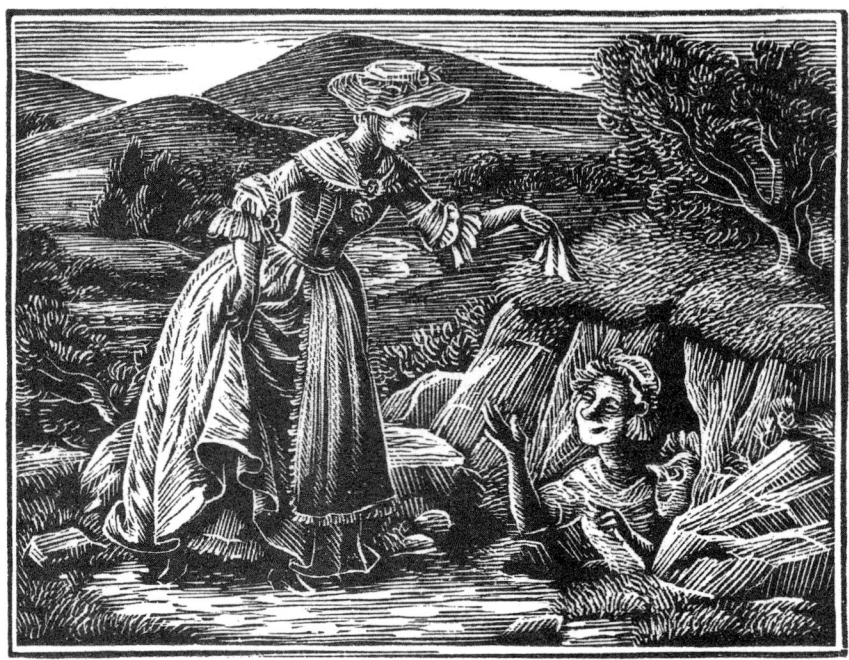

Historians of children's book illustration are familiar with both Bewick's and Joan Hassall's names and are likely to understand the artists' cultural significance in terms of a gendered history of illustrated book publication. As discussed in the Introduction, women artists experienced professional success in the commercial art and book industries, and white-line wood engraving by Hassall, Gwen Raverat, and Agnes Miller Parker is seen as an exciting development in children's illustration aesthetic and design during the years of the Great Depression and World War II.[48] In connection with this development, Whalley and Chester, for example, look back to Thomas Bewick, explaining that he is important to twentieth-century children's book illustration because he "completely changed the art of engraving on wood, and hence the attitude to it—it was no longer the medium to be used for only the humblest and cheapest work, but had proved

FIGURE 4.15 Joan Hassall's irresistible wood engraved header of "the little wifies" "aneath the stane." From *Whuppity Stoorie,* Saltire Chapbook No. 6 (Edinburgh: Saltire Society, 1946), 5. 2⁹⁄₁₆ × 1⅞ inches. Reproduced by permission of the Estate of Joan Hassall/Simon Lawrence.

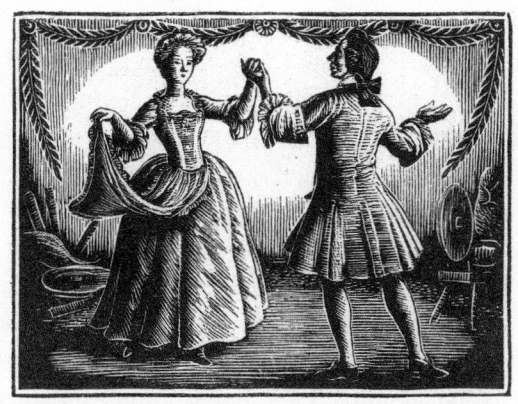

[*Here speak with the mouth turned to one side, in imitation of the ladies.*]

' Is that the case ? ' cried the gentleman. ' Then, John, Tam, and Dick, fye, go haste and burn every rock, and reel, and spinning-wheel in the house, for I'll not have my wife to spoil her bonny face with SPIN-SPIN-SPINNING.' [*Imitate again*]

And so the lady lived happily with her goodman all the rest of her days.

8

itself to be capable of great subtlety."[49] True enough, or true by parts. In Whalley and Chester's chapter on 1930s children's book history, Bewick's name comes to substitute for a full explanation of the women artists' diverse sources of inspiration and their entirely modern impacts on modern book arts. The modernity of the women engravers' art is similarly disguised or minimized by the concept of revival, the very concept that seems to promise women artists acclaim through borrowed aesthetic and cultural significance. But herein lies the problem with the otherwise attractive idea of revival: As discussed in the Introduction, any account of a modern art movement that is endorsed and legitimated as a revival will inevitably be received as another tale of loss, inviting yet another round of nostalgia for an art form that is figured as perpetually trapped in a cycle of death and rebirth. To be revived is to come back to life, but that life is seen as tenuous, fragile, always threatening to recede into the past of its origins. It is a half life, not a full life. In adopting the logic of revival without discussing its conceptual limitations, Whalley and Chester risk construction of a weakened, truncated women's art history.

In contrast, print historian Richard Benson argues that Bewick's real importance to book history is his happening upon a commercial solution to the problem of costly illustrated texts. Experimenting with steel engraving tools on the hard end of a wood block, he advanced a printing system that began with handwork but found its completion in a mechanical process that permitted binding up wood blocks in a chase with type, all of which could be inked and printed in one pass. This method reduced printing costs, and savings were passed on to consumers.[50]

Among Joan Hassall's books, the Saltire Chapbooks stand out for being among the least expensive volumes of beautifully illustrated text published in twentieth-century Britain, bringing the older values that Bewick endorsed in his popular books for children onto the modern page. McLean, for example, emphasizes that wood engraving has a "unique place high in the connoisseur's affections" precisely because, as a hand process, it is "out of date in the modern world of commercial book-production."[51] In a 1960 essay, he declares:

> The essential and original virtue of typography is the crisp impression of black type on white paper; and letter-press printing, the traditional technique of laying paper on inked type and pressing on it, is still the only way to achieve that end perfectly.

And wood-engraving . . . is the only way of making illustrations to match perfectly with type. An etched, lithographed, or steel-engraved illustration may be beautiful, but only a wood-engraving can have exactly the same qualities of black-and-white and crispness as type itself, because it is a relief printing surface identical in character with metal-cast type.[52]

All this to say that McLean values Hassall's work in part because his print aesthetic retains traces of a modernist aesthetic, with its premium on works of art that are received as unique, unified, elite, noncommercial, and pure of form. McLean's formalist values, his way of looking at wood engravings apart from their social contexts, does not help us to understand the popular and populist motives, forms, methods, and markets of the chapbooks.

"A VAST NEW PUBLIC OF READERS"

In 1932, the first edition of Clare Leighton's *Wood-Engraving and Woodcuts* appeared as part of The Studio Publications How to Do It series. Reprinted twice in the 1940s, once in 1944 while Hassall was still in Edinburgh and again in 1948, Leighton's book testifies to the popularity of wood engraving as a medium of artistic expression pursued by nonspecialists well after the end of the so-called 1930s wood engraving revival. Designed for readers interested in teaching themselves how to create wood engravings, the book includes an introductory section on method written by Leighton and illustrated with photographs demonstrating her techniques and tools (Figures 1.10 and 3.7), a robust middle section of reproductions of twentieth-century wood engravings by British and European artists, and a "Finale" by Leighton in which she tries to explain the reasons for "the modern use of [wood engraving] as the artist's direct means of expression."[53] It is this last section that points most surely to the possible identity and role of the largest public to receive the wood engraved Saltire Chapbooks: lower-middle-class and newly middle-class British homemakers and homeowners.

Leighton theorizes that the first cause of the public's enthusiasm for wood engravings is economic. She was sensitive to the poverty of Britain's new public of readers, who found their newly acquired enthusiasms for art and literature constrained by the dire impacts of the Depression. Leighton encourages these readers to pursue the purchase and practice of economical arts, among them wood engraving, which requires only relatively inexpensive boxwood blocks and ten to thirteen tools for the generation of an almost "indefinite number of perfect prints."[54] Wood engraving shares the virtues of the Saltire Chapbooks—cheapness and beauty—and thus suggests parallel implications for public engagement.

Archives record the popularity of Hassall's Saltire Chapbooks and support Leighton's belief that Britain's vast new public of readers "has brought an immense stimulus to wood-engraving."[55] This comment constructs her modern readers as consumers of wood engraved books and wood engraved "wall pictures," objects that Leighton endorses not in terms of connoisseur aesthetics but in terms of public taste. They are in keeping "with modern ideas of interior decoration."[56] Leighton's modern readers are also do-it-yourselfers, aiming to learn from her not only why they should buy wood engravings but also why they should make them. Leighton's answer to this question constructs "the modern public" as a potential art market as well as a body of potential art producers, sensitive recorders and responders to modern life, "more exacting and scientific" than their predecessors, seeking "far greater precision of tone" and "a much stronger rendering of form" than is available in other kinds of reproductive media.[57]

The vast new public of readers that Leighton imagines in 1932 as newly appreciative of wood engraved prints and books is also the readership addressed by the Pelican book *Art in England,* published in 1938 by Allen Lane as part of his Penguin book enterprise.[58] Each Pelican book was an inexpensive, pocket-size, nonfiction paperback intended to attract intellectually adventurous readers with accessible writing by prominent authors who addressed topical concerns. Radically populist in design and price, *Art in England* is also populist in subject and narrative style. In a chapter titled "Patronage in Art To-Day," for example, Sir Edward Marsh attempts to "show how a man who has never had anything at all that could possibly be called Money, may in the course of years get together a collection which is a continuous joy in the making, and in the end a source of pride and enduring content."[59] Barnett Freedman in "Every Man His Own Lithographer" confronts the problems facing artists and art consumers whose modest means direct them to mechanically reproduced prints as the only viable way of engaging with art. Rather than scorning mechanically reproduced art altogether, Freedman, with whom Hassall corresponded, tries to persuade his readers to produce or buy lithographic prints and to reject photographically reproduced art. Freedman's emphasis on artistic self-empowerment, art education, and art accessibility is symptomatic of shifts in public art discourse. Though his attraction to color puts him at odds with Leighton's advocacy of wood engraving, both writers regard "this problem of multiplying a picture" as central to great art and to contemporary British culture.[60]

A final example from the Pelican volume suggests the extent to which contemporary art critics were very much concerned with "art for the people." This last phrase is the title of W. E. Williams's chapter describing his involvement with the British Institute of Adult Education, an organization dedicated to bringing great art to small, out-of-the-way British places through mobile art exhibitions. Like Freedman and Marsh, Williams is worried about public access to art in hard times and rural places, focusing on a central difficulty of the institute's initiative: Ought he to provide the people from, say, "a small Yorkshire or Lancashire town" with experts to help them understand the art on display, or should the art be allowed to speak for itself? He writes that he and his colleagues compromised by adopting as a first priority the goal of simply exposing people to art. Secondarily, they decided to offer these same people the opportunity to attend talks by experts. Williams describes these experts as "the kind of people . . . who are accustomed to giving popular talks on art and who really understand the plain man's problems."[61]

Williams's "plain man" is also Freedman's "Every Man" and Marsh's "ordinary man," and while it is not clear whether these men are imagined as standing in for or standing beside their wives, girlfriends, sisters, and mothers, they are part of Leighton's "vast new public of readers," what she also describes as the "modern public." The modern public, as it was imagined, constructed, and addressed in the 1930s by The Studio's How to Do It series and Penguin's Pelican books, had by the 1940s expanded in size and power through readers' repeated encounters with the popular writings that constructed them as "the modern public" in the first place. By the time the Saltire Society undertook to publish its chapbooks, a British print culture originating in London had helped diverse markets and readerships understand themselves in terms that included and often transcended regional loyalties and identities. As a result, there was a Scottish reading public more likely than even a decade previously to see itself as "modern," active, intelligent, tasteful, engaged, and consumerist, able to understand as well as consume objects and ideas once reserved for elites. Among the objects worthy of consumption were art objects, and among those art objects were wood engravings. Many of Hassall's Saltire Society wood engravings would have, in Bewick's words, "kept in remembrance . . . the songs and tunes of old times," demonstrating that a woman's hand and art could serve in one project contradictory social impulses; they represented a new, future-looking nationalist literary and print enterprise and also backward-looking nostalgic yearnings for safe "reflection or amusement" far away from the "ferocious battles" Bewick imagined while tramping the Scottish borders. As the simultaneously popular, populist, and heritage artist of the chapbooks' wood engravings, Joan Hassall was integral to the chapbooks' success, but so too were members of the Saltire Society Publications Committee. Their work may seem like a modest, local success story, a wartime effort of Edinburgh civilians, yet the chapbooks also participate in a broader story about the midcentury expansion of print culture in Britain driven by London publishers who discovered and engaged with a public receptive to art and art discourse. This vast new public of readers, conceived in abstract terms but generated by real historical changes, was composed of ordinary, plain, everyday people who were invited to receive and consume national intellectual discourse and to see themselves as the primary cause or motivation of that discourse. Studied in relation to national as well as regional publics, the Saltire Chapbooks' participation in a modern art cycle of cheap production, swift circulation, and broad consumption has implications for literary and book history at least as radical as those of the chapbook tradition of Jacobite Scotland.

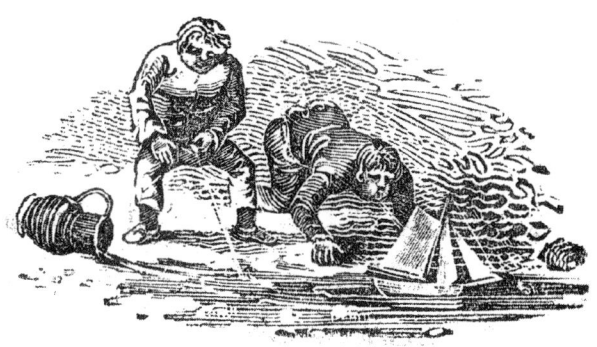

"I inwardly bid farewell, to the whinney wilds"

Thomas Bewick's memoir records from the perspective of old age his feelings on the day in 1767 that he left his childhood home of Cherryburn at the age of fourteen to take up a position as apprentice to Mr. Ralph Beilby, Newcastle's foremost silver engraver and copperplate printer:

> The eventful day arrived at last, and a most grievous day it was to me—I liked my master, I liked the business, but to part from the country & to leave all its beauties behind me, with which I had all my life been charmed in an extreme degree, & in a way I cannot describe—I can only say my heart was like to break, and as we passed away—I inwardly bid farewell, to the whinney wilds—to Mickley Bank, the Stob Cross hill, to the water banks, the woods, & to particular trees, and even to the large hollow old Elm which had lain (perhaps) for centuries past, on the haugh near the ford we were about to pass & had sheltered the Salmon-fishers while at work there, from many a bitter blast. (36)

Thomas Bewick, *A History of British Birds,* vol. 2, *Water Birds* (1804, 1826), 285. 1¾ × ⅞ inches.

Bewick would never again regard his beloved Cherryburn or the countryside of the Tyne Valley as his permanent home.

For much of the first decades of the twenty-first century, anyone wandering through Mickley village on a summer Saturday could drop by Cherryburn and find a volunteer printer giving demonstrations in the print workshop of methods employed two hundred years ago. This volunteer would lock up one of Bewick's wood blocks in a chase with lead type and press the inked whole onto individual sheets of paper to produce a picture from one of Bewick's handsomely illustrated children's books or perhaps from one of his books of natural history. Yet Cherryburn's presses are more often silent than chattering, unable to evoke for the casual Mickley visitor the kinds of images, experiences, or knowledge that scholars of print and scholars of empire—what we might call scholars of print empire—would hope to communicate to the general public, perhaps especially youthful members of that public.[1] Any exhibition space without activity becomes a dusty heritage secured by dead objects behind wooden railings.

Had we entered the Newcastle printshop of Bewick's talented printer-collaborator, Edward Walker, back in the year 1804, we could have witnessed the production of Bewick's most famous and visually accomplished book, the second volume of *A History of British Birds*. We would have smelled the ink and damp paper, and heard Bewick, the book's author-designer-illustrator, directing, intervening, and criticizing. In other words, we would have seen, smelled, heard, and felt what it was like to be in a successful local printshop in a northern regional city. At the same time, we would have found ourselves experiencing what it was like to be inside a small engine of empire. For in addition to coal, Newcastle's thriving print culture drove the circulation of words, ideas, men, and money that was integral to the region's and nation's industrial growth. Nigel Tattersfield creates a lively picture of Bewick's changing Tyneside with his list of new industrialists replacing the traditional salmon picklers: "steam engine manufacturers, boilermakers, chemical works proprietors, . . . those at the forefront of the financial revolution such as banks and insurance companies, and . . . manufacturers and suppliers of products catering to the newly-emergent consumer demand for luxury commodities such as tea, coffee, spirits and soda water."[2] This industrial-commercial growth fueled Bewick's career, his art, and his innovation, just as it fueled British imperial economies and ideologies of exploration, conquest, and control. To put this plainly, without industry and without empire, no charming Bewick engravings of rural Northumbrian human or wildlife and no turn-of-the-century volumes of his masterwork, *A History of British Birds*.[3]

This is not to suggest that Bewick was an apologist for empire. He was an ordinary Englishman, an artisan, a loyal husband and loving father, a teacher and friend and ardent explorer of Northumbria's wild places. His art and politics were the products of a country education and a happy, if crowded, childhood in the humble rooms of Cherryburn and broad spaces of Cherryburn's surrounding fields, woods, and waterways. As an adult, he earned his living through hard and unceasing labor. A politically engaged citizen, a reader and debater, he supported the working people of empire, including rebellious American colonists. His politics were consistent with his role as one of the world's grand democratizers of print information and literacy. Print historian Richard Benson argues that Bewick's real importance to book history is his solution to the problem of combining words and pictures on press for commercial systems. Benson cites the great print scholar William Ivins, who once said that "all civilization grew out of written language pointing to a picture."[4] If this is true, Bewick's role in Western civilization is tremendous because his experiments with wood engravings and metal type made it possible for just about everybody, even children and illiterate adults, to see written language pointing to a picture. Regarded in this historical context, Bewick is important not because he was "an artist of nature's own making" but because he started a printing revolution that produced mass quantities of "inexpensive volumes of illustrated text."[5]

Benson's reading of Bewick as a print revolutionary and this book's reading of Bewick as a white Englishman at home with the images and ideologies of print empire are not mutually exclusive. Indeed, both are true and both are necessary if we are to be free to seek the history of empire imprinted in images of rural England. To the extent that we keep our gaze on Bewick's vignettes, on the possibility that children and their books and toys may lead us to knowledge about empire at its height and in its decline, we also affirm that real and represented children belong in our conversations about rural England, rural nostalgia, and the imperial nation that defined them.

Two of those children are portrayed in Bewick's *Water Birds* vignette *Making Up the Difference,* a tiny, naughty reply to the sometimes quiet, cordoned-off spaces of twenty-first century Cherryburn. It is alive with mischief, inviting laughter and delight in part because it is so entirely inappropriate to great works of natural history or scholarly books. One has to imagine this vignette as a miniature impression of only 1¾ × ⅞ inches, located on a narrow page otherwise filled with earnest sentences about the migration patterns of wild geese (285). One of the boys is blowing vigorously, trying to fill the sails of a toy boat, while the other is peeing into their puddle, hoping to make up the difference needed to sail their ship on an imaginary ocean. What better metaphor could we seek for Britain's ideologies of empire than boys watering the inadequate seas with their own waste waters of ambition and playful desire?

At the turn of the nineteenth century, no one in Walker's printshop would have spared a thought about theories of print empire, its global impacts, or the role of children within it. They were consumed by enthusiasm for what they saw as a local project with the potential to influence national book markets: Bewick, his apprentices, and his printer knew that they had an utterly innovative, utterly original book on their hands, one that would sell quickly to Britain's landowning sportsmen, natural history enthusiasts, and the nation's rare and fine book collectors. Yet on off days in twenty-first century Cherryburn, this vital and conflicted past is hidden in the dusty exhibits celebrating Bewick's aesthetic and technical legacy. Bewick's home in rural Northumbria and his books of British birds seem distant from empire and imperial critique, a distance symbolized by words like "charming," "quaint," and "scenic" that are typically used to describe Bewick's rural cottage and rural art and that equally typically signify visitors' and viewers' feelings of nostalgia in the face of historic rural scenes. Yet for scholars of Bewick, of British print culture, and of rural modernity more generally, the stakes of remaining distant from imperial critique are high. In the age of the National Trust's *Interim Report on the Connections* between their properties and colonialism and of increased commitment on the part of virtually every American and British cultural institution to reparative examination of histories of relations with colonized and enslaved people, what opportunities and obligations await us?

Study of women wood engravers, the first female Bewicks, is one partial answer to this pressing moral and methodological question of how we can make the history of empire relevant to the history of Bewick and Cherryburn. Discussion of rural nostalgia and rural modernity can lead us from the spectacle of imperial decline offered up by present-day Cherryburn to the images, exhibitions, and aesthetics of Bewick's high imperial books as they simultaneously prompt us to look to the future, imagining what Bewick and his books might offer to very different kinds of young, postimperial, postcolonial readers. If Gwen Raverat, Agnes Miller Parker, Clare Leighton, and Joan Hassall could find in Bewick a mentor, friend, and aesthetic and intellectual guide to the meaning of their modern women's lives, then young artists working today, from diverse racial, class, sexual, gender, and ethnic backgrounds, may also hope to find in Bewick and those who have followed in his white-line English wood engraving tradition inspiration for continued engagement with changing scenes of rural modernity.[6] They, too, can aspire to democratic circulations of their visions of human life in nature, of humane life with nature, as they simultaneously respond to the disastrous legacy of high imperial attitudes and colonial-industrial practices for our small, green, and burning world.

FIVE

Pastorals and Petticoats

Portraits of the Artists as Young Women

In 1924, Virginia Woolf wrote a letter to Jacques Raverat that described his wife as "that granite monolithic" Gwen, capturing in these words the solid, sensible qualities of Raverat's character while hinting of Gwen's failures to adopt Woolf's diaphanous codes of Bloomsbury glamour.[1] Clare Leighton, routinely photographed in coiled braids and embroidered peasants' smocks, shared Raverat's earnestly bohemian fashion sense (Figure 1.10). The women wood engravers, in departing from Woolf's metropolitan modernist style, were choosing to perform eccentric versions of artistic femininity and female celebrity. The gender associations inspired by these departures and Woolf's metaphors are almost too obvious to merit review: Women artists choosing to work with a hard medium—wooden blocks, steel tools—while declining to wear soft, gender-compliant fabrics or adopt soft, flowing silhouettes and gestures are hard women, granite women. Such women are less like women and more like men; they are singular, upright, monolithic. For Leighton, at least, a refusal of flowing feminine fashion was itself a sign of her modernity, evidence of her distance from the efflorescent style of her mother, Marie Connor Leighton, the romance writer for Lord Northcliffe's papers who was introduced in chapter 1. Leighton described some of the elements of her complicated, difficult relationship with her mother in a memoir of her childhood, *Tempestuous Petticoat: The Story of an Invincible Edwardian.* This book came out in 1947, five years before Raverat published her childhood memoir, *Period Piece.* Raverat's is the happier book, the one more likely to enchant readers with its doodles and comic charms; it is also the more overtly pastoral and nostalgic book.[2] In part because of these narrative qualities of happiness, charm, and pastoral nostalgia, qualities destined to appeal to girls and other susceptible, sentimental people, *Period Piece* has not been recognized for what it is: a *modern* portrait of the *modern* artist as a young woman.[3]

Remedying the critical neglect of years, this chapter reads Raverat's and Leighton's childhood memoirs as portraits of modern artists as young women and as remarkable works of modern art, arguing that twentieth-century British women wood engravers and their white-line wood engravings are especially rewarding, dense, "hard" sources of knowledge about modern girlhood, modern artistry, and their simultaneously enriching and alienating associations with the pastoral places of British literature. Focusing on narrative qualities that make most intellectuals and scholars uncomfortable—happiness, charm, and pastoral nostalgia—it analyzes the artist-authors' gendered relations to nature, image, and childhood in order to complicate assumptions about the proper forms and feelings we can expect from our portraits of and by modern artists. Comparing Raverat's and Leighton's postwar memoirs of childhood to their interwar children's fictions, Raverat's *Four Tales from Hans Andersen* (1935), *The Runaway* (1936), and *The Bird Talisman: An Eastern Tale* (1939), and Leighton's *The Wood That Came Back* (1934), this chapter traces the ambiguously, contradictorily progressive and regressive origins and effects of these pastoral portraits of girls and women, characters who wander in word and image through thicket, wood, and garden before they and we arrive at last at their well-deserved happy endings.[4]

PASTORAL PROBLEMS

Classic pastoral "always" offers two kinds of happy endings or types of "return" from "idyllic retreat."[5] The first is a represented return within the world of the literary text of the restored and renewed hero-poet to the modern city. The second is the return of the pastoral text as a whole object to its intended urban readership. *The Bird Talisman*, for example, returns its princess heroine from her retreat in a garden tower to her rightful position at the center of the court and itself returns as a cultural object, a book, to the appreciative, implicitly metropolitan reader.[6] In *Some Versions of Pastoral* (1935), the contemporary critic William Empson defined "pastoral" as a "trick of thought" that culminates in the process "of putting the complex into the simple."[7] Nick Hubble explains that

"Empson was not just arguing that proletarian literature was a version of pastoral" but rather that it was a "culmination" of the meeting of "pastoral form and the historic emergence of a mass readership" whose members are not "simply confronted with themselves in the texts they read [as shepherds, as workers] but with the 'double attitude of the artist to the worker, of the complex man to the simple one.'"[8] This means Empson's proletarian literature is produced in conditions that mirror those of the period's popular, mass-reproduced children's literature; children's books, like Empson's proletarian pastoral, refer us simultaneously to "the constituent double irony of the [pastoral] plot" and "the material processes that turned it [the pastoral plot] into printed texts written by authors for a mass readership."[9]

The point of tracing this pastoral critical history is to echo, with Hubble, the hopeful idea that Empson's conception of pastoral promotes "the imaginative lives of readers and the interests of the workers [shepherds, children] themselves."[10] Beyond this, the only thing we can determine *in advance* about pastoral art is that it is always ambivalent. Historically contingent meanings will exceed the bounds of any particular subject, such as a cow, a daisy, or a dairymaid; of any particular form, such as white-line wood engraving; of audiences, such as girls or women; or of genre, such as children's or countryside literature. Hubble affirms that "Empson's own position actually offers the way out" of what we would describe as a modernist poetic impasse: the critic's refusal of the "common delusion" that "poetry is good in proportion as it is complicated," and the modernist poet's search for "a poetic idiom adequate to the complexity of modern life."[11] For Hubble, writing in the early twenty-first century, this "way out" is called intermodernism.[12]

Alexandra Harris suggests another way out in her attempts to theorize the interdisciplinary meanings of a residual English pastoral tradition within an emergent English midcentury modernism. Sensitive to the ways artists' movements between city and country inspired some of the period's most vibrant art, Harris takes up a classical pastoral (i.e., professorial) stance: She is the educated observer, writing from a place of cultural privilege, capable of revealing to nearly equally privileged readers (i.e., students) the enriching and ennobling complexities of country people and places.[13] This study, in adopting, as it must, Harris's pastoral stance, optimistically assumes, with Hubble, Empson, and Peter

Marinelli, that "a note of criticism is inherent in all pastoral from the beginning of its existence."[14] Even as some versions of pastoral attempt to use features of the form to advance an idealized, conservative worldview,

> it is this very versatility of the pastoral to both contain *and appear to* evade tensions and contradictions, between country and city, art and nature, the human and nonhuman, our social and our inner selves, our masculine and our feminine selves, that made the form so durable and so fascinating.[15]

The appearance of evasion of tension and contradiction, the apparent full retreat to Arcadia, is, of course, the evidence of "bad" pastoral derided by critics who assume that pastoral's geographical divide of city from country, extrapolated from the classic occupational divide of poet from shepherd, reinforces socially destructive divides between rich and poor, fashionable and rustic, men and women. Yet even the most willfully, fantastically escapist version of pastoral literature will, in its return to real readers as a literary object, reproduce good pastoral's potential for self-critique, that is, its production of antipastoral feeling. The real danger of pastoral discourse is not its purported neglect of political reality but its critics' inattention to the productive ambivalences and contradictions that attach to binary structures.[16] For example, Leo Marx argues in his early and well-regarded study *The Machine in the Garden* (1964) that there are two kinds of pastoral: "the pastoral of sentiment [bad pastoral] and the pastoral of mind [good pastoral]."[17] In *Pastoral,* Terry Gifford points out that these terms and their values map onto the "soft pastoral" and "hard pastoral" that Richard Jenkyns describes in a very different kind of study, *The Legacies of Rome* (1992).[18] Such sortings of bad from good, soft from hard literature, are integral to the modern history of pastoral criticism but are vulnerable to the same biases, including gender biases, that assist in the sorting of Svetlana Boym's "restorative [or bad] nostalgia" and "reflective [or good] nostalgia."[19] In each instance, "complexity," a masculinized binary term, signals and performs cultural elevation, while simplicity and its feminized correlates signal and perform cultural degradation.

If critics are prone to think of bad pastoral as that which is characterized by thoughts and feelings that are simple, soft, and sentimental, children's books, presumed to be the simplest, softest, most sentimental forms of literature, must deliver (so the logic goes) some of the worst, most dangerous forms of pastoral.[20] Adult nostalgia for a pastoral *place* of supposed unchanging, unthreatened innocence—the country—becomes confused with adult nostalgia for a *time* of supposed unchanging, unthreatened innocence—childhood—making it difficult to find signs of a contemporary history within the pages of many favorite children's books.[21] In the words of Anne Higonnet, "We long for a childhood we cannot reach."[22] Kimberley Reynolds points out that by the late nineteenth century, when most real children in Britain were threatened by deprivation, disease, and death, the Victorians were busy creating texts and images that idealized childhood into a "cult."[23] Only when childhood was seen as "immensely powerful and good" could it become "the proper subject for nostalgia."[24] Saintly, suffering, redeeming children wander the fictions of Charles Dickens, Hesba Stretton, John Ruskin, and William Morris. They encouraged mass readerships composed of children and adults to look back and yearn, with tears in their eyes, for pastoral escape from modernity's troubles.[25] Sometimes readers found comfort in private pasts of childhood memories, and sometimes they found comfort in public narratives about their nation's past in "a notional Golden Age."[26] Regardless, by the time late nineteenth-century educational reforms had legislated a distinct period of childhood, marketplace separation of adults' and children's books had produced the literary phenomenon known as the first Golden Age of children's literature.[27] This Golden Age, as illusory and mystifying as any other Golden Age, signifies the commercial success in a relatively concentrated period of time of what book-sellers and buyers still call children's classic literature: pastoral fantasies by Lewis Carroll, Edward Lear, Kenneth Grahame, Frances Hodgson Burnett, J. M. Barrie, A. A. Milne, and E. Nesbit.[28] The earliest of these classics are the secret garden books of Raverat's and Leighton's childhoods, the very kinds of books they chose to illustrate decades later when, as celebrated wood engravers, they sought to earn their livings in part by fulfilling publishers' illustrative commissions.

EARTHLY, NOT CELESTIAL PARADISE

Raverat had suffered a stroke before she began *Period Piece* and could no longer manage the physical demands of wood engraving. Instead, she created dozens of pen-and-ink drawings for her memoir (Figure 1.8). Her drawings or doodles of her childhood home in Cambridge, Newnham Grange, which her father, the astronomer Sir George Darwin, purchased in 1885, contribute in important ways to our understanding of pastoralism in her earlier work (Figure 5.1). Raverat emphasizes her joy in the water and trees that pressed up so closely to the Grange, and the sense of proximate natural adventure that made the safety of the children's nursery so delicious. She also emphasizes domestic spaces that function as interior Edens, describing for example her Great-Aunt Etty Darwin's old house at Kensington Square, London, as a place that "had a very strong flavour of its own. It was a peculiar kind of earthly paradise—earthly, not celestial. . . . The food was delicious, the beds were soft, the rhythm ran smoothly, everyone was kind and good and true and happy; and it seemed as if evil could never come near" (130).

This passage self-consciously utilizes the imagery and language of fairy tales to describe real places and experiences of Raverat's Victorian girlhood. Raverat in 1952 re-creates in her great-aunt's house the same cosseted, rosy, and eccentric world of upper-middle-class London evoked in those children's classics mentioned above. Humphrey Carpenter observed many years ago that the "authors of the outstanding English children's books that appeared between 1860 and 1930" were each and every one creating secret gardens for English youth, idyllic places of green escape, what Raverat would have called "earthly, not celestial paradise[s]" (Figure 5.2).[29] Carpenter theorized that these literary Arcadias were meant to replace Eden, the Golden Age children's writers having despaired of Christian havens amid the degradations and disillusionments of late Victorian modernity. Virtually all the great children's writers Carpenter claimed for his Golden Age, from Edward Lear to A. A. Milne, were doubters, atheists, or agnostics. So was Gwen Raverat. This is one reason her depictions of the Great Good Place in her memories of urban and suburban Darwin homes is an Arcadian recovery, a return to secular Edens. Great-Aunt Etty's Kensington Square home materializes as displaced pastoral in *Period Piece* in part because of Raverat's enraptured encounter there with the art of Thomas Bewick, an adventure discussed in the Introduction (Figure 1.6).

The timing of Raverat's discovery of Bewick is important. Not quite child, not yet young lady, the awkward and passionate Gwen both recognizes and misrecognizes her calling. Bewick's art of wood engraving was to remain her life's passion, but anonymity in the service of masculine genius was not. Instead, as we know from the brief biography rehearsed in chapter 1, Raverat arrived in

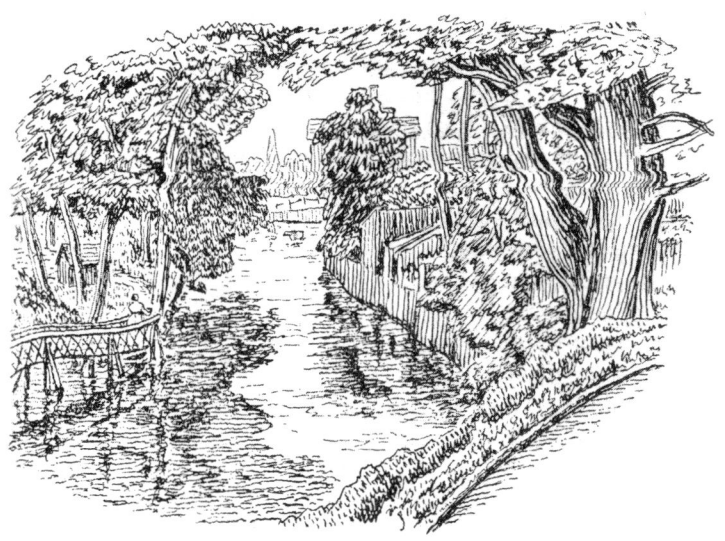

Bloomsbury in 1925 as a young widow with two children, and then moved back to Cambridge, where she consolidated her reputation as one of the nation's most successful and sought-after illustrators. *Period Piece* was her last great gift to English arts and letters. It has been continuously in print since its first publication, repeatedly hailed by critics as a "minor classic."[30] However, Raverat and *Period Piece* deserve better than that, and Clare Leighton's *Tempestuous Petticoat* provides additional evidence of the new materials and perspectives women artist-illustrators can bring to a British art history still weighed down by masculinist values. Almost as though she anticipated Harris's endorsement of a romantic vocabulary for purposes of understanding midcentury modernist art, Leighton remembers her earliest childhood home, Vallombrosa, in the following way:

FIGURE 5.1 Gwen Raverat's pen-and-ink drawing with extended caption, including the pastoral reflection, *Cows used to ford the river here . . . coming and going to and from their pasture on Sheep's Green.* From Gwen Raverat, *Period Piece* (London: Faber and Faber, 1952), 35. 3⅞ × 2⅝ inches. Copyright 2025 Estate of Gwen Raverat. All rights reserved. DACS/Artists Rights Society (ARS).

> We lived in a part of London called St. John's Wood. The actual neighborhood can still be found on the map, just beyond Baker Street and Regent's Park; but its spirit vanished many years ago. For St. John's Wood belonged to the age of Romance. . . .

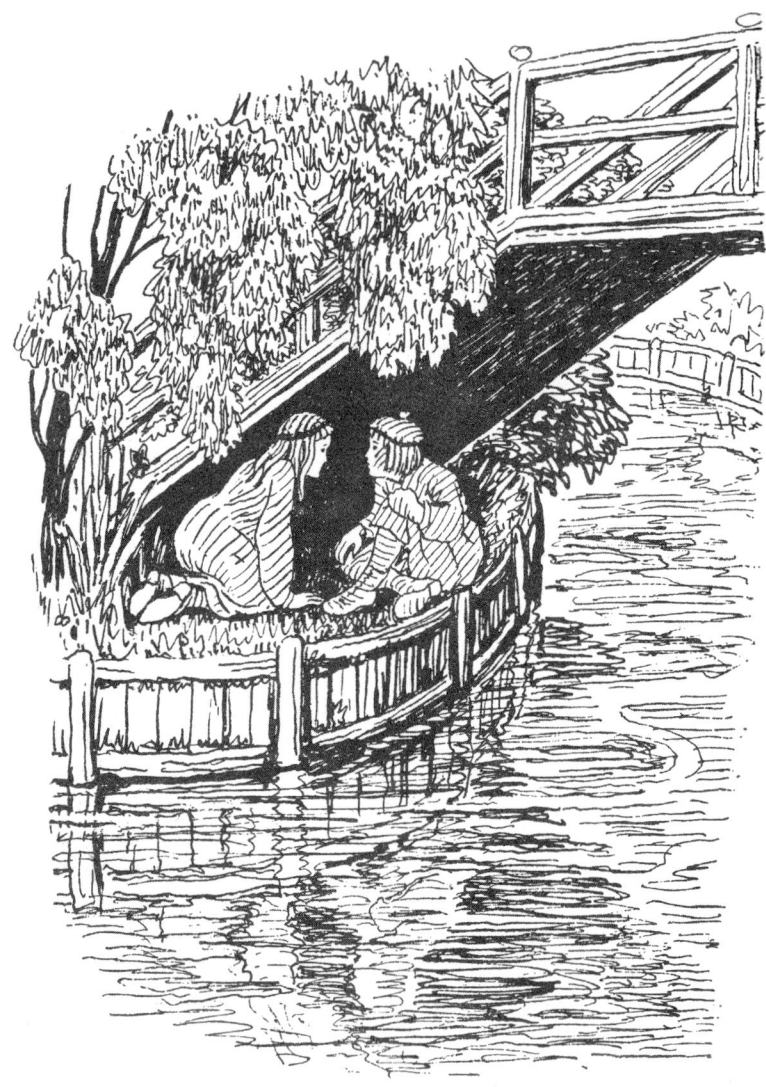

Frances (left) converting me under the bridge.

FIGURE 5.2 Gwen Raverat's full-page pen-and-ink drawing *Frances (left) converting me under a bridge.* From "Religion," in *Period Piece* (London: Faber and Faber, 1952), 220. 4⅛ × 5½ inches. Copyright 2025 Estate of Gwen Raverat. All rights reserved. DACS/Artists Rights Society (ARS).

It was a world of individual seclusion. Houses stood hidden behind high garden walls. Garden walls were dwarfed by massive trees. Whatever might take place within these walls was shielded from the eyes of the public. (23)

Gardens and privacy, eccentricity, but especially romance: These are the qualities of Edwardian London that the adult artist Leighton associates with her childhood. She characterizes her mother, the professional, obsessive writer of serial romances who stirred the tempestuous petticoat of her memoir's title, as the emotional pivot around which the entire household circled amid confusions of ink, silk, and lace. Leighton's descriptions of the humid devotions to art and romance created by her mother are invested with an ambivalent, not idealized, pastoralism. Feelings of shame and love, for example, are bound up with Leighton's earliest memories of their walled St. John's Wood garden:

We used to feel ashamed as we compared our wilderness with the lovingly tended gardens of other houses in the neighborhood. The grass of our lawns blossomed and seeded. Tall weeds flourished in the flowerless beds. It was lucky for us that the main charm of Vallombrosa lay in the thirty-six lilac bushes and the row of linden trees, which needed no care. (92)

Leighton's resistance in her memoir and her wood engravings to misty St. John's Wood romance and her mother's romantic ideals is an affirmation of alternate pastoral spaces of her youth. In particular, she idealizes Swallowfield, a quaint village in Berkshire where her paternal grandmother lived. Looking back after many years, Leighton describes Swallowfield as

a paradise of strawberries and roses. The lanes and woods in spring were sulphur with primroses, and sweet with the songs of nightingales. The Meadow, where the Leightons lived, was far up a leafy lane called Spring Piddle, beyond sight of any other house. (130)

Spring Piddle seems a name right out of Beatrix Potter. One cannot believe it is quite real, just as one cannot believe the worldly Leighton writes this with adult sincerity, rather than with modernist irony. But no, Leighton's memories of childhood visits to the Meadow are much like Raverat's memories of Great-Aunt Etty's earthly paradise in Kensington Square: sincere, sentimental, nostalgic. Rather than dismissing such sentiment or being embarrassed by it, scholars of modernist art and literature can embrace and examine it, discovering in such "soft" feelings and pastoral effects the childhood sources of Raverat's and Leighton's unique accomplishments as "hard" modern women. Once we understand their adult representations of girlish affection, sentiment, and nostalgia to be sophisticated strategies of modernist self-creation rather than signs of merely regressive Victorian and Edwardian excess, we not only have a scheme of aesthetic and cultural values that brings women wood engravers into the central conversations about modern art, but we can also construct a gendered theory of pastoral memory that may expand what we see as modern art in the first place. This study brings feminist analysis of cultural attitudes toward children and their literature to bear upon conventional histories of modern art in order to expose gendered biases in traditional and feminist criticism distrustful of "soft" ties between pastoral scenery, images of children, and children's books and the women who write and illustrate them.

WOMEN WRITERS AND THE ENLIGHTENED CHILD

At the same time in the late eighteenth century that Bewick was busily researching, writing, and illustrating his books of natural history, women writers were cementing their positions as the most prolific writers of British children's literature. In Julia Briggs's account of women's rise to dominance in this new but firmly established literary market, "hard" qualities of rationality, moral judgment, and reasoned pursuit of justice characterize the ideals and destinies of the heroines of their narratives. Any revisionary effort to break down academic barriers between adult modern and modern children's pastoral literature and art must take into account the long history of critical derision that has attended these successful women writers' books for children. Briggs explains that the women writers' "disregard for the imaginative needs of children" was "symptomatic of a desire felt by many . . . to free themselves, and their offspring too, from weaknesses regularly associated with their sex—being too emotional, too fickle, too affectionate, too doting."[31] Far from preparing the cultural ground for the sentimental, idealizing images of children that populated Victorian media, women

who were writing children's books in Bewick's day felt they had to distance themselves from feelings and behaviors that, then as now, are assigned most readily to
the devalued feminine gender and female sex. Sarah Fielding, Maria Edgeworth,
and Mary Wollstonecraft, for example, peopled their children's books with in-
structresses, parents, and guardians who might appear cold and anemic to a fin
de siècle reader raised on the pedagogical parodies of *Alice in Wonderland,* but
who communicated "the author's desire to identify herself with what had previously been thought of as masculine attributes."[32] Women writers' "concern with
education at the end of the eighteenth century helped to define their roles, both
as writers and women, as serious and important."[33] Serious and important: These
are the qualities of good literature, hard and difficult literature. They are the
"masculine" qualities that marginalized Fielding, Edgeworth, and Wollstonecraft
within twentieth-century canons of women writers and children's literature but
ensured the centrality of male and female modernists who rejected exactly those
excesses identified with feminine and literary weakness: the romantic qualities
of being "too emotional, too fickle, too affectionate, too doting."

The defeating double standard of this shifting, binarized sexual-aesthetic
code is evident in Leighton's account of her youthful loss of credibility as a
woman modern artist adopting a masculine modern style. In *Tempestuous Petticoat* she recalls that she earned as much criticism as praise from the many
artists in her family whom she elsewhere credits with inspiring her pursuit of
art as a profession. Even her beloved Aunt Sarah Leighton joins in, regretting
the lack of subtlety in the paintings of "you young moderns" (147). Reminisc-
ing about her and her brother Jack Leighton's days in the South Kensington Art
Schools, Aunt Sarah emphasizes that "we never used such harsh colors or sharp
contours. We were taught always to bring a gentle tone of brown into all our pictures, for harmony. And we knew the beauty of dim outlines" (147).

As we know, Clare Leighton, rather than endorsing her aunt's—and her
mother's—values of blur and intrigue, grew up to be one of her generation's most
talented purveyors of clarity, contrast, and commitment. Her record in *Tempestuous Petticoat* of her battle to fashion herself as a modern artist out of the
soft materials of her mother's corsets and lilacs testifies to the extraordinary
pressures exerted upon Edwardian girls to adopt Victorian codes of femininity.
Leighton's resistance to those pressures, her battle against the forces of haze,

gauze, and romance, hints of Raverat's even greater gender challenges as a girl growing up at the peak of Victoria's reign and the reign of the cult of the child. To triumph as Raverat did, defining her own codes of femininity and artistry and recording them in terms that spoke to *Period Piece*'s postwar readership, is an accomplishment that belongs in feminist and mainstream art and literary histories. Raverat's and Leighton's memoirs of their difficult struggles to become artists and women, communicated in an easy style that impresses critics with the subjects' happy charm and pastoral nostalgia, are unjustly forgotten classics of conflicted modern girlhood.

"THE TINDER-BOX" AND OTHER MODERN FAIRY TALES

The fairy tale as a *literary* genre, Jack Zipes reminds us, "was never told or written explicitly for children."[34] Appropriations of oral folktales of wonder and magic to modern conditions of morality and literacy, fairy tales are ambiguous forms, incorporating story elements ancient and modern, peasant and aristocratic, bearing witness to encounters between ahistorical "once upon a time" devices and specific historical developments of the printing press and the growth of a European middle class.[35] Such ambiguities of audience, history, and class resonate perfectly within and without Gwen Raverat's wood engravings for *Four Tales from Hans Andersen* and *The Bird Talisman,* perhaps because white-line wood engraving as an illustrative form had, by the twentieth century, taken on ambiguous cultural meanings akin to those of the literary fairy tale. It was associated with literature for adults and children, in books for rich and poor, produced through combinations of technologies antique and modern. Of course, in the Victorian period white-line wood engraving disappeared altogether from mass-reproduced books, replaced by the reproductive black-line factory-style wood engravings perfected by the Dalziel brothers.[36] As Zipes points out, these are the very years, from 1830 to 1900, that "the fairy tale came into its own for children" in the work of Hans Christian Andersen, who "brilliantly combined humor, Christian sentiments, and fantastic plots to form tales that amused and instructed young and old readers at the same time."[37] When white-line wood engraving was reinvented in the early twentieth century as an experimental, elevating form of illustration for children's trade books, the fairy tales of Andersen were there waiting for treatment in the hands of this new generation of wood engravers. Is it any wonder that Andersen's witches, princesses, and "miraculous transformations . . . [of] disadvantaged protagonists" won the sympathetic interpretation of Raverat, who, as "The Génie" described in the Introduction, had fallen miserably into the role of marginalized outsider before enacting her own miraculous transformation into acclaimed artist (Figure 1.5)?[38]

Raverat's edition of *Four Tales from Hans Andersen* is a beautiful little book, and beautiful in part because it is little. It wins the praise of art historians for its dramatic frontispiece, a colored wood engraving illustrating "Little Claus and Big Claus," four perfectly realized wood engraved initials beginning each of the four tales, and thirty-five white-line wood engraved illustrations distributed throughout.[39] Sized for little hands at 4½ by 7½ inches, *Four Tales,* like Joan Hassall's Saltire Chapbooks, is so skillfully designed, illustrated, and produced that it reworks our standard literary critical categories (Plate 8). Raverat's illustrations seem to turn this Depression-era mass-reproduced book into a fine edition, its children's fantasy contents appealing to adults, its old plebeian plots of magical transformation themselves transformed into something appropriate for publication by an elite university press.

"Little Claus and Big Claus" is the only tale to earn full-page wood engravings, but it is "The Tinder-Box," the first tale, that best communicates the energies of a revised or reversed pastoral, with its protagonist foot soldier encountering in the dark woods an old witch who makes his fortune (Figure 1.1). As in all the best fairy tales, this soldier, walking home from the war, is brave enough to make a bargain with the powers of darkness. The "ugly" witch whose "lower lip hung right down on her chest," promises him good fortune if he returns with her tinderbox, then buried deep in a hollow tree inhabited by three frightful magical dogs with spinning eyes. The sensible fellow, upon his return from the tree with coins of gold filling all his pockets, asks the witch, "What are you going to do with this tinder-box?" As sensible as the soldier, she replies, "That's no business of yours! . . . You've got your money; now just give me my tinder-box!" (ellipses in original). He refuses to do so, telling the witch that he will cut off her head with his soldier's sword if she does not let him in on the secret of her intentions.

"No," said the witch.
So he cut off her head. . . . There she lay!

But the soldier tied up all his money in her apron and made a bundle of it, to go on his back. He put the tinder-box in his pocket and went straight on into the town. (9; ellipses in original)

This is how R. P. Keigwin translates Andersen's Danish sentences for Raverat's new edition of *Four Tales*. His delicately poised "But" draws our attention to a gap, a silence, between the narrator's astonished exclamation "There she lay!" and the soldier's action of pocketing her tinderbox. We are meant and not meant to register that gap, the white space between our vision of the old witch's prostrate body and the soldier's upright youthful one, a space that contains a violent feeling equal to the violence of the witch's beheading. Indeed, what the "But" hints of is a missing expression of horror by the two men, the young soldier and the narrator, "Andersen," anchoring this particular narrative triangle.

The scene, delicious in its vindication of the disadvantaged protagonist, inspires an uncomfortable doubt. Maybe the witch is not really a witch. Maybe she is merely a woman. "There she lay!" we read. Would not a real witch anticipate and avoid such an ignominious end, perhaps casting a spell, waving a wand, arresting the arm of the soldier mid-swing, or at the very least enacting some kind of revenge after death that refuses him the power of the stolen tinderbox? "But" no, or, to quote the witch, "No." There is no retribution, no penalty to be paid for the exercise of youthful masculine might upon aged feminine wits, of male punishment for female opposition. The soldier travels out of the wood without a second glimpse at the corpse, into a "fine town, and he put up at the finest inn" (9). Having discovered the secret of the tinderbox without the witch's help, he is able to summon the magic dogs from the hollow tree to fulfill his wishes, the most powerful of which is to see and then marry the beautiful neighborhood princess locked up in a copper castle by her parents. The king and queen must, by fairy-tale logic, be disposed of, so they like the witch are killed in order to facilitate our happy pastoral ending. The soldier gets his princess and her castle, the princess is "pleased" to be put in her mother's place, and we all move on to the next tale, as pleased as the princess that the soldier assumed the witch's magical powers when he took her life and her tinderbox.

This is antipastoral pastoral at its very best. The young hero in a wood full of secrets is a rough sort of Adam in a dark kind of Eden. Rather than finding Eve there, he finds her hag-like double, the ugly old witch, who must be killed before the beautiful princess can take her place at his side. The wood is the countryside place of regeneration and transformation, which is confirmed with the hero's return to the city, with its delighted people who proclaim him king. Raverat responded to this tale with equal delight, her illustrations of the witch especially ingenious, vigorous, and compelling. It is hard not to receive this wood engraved figure as a good witch, an enchanting woman, perhaps a feminist heroine if we recall Raverat's fond description in *Period Piece* of her five-year-old granddaughter Anne's feelings about witches:

> "Grandmamma, when I am grown up, I think I shall be a witch. There are too many ladies, don't you think?" Well, I suppose there are still too many ladies; but there were many more too many ladies when I was young. My whole life was surrounded by them; but from the very beginning I was determined, like Anne, never, never to be one. (75)

Raverat's witch, who could never, never be mistaken for a lady, greets us with smiling face and open arms, welcoming us into the story and the book as she welcomes the soldier into her tree. Her status and her threat are revealed in her outsize hands and feet, while the soldier remains a cypher, an anonymous man in uniform, depicted throughout the tale mainly from the back or in profile and always in miniature. He is most clearly revealed as a man, as an individual human, in a wood engraving positioned two-thirds of the way through the "The Tinder-Box" that illustrates his first stolen candlelit vision of the sleeping princess. Yet even here, in a small engraving that involves us as guilty voyeurs in the intimate encounter between the squished couple within their confining frame, it is the female figure that draws our eyes rather than the regarding soldier, who holds the candle and the power (Figure 5.3). Raverat turns the princess into an everywoman, her hair devoid of crown or ornament, her gown simple and flowing. She is close to us in perspective, time, and appearance; she is one of us, and we, like her, are subject to the soldier's gaze.

Raverat's princess in "The Princess and the Pea" suffers a similar kind of surveillance. We meet this princess in the position of the soldier in the first tale, wandering alone through wild countryside, suspect in her solitude and desperation (Figure 5.4). We know before we meet her, having absorbed in our own childhoods the sexual logic of Western myths, that a woman woods walker is

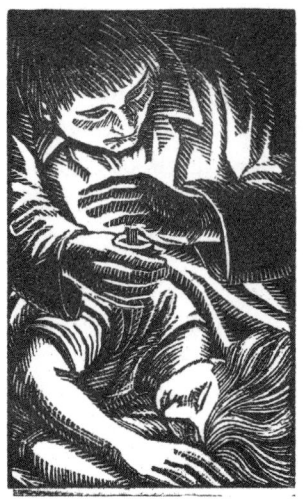

FIGURE 5.3 Gwen Raverat's wood engraving of the sleeping princess, compressed with the soldier in her back frame. From "The Tinder-Box," in *Four Tales from Hans Andersen* (Cambridge: Cambridge University Press, 1935), 13. 1⅝ × 2½ inches. Copyright 2025 Estate of Gwen Raverat. All rights reserved. DACS/Artists Rights Society (ARS).

hardly better than a city streetwalker. Andersen's tales repeatedly pose the problem of women's solitude, which they resolve in classic pastoral endings that bring us and the heroes out of the woods into civilization, even as the women characters suffer very different fates of instant death and thoughtless marriage by the ends of their respective tales. Raverat's wood engravings simultaneously advance and retard the patriarchal logic of this plot. On the one hand, they accelerate the narratives' compulsive devotion to binary oppositions in opposing colors of black and white that confirm what we think we know and need: a witch who is old and ugly, a soldier young and disciplined, a princess tender and graceful. On the other hand, Raverat's characters exceed these binary terms, their minute linear components creating faces, hands, hair, and light that interpose gaps between visual and verbal figures, spaces for our feminist questions and objections.

We see this contrary impact of Raverat's illustrations in "Little Claus and Big Claus," another tale about a poor and lonely wanderer. The Little Claus of the title, dispossessed of his worldly goods by Big Claus, must seek his fortune, traveling through "a big, gloomy wood" where, like the princess who will discover the pea, he gets lost in a terrible storm (25). Caught in a scary, dangerous pastoral place between home and town, he approaches a large farmhouse hoping to find a bed for the night. The farmer's wife is home, but she refuses to shelter Little Claus because, while her husband is away, she is secretly entertaining the parish clerk with "wine and roast meat and oh! such a delicious-looking fish" (26). Little Claus tricks the erring wife and displaces her male admirer, and when the farmer returns to the head of his table, Little Claus enjoys with him the wine, roast, and fish prepared for the parish clerk, who is by then hidden away in a large chest (Plate 8). Ultimately, Little Claus fulfills the heroic destiny of every

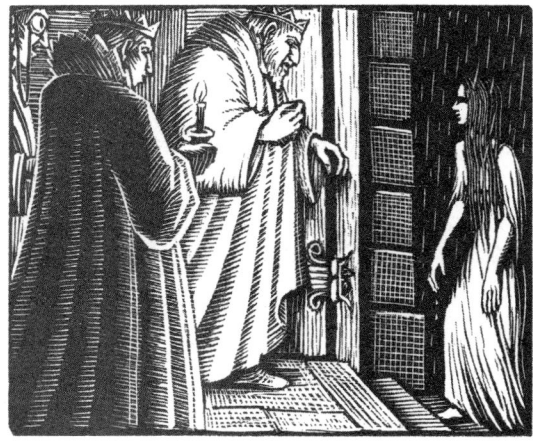

FIGURE 5.4 Gwen Raverat's wood engraving *The Wet Princess,* a princess more famous for finding a dry pea than for wandering the wild woods. From "The Princess and the Pea," in *Four Tales from Hans Andersen* (Cambridge: Cambridge University Press, 1935), 52. 2⅞ × 2¼ inches.

disadvantaged fairy-tale protagonist by outwitting and defeating a series of ever more powerful men before returning home, in classic pastoral fashion, to civility and public admiration.

Raverat's engravings of the farmer's wife divert a pastoral plot of male–male violence, retribution, and transformation with scenes of static, stolid femininity.[40] The farmer's wife is a kind of Gwen Raverat double, shaped like a granite monolith, sturdy as the witch in the woods, even dressed in an identical checked apron. We know that Andersen's farmer's wife is a narrative device propelling Little Claus on toward more dangerous, more masculine challenges. Raverat's farmer's wife, on the other hand, is a substantial body who arrests the narrative's heroic momentum as she arrests our gaze. Big, broad, irresistible, she commands her feast and the parish clerk who sits below her, a formidable force at the center of home and farm.

The last illustration in "Little Claus and Big Claus," a full page within a rectangular border, provides a pastoral antipastoral, tragicomic ending guaranteed by the wandering hero's discovery of freedom from want through innocent murder in the countryside (Figure 5.5). In a scene of overtly pastoral, bovine resolution, Little Claus brings about the drowning death of Big Claus by convincing him that there are lovely, lowing sea-cattle on the bed of the local river. Distracted by Raverat's wood engraving of living cows and pacific scenery, readers may not at first notice the visual signs of Big Claus's comic end; they are there in Little

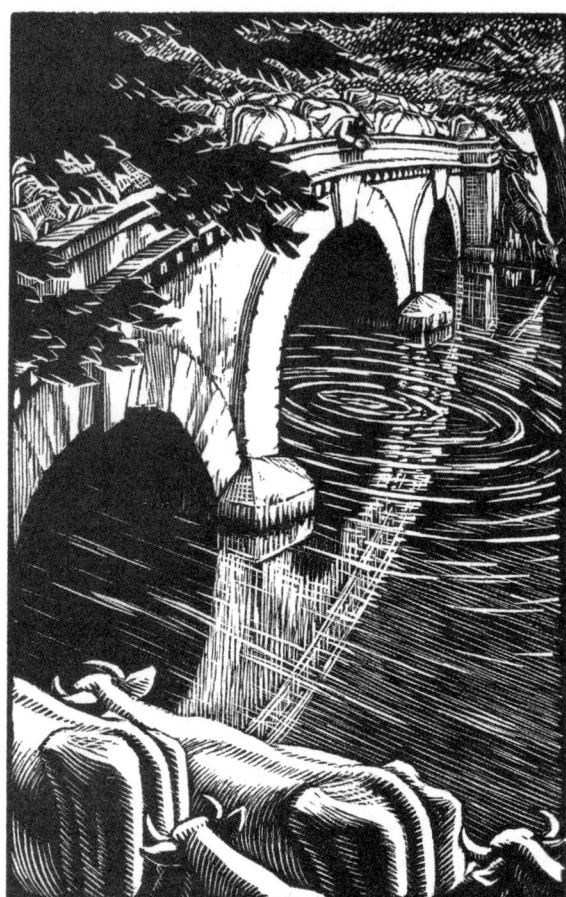

FIGURE 5.5 Gwen Raverat's full-page wood engraving *The Bridge/Great Claus Is Drowned* is a visual pastoral joke that hides murder in the midst of quiet cows and gentle streams. Can you find signs of the corpse? From "Little Claus and Big Claus," in *Four Tales from Hans Andersen* (Cambridge: Cambridge University Press, 1935), 48. 3¹⁄₁₆ × 4¹¹⁄₁₆ inches. Copyright 2025 Estate of Gwen Raverat. All rights reserved. DACS/Artists Rights Society (ARS).

Claus's arms, still outstretched, and in ripples on the surface of the river where Big Claus must have, moments before, entered the water. The drama of death, of Cain and Abel outside Eden, is secondary to the peace of the wood engraved country scene, a scene that is strikingly reminiscent of Raverat's pen-and-ink drawings of her happy childhood home beside the Cam composed decades later for *Period Piece*. In each case, Raverat's illustrations emphasize the pastoral beauty of rivers and woods that we know from the surrounding narratives are mediating spaces of human change and thus possible sites of danger. These changes ultimately lead to happy endings but bring with them all the ambivalence of doubt and, in the fairy tales, of deadly violence encountered along the way.

RUNNING AWAY

Bernard Darwin promoted his cousin Gwen Darwin Raverat's 1936 edition of Elizabeth Anna Hart's *The Runaway,* subtitled *A Victorian Story for the Young,* in these terms:

> There never was a happier book. What is surprising is not how well it wears, but how intrinsically modern it is. There is a total and blessed absence of piety and sentimentality; there is a genuine and engaging humour, and there is no moralizing worthy of the name.

His review ran in *Country Life* and is cited on the inside front cover of Duckworth's 1953 reprint, aimed to sell a pastoral comedy about girls in gardens to a midcentury readership recovering from industrial war-induced traumas. The blurb from Darwin's review emphasizes many of the qualities of the novel that Raverat mentions in her 1936 preface to the book. She, too, is eager to assure readers that the book is "modern," "not really old-fashioned," with its modernity best represented by the mobility of its thirteen-year-old runaway heroine: "Indeed I am sure that no heroine, however modern, ever climbed trees or walls as well as Olga did" (v) (Figure 5.6). For illustrator and editor Gwen Raverat and reviewer Bernard Darwin, a modern book and modern heroine are defined through their freedom from piety and sentimentality and other signs of feminine weakness. Without "prayers or death-beds" and "only such few tears as are very quickly dried" (v), we are told by Raverat that *The Runaway* escapes the worst qualities of historic British children's literature written by women. On the one hand, we are assured that it avoids the excesses of emotion—tears and kisses—associated with the overwrought sentimental fictions stoking the Victorian cult of the child; on the other hand, we are assured that it avoids the excesses of morality and propriety—prayers and duty—associated with earnest women's fictions of an earlier century that promulgated Enlightenment pedagogies. Yet Raverat's wood engravings do not renounce but rather highlight the novel's sentimental scenes. In illustration after illustration, Raverat represents through precise and tender inscriptions of black and white lines the very things that modern readers were likely to regard as evidence and instigators of "old-fashioned" feelings: the love, tears, and embraces shared by Olga, an adorable, mischievous

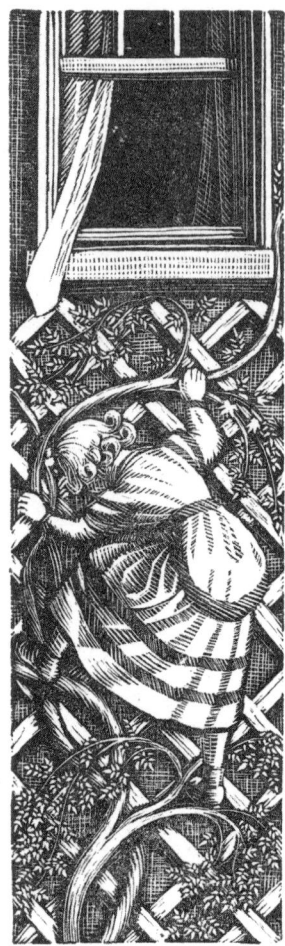

FIGURE 5.6 Gwen Raverat's wood engraving of a mobile modern heroine, who "had descended by aid of the jessamine branches nailed against the houses, with an agility that took away the breath of her more sober companion." From Elizabeth Anna Hart, *The Runaway: A Victorian Story for the Young* (London: Gerald Duckworth, 1936, 1953), 49. 1½ × 4⅞ inches. Copyright 2025 Estate of Gwen Raverat. All rights reserved. DACS/Artists Rights Society (ARS).

thirteen-year-old runaway, and Clarice, Olga's more rational fifteen-year-old rescuer and coconspirator. What is one to make of the narrative's excesses of kisses and pouts, the lingering evidence of Victorian sensibility and sentimentality, in the context of the interwar illustrator's commitment to modern bookmaking?

If we look beyond kisses and tears to scenes of tricks, disguises, and pranks, Raverat's sixty-one wood engravings in *The Runaway* provide the modern book promised by her and her cousin's words. They are among the most joyful or "fun" of her illustrations for children's books, delighting in representation of the

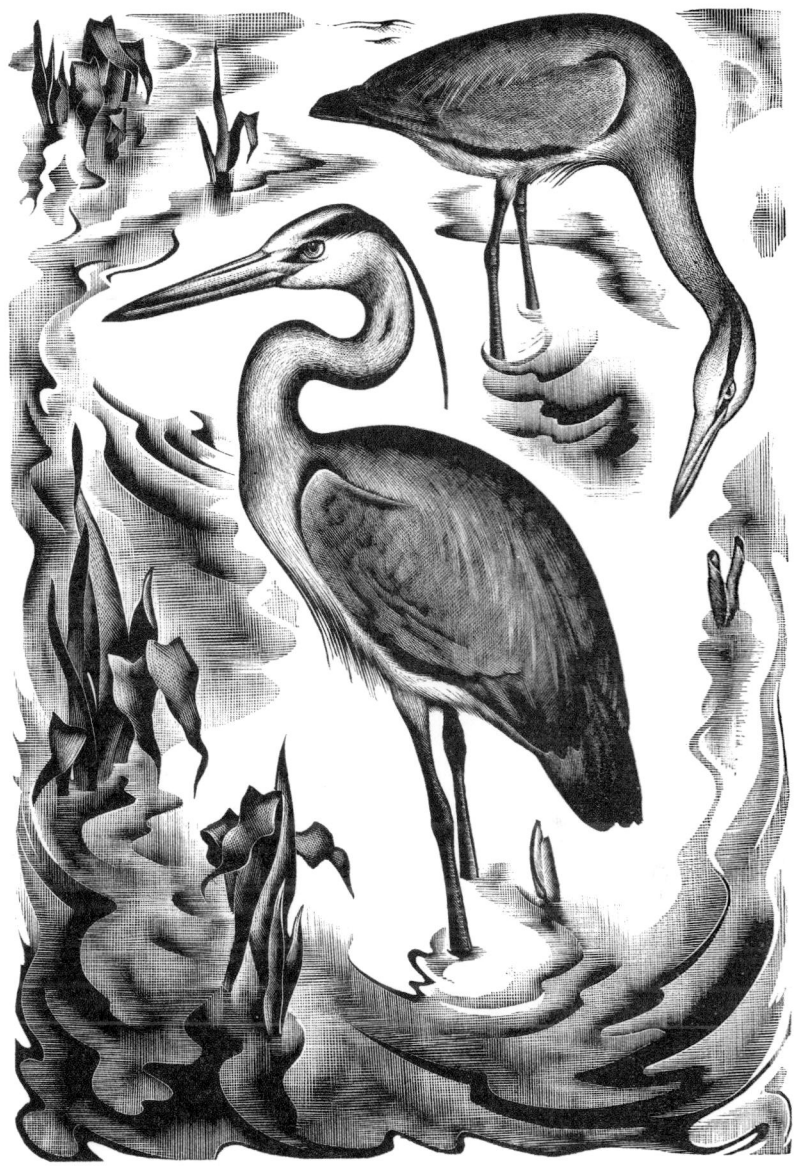

PLATE 1 Agnes Miller Parker's full-page wood engraving *Herons.* The cross-hatching is exemplary, achieving effects of shimmering tones unsurpassed by the work of any other wood engraver, modern or ancient. From H. E. Bates, *Down the River* (London: Gollancz, 1937), 23. 4¾ × 6¹⁵⁄₁₆ inches. Reproduced by permission of the Estate of Agnes Miller Parker.

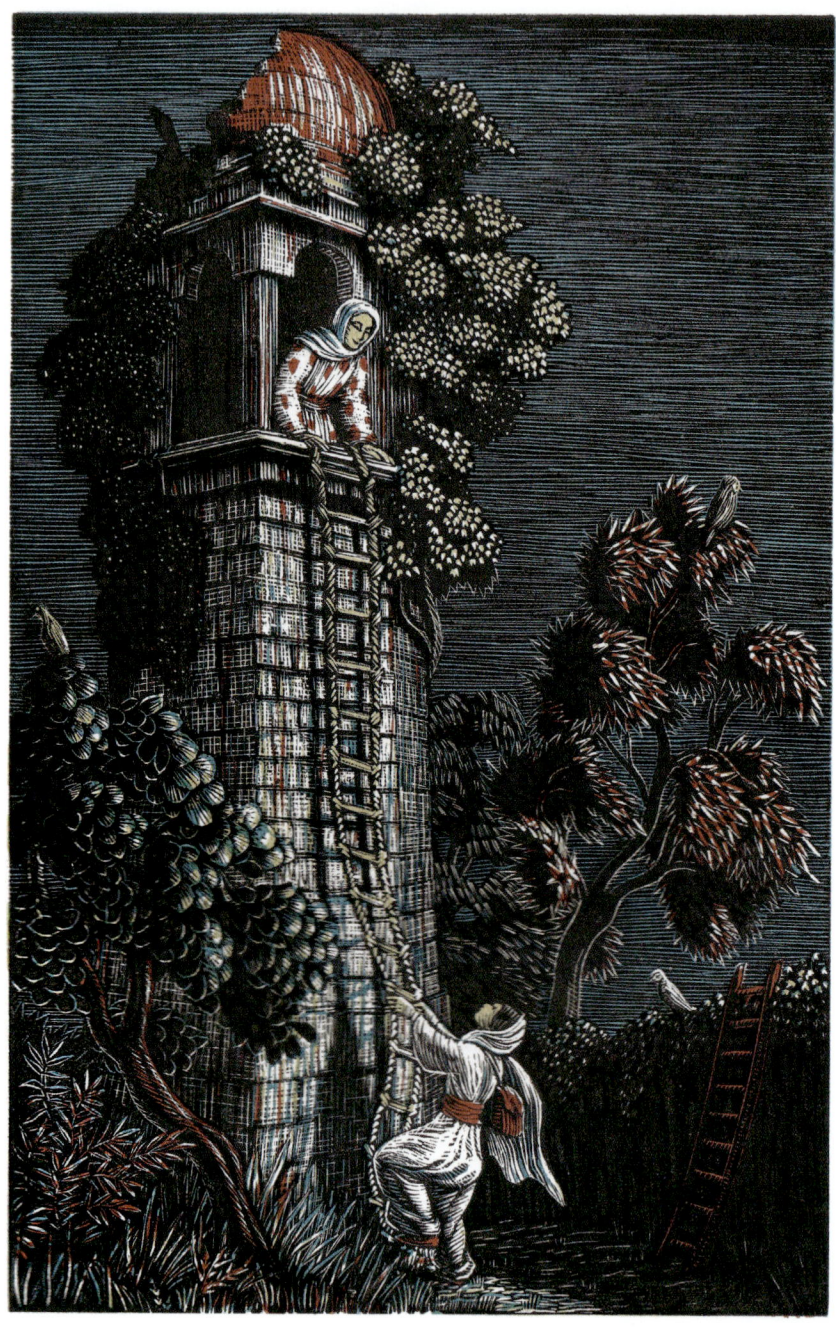

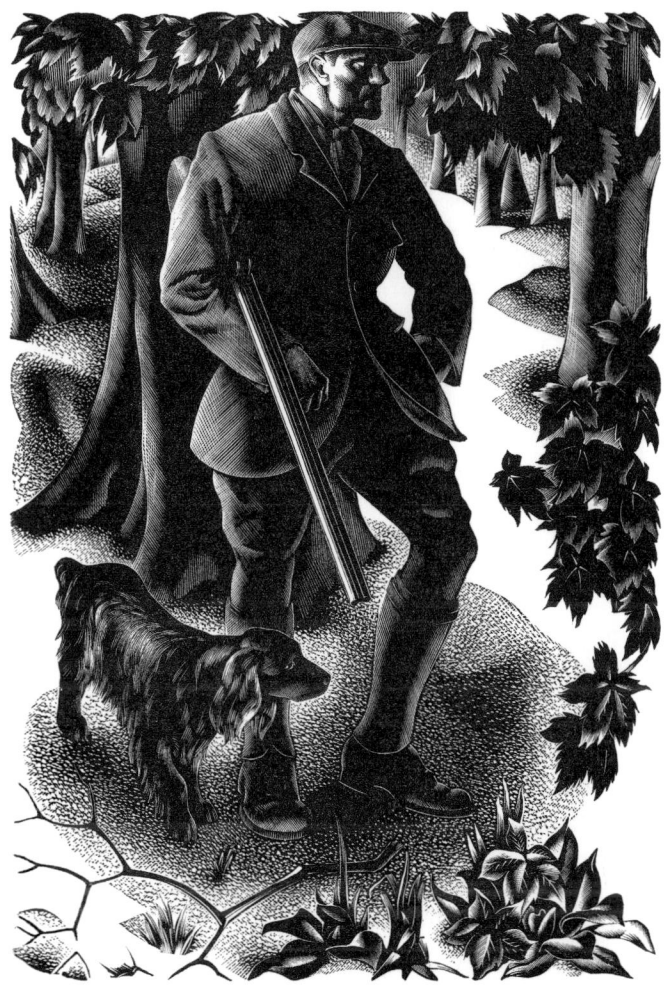

PLATE 3 Agnes Miller Parker's wood engraving *The Villain and His Dog,* depicting the "evil spirit" of the English woodlands. From H. E. Bates, *Through the Woods* (London: Gollancz, 1936), 55. 4½ × 6⅞ inches. Reproduced by permission of the Estate of Agnes Miller Parker.

PLATE 2 Gwen Raverat's full-page color wood engraving of Zuleika climbing a silken ladder to reach the heroine princess in her hiding place at the top of a minaret revises as it reproduces the classic fairy-tale scene of the eager prince ascending Rapunzel's tower in the woods. From Henry Allen Wedgwood, *The Bird Talisman: An Eastern Tale* (London: Faber and Faber, 1939), n.p. 4⅜ × 6¾ inches. Copyright 2025 Estate of Gwen Raverat. All rights reserved. DACS/Artists Rights Society (ARS).

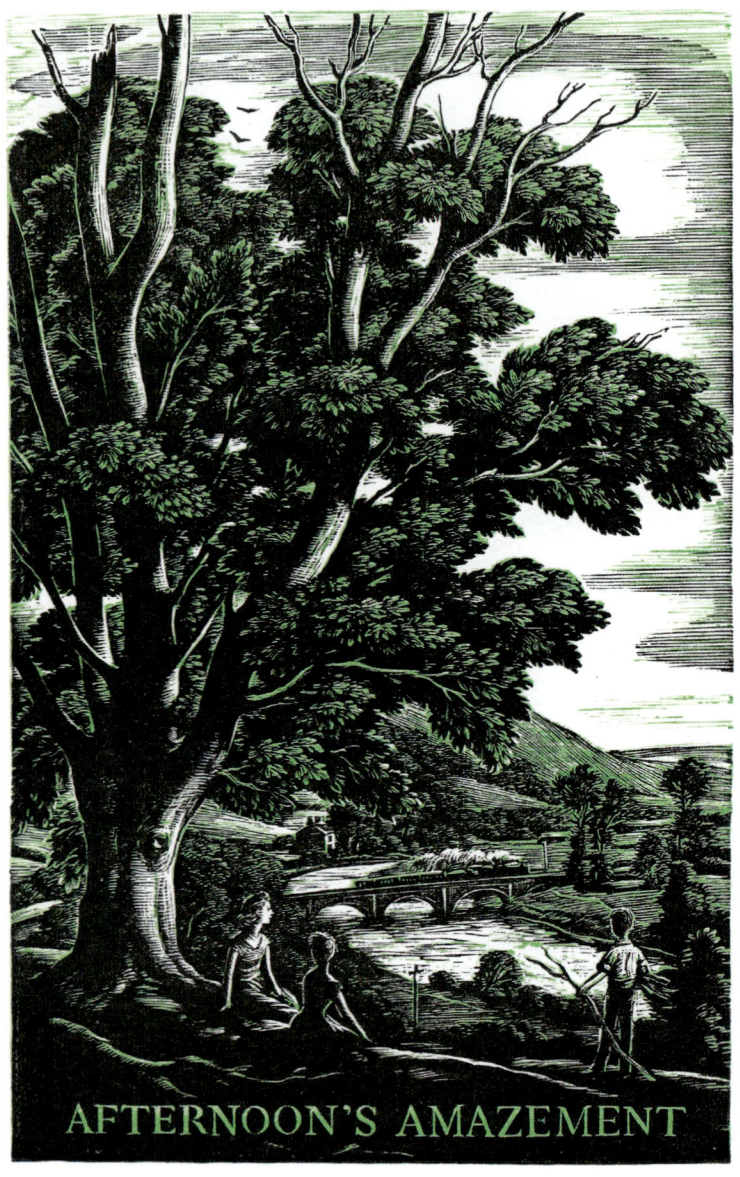

AFTERNOON'S AMAZEMENT

PLATE 4 Joan Hassall's color wood engraving *Afternoon's Amazement,* an illustrated full-page divider at the beginning of a section titled "The World of People." From Pamela Whitlock, *All Day Long: An Anthology of Poetry for Children* (Oxford: Oxford University Press, 1954), n.p. 3¾ × 5¾ inches. Reproduced by permission of the Estate of Joan Hassall/Simon Lawrence.

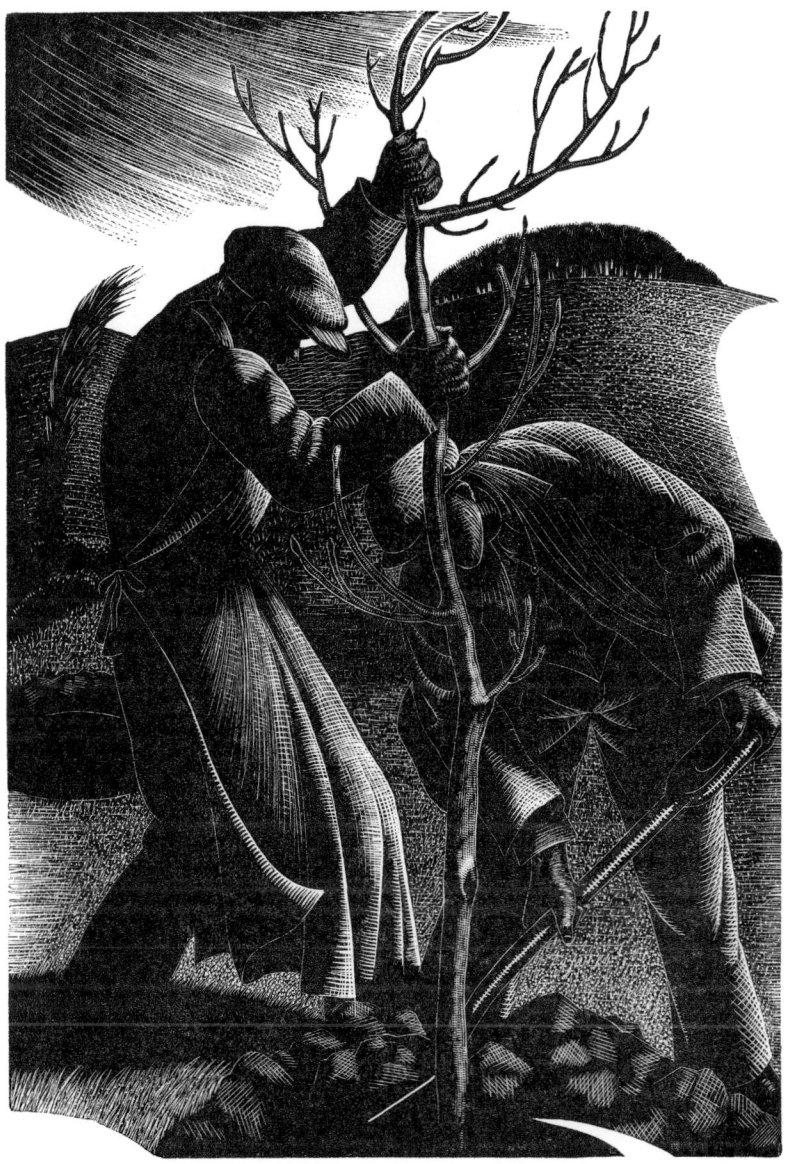

PLATE 5 Clare Leighton's full-page wood engraving *Planting Trees,* showing her lover, Noel, and gardener, Alf, working in the chalky soil of the Chiltern Hills of Buckinghamshire. From Clare Leighton, *Four Hedges: A Gardener's Chronicle* (London: Gollancz, 1935), 119. 4¾ × 6⅞ inches. Copyright 2025 Estate of Clare Leighton. All rights reserved. DACS/Artists Rights Society (ARS).

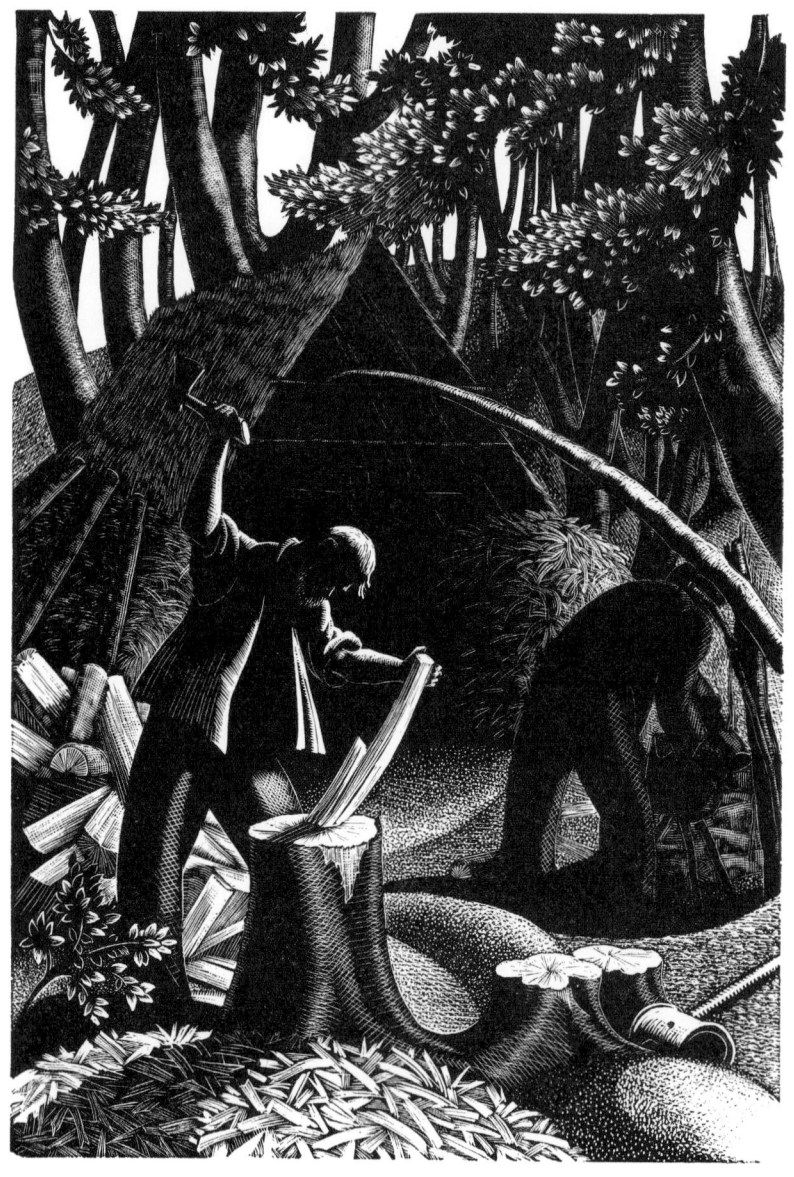

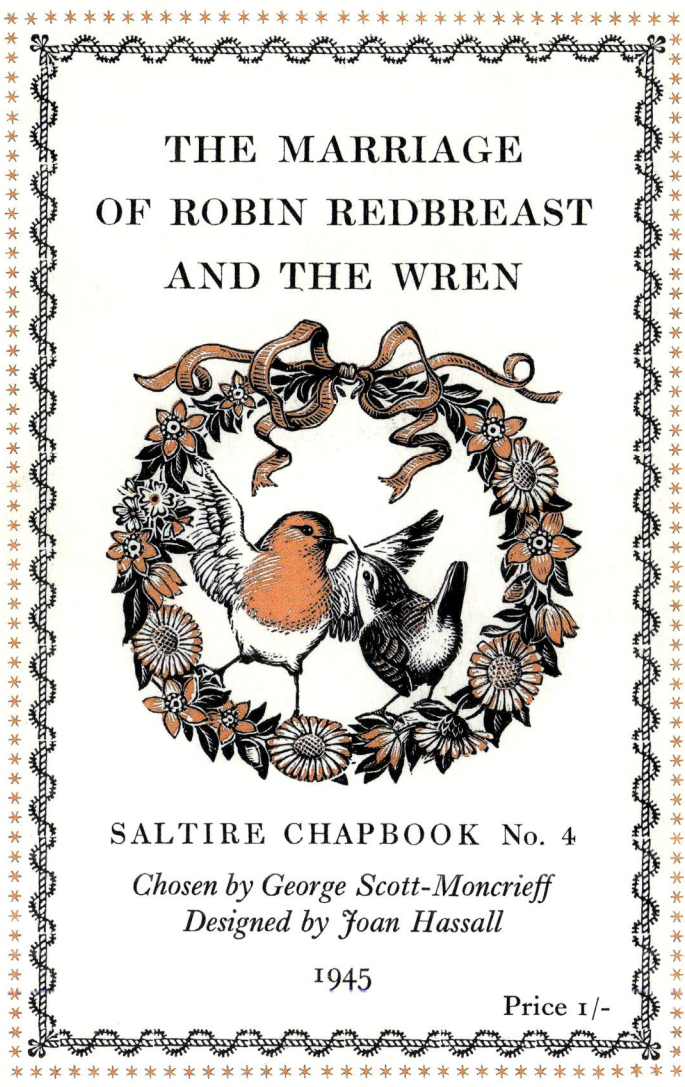

THE MARRIAGE
OF ROBIN REDBREAST
AND THE WREN

SALTIRE CHAPBOOK No. 4

Chosen by George Scott-Moncrieff
Designed by Joan Hassall

1945

Price 1/-

PLATE 7 Arguably Joan Hassall's masterpiece: a perfect wood engraving and front cover design for Saltire Chapbook No. 4, *The Marriage of Robin Redbreast and the Wren* (Edinburgh: Saltire Society, 1945). 3½ × 5¼ inches. Reproduced by permission of the Estate of Joan Hassall/Simon Lawrence.

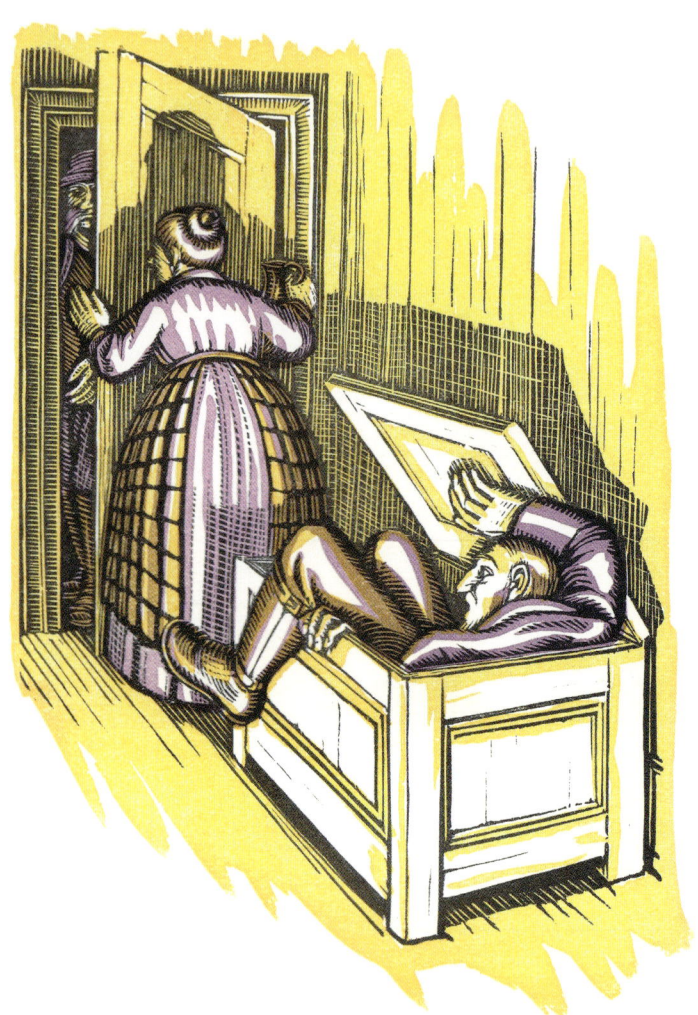

PLATE 8 Gwen Raverat's colored frontispiece, a wood engraving of the farmer's wife and her dinner companion, the parish clerk, whom she has hidden in a big empty chest upon the return of her husband, who waits at the door. From "Little Claus and Big Claus," in *Four Tales from Hans Andersen* (Cambridge: Cambridge University Press, 1935). 3⅜ × 5⅛ inches. Copyright 2025 Estate of Gwen Raverat. All rights reserved. DACS/Artists Rights Society (ARS).

"volatile, capricious" antics of the runaway Olga as they sympathetically interpret the conscientious doubts of the more sober, but equally loving Clarice (v, 91)
(Figure 5.7). The novel begins, "Clarice Clavering—young, ardent, and happy—
strolled alone, by twilight, among the shrubberies in her father's garden. 'Oh, the
dullness of life!' cried the young philosopher" (1). Boredom is banished once Clarice discovers in a favorite thicket of "hazel, laurels, ferns, fox-gloves, and furze"
the small, fair, bewitching Olga, whose head is covered with angelic golden curls,
her rosy lips laughing when they are not pouting for a kiss (4). Yet Olga's and
Clarice's kisses, often following quickly upon tears, throw into question the dry-
eyed modern aesthetics we have been encouraged by Darwin and Raverat to find
within the text. Again and again, kisses and tears prove the girls' capacity for opposing qualities of devotion and danger, duty and flight, union and solitude, that
sustain the "romance and excitement" that Raverat recalls experiencing when
listening to the story read aloud in the 1890s (v). For example, having persuaded
Clarice that she, Olga, is a heroine rather than a thief, Olga exclaims:

> "But oh Clarice! let us go to sleep now, and give me a kiss—there's a dear; nobody
> ever kissed me that whole time I was at school—not anybody ever once!"
>   Clarice kissed her heartily, and Olga returned the kiss with pretty childish ca-
> resses. (38–39)

This beginning of girlish intimacy is repeated throughout the narrative, perhaps
in its most excessive, overdetermined form in this scene:

> Olga . . . pouted out her rosy lips kissingly like a penitent saucy child . . . and she
> said, "I thought you loved me, Clarice!" and pouted out her lips again for a kiss.
>   "Oh, Olga, I do love you, but you must be good!" said Clarice, and took her in
> her arms, and gave the kiss so sweetly demanded, which the little creature returned
> twenty times. (79)

In addition to the startling adverb "kissingly," *The Runaway* boasts thirty additional instances of nouns or verbs built around the word "kiss." Indeed, it is from
kiss to kiss, sweetly demanded, that emotional, affectionate, and doting behaviors determine the modern plot of female rebellion, which resolves, in classic

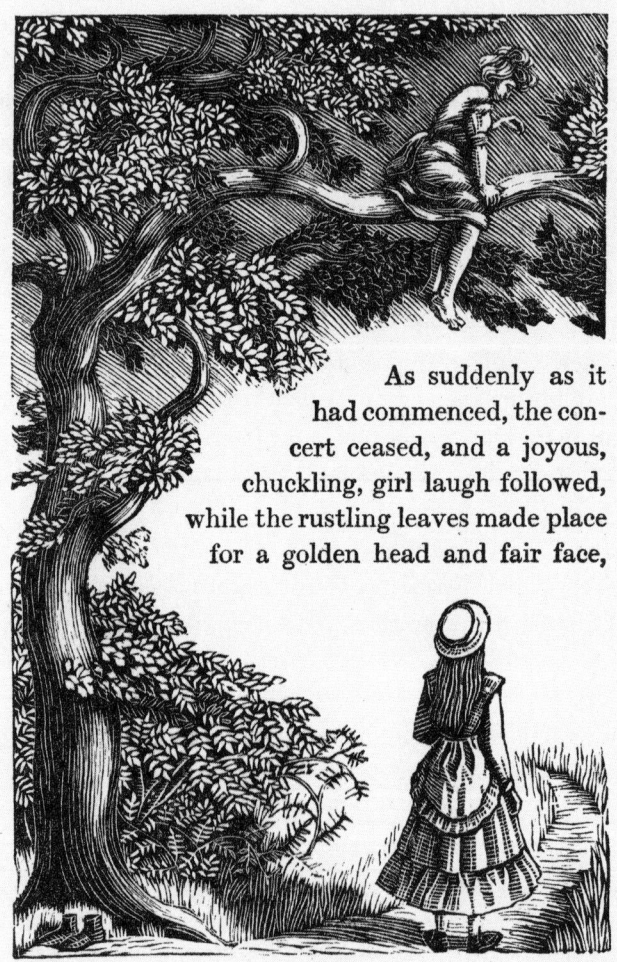

As suddenly as it
had commenced, the con-
cert ceased, and a joyous,
chuckling, girl laugh followed,
while the rustling leaves made place
for a golden head and fair face,

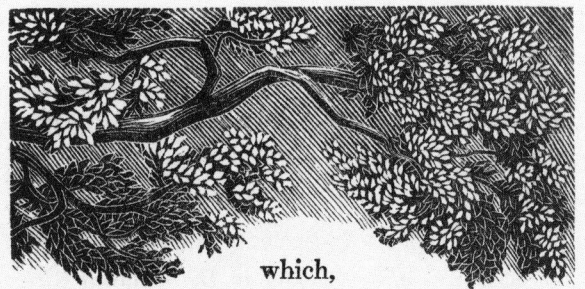

which,

peeping out at her,

looked like the bodiless angel heads in old pictures, wanting only the wings instead of a neck to be the angel-head complete. "I can imitate animals just as well as birds," cried a gay sparkling voice, "so that they all come flocking round me, only I dare not do it here, you know, as cows and horses cannot be supposed to live in this glade."

"Come down, naughty child," said Clarice quite fondly, and down ran Olga like a squirrel, and nestled by her side.

"I have found my bag," cried she, "and only think, the mouth was open, and half the things had tumbled out, but I hope I have collected them all; and Oh, Clarice! as I was picking them up, only just fancy, I saw a man looking at me over the hedge—he was in the lane outside you know; but wasn't it rude?"

"I don't know," answered Clarice; "he must

fairy-tale fashion, with a happy restoration of the heroine to her rightful place in family and community. Rather than a vagrant, servant, and thief, the suspect status of any girl lost in the verdure, Olga is what she has always claimed to be, the daughter of the dashing Colonel Leslie, inhabitant and inheritor of Glenkeen Castle in Scotland.

In early chapters of *The Runaway*, Raverat includes four illustrations of Olga in Clarice's bed, where, like Snow White, Goldilocks, or the princess with the pea, Olga falls after her rescue from the thicket (31, 80, 117, 121) (Figure 5.8). These illustrations, which are textually layered with dense sentimental meanings, suggest that Raverat misrecognizes in her preface to *The Runaway* the source of modernity when she looks back at her favorite Victorian tale of childhood. Modernity does not lie in the illustrations' refusals of sentimentality but in those exuberantly worked-out wood engravings representing girls' intimacy. Feminist affirmation of the novel's textual and visual scenes of love between girls, affirmation of scenes of pubescent kisses and embraces, can persuade yet another generation of modern readers that modernity does not abide in the novel as a negative quality, an absence of piety, propriety, and tears. Raverat's images of what is meant to be understood as a kind of presexual female intimacy confirm and maintain a vision of modern girlhood through precisely those doting, pouting, too-sweet kisses that modernism spurns as soft and sentimental. This feminist interpretation is latent in Hart's text, but it becomes manifest in Raverat's wood engravings; it is Raverat who turns this Victorian fairy tale into protofeminist modern fiction.

The Bird Talisman, another Victorian fairy tale that Raverat transformed into modern fiction, has earned critics' praises for its innovative illustrations, in particular its eight color wood engravings.[41] Yet like *The Runaway*, it has never attracted literary scholars of modernist or children's literature who could provide the kinds of deep readings of words and images that such a curious and

FIGURE 5.7 Gwen Raverat's wood engraving of Olga hidden high in a garden oak tree, imitating bird calls, as Clarice wanders disconsolately below. The flawless design of this two-page spread breaks the sentence beginning on the first page, subtly turning the disguised Olga from "a golden head and fair face" into a "which" (witch) in the center of the second page. From Elizabeth Anna Hart, *The Runaway: A Victorian Story for the Young* (London: Gerald Duckworth, 1936, 1953), 52–53. Verso, $3\frac{3}{16} \times 4\frac{7}{8}$ inches; recto, $3\frac{1}{8} \times 1\frac{1}{2}$ inches. Copyright 2025 Estate of Gwen Raverat. All rights reserved. DACS/Artists Rights Society (ARS).

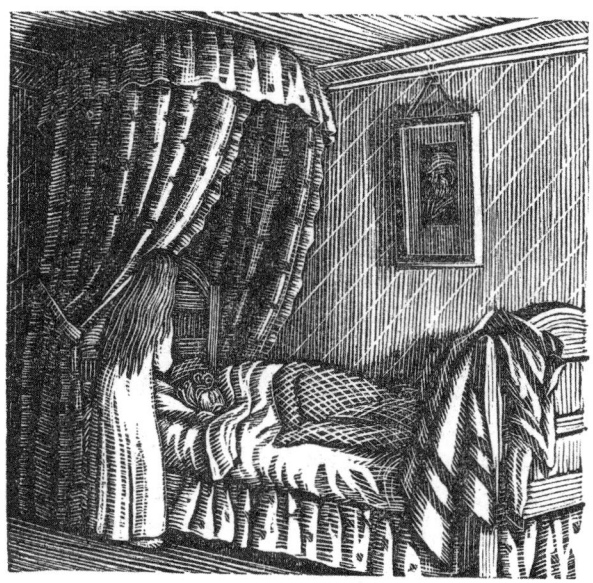

FIGURE 5.8 Gwen Raverat's wood engraving depicting the moment Clarice discovers that "Olga had taken possession of her bed." From Elizabeth Anna Hart, *The Runaway: A Victorian Story for the Young* (London: Gerald Duckworth, 1936, 1953), 31. 3⅛ × 3 inches. Copyright 2025 Estate of Gwen Raverat. All rights reserved. DACS/Artists Rights Society (ARS).

beautiful book deserves. First among its curiosities is its subtitle, *An Eastern Tale*. Although set in India, *The Bird Talisman* is obviously a Western tale, containing many of the same elements of character, theme, and plot that attracted Raverat to *The Runaway*—mobile girl heroines, their escapes to trees, thickets, and gardens, their tears, and their kisses—and the same dangers, death, and uncanny magic that must have attracted her to Andersen's *Four Tales*. With an evil queen, an endangered princess, and a magic ring that allows its bearer to understand and command all birds, it is no wonder that this Victorian children's book prompted Raverat, a devoted reader of Bewick who shared by proxy if not in fact his devotion to birds, to create some of her most arresting wood engraved illustrations (Figure 5.9). Produced with consummate attention to book design, materials, and printing in the last year of interwar peace, *The Bird Talisman* was never declared by critics a "minor literary classic," although arguably it is as worthy as *Period Piece* of being kept continuously in print by Faber and Faber, the publisher of both books.[42]

Raverat's most unusual and experimental wood engraving in *The Bird Talisman* illustrates the princess heroine grasping the feet of two owls as she leaps at their command from a minaret window into the leafy tips of branches just

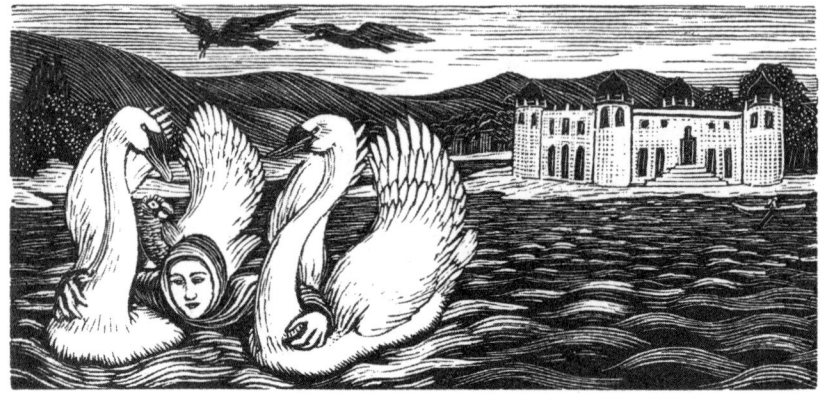

peeking up from the triangular bottom of the engraving that is aligned with the page number below (Figure 5.10). The words of the narrative, exactly matched to the action depicted in the wood engraving, create a kind of double frame of text around the angle of the wood block that points down, the direction of the princess's escape through the garden:

No sooner said than done. The princess grasped the legs
of the friendly owls, and threw herself from the balcony;
down they went all three with a tremendous rushing of wings, and the princess fell
on the springy branches of the bush without receiving any hurt at all. (59)

To quote these words in an unbroken paragraph, as above, eliminates a visual meaning that emerges not only from Raverat's picture but also from the page design—the precise coordination of black type and black lines that together create a modern impression of female freedom.[43]

Raverat tells us in a brief preface that *The Bird Talisman* was written and illustrated by her great-uncle Harry Wedgwood for his children and was privately printed for the Wedgwood and Darwin families in 1852 and then in 1887. She adds that "the author was never in the East in his life; and . . . neither he nor I have made any effort to be accurately Indian" (v). In other words, Raverat prepares us to receive the book as an Oriental tale, a Western fantasy of the East that is interesting to the degree that it simultaneously confirms and complicates the classic cultural values and racial hierarchies of better-known Golden Age fictions.[44] Among those classic cultural values are idealizing associations of children in gardens with innocence and the threat of the loss of that innocence. *The Bird Talisman,* like *The Runaway,* is deeply informed by these familiar ideals and assumptions. Yet it departs from classic pastoral tropes when it, like *The Runaway,* populates its gardens with two girls rather than Adam and Eve, a prince and princess, or soldier and witch. Raverat, the mother of two daughters, seems to have been drawn to pastoral children's fiction that aligned its romance and worked out its redemptive returns through the preadolescent, presexual love, devotion, and sacrifice of one girl for another: Clarice and Olga in *The Runaway* and a little princess and her friend Zuleika in *The Bird Talisman.*

Like other pastoral landscapes, those in *The Bird Talisman* are ambivalent places. The garden, for example, is a dark retreat, providing cover to the princess, the friendly owls, her faithful parrot, and the loyal Zuleika (Plate 2). It is also a symbol of danger, of the threat of captivity rather than liberty, as the princess enters the garden as a runaway from the palace and its usurping, jealous queen of Cashmere. When the owls help the princess leap from the minaret, her flight from the garden into the city streets eventually leads to pastoral-antipastoral closure in another garden, the palace garden of her grandfather, the restored king of Cashmere. Here the princess's bird friends "flew joyously overhead, to resume their old roosting-place" while the princess returns to her rightful place in the palace. And the evil queen? She, like Andersen's witch, has lost her head with one swift stroke of a man's sword, the scimitar of her henchman and onetime favorite, the enslaved Baboof. The palace, thus rid of adult female evil, resumes its symbolic role as the center of civility, maintained through the gentle daily conversations of the princess and Zuleika.[45]

THE WOOD THAT CAME BACK

Clare Leighton's *The Wood That Came Back* (1934) is a children's book about plants and animals without a garden or a princess—without even a child—yet, as much as Raverat's children's books, it self-consciously engages with pastoral literary traditions. Published at the same time that Leighton was working with

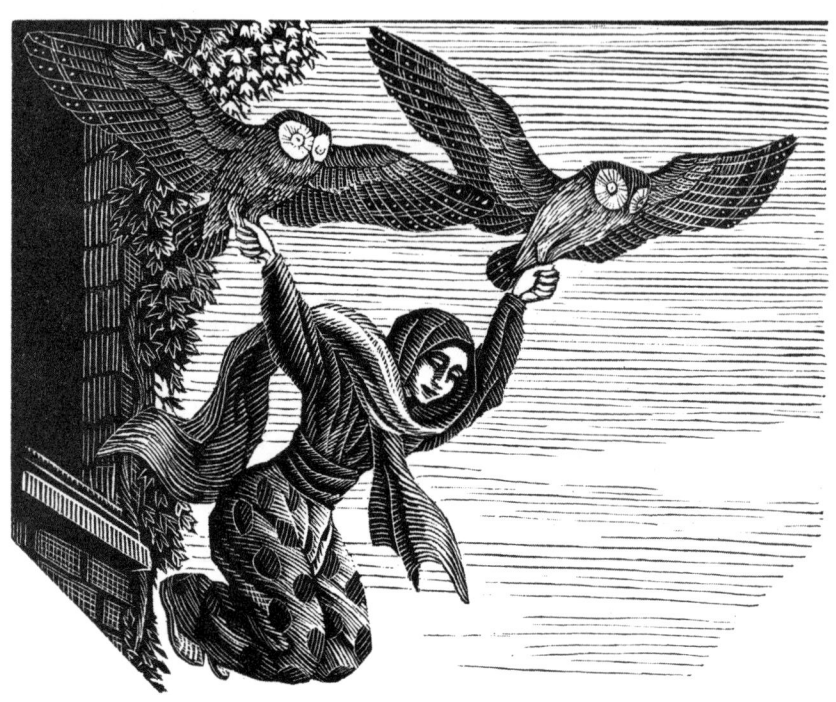

No sooner ——————— said than
done. The prin- ——————— cess grasped
the legs of the friendly owls, and
threw herself from the balcony; down
they went all three with a tremendous rushing
of wings, and the princess fell on the springy branches

FIGURE 5.10 Gwen Raverat's wood engraving *The Owls' Parachute,* showing another mobile heroine in a garden. The page design is as remarkable as the wood engraving. From Henry Allen Wedgwood, *The Bird Talisman: An Eastern Tale* (London: Faber and Faber, 1939), 59. 4⅜ × 5 inches. Copyright 2025 Estate of Gwen Raverat. All rights reserved. DACS/Artists Rights Society (ARS).

Victor Gollancz on *Four Hedges,* this environmentalist fable is about human desecration of a wood, the displaced woodland creatures' schemes of revenge, and the restoration of the wood to a natural state. It is Eden relieved of Adam and Eve, moral innocence assured through human exile. At the beginning of the story the Adam figure, a man who has built a charming little house on the hill where the wood once stood, tells his wife, "Now we shall be able to live happily ever after." The narrator immediately extinguishes this hope: "But it was not to be! Little did they know that even while they sat there things were happening. The very birds were whispering everywhere of the Great Plan!" (n.p.) (Figure 5.11). This is no classic pastoral tale, all human agents having been removed by the animals, and thus no children's version of Leighton's genial and lushly illustrated adult books about country gardening that promise human spiritual restoration through rural habitation. Pastoral consolation is reserved for readers, perhaps mainly adult readers with children wriggling on their laps, who receive Leighton's book as the wished-for return or replacement of rural landscapes lost to modern development.[46]

In the context of a study of Leighton's wood engravings for adult publications, the title and moral of this children's tale—the endurance of wood—seems an overdetermined allusion to her art of wood engraving. Yet the illustrations of *The Wood That Came Back* are not wood engravings but rather pen-and-ink lithographic images. The text is hand-lettered and incorporated into the illustrations, which are hand-colored with bright pink, green, and deep-black inks. Also curious is the identity of the book's publisher, Ivor Nicholson & Watson, rather than Leighton's usual 1930s publisher, Victor Gollancz. Nicholson & Watson was, like Gollancz, a trade firm based in London. It was not especially known for its children's books, but rather for its adult books about popular religion, gardening, dogs, treasure hunting, coronations, and military exploits. Leighton, by then building her reputation as a serious, difficult artist, was publishing a children's book with Nicholson & Watson at the very moment in the mid-1930s that Ivor Nicholson was triumphantly poaching best-selling writer Denise Robins from legendary romance publisher Mills & Boon.[47]

Reading Leighton's environmentalist fable in the publishing context of Robins and Nicholson & Watson, we may be surprised to discover how close it brings us to Marie Connor Leighton's confections and Raverat's sentimental children's

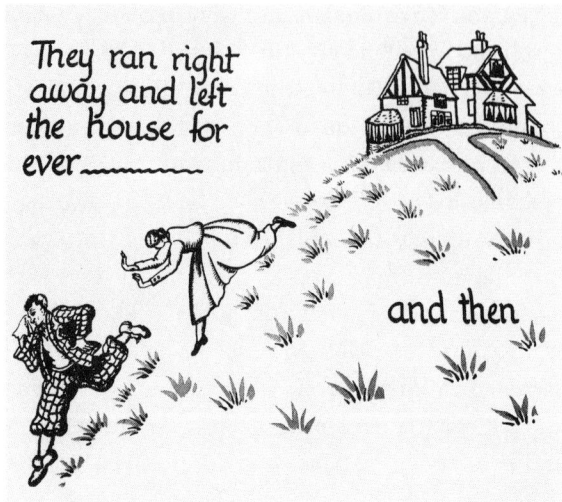

They ran right away and left the house for ever———— and then

FIGURE 5.11 Clare Leighton's drawing of the man and his wife who "ran right away and left the house for ever" in the face of a conspiracy of nettles, spiders, birds and "all the living things" who had been chased from the wood. From Clare Leighton, *The Wood That Came Back* (London: Ivor Nicholson & Watson, 1934), n.p. Copyright 2025 Estate of Clare Leighton. All rights reserved. DACS/Artists Rights Society (ARS).

books with wood engravings. The proximity of differently gendered and valued adjectives like "sentimental" and "serious," "soft" and "hard," "easy" and "difficult," "antique" and "modern," "bad" and "good" in descriptions of the same artists and art exposes the failures of existing critical frameworks to capture the living reality of any given wood engraved illustration or illustrated book in its reception by diverse readers in diverse situations. The contrasting terms that we use to describe relief engraving and printing—of white and black, wood surface and engraved depth, letterpress and illustration—tempt us to adopt contrasting terms in our descriptions of our own and others' experiences of this art. Yet feminist analysis of Raverat's and Leighton's memoirs about their childhoods and books for children suggest that new, more empowering ways of knowing and being lie in the ambiguous, contradictory material signs and epistemological spaces that open up on the page beside or between the opposed features and qualities that we have assigned to the texts.

What, then, is the relation of women wood engravers' children's books to feminist modernity? What kind of happy endings—if any—do they promise twenty-first-century women and girls? Leighton's *The Wood That Came Back* hints that answers to these questions might reside outside the words of our texts, even beyond the contents of their pictures, in the contexts and processes of her books' making. Her forgotten children's book, devoid of wood engravings or other signs of modernist aspiration, gestures toward a return in our studies of modernity to wood and woods. This return, which is both real and metaphorical, historical and pastoral, not only promises new knowledge about women artists, rural Britain, and the twentieth-century wood engraving revival but also, in its embrace of whatever lies between the beguiling symmetries of black and white, high and low, adult and child, may bring unanticipated sources of hope for a green future in which we all may live together happily ever after.

Acknowledgments

Many years ago, in 2011, I delivered my first paper on British women wood engravers at a Modernist Studies Association conference in Buffalo, New York. Karin Westman was among the small group of scholars in attendance, and, with her encouragement, that conference paper turned into an article in *The Lion and the Unicorn,* marking my entrance into the field of children's literature. Without Karin's sustained editorial support, and later the support of the wonderfully expert and enthusiastic children's literature scholar and rare-book librarian Laura Wasowicz, I might never have extended my research on interwar women wood engravers. I am grateful to other, more skeptical readers for leading me to the rich debates about rural Britain, modern culture, women's art, and children's books that inspired not only this book but also my previous book *Rural Modernity in Britain: A Critical Intervention,* coedited with Michael McCluskey. I thank Michael for introducing me to the idea of rural modernity in the first place, and for convincing me, later, to return to what was my abandoned monograph on women wood engravers. I would also like to acknowledge other members of the Space Between Society for their friendship and intellectual challenge, particularly Claire Buck, Debra Rae Cohen, Sarah Cornish, Faye Hammill, Allan Hepburn, and Phyllis Lassner. You are still, after so many years, my role models, my stars.

Research for this book was undertaken on many trips to archives in Britain and through creation of my own archive of forgotten books and chapbooks illustrated with wood engravings, all funded by Monmouth University and the Wayne D. McMurray and Helen Bennett Endowed Chair in the Humanities.

Thank you to Monmouth University and the many colleagues and administrators who supported my research over the years, including Deans Stan Green, Ken Womack, and Rich Veit, and, during the final stretch, my mentor and companion in the McMurray School, Dean David Golland. I would also like to acknowledge Monmouth University English Department Chairs Susan Goulding and J. P. Hanly, who maintained their belief in the value of my seemingly obscure research and its importance for students and faculty at Monmouth. I would especially like to thank then-Interim Provost Rekha Datta and faculty union (FAMCO) President Johanna Foster, both friends of long standing, for making it possible for me to suspend and then resume a one-year sabbatical that coincided with the Covid pandemic, enabling me to accept the deferred award of a Leverhulme Visiting Professorship at Newcastle University in January 2022.

My seven-month Leverhulme Visiting Professorship supported new research on wood engraving and rural culture in the Archives and Special Collections of Newcastle University, Oxford University, the University of Surrey, and the University of Reading. I am grateful to the Leverhulme Trust and my energetic and inspiring Newcastle University sponsoring scholar, Professor Matthew Grenby, Pro-Vice-Chancellor, Research and Innovation, for making these visits possible. Thanks also to Matthew for making possible delightful conversations with two influential scholars of children's literature: Kim Reynolds, on a coastal footpath to Dunstanburgh Castle, and Brian Alderson, in his North Yorkshire home-cum-rare-book-library. My thanks as well to Newcastle University School of English research administrator extraordinaire Laura Elliott, for making the navigation of British railways and academic bureaucracy simple—yes, simple—as I organized travel throughout England and Scotland to deliver lectures, hold workshops, and present conference papers. Another English friend who deserves special thanks is Andrew Frayn, for welcoming me into his classroom at Edinburgh Napier University and, as BAMS president, making the 2022 "Hopeful Modernisms" conference in Bristol such a success. Kathy Laing, who holds a faculty position at Mary Immaculate College in Limerick, Ireland, but lives outside Oxford in England, is another English (English? Irish? British?) friend to whom I am deeply grateful for ideas, companionship, sympathy, and spirited conversation. Thanks too to Bethan Stevens for sharing with me her more developed expertise on Victorian reproductive wood engraving as my own project took shape and to Jan Montefiore for sharing with me her wisdom, strawberries, and love of wood engraving.

My Leverhulme Lectures on British women wood engravers as rural modernists took place at the Stirling Maxwell Centre for the Study of Text/Image Culture, University of Glasgow, the Lit & Phil Library, the National Innovation Centre for Rural Enterprise, Newcastle University, the Museum of English Rural Life, University of Reading, and Seven Stories: The National Centre for Children's Books, and I am indebted to audiences at these events for questions and suggestions that improved arguments incorporated into this book. I am also grateful for the welcome of my hosts and sponsors at these lectures, including especially Laurence Grove, Luis Gomes, and Faye Hammill (again and again Faye Hammill) at the University of Glasgow, Kay Easson at the Lit & Phil, and Ollie Douglas at MERL.

For the most intelligent of introductions to everything and anything related to Bewick, I am indebted to Peter Quinn, president of the Thomas Bewick Society, and his wife, Dr. Josiette DeBono. I would also like to thank June Holmes, archivist and long-serving membership secretary of the Bewick Society, for her research support, and wood engraver Chris Daunt for an unforgettable day of instruction in the basics of wood engraving at his kitchen table in Dunston.

I am grateful for the stimulating conversations about possible futures for rural modern and rural British studies with Newcastle University social scientists Alastair Bonnett, Menelaos Gkartzios, and Mark Shucksmith, Northumbria University historians Matt Kelly and Gareth Roddy, and my longtime collaborator and friend art historian Ysanne Holt, also at Northumbria. A special thanks to the University of Reading's invaluable Jeremy Burchardt for a memorable, leisurely outdoor tea at MERL, where we discussed all things rural. For lively literary conversations with Newcastle University English colleagues, I cannot thank warmly enough Jo Robinson, Stacy Gillis, Ella Dzelzainis, Kirsten MacLeod, and Kate Chedgzoy, who became good walking, eating, and drinking friends. And speaking of eating and drinking: No acknowledgments for this book would be complete without mention of my gregarious, clever landlady at 19 Sanderson Road, Emma Weetch.

As the manuscript of *Enchanted Wood* reaches publication, I would like to thank those who have helped with the last stages of its preparation. I am happy to acknowledge that this work was made possible with the generous support of the Publication Grant Fund of The Leonard A. Lauder Research Center for Modern Art, The Metropolitan Museum of Art. J. R. Pepper and Siobhan Donnelly of the Artists Rights Society, New York, deserve my heartfelt thanks for their assistance obtaining permissions to reprint wood engravings by Gwen Raverat and Clare Leighton. I am deeply grateful to the estates of all four women wood engravers, including Mrs. Anne Quickenden, who manages the Miller Parker estate, and Mr. Simon Lawrence, who manages the Hassall estate, for permission to reproduce the artwork and illustrations reprinted in these pages. I am also grateful for the kindly assistance of Ian Rogerson, the foremost scholar of Agnes Miller Parker's work, for help obtaining permission to reproduce her wood engravings. Thanks to Jen Rivera, Monmouth University graduate research assistant and now MFA graduate, for reading the entire manuscript and cross-referencing sources with my bibliography, and to Zafira Demiri, graduate research assistant and Monmouth English MA student, for her eleventh-hour help researching the Appendix. I thank my editor at the University of Minnesota Press, Leah Pennywark, for her guidance, patience, and support, and the invaluable Anne Carter for her kind and keen editorial eye for detail. The design and production team at the Press, including production editor Carla Valadez, book designer Sandra Friesen, managing editor Laura Westlund, and copy editor Judy Selhorst, is unequaled. Any errors or infelicities that remain in the book are my sole responsibility. I also extend grateful thanks to my external readers, one of whom generously revealed herself to be the book historian and children's literature expert Hannah Field. A warm and grateful thanks to Doug Armato, director at the University of Minnesota Press, for directing me to Leah when I initially inquired about Press interest in my research. Doug was my first real boss when I worked as a twenty-one-year-old publicity assistant at the University of Georgia Press late in the twentieth century, which just goes to show how important it is to keep crossing rather than burning your old scholarly bridges.

Finally, I would like to acknowledge the four people to whom I am dedicating this book. As always, thank you George, Helen, and Vera Witte, my immediate and most beloved and loving family members, for your heroic tolerance of my eccentric Anglophilic passions that have taken me so often so very far away from you. This book cannot make up for my absences, but at least the absences will come to an end with its publication. The book ends as it begins, with a dedicated acknowledgment to the friendship beyond friendship, of kinship in art and spirit, to the wood engraver, printmaker, and cherished English companion Caroline Coode, whom I met at the Lit & Phil in April 2022. I miss many things about Newcastle and Northumberland, but nothing more than our morning waves across the lane separating our homes in Jesmond, me hollering with American accents "Hello!" out my bedroom window, and Caroline greeting me joyfully, "Hello!" from her garage-top garden.

Appendix

Midcentury British Women Wood Engravers

The women artists included in the following list all achieved distinction as wood engravers in the middle decades of the twentieth century. Some were wealthy and engraved wood for the love of it, others were working women who relied on illustrative commissions from publishers or teaching positions in art schools to earn their livings from their wood engraving practice. The four women wood engravers who are the subjects of the earlier chapters in this book are included here because, once introduced as entries in an alphabetical listing, their exceptional and seemingly unrepeatable achievements as female Bewicks are revealed to be consequences of shared political history, social policy, and cultural habit. Their experiences were common, mainstream, part of a modern movement that brought education to girls and professions to women. Their achievements are no less significant because they took place at a time when large numbers of girls and women aspired to recognition and independence as artist wood engravers.

LADY MABEL ANNESLEY (1881–1959) Born in Regent's Park, London, died in Clare, Suffolk. Daughter of landowning aristocrats, she was the great-great-granddaughter of Sir Francis Grant, a portrait painter and president of the Royal Academy. Trained as a painter, she learned wood engraving from Noel Rooke at the Central School of Arts and Crafts in the early 1920s. She illustrated with wood engravings the Golden Cockerel Press edition of *Songs from Robert Burns* (1925) and two Duckworth volumes, *County Down Songs* (1924) and *Apollo in Mourne* (1926). She was elected a member of the Society of Wood Engravers in 1925 and exhibited her work in her own studio in Belfast. Her husband, Gerald Sowerby, died in 1913, and the next year she inherited Castlewellan Castle and took back her maiden name. She immigrated to New Zealand in 1945, but returned to England in 1953. Her unfinished autobiography is *As the Sight Is Bent* (1964). Her artwork is featured in various museums in the United Kingdom, Canada, and New Zealand.

HELEN BINYON (1904–1979) Born in Chelsea, London, died in Chichester, England. Wood engraver, writer, watercolor painter, illustrator, puppeteer, and teacher. She attended the Royal College of Art with notable artists and wood engravers Eric Ravilious and Edward Bawden, and after attending the Central School of Arts and Crafts and studying with W. P. Robins, had a three-person show with Ravilious and Bawden at the Redfern Gallery. She established and performed in a traveling puppet theater, Jiminy Puppets, with her twin sister, Margaret. She worked with her sister largely on children's books that she illustrated with pen-and-ink, and she taught at a number of art schools. Her wood engravings illustrate *Brief Candles* (1938), a play written by her father, Laurence Binyon, and published by the Golden Cockerel Press, as well as Maria Edgeworth's *Angelina; or, L'Amie Inconnue* (1933) with the Swan Press and an edition of Jane Austen's *Pride and Prejudice* (1938) for Penguin. Her correspondence is in the Tate Gallery Archive.

DOROTHEA PAUL BRABY (1909–1987) Born in Wandsworth, London, place of death undiscovered. Wood engraver, designer, illustrator, and eventually full-time social worker. She studied at the Central School of Arts and Crafts and from 1928 to 1930 at the Heatherley School of Art, supplemented by studies in Paris and Florence. She was one of Christopher Sandford's most trusted wood engravers, illustrating numerous Golden Cockerel Press books, including *The Mabinogion* (1948) and *Sir Gawain and the Green Knight* (1952). She contributed line drawings to Noel Streatfeild's children's book *The Fearless Treasure: A Story of England from Then to Now* (1953), which came out the same year as her How to Do It series book, *The Way of Wood Engraving*, published by The Studio. Married to Douglas Paul, she had two children. She left her career as an artist in 1959 to become a social worker. Her papers are at the British Library's Manuscript

Collections, the Archive of Art & Design at the Victoria and Albert Museum, and the Department of Collection Services, National Library of Wales.

CELIA FIENNES (CELIA MARY TWISLETON-WYKEHAM-FIENNES) (1902–1998) Born in Ealing, London, died in Culworth, England. Wood engraver, painter, printmaker, and illustrator. She attended the Central School of Arts and Crafts, studying wood engraving with Noel Rooke, whom she married in 1932, at which point she also went by the name Celia Rooke. Her most significant wood engraved illustrations appear in *The Fables of Aesop* (1926), published by Robert Gibbings at the Golden Cockerel Press, and *The Twelve Moneths* (1929), published by Cresset Press. A direct descendant of the seventeenth-century travel writer Celia Fiennes, her work is in the Central St. Martins Museum and Study Collection of the University of the Arts London.

MARCIA LANE FOSTER (1897–1983) Born in Seaton, Devon, died in Wincanton, England. Wood engraver, printmaker, illustrator, and portrait and commercial artist. She studied at the St. John's Wood Academy of Art and the Royal Academy Schools, learning wood engraving with Noel Rooke at the Central School of Arts and Crafts. Her wood engravings illustrate Kenneth Grahame's *Headswoman* (1923), published with Dodd, Mead, and Anatole France's *The Merrie Tales of Jacques Tournebroche* (1923), published by John Lane–the Bodley Head. She illustrated dozens of children's books, often with black-and-white line drawings, and remained active as a bookmaker well into the 1960s. She married another artist, Howard Dudley Jarrett, and never had any children. There does not appear to be any archive devoted to her life and work.

TIRZAH GARWOOD (1908–1951) Born in Gillingham, Kent, died in Colchester, England. Wood engraver, painter, paper marbler, and author. She studied wood engraving under Eric Ravilious at the Eastbourne School of Art and later at the Central School of Arts and Crafts. She and Ravilious married in 1930, forming one of the most talented and popular artist couples working in interwar Britain. Her wood engravings appear in Golden Cockerel books, among those of other publishers. As Tirzah Ravilious, she focused on raising her and Eric Ravilious's three children. During World War II, she was diagnosed with breast cancer, and her husband, working as a war artist, died in a plane crash around the same time. After her surgery, she wrote the autobiography *Long Live Great Bardfield and Love to You All,* which was published posthumously in 2012 by her daughter, Anne Ullman. In 1946 she married Henry Swanzy and resumed her career as a painter. However, this new love and art came to a tragic end when she was diagnosed with cancer a second time and died shortly thereafter. A first retrospective exhibition of her work was organized by the Dulwich Picture Gallery in 2024.

BARBARA GREG (1900–1983) Born in Styal, Cheshire, died in Enfield, London. Wood engraver, illustrator, and linocut engraver. She learned wood engraving at the Central School of Arts and Crafts and pursued instruction in more canonical media at the Westminster School of Art and the Slade. At the latter she met Norman Janes, a teacher who would later become her devoted husband and with whom she would raise three children. Her wealthy family supported her career as a professional artist as well as that of her husband. Critics speculate that her grandfather's collection of Thomas Bewick's work inspired her love of wood engraving. She specialized in providing illustrations for nature books and magazines, contributing wood engravings into the 1960s, well beyond the so-called wood engraving revival of the 1920s. She illustrated a number of books for Cresset Press, including *Enigmas of Natural History* (1936) and *More Enigmas of Natural History* (1937), though she is most highly esteemed today for her wood engravings in Ian Niall's books, including *Fresh Woods* (1951) and *Pastures New* (1952). She was elected to membership of the Manchester Academy of Fine Arts in 1925, and other awards followed, culminating with her full membership in the Society of Wood Engravers in 1952. In 2015, Quarry Bank held an exhibition titled *Drawn Out of Love* featuring the work of Greg and her artist husband. There appears to be no archive devoted to her work, although a few of her letters are preserved in the Chatto & Windus files at the University of Reading's Special Collections.

VIVIEN MASSIE GRIBBLE (1888–1932) Born in Chelsea, London, died in Higham, Suffolk. The daughter of the Slade-trained artist Norah Royds, she also studied at the Slade School of Art. By 1919, she was one of four women artists praised by Malcolm Salaman in *Modern Woodcuts and Lithographs by British and French Artists* for her work with Noel Rooke at the Central School of Arts and Crafts. Her most notable works include black-line wood engravings for *Odes* (1923), by John Keats, and *Songs from "The Princess"* (1924), by Alfred Lord Tennyson, both published by Thomas Balston at Duckworth Books; and, most famously, *Tess of the D'Urbervilles* (1926), published by Macmillan. Gribble and her husband, Douglas Doyle-Jones, tried to have children, but after several miscarriages, they decided to adopt a child. After welcoming the child into their lives, Gribble lost interest in her artistic work and, tragically, died shortly thereafter of cancer. A limited amount of her correspondence is in the collections of the Paul Mellon Centre for Studies in British Art.

MARY ELIZABETH GROOM (1903–1958) Born in Corringham, Essex, died in Norwich, Norfolk. Wood engraver, printmaker, illustrator, and sculptor in wood. She studied printmaking at the Grosvenor School of Modern Art before focusing on wood engraving instruction at Leon Underwood's Brook Green School. She produced wood engraved illustrations for Golden Cockerel Press limited editions, including *Paradise Lost* (1937) and *Roses of Sharon* (1937). She was a member of the rival groups the Society of Wood Engravers and the English Wood Engraving Society. An unmarried professional artist, she lived with her widowed mother in Suffolk. Her wood engravings are held in major public collections, including the British Museum and the Victoria and Albert Museum, with the largest collection of her prints at the Ashmolean Museum in Oxford.

JOAN HASSALL (1906–1988) Born in Notting Hill, London, died in Malham, Yorkshire. Wood engraver, typographer, and illustrator. The daughter of the famous poster artist John Hassall, she worked at her father's London School of Art before enrolling as a student at the Royal Academy Schools. She learned wood engraving with R. J. Beedham at the London County Council School of Photo-Engraving and Lithography. Her first illustrative commission for a wood engraving was the title page for the book of poems *Devil's Dyke* (1936), written by her brother, Christopher Hassall. During the war years, she taught wood engraving at the Edinburgh College of Art and designed and illustrated the Saltire Chapbooks, published by the Saltire Society. Her wood engravings for children's books can be found in *A Child's Garden of Verses* (1947), by Robert Louis

Stevenson, Pamela Whitlock's *All Day Long: An Anthology of Poetry for Children* (1954), and *The Oxford Nursery Rhyme Book* (1955), compiled by Iona and Peter Opie. Her wood engravings for George Harrap's edition of Mary Russell Mitford's *Our Village* (1947) are even more beguiling than those featured in the Folio Society's seven-volume series of Jane Austen's novels produced from 1957 through 1962. She never married and retired to Malham, where she lived in a cottage inherited from an old friend and enjoyed performing music at both the local chapel and the Anglican church. In 1987 she traveled to Buckingham Palace to receive the OBE from the queen. Her correspondence is in the University of Reading Special Collections, British Library Manuscript Collections, Edinburgh Library Special Collections, the Tate Gallery Archive, and the University of Birmingham's Cadbury Research Library Special Collections, with additional papers and drawings at the University of Cambridge's Fitzwilliam Museum.

GERTRUDE HERMES (1901–1983) Born in Bromley, Kent, died in Bristol, England. Wood engraver and sculptor. She studied at Beckenham School of Art and at Leon Underwood's Brook Green School of Painting and Sculpture. In 1926 she married the celebrated wood engraver Blair Hughes-Stanton, who joined her and Agnes Miller Parker and William McCance at the Gregynog Press in Newtown, where they formed a rural avant-garde of wood engravers and bookmakers. She divorced Hughes-Stanton in 1933. During the war years, she traveled to and worked in the United States and Canada. After the war, she returned to England and taught wood engraving and linocutting at the Central School of Arts and Crafts and the Royal Academy Schools. A member of the English Wood Engraving Society in the 1920s and 1930s, she earned many honors and awards during her artistic career, including election to the Royal Society of Painter-Etchers and Engravers, and associate and then full membership in the Royal Academy by 1971. Unfortunately, in the late 1960s she suffered a stroke that prevented her from working further. She was dedicated to her career and was appointed OBE in 1981. The first retrospective of her work, *Wild Girl: Gertrude Hermes,* was held in 2015–16 at the Hepworth Wakefield. Her papers and correspondence are at the Henry Moore Institute Archive and at Oxford University's Bodleian Library Special Collections.

MURIEL BLOMFIELD JACKSON (1901–1977) Born in St. Pancras, London, died in Camden, London. Wood engraver, painter, lithographer, poster artist, and muralist. She studied with Noel Rooke at the Central School of Arts and Crafts and exhibited with the Society of Wood Engravers. She was a finalist in the British Prix de Rome scholarship competition in 1925, and in 1931 she was awarded the Logan Medal of the Arts for her print *Wagon on the Heath* at the International Exhibition of Lithography and Wood Engraving in Chicago. She never illustrated any books, but she was included in Malcolm Salaman's influential 1930 book on wood engraving, *The New Woodcut,* and her wood engraved prints appeared in later issues of *The Studio* and *Drawing and Design.* In 1928 she married Francis Courtenay Mason, a surgeon, and they had two children. Her work and correspondence do not appear to be preserved in any archive; indeed, there are virtually no records of her work.

HELEN BABETTE KAPP (1901–1978) Born in Hampstead, London, died in Leiston, Suffolk. Wood engraver, illustrator, painter, curator, gallery director, and writer. Her parents were immigrants, her mother from the United States, her father from Germany. She trained at the Slade School of Art and the Central School of Arts and Crafts, with additional art studies in Paris. She exhibited widely, including at the Royal Academy, with the Society of Wood Engravers, the Artists' International Association, the London Group of Artists, and the Society of Women Artists. After the war, she had a solo show at Haifa, Israel, with the British Council. She illustrated books with wood engravings and line drawings, the former including *The Scandal and Credulities of John Aubrey* (1931), with Peter Davies, and the latter including *Take Forty Eggs: A Comprehensive Guide to Cookery and Household Mismanagement* (1948), with Victor Gollancz. Other books, such as *Toying with a Fancy: A Book of Drawings* (1945) and *Young People's Guide to Art* (1960), issued by the Society for Education through Art, she wrote and illustrated herself. During the war she was a touring lecturer with the Harrogate Art Gallery. In 1951 she was appointed director of the City Art Gallery in Wakefield (now Hepworth Wakefield), Yorkshire, where she also exhibited her works. From 1961 to 1967, she was director of the Abbot Hall Art Gallery, Kendal. She never married, and after retiring to Leiston, Suffolk, she remained active, including writing and designing *Enjoying Pictures* (1975), produced for the Local Search Series. Her archives are at the Hepworth Wakefield.

ANNABEL KIDSTON (1896–1981) Born in Hillhead, Glasgow, died in North Berwick, Scotland. Wood engraver, painter in oils and watercolors, and illustrator. She attended the Glasgow School of Art, trained in Paris at the Académie de la Grande Chaumière, taught art at the Laurel Bank School in Glasgow, and then learned wood engraving as a student at the Slade. She worked as an art and painting teacher for troops stationed in St. Andrews during World War II. With artist-engravers Alison McKenzie and Winifred McKenzie, she formed the St. Andrews School of artists and promoted wood engraving. Her best-known illustrative commission was for Matthew Arnold's *"The Forsaken Merman" and "The Scholar Gipsy"* (1927), published by John Lane–the Bodley Head in the Helicon series. Her two sisters were also artists. There does not appear to be a Kidston archive.

CLARE LEIGHTON (1898–1989) Born in London, died in Waterbury, Connecticut. Wood engraver, illustrator, writer, and stained glass artist. She was the daughter of Marie Connor Leighton, a successful writer of romances for the Lord Northcliff newspapers, and niece to the painter Jack Leighton. She studied at the Brighton College of Art, the Slade School of Art, and the Central School of Arts and Crafts, where her teacher was Noel Rooke. She popularized unlimited editions of rural subjects during the interwar years and was the first woman to write a book on wood engraving, *Wood-Engraving and Woodcuts* (1932). She immigrated to the United States in 1939, where, during the war, she worked as a member of the Department of Art, Aesthetics, and Music at Duke University. In 1949, she became a full member of the National Academy of Design. In 2022–23, her work was included in *Print and Prejudice: Women Printmakers, 1700–1930,* an exhibition at the Victoria and Albert Museum. Her devotion to rural arts, rural living, and gardening is evident in many of her wood engraved illustrations, including in *Four Hedges* (1935), which describes her relationship with her partner of many years, H. N. (Noel) Brailsford, and *Country Matters* (1937). Her six wood engravings depicting winter work in the Canadian International Paper Company's lumber camp in the Laurentian Mountains of Quebec, which she visited in the depths of winter and the depths of the Great Depression, are among her most striking. Her correspondence, papers, and artworks are in collections in the United Kingdom and the United States, including at the University of Connecticut Library's Archives and Special Collections, Duke University Libraries Archives and Manuscripts, the Smithsonian Museum's Archives of American Art, the Yale Center for British Art, the National Archives at Kew, the Metropolitan Museum of Art, the Victoria and Albert Museum, and the British Museum.

AVERIL MACKENZIE-GRIEVE (1903–1975) Born in Uckfield, Sussex, died in Robertsbridge, East Sussex. Also known as Averil Salmond MacKenzie Grieve, Averil Le Gros Clark, and Mrs. John Keevil. Wood engraver, illustrator, translator, and author of fiction, biography, and autobiography. While she was growing up in Castle Hill House, Devon, her private tutor, Francis James, inspired her interest in art with his flower painting. After the death of her father in 1918 she went to Florence to study at Marfori Savini's studio. She returned from Italy with her mother when Mussolini and fascism became dominant forces, settling in St. Ives, Cornwall. In 1925 she married Cyril Drummond Le Gros Clark, and they traveled to his postings in China and Sarawak. Her book *A Race of Green Ginger* (1959) recalls British colonial life in Gulangyu in the late 1920s. She exhibited in the 1928 summer exhibition at the Newlyn Art Gallery under her married name, Le Gros Clark. In the 1930s, she made wood engraved illustrations for Golden Cockerel books, including her husband's edition of *Selections from the Works of Su Tung-p'o* (1931). She divorced her husband, and two months before the end of the war, he was executed by the Japanese. In 1946, she married John Keevil, a medical historian. Her autobiography is *Time and Chance* (1970). There is no archive of her work, although there is a robust textual record of her artistic life.

RACHEL "RAY" MARSHALL (1891–1940) Born in London, place of death undiscovered. Wood engraver and illustrator. The sister of famous diarist Frances Partridge, she was a peripheral member of the Bloomsbury Group. She studied wood engraving with Noel Rooke at the Central School of Arts and Crafts in his early years there, later publishing her wood engraved illustrations as R. A. Garnett, largely with Chatto & Windus and mostly in works written by her husband, the writer, editor, and publisher David Garnett, including *Lady into Fox* (1922),

A Man in the Zoo (1924), and *The Grasshoppers Come* (1931). As R. A. Marshall, she wrote and illustrated *Archibald* (1915) and *A Ride on a Rocking Horse* (1917). She and Garnett had two children, and family commitments took her away from her art; by the late 1930s she became extremely ill, leading to her death from breast cancer. A limited collection of her papers is at the Harry Ransom Center at the University of Texas at Austin.

ENID MARX (1902–1998) Born and died in London. Wood engraver, painter, and designer. She studied painting, drawing, ceramics, and textile design art at the Central School of Arts and Crafts and at the Royal College of Art, with Paul Nash and Leon Underwood serving as formal teachers and Eric Ravilious as an informal teacher of wood engraving. She wrote and illustrated with lithographs some of her own children's books during World War II, such as *Bulgy the Barrage Balloon* (1941) with Oxford University Press and *The Pigeon Ace* (1943) with Faber and Faber. After the war she spent time designing covers and engraving for Penguin Books, although she was best known as an industrial textile designer and was the first woman engraver designated a Royal Designer for Industry. She taught at several art schools, including the Ruskin School of Art, Oxford. Very late in life she published *Some Birds and Beasts and Their Feasts: An Alphabet of Wood Engravings* (1996), which appeared in a limited edition with Incline Press. She lived with her partner, Margaret Lambert, a history lecturer, in Scotland. Her correspondence is archived at the University of Reading's Special Collections.

ALISON MCKENZIE (1907–1982) Born in Bombay, India, died in Dundee, Scotland. Wood engraver, printmaker, and painter. She attended the Glasgow School of Art before moving to London to study wood engraving with Iain Macnab at the Grosvenor School of Modern Art with her sister, Winifred McKenzie, with whom she exhibited on numerous occasions throughout the 1930s. Her best-known illustrations are the wood engravings for a limited edition of Milton's *On the Morning of Christ's Nativity* (1937), published by Gregynog Press. During World War II, with Winifred and Annabel Kidston, she led drawing, painting, and engraving classes for Allied troops stationed in St. Andrews. With Winifred, she moved to Dundee to teach part-time at the Dundee College of Art, from which she retired in 1958 to care for her elderly mother. She continued to paint and exhibit during the last decades of her life.

WINIFRED MCKENZIE (1905–2001) Born in Bombay, India, died in Dundee, Scotland. Wood engraver, printmaker, and painter. She studied with her sister, Alison, at the Glasgow School of Art, focusing on color wood engraving. With her family, she moved to London in 1930 and enrolled in the Grosvenor School of Modern Art. She worked closely with her sister during their studies and afterward, on exhibitions and in art schools, including her teaching of art classes for Allied troops during World War II and wood engraving classes at Dundee College of Art. She left her teaching post in 1958 to take care of her elderly mother alongside her sister and, also like her sister, continued painting and engraving until her death.

AGNES MILLER PARKER (1895–1980) Born in Irvine, Ayrshire, died in Greenock, Scotland. Wood engraver, illustrator, and painter. Trained at the Glasgow School of Art, she is thought to have learned wood engraving informally from artists gathered around Leon Underwood. She is famous for her wood engraved illustrations in the limited edition of *The Fables of Esope* (1931), designed by her husband, William McCance, and published by the Gregynog Press. The 1930s brought her wood engraving to the general public through author H. E. Bates's *Through the Woods* (1936) and *Down the River* (1937), published by Victor Gollancz. She was one of George Macy's favorite illustrators, contributing wood engravings to his New York Limited Editions Club and Heritage Press classics. She was married for nearly four decades to McCance until they separated and divorced. Her papers are in the Manuscript Collections at the National Library of Scotland and the National Art Library at the Victoria and Albert Museum.

GWENDA MORGAN (1908–1991) Born and died in Petworth, Sussex. Wood engraver and writer. Like Elizabeth Rivers, she studied at Goldsmiths' College of Art and the Grosvenor School of Modern Art, where she was influenced by the school principal, leading wood engraver Iain Macnab. She contributed wood engravings to private press books, including *Pictures and Rhymes* (1936) for

Samson Press, and T. F. Powys's *Goat Green* (1937), Thomas Gray's *Elegy Written in a Country Churchyard* (1946), and *Grimms' Other Tales* (1956) for the Golden Cockerel Press. She spent the war working as a land girl near Petworth. After her death her memoir, *The Diary of a Land Girl, 1939–1945* (2002), was published by the Whittington Press in a very limited edition illustrated with thirty-one wood engravings. She exhibited widely in Britain, with works in various public collections including the British Museum and the Victoria and Albert Museum. She gave a significant bequest to Leconfield Hall, Petworth, where her prints are on permanent display.

MARGARET PILKINGTON (1891–1974) Born in Pendleton, Manchester, died in Alderley Edge, Cheshire. Wood engraver, painter, humanitarian, and philanthropist. She studied at the Manchester College of Art and the Slade School of Art, and then at the Central School of Arts and Crafts with Noel Rooke and Lucien Pissarro. She exhibited with the Society of Wood Engravers in its earliest years, becoming honorary secretary of the group in 1924 and chair from 1952 to 1967. Many of her best wood engravings can be found in books written by her father, Lawrence Pilkington, including *"An Alpine Valley" and Other Poems* (1924), *Tattlefold* (1926), and *The Chimneys of Tattleton* (1928), published by trade houses. She never married and was very close to her sister Dorothy; both served as directors of the firm their father and uncle Charles started, Pilkington's Lancastrian Pottery and Tile Company. She was awarded an honorary MA from the University of Manchester in 1942 and appointed an OBE in 1956. Her correspondence and papers are in the John Rylands Research Institute and Library of Manchester University.

GWEN RAVERAT (1885–1957) Born and died in Cambridge. Wood engraver, painter, and writer. The granddaughter of Charles Darwin, she attended the Slade School of Art, although it was her cousin's wife, Elinor "Eily" Monsell, who taught her wood engraving. She married fellow Slade artist and Cambridge University mathematician Jacques Raverat in 1911. In 1920 she joined nine others to found the Society of Wood Engravers. She and her husband raised two daughters in southern France until Jacques's untimely death in 1925 led Raverat to return to England. Most of her wood engraved book illustrations were completed for trade publishers in the 1930s, including, for adults, A. G. Street's *Farmer's Glory* (1934), and for children, *The Cambridge Book of Poetry for Children* (1932), *The Runaway* (1936), and *The Bird Talisman* (1939). Her line drawings appear in several books, including Alison Uttley's *Mustard, Pepper and Salt* (1938), Charlotte M. Yonge's *Countess Kate* (1948), and her own childhood memoir *Period Piece* (1952). Her papers are in the Tate Gallery Archive and King's College Archive Centre of Cambridge University.

RACHEL RECKITT (1908–1995) Born in St. Albans, Hertfordshire, died in Somerset, England. Wood engraver, sculptor in wood and stone, wrought iron designer, and artist. She studied at the Taunton School of Art and Grosvenor School of Modern Art, the latter from 1933 to 1937, when she was instructed by Iain Macnab in wood engraving. She studied lithography at the Central School of Arts and Crafts and, in the mid- to late 1940s, stone sculpture at Hammersmith School of Building Crafts. She exhibited stone and wood carvings with the London Group and her wood engraved prints with the Society of Wood Engravers. She lived in Somerset in her family home known as Golsoncott, which was very special to her. During World War II, she assisted with evacuations of London children to Golsoncott. In the late 1960s, she studied metal sculpture and became a member of the British Artist Blacksmith Association. Books with her wood engraved illustrations include *Voices on the Green* (1945), published by Joseph; *London—South of the River* (1949) and *English Country Short Stories* (1949), both published by Paul Elek; and *People with Six Legs* (1953), published by Faber and Faber. Evocative glimpses of the artist at work are offered in the memoirs *Oleander, Jacaranda* (1994) and *A House Unlocked* (2001), both by her niece, the writer Penelope Lively. There does not appear to be a Reckitt archive.

ELIZABETH RIVERS (1903–1964) Born in Sawbridgeworth, Hertfordshire, died in Dalkey, County Dublin. Wood engraver, illustrator, painter, printmaker, stained glass designer, and author. She studied at Goldsmiths' College of Art and the Royal Academy Schools, where in 1926 she won a scholarship. Beginning in 1931 she studied art at the École de Fresques in Paris. She then joined her artist friend Amy Elton in Inishmore, where she made art and ran a guesthouse. There she authored and illustrated several of her own works, including *This Man*

(1939), published by the Guyon House Press, and a memoir, *Stranger in Aran* (1946), published by the Yeats sisters' Cuala Press. During the war, she moved to London and worked as a fire warden. When she returned to Ireland after the war, she met the stained glass artist Evie Horn, with whom she worked until the latter's death in 1955. A retrospective exhibition of her work was held at the Gorry Gallery, Dublin, in 1989. Her archives are in the National Library of Ireland.

HESTER SAINSBURY (1890–1967) Born in London, died in Berkshire, England. Wood engraver, illustrator, modern dancer, poet, and performance artist. Trained as a dancer by Margaret Morris, she was influenced by Bloomsbury artists, including Roger Fry and Gwen Raverat. Her brother founded two publishing houses for which she produced work, including her illustrated edition of the children's book *The Lady's New-Years-Gift; or, Advice to a Daughter* (1927), published by Cayme Press. She also illustrated Golden Cockerel books and a limited edition of *Tales from Hans Andersen* (1929), published by F. Etchells & Macdonald. A real bohemian, she lived with the playwright Kori Torahiko until his death in 1924. In 1932 she married Frederick Etchells, her publisher with Hugh Macdonald; Etchells was better known as an avant-garde painter, illustrator, architect, and translator of Le Corbusier. Sainsbury illustrated several books for Etchells's Haslewood Press. After moving to Berkshire with her husband and daughter, she faded away from the artistic scenes that she had once influenced, except for one illustrated edition of her former lover Torahiko's works in 1936. There does not appear to be a Sainsbury archive.

LETTICE SANDFORD (1902–1993) Born in St. Albans, Hertfordshire, died in Herefordshire, England. Wood and metal engraver, illustrator, watercolor painter, writer, publisher, and corn dolly revivalist. She studied at the Byam Shaw and Vicat Cole School of Art and later at Chelsea Polytechnic, where Robert Day taught her wood engraving. In 1929 she married Christopher Sandford, and together they ran the Boar's Head Press until Christopher bought the Golden Cockerel Press in 1933. They had three children. She contributed many wood engravings to Boar's Head, Golden Cockerel, and Golden Hours limited editions of the 1930s, with her best white-line work evident in books like *Sappho* (1932), *Thalamos* (1932), and *Hero and Leander* (1933). She wrote and illustrated with color lithographs the children's books *Roo-oo and Panessa* (1938) and *Coo my Doo* (1943); after the war, she illustrated a number of Folio Society books with pen-and-ink drawings. When her husband sold the Golden Cockerel Press in 1959, they moved to the seventeenth-century Eye Manor in Herefordshire, where she took up country life with great enthusiasm, becoming famous for reviving, writing about, and teaching the traditional country art of decorative straw work and corn dollies. She also enjoyed watercolor painting in the last years of her life. There does not appear to be a Sandford archive.

MARY DUDLEY SHORT (1895–1986) Born in Birmingham, England, place of death undiscovered. Christened Laura, she was also known as Molly Freeman upon her marriage. Wood engraver, painter, and linocut artist. She studied at the Reading School of Art and the Central School of Arts and Crafts, where she was taught wood engraving and linocutting by Noel Rooke and Claude Flight. In 1930 she exhibited at the Redfern Gallery as part of the annual exhibition of the Society of Wood Engravers. During the wood engraving revival, she produced illustrations for St. Dominic's Press. She and her husband, Percy Freeman, were avid collectors of British modern art, and in 1959 they gifted £1,000 to the Tate Gallery, which was used to set up the Friends of Tate Gallery. On her death, she bequeathed £65,000 to the Ashmolean in Oxford to promote twentieth-century British art. Her wood engraving was featured in the 2015 exhibition *Women Wood Engravers: Discovering Mary Dudley Short,* held at the Ditchling Museum of Art and Craft.

NORA UNWIN (1907–1982) Born in Tolworth, Surrey, died in Wayland, Massachusetts. Wood engraver, illustrator, painter, and writer. A twin and one of five children, she was born into a family that founded three publishing houses, Unwin Brothers, Allen & Unwin, and T. Fisher Unwin, the latter two of which commissioned her illustrative work. In her eight years of specialized arts training at Leon Underwood's Brook Green School, the Kingston School of Art, and the Royal College of Art, she studied a wide array of arts and media, including wood engraving, pottery, embroidery, etching, and bookbinding. Her wood engravings were inspired and influenced by the work of Agnes Miller Parker, evident in her illustrations in *Exploring the Animal World* (1933), published by Allen

& Unwin, and *Footnotes on Nature* (1947), published by Doubleday. In 1937, at age thirty, she met the young American writer Elizabeth Yates, who was married to William McGreal, and the women's first collaboration on a children's book led to an artistic partnership that eventually brought Unwin to New England, where she found great success as a teacher and leader of a postwar American wood engraving revival. She created wood engraved illustrations for dozens of books written by other authors and wrote and illustrated fourteen books of her own, including her earliest production, *Lucy and the Little Red Horse* (1943), cowritten with her friend Gwendy Caroe and inspired by her wartime work with children evacuated to the English countryside. With Yates, she earned a Newbery mention for *Mountain Born* (1943) and a Newbery Medal for *Amos Fortune, Free Man* (1950). She had more than forty one-woman shows and won many major awards during her long career. The Monadnock Center for History and Culture in Peterborough, New Hampshire, houses more than 1,500 wood engravings, drawings, paintings, and sketchbooks in its Nora S. Unwin Collection and was the site of the first retrospective of the artist's work in 2024. Archives of her correspondence, manuscripts, and other materials are in the Nora S. Unwin Papers at the University of Oregon Libraries, Special Collections and Archives, with additional materials related to her collaborations with Elizabeth Yates at the de Grummond Children's Literature Collection at the University of Southern Mississippi's McCain Library and Archives.

MARGARET WEBB Virtually nothing is known. Wood engraver and illustrator. Her wood engravings appear in *Early English Recipes* (1937), published by Cambridge University Press; John Claridge's *The Country Calendar, or The Shepherd of Banbury's Rules* (1946), published by Sylvan Press; and John Hillaby's *Journey Through Britain* (1968; republished in the United States as *Walks Through Britain,* 1969).

Notes

INTRODUCTION

1   Eve comes first in a long line of enchantresses capable of inspiring others to produc-
    tion of great art but not themselves creating anything other than chaos and babies.
    Griselda Pollock, in her "Preface to the Bloomsbury Revelations Edition" of *Old
    Mistresses,* coauthored with Rozsika Parker and first published in 1981, writes that the
    book took its title from a 1972 exhibition that proved that European art of the thir-
    teenth through eighteenth centuries did include many beautiful paintings by women.
    Parker and Pollock demonstrated how their discipline of art history "was *structurally*
    sexist. It did not just ignore or neglect women. It actively made art history women-
    free, and did so most effectively only in the twentieth century." Pollock, "Preface," xxi.
    The first picture in their classic feminist study represents Eve in Adam's place in *And
    God Created Woman in Her Own Image* (1970) (2). Feminist literary studies had an
    earlier disciplinary impact. A partner literary study for Parker and Pollock's might
    be Virginia Woolf's 1929 *A Room of One's Own.* Wood engravers of Woolf's genera-
    tion, both male and female, were always protective of their reputations as artists
    as opposed to craftsmen. See, for example, Selborne, *British Wood-Engraved Book
    Illustration,* 9–10; Brett, *Wood Engraving,* 11.

2   Among the general histories of illustration and wood engraving that are of
    special relevance to this study are Balston, *English Wood-Engraving*; Balston,
    Wood-Engraving in Modern English Books; Benson, *Printed Picture*; Bliss, *History
    of Wood-Engraving*; Hamilton, *Wood Engraving and the Woodcut*; Hodnett,
    Five Centuries of English Book Illustration; Jaffé, *Women Engravers*; Peppin and

Micklethwait, *Dictionary of British Book Illustrators*; Selborne, *British Wood-Engraved Book Illustration*.

3 For discussion of the origins and traditions of English white-line engraving, see, for example, Hamilton, *Wood Engraving and the Woodcut*; Hodnett, *Five Centuries of English Book Illustration*; Selborne, *British Wood-Engraved Book Illustration*.

4 John Ruskin quipped of Bewick, "He could draw a pig but not an Aphrodite." Ruskin, "Technics of Wood Engraving," 78. At the end of the nineteenth century, Morris's Kelmscott Press, along with the Ashendene, Doves, Vale, and Eragny Presses, paved the way in England for wood engraving's transformation from an industrial, factory-based, mass-reproduction process into an autographic art form, in which the author and engraver of an image were one. Fine private presses of the interwar period, including Gregynog, Golden Cockerel, Nonesuch, and again Ashendene, took over the late Victorian fine press market for wood engraved books. See Cave, *Private Press*. For an examination of interwar illustrated books as neglected components of the British "modernist mediascape," see Aymes, *Modernist Mediascapes*. Aymes finds in the materials and designs of Paul Nash's elegant little books with wood engravings evidence of a shift in print culture from the revivalist aesthetics and mournful nostalgia of 1920s private press books to the antipastoral experiments with technologies of mass reproduction in illustrated books of the 1930s. Sorensen describes small presses such as the Hogarth, Cuala, and Black Sun as "harken[ing] back to the politicized aspects of non-mass-produced and decorative printing advocated by William Morris in his Kelmscott Press." Sorensen, *Modernist Experiments*, 189. To the extent that the modernist small presses Sorensen mentions assumed the Kelmscott mantle, the mass-produced wood engraved books examined in this study are "anti-Kelmscott" productions.

5 In this study, I refer to artists primarily by their surnames. For discussion of the sexism embedded in the coy tradition of referring to women artists by their first names (e.g., the 2020 National Gallery exhibition titled *Artemisia*), see Pollock, "Preface," xxiii. For the most authoritative account of Bewick's life, publications, and historical significance, see Tattersfield's three-volume *Thomas Bewick: The Complete Illustrative Work*. For evidence that Bewick can delight and instruct a broad twenty-first-century readership, see Uglow's award-winning biography, *Nature's Engraver*.

6 In addition to treatments of these women wood engravers in studies of modern woodcuts and wood engravings, see Chambers, "Books and Bookplates"; Hickman,

"Clare Leighton's Art and Craft"; Belloc, "Introduction"; Jaffé, "Introduction"; David Leighton, "Clare Leighton Remembered by Her Nephew"; Stevens, "Clare Leighton"; Rogerson, *Agnes Miller Parker: Wood Engraver and Book Illustrator*; Selborne and Newman, *Gwen Raverat*; Spalding, *Gwen Raverat*.

7 The simple act of beginning a scholarly or professional reading of a book with its illustrations has consequences for literary and textual studies that extend beyond simple questions such as "How can one construct a bibliography around the name of the illustrator rather than the name of the author?" While even the most materialist of literary scholars tend to organize their thinking around authors rather than illustrators, there are certainly many who have grappled with the implications of diverse visual forms, print networks, and historical conditions of production for readings of literary texts. Victorianists are especially adept at this kind of thing, but even in the field of twentieth-century literary studies, during the giddy early days of New Modernist study, George Bornstein argued that "examining modernism in its original sites of production and in the continually shifting physicality of its texts and transmissions results in alternative constructions very different from current ones." Bornstein, *Material Modernism,* 1. More recently, Aymes and Sorensen have integrated media, book history, and genre studies into Bornstein's materialist formalist methods, with Sorensen asking, "What versions of modernism emerge through the kinds of reading that traversing publishing networks and illuminating dynamic material forms make available?" Sorensen, *Modernist Experiments,* 3; see also Aymes, *Modernist Mediascapes.* Aymes's and Sorensen's interesting answers to this question follow Bornstein to "alternative constructions" of modernism but do not dislodge modernism itself as an already recognized and constituted starting and ending point for expanded "modernist" study. In contrast, in this book I hold out the possibility that its feminist biographical-book historical-formalist methodology, in changing how we study, can change what we think we are studying in the first place. To this extent, I echo Collier in saying, "This is not a book about modernism. Or, rather, it is about modernism only insomuch as the aesthetic means and preoccupations that gradually became modernism would exert their pressure, formally and otherwise, on virtually everyone who was producing art in the decades surrounding [or, in this case, quite a bit after] the turn of the century." Collier, *Modern Print Artefacts,* 2. All these studies in print (non)modernism, knowingly or not, respond to Tickner's challenge to review "with hindsight . . . the canon of modernist works and attend to the processes that sift the

modern from the merely contemporary." They demonstrate with Tickner that "there is more than one kind of modernism (and modernity) at stake." Tickner, *Modern Life*, 184.

8   Selborne, *British Wood-Engraved Book Illustration,* 396.

9   British women had been successful illustrators of children's books before these four wood engravers' entry into children's publishing. Kate Greenaway and Beatrix Potter are the most famous Victorian women artist-illustrators, while Mabel Lucie Attwell and Honor Appleton dominated the interwar scene. See Whalley and Chester, *History of Children's Book Illustration.*

10   Bias against reproductive crafts and commercial arts—versus the aura arts of painting and sculpture—and a modernist preference for abstract rather than realist aesthetics have kept 1930s wood engravers working in the Bewick tradition on the margins of modernist art studies. In her monumental *British Wood-Engraved Book Illustration 1904–1940,* significantly subtitled *A Break with Tradition,* Selborne defies art historians who maintain a "dismissive view" of book illustration, approaching it from "the perspective of the history of painting," in which it "is usually regarded as a 'minor art' which labours under the constraint of representing a set subject" (16; Selborne quotes Gordon Ray). Hamilton confidently describes wood engravings of the midcentury revival as "a fine art medium," "at the cutting-edge of the avant-garde," and "new and experimental," words often associated with twentieth-century modernism. Hamilton, *Wood Engraving and the Woodcut,* 53, 63, 83.

11   There is an extensive feminist scholarship on modernist literature and early twentieth-century and Golden Age children's literature. Benstock's *Women of the Left Bank* is a foundational study, as are Gilbert and Gubar's *No Man's Land* and Scott's invaluable *The Gender of Modernism.* It could be claimed that Rose's *The Case of Peter Pan* launched the field of contemporary children's literary studies. Reynolds's *Left Out* and *Radical Children's Literature* and Dusinberre's *Alice to the Lighthouse* have forged interdisciplinary ties between studies of children's literature and studies of modernist literature. Pollock transformed art history with *Old Mistresses* and *Framing Feminism,* both cowritten with Rozsika Parker, and *Vision and Difference.* In 2020, Pollock was awarded the prestigious Holberg Prize for her contributions to the humanities through feminist revision of the discipline of art history. Yet as recently as 2019, Wiesner-Hanks reported in an *Art Herstory* guest post titled "Why Do Old Mistresses Matter Today?": "The number of monographs about women artists, past and

present, remains much lower than those about men, as is the price of their work. . . .
At the 2005 Venice Biennale, the indefatigable Guerrilla Girls counted all the works at
six of Venice's major museums; they found that of the roughly 1240 works, 40 were by
women. A bit better than [H. W.] Janson in 1986, but not much."

12 Roland Leighton, Clare Leighton's older brother, was killed in action in 1915. He was
eulogized by his distraught mother, Marie Connor Leighton, in *Boy of My Heart* and
by his fiancée, Vera Brittain, in *Testament of Youth*. One day after Raverat's friend
Rupert Brooke died, her first cousin Erasmus Darwin was killed in action in the Second Battle of Ypres. William McCance, Miller Parker's husband, was imprisoned as a
conscientious objector during World War I.

13 Jaffé attributes the scarcity of women engravers in England prior to 1900 to "economics, the apprenticeship system and the status of women." Jaffé, *Women Engravers*, 8.
When in 1856 publishers Ward and Lock produced *Elegant Arts for Ladies,* appropriate
feminine arts such as feather flowers and painting on velvet were illustrated in the
book with wood engravings, but wood engraving itself was not on the list. The Arts
and Crafts movement attracted women to wood engraving, but, as Jaffé notes, even
professionals like Georgiana Burne-Jones and Janey Morris were little more than
"unpaid adjuncts" (12).

14 In other words, they were invested in contributing to various phases and understanding diverse environmental relations of what Robert Darnton described years later as
the "communications circuit." Darnton, "What Is the History of Books?"

15 Macaulay's October 24, 1952, review of *Period Piece* was anonymous. Through the
mediating effects of Walt Disney, the phrase she used to describe Raverat's memoir
is now associated with another early twentieth-century enchantress, P. L. Travers's
Mary Poppins.

16 Donald could include the young Gwen Darwin among the "countless Victorians" who
"had first encountered Bewick's books as nursery reading, and wrote fondly of how
the pictures had captured their imagination at that age." She adds, "Child readership
of these books is a category largely neglected by historians." Donald, *Art of Thomas
Bewick*, 182.

17 The real Mrs. Bewick was Isabella Elliott, a country woman whom Bewick had known
since childhood and with whom he shared a long and loving marriage. They had
four children, a son and three daughters. Their second child, Robert, was trained in
Bewick's workshop as a wood engraver, and while destined to inherit the workshop,

was not equal to continuing his father's art or business. Their eldest, Jane, was inde-fatigable in defending, curating, and preserving her father's legacy. For biographical information on Bewick family members, see Tattersfield, *Thomas Bewick: Complete Illustrative Work*; Uglow, *Nature's Engraver*.

18   As Jaffé notes, "It is impossible to leave the subject of women engravers without a thought for all those hundreds of women in both nineteenth and twentieth centuries who have learned the craft and remained unknown." Jaffé, *Women Engravers*, 124. Surely there is the echo in both Raverat's and Jaffé's words of Virginia Woolf's invoca-tion of the lost female "Anon, who wrote so many poems without signing them." Woolf, *Room of One's Own*, 49.

19   This book joins those by Selborne and Jaffé in addressing the "curious phenomenon" of "the large number of significant women engravers in the twentieth century" that Daunt wonders about. Daunt, *Art and Craft of Wood Engraving*, 12. Selborne refers to the "small-scale, domestic nature of wood-engraving" as one of the reasons "a signif-icant number of female exponents were drawn to the medium, several of whom were among the most respected wood-engravers of the period." Selborne, *British Wood-Engraved Book Illustration*, 11. Jaffé associates "the domestic scale" of wood engraving with "female understanding" of the medium. Jaffé, *Women Engravers*, 8.

20   On the formation of the new public of readers, see Flint, *Woman Reader*; Hammond, *Reading, Publishing*; McAleer, *Popular Reading and Publishing*; Rose, *Intellectual Life*; Wild, *Rise of the Office Clerk*. For related studies on the formation of the middlebrow as a disparaged category of taste in Britain, see Brown and Grover, *Middlebrow Liter-ary Cultures*; Humble, *Feminine Middlebrow Novel*; Macdonald, *Masculine Middlebrow*.

21   Lowerson, "Battles for the Countryside," 262, 260. As with all so-called cults, including the Victorian cult of the child, "the cult of the countryside" is a label that functions as a kind of shorthand or caricature pointing to a complicated cultural and discursive preoccupation. The textual and historical subjects of such cults—the countryside, the child, the child in the countryside—are not as coherent or universal as their total-izing labels suggest.

22   Chase, "This Is No Claptrap," 129; Newby, *Country Life*, 175.

23   Howkins, "Discovery of Rural England," 67; Baldwin, "England," 6. See also Howkins, *Death of Rural England*; Howkins, "Death and Rebirth?"; Brassley et al., *English Coun-tryside*; Burchardt, *Paradise Lost*; Wild, *Village England*.

24   Baldwin, "England," 7.

25 Brassley et al., *English Countryside,* 240. Brassley, Burchardt, and Thompson conclude their revisionary study: "Whether we consider it from a social, cultural, political or economic point of view, the English countryside between the wars is better characterized by growth and innovation than by stagnation or decline" (235).

26 One of Leighton's "sporadic" American lectures, "Wood Engraving: A Lost Art Revived," delivered 1925–39, would have contributed to the association of the modern wood engraving movement with the contradictory notion of revival. See Stevens and Leighton, *Clare Leighton,* 6. Describing a similarly contradictory climate around rural subjects in photography, Bailey contends that editors of interwar mass-circulation publications used photographs of rural craftsmen at work to "provide a memento of the 'living relics' the reader might be expected to encounter on trips into the countryside" rather than "to instruct the reader," which was the intention of the photographers of the Rural Industries Bureau. Bailey, "Rural Industries," 136.

27 Boyes, *Imagined Village,* 2.

28 Mandler, "Against 'Englishness,'" 155.

29 Mandler, *Fall and Rise,* 169, emphasis added.

30 Boyes, *Imagined Village,* 2.

31 Mandler, "Against 'Englishness,'" 170.

32 Corbett et al., "Introduction," x.

33 Corbett et al., "Introduction," x.

34 Ruralist champion William Morris is everywhere in studies of 1920s and 1930s literature, art, craft, design, and printing; other scholars have ably traced his extraordinary impact and legacy for popular and specialist readerships. See, for example, MacCarthy, *Anarchy and Beauty;* Miele, *From William Morris;* Thomas, *Women Art Workers;* Mason et al., *May Morris.* All twentieth-century British wood engravers whose handmade block prints illustrated books, particularly those running along rural themes, are William Morris's direct descendants when judged as creators of beautiful objects designed for everyday use by ordinary people. Yet even a superficial knowledge of Morris's writings, teachings, tapestries, buildings, wallpapers, and politics quickly leads to diagnosis of key differences between Arts and Crafts and Pre-Raphaelite exercises in social renewal through an idealized and revived medieval past and twentieth-century artists' ideologically diverse motivations for seeking inspiration and income in moves to and representations of a contemporary countryside. For an influential consideration of modernist literary "inward" turning to countryside

spaces and ideals, see Esty, *Shrinking Island*. For a revisionary interdisciplinary study that assesses modernist and commercial arts and objects in terms of rural romanticism, see Harris, *Romantic Moderns*. For a sophisticated account of the ways modern markets incorporated Arts and Crafts–like notions of the preindustrial authentic into modernist texts and images, see Outka, *Consuming Traditions*.

35 For theorization of rural-urban art and social relations derived from analysis of relations between rural places, women's history, middlebrow genres, and amateur arts as well as modernist icons and institutions, see Bluemel and McCluskey, *Rural Modernity*. For data on regional variations in "aristocratic flight," see Howkins, "Landowners and Farmers." For a brief history of working-class rural activism, see Lowerson, "Battles for the Countryside."

36 On the class-based skirmishes over rural access and meaning epitomized by the 1932 mass trespass of Kinder Scout in Derbyshire by members of the communist-inspired British Workers' Sports Federation, see Lowerson, "Battles for the Countryside," 268–69.

37 A. G. Street's *Farmer's Glory*, illustrated with wood engravings by Gwen Raverat, represents thousands of British farmers who in the 1930s decreased pasture to rely on dairying. See Brassley, "British Farming," 193–95.

38 Howkins, "Discovery of Rural England," 67.

39 Lowerson, "Battles for the Countryside," 261.

40 *The Middlebrow Network* website quotes Woolf's comment in "Middlebrow," first published 1942, that "[Middlebrows are] the go-between; they are the busybodies who run from one to the other with their tittle tattle and make all the mischief" and Q. D. Leavis's call to arms for minority highbrows to withstand the influence of book clubs that were standardizing taste "at a middlebrow level." See "About: Defining the Middlebrow," Middlebrow Network, accessed March 7, 2025, https://middlebrownetwork .com. See also Sullivan and Blanch, "The Middlebrow."

41 Lowerson, "Battles for the Countryside," 262.

42 The phrase "Green Fascism" is Dominic Head's, summarizing arguments of Raymond Williams and Valentine Cunningham. Head, *Modernity and the English Rural Novel*, 28.

43 Publishers considered wood engraving an ideal illustrative medium for reprints of nineteenth-century classics of rural life. Miller Parker and Leighton fulfilled multiple commissions for wood engravings for novels by Thomas Hardy, including Miller Parker's editions of *Far from the Madding Crowd, Jude the Obscure, The Mayor*

of Casterbridge, The Return of the Native, and *Tess of the D'Urbervilles.* Leighton illustrated Hardy's *The Return of the Native,* his *Under the Greenwood Tree,* and Emily Brontë's *Wuthering Heights.* Along these same rural classic lines, Miller Parker illustrated five volumes of Richard Jefferies's essays, published in the period immediately following World War II, as well as an interwar edition of Thomas Gray's *Elegy Written in a Country Churchyard* and a wartime edition of A. E. Housman's *A Shropshire Lad.* Raverat provided wood engravings for Anthony Trollope, *The Bedside Barsetshire,* and Hassall illustrated multiple works by Anthony Trollope including *"Mary Gresley" and Other Stories* and *"The Parson's Daughter" and Other Stories.* Working through the late 1950s and into the early 1960s, Hassall provided wood engraved illustrations for Mary Russell Mitford's *Our Village,* all of Jane Austen's major novels, her friend Margaret Lane's *The Brontë Story,* Alfred Lord Tennyson's *In Memoriam,* and, in the mid-1960s, an edition of Robert Burns's *Poems.* McLean describes Hassall's wood engravings for a wartime edition of Elizabeth Gaskell's *Cranford* as "genius." McLean, "Joan Hassall as Illustrator," 13.

44   In contrast, modernist texts of the same period were judged to be hard (both difficult and masculine). The exclusions of women's writing from the canons of high (hard) modernism have withstood feminist revision. These sustained exclusions are presumably one of the motivating forces behind the founding in 2017 of the Feminist inter/ Modernist Association and its journal *Feminist Modernist Studies* by one of the first editors of the Modernist Studies Association's field-leading journal, *Modernism/ modernity.* See Laity, "Editor's Introduction." See also the 2017 *Modernism/modernity Print Plus* forum "Mind the Gap! Modernism and Feminist Praxis." In its opening salvo, issue editor Urmila Seshagiri states, "Feminist method should be as indispensable to the study of modernism as women were to the movement's multiple strands."

45   Hamilton, *Wood Engraving and the Woodcut,* 15.

46   Exceptions to this generalization include Harris's *Romantic Moderns,* which reproduces Gertrude Hermes's *Stag,* destined for a reprint of Gilbert White's *Selbourne,* as evidence of interwar interest in village life (170); Montefiore's *Men and Women Writers of the 1930s,* which discusses wood engraving as integral to the history of women's poetry books published in the 1930s (115); and Leaper's related study, *Sybil Andrews Linocuts.* See also Uglow, *Sybil and Cyril.* In an investigation of the material textuality of three early Hogarth Press books illustrated with woodcuts, Sorensen forwards readings of textual and visual relations, production history, and print networks but

does not comment on the meaning of woodcuts themselves as a peculiar, historically significant form of modernist or interwar production. Sorensen, *Modernist Experiments,* 188–251. Raverat also figures in Zimring, "Ballet, Folk Dance."

47 For an acute analysis of the semantic implications of the materiality of the book as a printed object and the peculiar agency of wood in production and reproduction of interwar illustrated books, see Aymes, *Modernist Mediascapes.*

48 This approach owes much to Light's groundbreaking feminist study *Forever England,* which examines the structures of feeling, society, and literature that made English women the standard-bearers of conservative modernity between the wars. For other models for this kind of scholarship, see Collier, *Modern Print Artefacts*; Gitelman, *Paper Knowledge*; Crain, *Story of A*; Hammill, *Sophistication*; Hammill, *Women, Celebrity, and Literary Culture.*

49 Hendrick explains how historians of childhood, following feminist models, put "'children's history' into 'history,'" treating "an 'age' dimension . . . as a 'fundamental category of analysis.'" Hendrick, *Children, Childhood,* 4. Sorensen is unusual in mentioning children's literature in a discussion of "modernism's material afterlives." Sorensen, *Modernist Experiments,* 252, 254. For an analysis of the relations among H. G. Wells's World War I–era war-gaming texts for children, the toy soldier industry in Britain, and cultural fantasies of masculine embodiment, see Flower, "Exemplary Game." For an early appeal for interdisciplinary collaboration between children's literature and modernist scholars, see Westman, "Children's Literature and Modernism."

50 Hammill and Hussey join Bornstein and Sorensen in producing some of the most theoretically sensitive readings of the meanings of material forms, media forms, and historical conditions of book production—what Bornstein calls "lost bibliographic and contextual codes"—for literary readings of early twentieth-century (high) modernist texts. Bornstein, *Material Modernism,* 2. Hammill and Hussey announce at the conclusion of their field-defining introduction that "attention to print culture has provoked a thorough rethinking of the history of modernism." Hammill and Hussey, *Modernist Print Cultures,* 35. Faye Hammill, Celia Marshik, and Andrew Thacker are the founding editors of the recently launched Palgrave Macmillan Material Modernisms book series.

Children's literature scholars have been at the forefront of theorizing verbal–visual, text–paratextual relations in modern picture books. See, for example, Moebius, "Introduction to Picturebook Codes"; Nodelman, *Words About Pictures*; and, more recently, Nikolajeva and Scott, *How Picturebooks Work*; op de Beeck, *Suspended Animation*; Sanders, "Chaperoning Words." See also Mitchell's foundational studies *Iconology* and *Picture Theory*.

"TRUTH IS TO BEND TO NOTHING, BUT ALL TO HER."

1 Quoted in Tattersfield, "Peculiar Spirit and Fancy," 22–23.

ONE GREEN WORLDS IN BLACK AND WHITE

1 Quoted in Spalding, *Gwen Raverat*, 160.

2 Spalding, *Gwen Raverat*, 170.

3 Quoted in Spalding, *Gwen Raverat*, 170.

4 See Delaney, *Neo-Pagans*.

5 For a fascinating record of this period of Raverat's life, see Pryor, *Virginia Woolf and the Raverats*.

6 See Andersen, *Four Tales*; Grahame, *Cambridge Book of Poetry*; Hart, *The Runaway*; Wedgwood, *Bird Talisman*; Pye, *Red-Letter Holiday*; Younge, *Countess Kate*. The last two of these works feature line drawings by Raverat.

7 Compare the brief biographies of John and Joan Hassall in Peppin and Micklethwait, *Dictionary of British Book Illustrators*. John Hassall's children's book illustrations were the inverse of his daughter's, featuring jolly characters defined by thick black outlines. In this he followed William Nicholson, whose *An Alphabet* (1898) introduced Victorian readers, accustomed to the elaborate decorative work of Walter Crane, Leslie Brooke, and Arthur Rackham, to simple designs inspired by English chapbooks.

8 McLean, "Joan Hassall as Illustrator," 9.

9 Hassall, "Introduction," vii.

10 McLean, "Summing Up," 32.

11 McLean, "Joan Hassall as Illustrator," 11. Beedham was one of only three wood engraving instructors active in the interwar period who had passed through the nineteenth-century mass-reproduction apprentice system. See Hamilton, *Wood Engraving and the Woodcut*, 15.

12 Hassall, "Introduction," viii.

13 The lecture was presented by Francis Dodd, who showed a slide of a Bewick illustration of an angler, greatly enlarged. See Hassall, "Introduction," ix; Jaffé, *Women Engravers*, 81.

14 Hassall, "Introduction," x. Hassell cites Selwyn Image's 1924 edition of Bewick's memoir, which had reproductions that were useful to an aspiring art student. The standard edition cited by Bewick scholars and in this study is the 1975 *A Memoir Written by Himself,* edited by Iain Bain.

15 McLean, "Summing Up," 32; McLean, "Joan Hassall as Wood-Engraver," 28. Hassall's first wood engraved book illustration was a frontispiece for her brother Christopher Hassall's book of poems, *Devil's Dyke* (1936). She went on to publish many books with so-called middlebrow publishers, including Cape, Dent, Harrap, Heinemann, Hopetoun Press, Hutchinson, the Limited Editions Club, Oliver and Boyd, and R. Hart-Davis.

16 Hassall, *Dearest Joana,* 2:158, quoted from a letter to Ruari McLean written circa 1951. Hassall's words reverberate in Macdonald's introduction to *The Masculine Middlebrow,* where the "middlebrow is shown to transcend the fixed linear cultural continuum, and to offer experiences not anchored to a desire to be considered intellectual or fashionable, but to the enjoyment of the individual" (8). Early scholars of middlebrow literature and middlebrow books were careful to enclose "middlebrow" in quotation marks to indicate that it was a flexible term of disparagement that could convey judgment of taste, readers, kinds of books, types of magazines, genres of literature, sorts (and sexes) of authors—in fact, pretty much what anyone wanted it to mean. In their introduction to *Middlebrow Literary Cultures,* Brown and Grover say the term is itself a "product of powerful anxieties about cultural authority and processes of cultural transmission. It is a nexus for prejudice towards the lower middle classes, the feminine and domestic, and towards narrative modes regarded as outdated" (1). For discussion of illustrated books as forms of mixed media historically subject to middlebrow diminishment, see Bluemel, "Illustrating *Mary Poppins.*"

17 Quoted in Leighton, "Growth and Shaping," 5.

18 David Leighton, "Clare Leighton: Her Family," 3.

19 David Leighton, "Clare Leighton: Her Family," 4–5.

20 Quoted in David Leighton, "Clare Leighton: Her Family," 5.

21 Leighton studied at the Slade from 1920 to 1923, roughly one decade after Raverat, who was in attendance from 1908 to 1911.

22 Hamilton, *Wood Engraving and the Woodcut,* 54.

23 Hamilton, *Wood Engraving and the Woodcut,* 85. Leon Underwood and several followers formed the English Wood Engraving Society, which held its first exhibition in 1925

at the St. George's Gallery, while the Society of Wood Engravers, under the "patrician" influence of Raverat, among others, held its annual show at the Redfern Gallery. See Hamilton, *Wood Engraving and the Woodcut*, 101–2.

24 Hamilton, *Wood Engraving and the Woodcut*, 97, 98. Hamilton's phrase "shaplier lines" is borrowed from Noel Brailsford's 1923 statement of world aims for socialists contributing to and reading the *New Leader,* the journal he edited that was owned by the International Labour Party.

25 Hickman counts sixty-five books illustrated by Leighton, fourteen of which she wrote. Hickman, "Clare Leighton's Art and Craft," 7.

26 For a historical study that examines why rural landscapes have had such powerful impacts on British people, see Burchardt, *Lifescapes*. Burchardt's project began as an investigation into what others might have called a cult of the countryside—the countryside's increasing popularity through the end of World War II—but shifted to analysis of change in individuals' lifetime relations to the rural landscapes they loved.

27 Leighton traveled throughout the United States in 1940 with the *New York Times* book review editor, Don Adams, working with cotton pickers in the South. This led to the publication of *Southern Harvest* in 1942. In 1931 she spent a week in a lumber camp of the Laurentian Mountains prior to completing her celebrated, exhibited, nonillustrative *Canadian Lumber Camp* series. See Hickman, "Clare Leighton's Art and Craft"; Stevens and Leighton, *Clare Leighton.*

28 Selborne, *British Wood-Engraved Book Illustration,* 381.

29 Leighton's most notable appointment was to a lectureship in Duke University's Art, Aesthetics, and Music Department from 1943 to 1945. Her commission to prepare wood engravings for the seven volumes of *The Frank C. Brown Collection of North Carolina Folklore* came at this time, in the midst of war.

30 Rogerson, "Agnes Miller Parker," 12.

31 Art historians are discreet, with Hamilton describing McCance as an "energetic and opinionated" art critic of the *Spectator* in the 1920s, "a figure of some influence in the art world"; Selborne remarking upon the professional qualifications and experiences of this "Scottish painter sculptor, and one-time art critic"; and Rogerson noting that "the three brief years at Gregynog [in the early 1930s] were among the happiest of their [his and Miller Parker's] marriage." Hamilton, *Wood Engraving and the Woodcut,* 88; Selborne, *British Wood-Engraved Book Illustration,* 146; Rogerson, "Agnes Miller Parker," 21.

32 See Peterson, *Kelmscott Press.* When McCance and Miller Parker moved to the Hammersmith-Chiswick area in the mid-1920s, they would have joined the area's writers Naomi Mitchison, Robert Graves, and A. P. Herbert, sculptor Eric Kennington, theater director Nigel Playfair, and the Central School calligrapher and teacher Edward Johnston. See Hamilton, *Wood Engraving and the Woodcut,* 88.

33 Article quoted in Rogerson, "Agnes Miller Parker," 13. Rogerson locates Miller Parker at Maltman's Green School, Gerrards Cross, at the beginning of the 1920s and at Clapham High School from 1928 to 1930.

34 Miller Parker's early editioned prints *Pigsty* and *Stevedores* of 1926 show the influence of McCance, who was himself influenced by Wyndham Lewis's vorticism. See Rogerson, "Agnes Miller Parker," 13. Hamilton contrasts Rooke's and Underwood's schools, describing the "Conservatism vs. Modernism controversy" that the London press "unsuccessfully" tried to stir up. Hamilton, *Wood Engraving and the Woodcut,* 102.

35 Rogerson, "Agnes Miller Parker," 22.

36 Rogerson, "Agnes Miller Parker," 23.

37 Friends writing in September 1955 refer to Miller Parker's "wonderful" news of her break from Mac and joyfully share the assumption that she "must be like a new born person, to now be surrounded by love and peace instead of that too awful atmosphere, stuck with such a selfish being." They wonder how long she had to "endure such a wretched state of things" and admit that "sometimes we felt terribly worried about you, the prospect for you seemed so grim." They continue: "Thank Goodness your brothers came to your rescue, and they will surely see to it that whatever unpleasantness may come in the near future, and knowing the brute, he may try something—anything, you are now in safe, good hands, and will be protected from the worst that he might do." Jessica and Serge Knish to Agnes Miller Parker, September 20, 1955, File 2, Agnes Miller Parker Archives, National Library of Scotland (NLS).

38 Clipping, *The Bulletin,* September 19, 1958, File 2, Agnes Miller Parker Archives, NLS.

39 Describing Miller Parker's catlike, "silent, solitary, and inscrutable nature," Jaffé comments, "It comes as no surprise that her recreation was fly fishing." Jaffé, *Women Engravers,* 58

40 Raverat's first book illustration project consisted of seven wood engravings for her cousin Frances Cornford's volume of poems for adults, *Spring Morning* (1915).

41 For a literary study that begins with consideration of illustration by a child, the ten-year-old artist, Willie Macready, as a means of rereading the material and critical

histories of Golden Age children's literature, see Smith, *Between Generations,* 3. Op de Beeck "situates the American picture book and its visual-verbal sequences" in the same kinds of cultural and critical contexts of "modernity and the machine age" that shaped the work and reception of the British women wood engravers examined in this study; see op de Beeck, *Suspended Animation,* ix. For foundational work in visual poetics and graphic materialist approaches to writing and literature, see Drucker's trailblazing studies, including *The Visible Word* (1994), *Figuring the Word* (1998), *Graphesis* (2014), and *Inventing the Alphabet* (2022).

42 In order to claim the status of "a field of scholarly interest" for children's literature, scholars have had to adopt contradictory positions. On the one hand, they have had to distinguish, sometimes unwillingly and often defensively, between adults' and children's literatures. See, for example, Lundin, *Constructing the Canon.* On the other hand, their efforts to position "research in children's literature within the context of general literary and cultural theory" has been "essential" for the survival of the field. Kümmerling-Meibauer and Müller, "Introduction," 6.

43 Hunt begins with an anxious rehearsal of Anita Moss's 1981 assertion that "children's literature occupies a place in the tradition of all literature." Hunt, *Criticism, Theory,* 1.

44 Hunt, *Criticism, Theory,* 3.

45 On children's book illustration, see, for example, Nodelman, *Words About Pictures;* Nikolajeva and Scott, *How Picturebooks Work;* op de Beeck, *Suspended Animation.* On children's classics and the Golden Age, see Kümmerling-Meibauer and Müller, "Introduction"; Lundin, *Constructing the Canon;* Styles, *From the Garden to the Street;* Carpenter, *Secret Gardens;* Wullschläger, *Inventing Wonderland;* Gubar, *Artful Dodgers.*

46 Whalley and Chester, *History of Children's Book Illustration,* 183, 185. These authors admire contemporary male wood engravers of children's books Eric Fitch Daglish, Raymond Sheppard, Rex Whistler, and Clifford Webb. Of these, Daglish is allied most closely with Raverat, Miller Parker, and Hassall as an illustrator for children because he worked with the same materials, natural subjects, traditional designs, and popular trade publishers.

47 Most famous among the experimentalist wood engravers are Edward Wadsworth, Paul Nash, Blair Hughes-Stanton, and Eric Ravilious. Hamilton favors the work of Gertrude Hermes and generally prefers the "excitement" of the Underwood school members' characteristic search for "sculptural form" over the Rooke–Central School

members' devotion to integrity of total book design. Hamilton, *Wood Engraving and the Woodcut*, 85, 81. One should be cautious about dividing generations and schools of wood engravers too absolutely in the interwar years, as the expressionist-influenced Paul Nash trained the traditional ruralist Eric Daglish, and the avant-garde Eric Gill published with his St. Dominic's Press the traditionalist Ralph Beedham's manual *Wood Engraving*. Modernist experimenter Underwood trained Blair Hughes-Stanton and Gertrude Hermes, who in turn influenced rural realist Agnes Miller Parker.

48 Whalley and Chester, *History of Children's Book Illustration*, 185, 193, 186.

49 Whalley and Chester, *History of Children's Book Illustration*, 184.

50 Power, *How It Happened*, 169.

51 Power, *How It Happened*, 166.

52 Hunt omits this reading situation—of children reading adults' books—from his taxonomy of possible relations between adults, children, and books. He mentions adults reading books intended for adults, adults reading books intended for children, and children reading books intended for children. See Hunt, *Criticism, Theory*, 45. Literature by children for children, an underresearched category, has tended to receive attention from experts in literacy and education. For a happy exception to this trend, see Smith, *Between Generations*.

53 Rogerson, "Agnes Miller Parker," 70.

54 Selborne's record of her conversations in the early 1980s with Leighton about her rivalry with Miller Parker, along with Selborne's citation of correspondence between Leighton and Gollancz from the Victor Gollancz archives, provides evidence of the complex relations between the most successful 1930s women wood engravers. See Selborne, *British Wood-Engraved Book Illustration*, 379–81.

55 Miller Parker and Bates's first collaboration was *"The House with the Apricot" and Two Other Tales* (1933). This very limited edition of three hundred copies was designed and published by Robert Gibbings at the Golden Cockerel Press. According to the H. E. Bates Companion website, from 1935 to 1940 "Bates wrote the ["Country Life"] column in place of its chief writer, William Beach Thomas." "Country Life," H. E. Bates Companion, accessed April 26, 2023, http://www.hebatescompanion.com. Gollancz had first approached Thomas as a possible author-collaborator for *Through the Woods*. See Rogerson, "Agnes Miller Parker," 36.

56 Agnes Miller Parker to Philip Gibbons, March 3, 1936, MSL/1983/26, National Art Library, Victoria and Albert Museum, London.

57 Agnes Miller Parker to Philip Gibbons, [April] 20, 1936, MSL/1983/26, National Art
    Library, Victoria and Albert Museum, London.

58 Agnes Miller Parker to Philip Gibbons, October 18, 1937, MSL/1983/26, National Art
    Library, Victoria and Albert Museum, London. See also Bluemel, "Windmills and
    Woodblocks."

59 Agnes Miller Parker to Philip Gibbons, October 9, 1936, MSL/1983/26, National Art
    Library, Victoria and Albert Museum, London.

60 Agnes Miller Parker to Philip Gibbons, February 8, 1937, MSL/1983/26, National Art
    Library, Victoria and Albert Museum, London.

61 Bates, *Down the River,* 95.

62 Rogerson "Agnes Miller Parker," 60. Rogerson echoes his concern with Miller Parker's
    "lack of social realism" in his more recent "Creative Wood-Engraved Illustration,"
    although he also notes that in 1962 John Dreyfus, the Limited Editions Club's British
    designer, wrote to the club's owner, then Helen Macy, that "he was 'stunned by the
    beauty and brilliance' of Parker's engravings" (70). Compare Bewick's fearless
    representation of everything from pigsties to privies and the humans using them.
    These are read as signs of his "startling realism . . . confirm[ing] Bewick's credentials
    as an accurate field naturalist, and as an author of integrity." Donald, *Art of Thomas
    Bewick,* 93.

63 Quoted in Rogerson, "Agnes Miller Parker," 37.

64 Bates, *Through the Woods,* 21.

65 Agnes Miller Parker to Philip Gibbons, November 28, 1935, MSL/1983/26, National Art
    Library, Victoria and Albert Museum, London.

66 Grossman, *History of the Limited Editions Club,* 244.

67 Rogerson, "Creative Wood-Engraved Illustration," 62. Macy died on May 20, 1956,
    before Miller Parker published her most important LEC commission, Thomas Hardy's
    Tess of the D'Urbervilles. Miller Parker saved a telegram (undated) from Helen Macy,
    sent to "Miss Agnes Miller Parker 31 Riddrie Knows Glasgow Scotland," that reads, "I
    think you will want to know that George died here this morning." Helen Macy took
    over George's position as director of the LEC and the Heritage Press, with her first
    letter to Miller Parker announcing this decision arriving less than a month after her
    husband's death. Here she described George's books as "brain children," explaining
    that "during our [the Macys'] twenty-eight years of marriage, I was fortunate enough
    to know—either personally or through his talking to me of them—the many artists,

designers, printers, binders and other fine book craftsmen whose creative skills made possible the realization of my husband's brain children. I know I can count on you as one of these to continue to make available to us your cooperation, your interest and your skills." Helen Macy to Agnes Miller Parker, June 15, 1956, File 2, Agnes Miller Parker Archives, NLS. Just over one and a half years later Helen Macy would write with sincere warmth and friendship: "You have done it again! I would have sworn that you couldn't make more beautiful engravings for any book than those for our Tess, but the proof is before my eyes [blocks for *Far from the Madding Crowd*]. I am filled with admiration once more at the way in which you manage to combine force and strength with tenderness and delicacy. I am truly enchanted." Helen Macy to Agnes Miller Parker, December 1, 1957, File 7, Agnes Miller Parker Archives, NLS.

68 Grossman, *History of the Limited Editions Club*, 175.

69 Rubin, *Making of Middlebrow Culture*, xi.

70 Grossman, *History of the Limited Editions Club*, 175.

71 Miller Parker to Gibbons, October 18, 1937. By "this more precious stuff" she meant the LEC edition of Thomas Gray's *Elegy Written in a Country Church-Yard* (1938). Multiple editions, including most recently a 2021 edition published by the Bodleian Library, testify to this work's popularity with readers even as critics have been less impressed. See Rogerson, "Agnes Miller Parker," 43.

72 Grossman, *History of the Limited Editions Club*, 4.

73 Grossman, *History of the Limited Editions Club*, 13.

74 Quoted in Grossman, *History of the Limited Editions Club*, 13.

75 Grossman, *History of the Limited Editions Club*, 2.

76 Exceptions are Benstock, "The Double Image of Modernism"; and Goodwin, "'A Very Pretty Picture M. Matisse.'"

77 Grossman, *History of the Limited Editions Club*, 78.

78 See also Radway's monograph on the Book of the Month Club, *A Feeling for Books*; and Lewis's history of Allen Lane, *Penguin Special*.

79 Goodman, "Words and Pictures," 298.

80 Nodelman, *Words About Pictures*, 193. For assessment of the influence of Nodelman's book on more than two decades of scholarship in multiple fields, advanced by scholars located in diverse institutions and nations, see Hamer et al., *More Words About Pictures*.

81 Nodelman, *Words About Pictures*, 196.

82 Berger, *Ways of Seeing*, 28, 29.

83 Rogerson, "Agnes Miller Parker," 59–60, 63.

84 On color printing in the LEC *Tess*, see Grossman, *History of the Limited Editions Club*, 175.

85 Lubbock, "Defining the Vignette," 48, 42.

86 Lubbock, "Defining the Vignette," 48.

87 Mitchell, *Picture Theory*, 69–70.

88 Charlotte Brontë. *Jane Eyre*, 21.

89 The *Sandglass* article "In Praise of Mrs. McCance," which accompanied Miller Parker's edition of Hardy's *Return of the Native*, makes explicit Macy's assumption that readers read pictures before they read words, stating that the "remarkable" wood engravings by Agnes Miller Parker "will serve as the majestic overture to your reading of the story" (n.p.).

90 Hunt, *Criticism, Theory*, 192, following Paul, "Enigma Variations."

"FIGURES DELINEATED WITH ALL THE FIDELITY AND ANIMATION I WAS ABLE TO IMPART"

1 Carpenter, *Secret Gardens*, 2. O'Malley says that in the last two decades of the eighteenth century, "'transitional' books" that "acknowledged the trend towards middle-class values and ideology in young readers" but still employed earlier popular chapbook forms "flooded" the English book market. O'Malley, *Making of the Modern Child*, 17. Grenby traces the changing definition of chapbooks, arguing that by the late eighteenth century, "with better communication networks allowing more people access to fixed retail facilities, and with those retailers having expanded into material and markets which were previously the domain of the pedlars," it was the "plebeian associations of the texts" that had more influence on their status as chapbooks than their distribution by traveling hawkers. Grenby, "Before Children's Literature," 33, 38. See also the following classic studies of chapbooks: Neuberg, *Chapbooks*; Neuberg, *Penny Chapbooks*; Weiss, *Book About Chapbooks*.

2 Tattersfield, *Thomas Bewick: Complete Illustrative Work*, 1:76.

3 Many of his early critics agreed. Donald cites a piece in the *Analytical Review* that recommends Bewick's *Quadrupeds* as particularly suited to young readers, the pictures "leading them on gradually to a more intellectual understanding of the natural world." Donald, *Art of Thomas Bewick*, 30.

4 The sixth editions of both volumes of *A History of British Birds, Land Birds* and *Water Birds,* were published simultaneously.

5 Darton, *Children's Books in England,* 3rd ed., 9. Darton's is still considered the authoritative account of the history of early English children's literature. In addition to Alderson's 1982 revision of this classic study, see Alderson and de Marez Oyens, *Be Merry and Wise.* Immel reminds us that Locke ignored contemporary children's books, regarding "traditional texts" like Aesop's fables as "perfectly adequate as a child's first reading assignment." Immel, "Children's Books," 30.

6 Tattersfield, *Thomas Bewick: Complete Illustrative Work,* 1:163. Bewick notes in his *Memoir* that he completed the first two and a half chapters of that book in 1822 (29). A cautious Jane Bewick withheld publication of the *Memoir* until 1862.

7 For an extended excerpt of Audubon's account of Bewick, originally published in Audubon's 1831 *Ornithological Biography,* see Bain, "Introduction," xxii.

8 Bain, "Introduction," xxii.

9 Quoted in Bain, "Introduction," xxii.

10 Rayner, a later Bewick mythologizer, assembles in one tiny, beautiful book, *Wood Engravings by Thomas Bewick* (1947), these Victorian critics' most familiar words of praise for Bewick. Per Donald, "interpretations of his work are inevitably associated with notions of Bewick *the man.*" Donald, *Art of Thomas Bewick,* 14; see also chap. 4, on "the Victorian inheritance."

11 Ruskin, "Technics of Wood Engraving," 80, 78.

12 Ruskin, "Appendix," 170.

13 For a detailed account of the process by which nineteenth-century critics turned Bewick from northern artist into wild nature, see Quinn, "'Their Strongest Pine.'" Quinn notes that "Bewick, to Ruskin, is himself a pine" (112).

14 Ruskin, "Appendix," 170.

TWO "A HAPPY HERITAGE"

1 These words are Raverat's to Richard de la Mare, December 20, 1947, quoted in Spalding, *Gwen Raverat,* 390. By the time *Period Piece* came out, Raverat had published with Faber and Faber two other Victorian works with line drawings: Charlotte Yonge's children's novel *Countess Kate* (1948) and the anthology *The Bedside Barsetshire* (1949). In the previous decade she had provided line drawings for Alison Uttley's wonderful *Mustard, Pepper, and Salt,* published by Faber and Faber (1938). Raverat's

illustrated edition of *The Runaway* may yet attain "minor classic" status through its reappearance as a Persephone Books paperback in 2002. Persephone's marketing to adults of the Hart–Raverat children's book coincides with the crossover phenomenon that Falconer associates with publication of adult editions of J. K. Rowling's *Harry Potter* books (1997–2007) and Philip Pullman's winning of the Whitbread Book of the Year for *The Amber Spyglass* (2000). See Falconer, *Crossover Novel*.

2 For full bibliographic information, see Selborne and Newman, *Gwen Raverat*, 87.

3 Raverat's 1932 *Cambridge Book of Poetry for Children* is mentioned in David McKitterick's history of Cambridge University Press as an example of the press's skill as a printer of wood engravings, even as McKitterick does not treat the press's children's books as a dimension of Cambridge's publishing program. McKitterick, *History of Cambridge University Press*, 255. For analysis of institutional publishing histories, including Sutcliffe's history of Oxford University Press, that grant children's publishing a page or two, reflecting the diminished status of children's or juvenile book publishing within mainstream publishing houses, see Reynolds, "Publishing Practices," 23–24.

4 Grahame, *Cambridge Book of Poetry for Children*, 27.

5 "Buttercups and Daisies" appeared in Howitt's 1837 collection *The Christmas Library: Birds and Flowers and Other Country Things*.

6 The July 1916 issue of *Poetry*, vol. 8, no. 4, includes "Poems by Children" (what might be more accurately titled "Poems by Girls"): Arvia Mackaye's "The Purple Gray," four-year-old Hilda Conkling's "Songs I–VIII," and five-year-old Elsa Conkling's "Summertime I–X."

7 Scholarly treatments of Puffin Picture Books are few and far between. The legendary book historian Iain Stevenson presented his research on this series in "The Children's Front: Puffin Books and the Second World War" at the 2012 annual meeting of the Society for the History of Authorship, Reading and Publishing in Dublin. Stevenson died tragically in 2017.

8 Carrington, "Puffin Picture Books," xi.

9 Alderson, *Sing a Song for Sixpence*, 102.

10 Rogerson, *Noel Carrington*, vi.

11 Rogerson, *Noel Carrington*, vi.

12 The importance of Allen Lane and the paperback revolution for consideration of post-1930 British publishing, including children's publishing, cannot be overstated. In

Book Makers, a study of British publishing in the twentieth century, Stevenson titles his chapter on the 1930s "'The Penguins Are Coming!'" and notes that he could have devoted it exclusively to Allen Lane (73).

13 Carrington, "Puffin Picture Books," xii.

14 Carrington, "Puffin Picture Books," xii.

15 Rogerson, *Noel Carrington*, 2.

16 Stevenson indirectly brings a discussion of Cambridge University Press and Oxford University Press into his conversation about Penguin and Puffin books in his chapter on 1930s bookmakers, but only to emphasize the differences between scholarly and trade publishing. He notes among other things that both cup and oup were considered university departments and were thus working in very different financial climates than trade publishers; even as Oxford was more commercially minded than Cambridge, both were governed by policies established by ruling committees of university academics. See Stevenson, *Book Makers*, 78–81.

17 For a tendentious account of the material, historical, and ideological processes that determine the making of children's classics and canons, see Lundin, *Constructing the Canon*.

18 On the complex and culturally specific social factors that led to the devaluation of children's publishing in Britain, see Reynolds, "Publishing Practices," 21, 24. Reynolds's argument is indirectly continued in Stevenson's chapter "'No More Gentlemen,'" an account of women's rise to management in British publishing of the late 1970s. Stevenson, *Book Makers*, 203–43.

19 Grahame's section subtitles also fall into these rough divisions of pastoral ("Seasons and Weather," "Fur and Feather"), romantic ("Arms and the Man," "Dream-Land"), or both ("Green Seas and Sailor Men").

20 Only seven poems appear in both volumes: Thomas Beddoes's "Dreams to Sell" ("From *Dream-pedlary*" in Whitlock's volume), Richard Hovey's "The Sea Gipsy," Wordsworth's "Written in March," Tennyson's "Blow, Bugle, Blow" ("Song from *The Princess*" in Whitlock's volume), Bridges's "London Snow," and Thomas Hardy's "Weathers," with Lord Macaulay's "Horatius" represented in full in Grahame's Cambridge anthology and in part in Whitlock's Oxford anthology.

21 For analysis of the sometimes ludicrous values that have guided compilers and publishers who wanted their poetry anthologies to be taken seriously as potential "classics," see Styles, "'From the Best Poets'?"

22 The Opies authored or edited more than thirty other texts on children's literature and culture, including collections with Allen Lane's decidedly more middlebrow Penguin house, but Hassall did not contribute wood or scraperboard engravings to any of these.

23 The Opies may describe Hassall as "the ideal collaborator" (x), but their closing section, "Sources of the Illustrations" (211–15), renders her contributions nearly invisible by identifying sources for only the eighteenth- and nineteenth-century woodcuts and wood engravings reproduced within the volume. It would take the most assiduous of readers to work their way through hundreds of pages and woodcuts to determine by a process of elimination which illustrations are Hassall's. The contradictory nature of Hassall's achievement is evident in her status as the illustrator whose modern genius is proven by her ability to pass as an eighteenth-century male engraver. It is important to remember that the Opies' amateur interdisciplinary enterprise was itself contradictory, both supremely conservative and utterly new and subversive.

24 OUP was more fully committed than CUP to general and trade publishing, though its mandate, like Cambridge's, was to advance academic monographs and treatises, not popular publishing. See Stevenson, *Book Makers,* 238–39. It is telling that McAleer doesn't mention CUP in *Popular Reading and Publishing* and mentions OUP only twice, both in connection with Captain W. E. Johns's "Biggles" aviation and war books (58, 142). For an analysis of the dominant weekly letterpress children's papers such as *Magnet, Gem,* and *Boys' Friend* that takes into account the reading habits of lower-middle-class and working-class youth, see McAleer, *Popular Reading and Publishing,* chap. 5, "'We Must Prevent the Leakage.'" As with Stevenson's history, McAleer's implies the incongruity of scholarly publishers adding children's trade books to their lists.

25 In *The Wood Engravings of Joan Hassall,* Ruari McLean, described by Stevenson as "the leading typographer of his generation," who after the war worked at Penguin, includes selected reproductions of Hassall's engravings from these tiny "beguiling" volumes. McLean, "Joan Hassall as Illustrator," 15; Stevenson, *Book Makers,* 135. McLean's brief critical biography, "Joan Hassall as Illustrator," is also valuable. See also Chambers, "Hassall, Joan."

26 These titles were Puffin Picture Books no. 12, Enid Marx's *Book of Rigamaroles or Jingle Rhymes* (1945), and no. 91, H. A. Rey's *"Mary Had a Little Lamb" and Other Nursery Songs* (1951). Penguin extended Allen Lane's early commitment to children's poetry

with publication of the Opies' *Puffin Book of Nursery Rhymes* (1963, reissued 1999) and Brian Patten's *The Puffin Book of Twentieth Century Verse* (1991).

27 See Whalley and Chester, *History of Children's Book Illustration*, 177–213. These authors mourn the end of the gift-book age brought about by the cutbacks of World War I. They claim World War II proved most disastrous for quality children's illustration in Britain, even as they note the appearance in the 1950s of the illustrators who would transform British children's books in the 1960s: Charles Keeping, Brian Wildsmith, and Dr. Seuss.

28 McAleer, *Popular Reading and Publishing*, 148.

29 Quoted in McAleer, *Popular Reading and Publishing*, 148.

30 McAleer, *Popular Reading and Publishing*, 152.

31 For an inspired model of how to read framed engravings and unframed vignettes in terms of contemporary culture and attitudes toward children and children's books, see Thompson, "Enclosure and Childhood."

32 Hassall herself subscribed to the idea that the text is primary, illustration secondary, but that the best illustration allows "a commentary or extension of the text such as is possible with poetry or natural history." Hassall, "Introduction," xii.

33 Styles, "'From the Best Poets'?," 193.

34 Women were not considered to be full members of Oxford University until 1920 and of Cambridge University until 1947. For representation of women's positions in Cambridge at the time when university celibacy rules were beginning to relax, see Raverat, *Period Piece.*

35 McKitterick, *History of Cambridge University Press*, 374.

36 McKitterick, *History of Cambridge University Press*, 22.

37 McKitterick, *History of Cambridge University Press*, 15. As McKitterick explains, in the early decades of the twentieth century, the press established a general list in accordance with national trends, but in the 1920s this meant publication of Cambridge titles such as G. F. Browne's *A Year Among the Persians,* and in the 1930s, it meant publication of the heavily illustrated survey *Greek Sculpture and Painting.* "Enormous popular success" was reserved for Cambridge author Sir Arthur Eddington's *Space, Time and Gravitation* and James Jeans's expanded lecture *The Mysterious Universe* (265).

38 Sutcliffe, *Oxford University Press*, 250. American university presses rarely publish children's books, in good taste or bad, and many American academics would be

surprised to learn that OUP and Oxford University, with its incomparable Opie Collection, are regarded as synonymous with good children's literature and good children's books. The Opies' association with OUP and Oxford began after a credentialed member of the academic community, Dr. Richard Hunt, the Bodleian's keeper of Western manuscripts, "personally effected the crucial introductions." Avery and Briggs, "Introduction," 1.

"THE OVERFLOWINGS OF AN ACTIVE, WILD DISPOSITION"

1 Bewick's 1804 preface to *Water Birds* concludes with the plea that "the reader, impressed with sentiments of humanity, on viewing the portraits [of birds], spare and protect the originals" (vi).

2 A gallows in the background of a vignette of two boys who are cruelly hanging a dog predicts their fates. See Tattersfield, *Thomas Bewick: Complete Illustrative Work,* 1:40. For a historian's description of rural boys' pleasures that confirms Bewick's memories of his rural childhood, in which "first came bird's nesting . . . and after that chasing small animals," see Thomas, "Children in Early Modern England." Thomas notes that in the eighteenth century, middle-class attitudes toward animals were changing, making Bewick one among many "enlightened adults" of the period who registered horror at children's torture of animals (61).

3 Tattersfield, *Thomas Bewick: Graphic Worlds,* 117. *Cottage Tales for Little People; or, The Amusing Repository for All Good Boys and Girls* was published in Glasgow by Lumsden & Son sometime between 1815 and 1820. Its illustrations are often attributed to Bewick, although that has not been established definitively.

4 See Tattersfield's reproductions of several Bewick children's book cover designs in *Thomas Bewick: Complete Illustrative Work,* vol. 2. There are illustrations of girls outside, but in each case the boys are more active than the girls. Examples include images of "two boys pushing a girl on a swing" (744), "boys playing shuttlecock, watched by a girl nursing a doll" (742), and "three boys playing leapfrog, watched by a bonneted girl peeking from behind a tree" (744). Compare, for instance, the hopelessly vigorous pursuer of outdoor games, Catherine Morland, in Jane Austen's *Northanger Abbey.*

5 There are only two illustrations of boys indoors in Bewick's *British Birds,* both in *Land Birds.* One depicts a ragged country boy having nits combed out of his hair, the other shows a well-dressed boy riding to hounds on a rocking horse.

THREE THE FINE ART OF MASS REPRODUCTION

1 Selborne, *British Wood-Engraved Book Illustration,* 379.

2 Hamilton, *Wood Engraving and the Woodcut,* 136.

3 Selborne, *British Wood-Engraved Book Illustration,* 381.

4 See Marcus, "'Creative Treatment of Actuality'"; Mellor, "Documentary Impulse"; Bluemel, "Ordinary Places."

5 Baxendale and Pawling, *Narrating the Thirties,* 18. For a case study of another 1930s cultural response to the growing crisis, the Arts League of Service's Travelling Theatre, see West, "'Within the Reach of All.'" As West notes, the theater was one of many democratizing arts organizations that, like the films, novels, reportage, and other narrative forms Baxendale and Pawling discuss, sought "to bring art to *all* the people" (227).

6 Baxendale and Pawling, *Narrating the Thirties,* 18. Baxendale and Pawling caution against the idea that realism and documentary are "just transparent windows on the 'real world' of the people." Rather, as Stuart Hall and Pierre Bourdieu remind us, they are "*encodings* of meaning which actively construct the object of their gaze, as well as recording it" (20).

7 See, for example, Baxendale and Pauling, *Narrating the Thirties*; Bryant, *Auden and Documentary*; Montefiore, *Men and Women Writers.*

8 Feminist critic Marsha Bryant argues that the "'homosocial' structure of thirties documentary practice" pursued by Grierson, Paul Rotha, W. H. Auden, George Orwell, J. B. Priestley, and others in the "largely male network" of British documentarists constructed an aggressively masculine discourse of reality that has ever since defined documentary forms and politics. Bryant, *Auden and Documentary,* 12–13, 23. For an important feminist treatment of Orwell's *Road to Wigan Pier* and other 1930s men's texts that deployed "a brilliant rhetoric of authenticity," see Montefiore, *Men and Women Writers,* 11.

9 See Edwards's authoritative biography, *Victor Gollancz.*

10 Hamilton, *Wood Engraving and the Woodcut,* 145; Selborne, *British Wood-Engraved Book Illustration.*

11 Selborne, *British Wood-Engraved Book Illustration,* 2.

12 Selborne, *British Wood-Engraved Book Illustration,* 2.

13 Selborne, *British Wood-Engraved Book Illustration,* 2.

14 For a parallel argument advocating increased critical attention to the linocut prints of Ethel Spowers and other Australian women artists, see Sim, "The Linocuts of Ethel Spowers." Sim analyzes the critical biases that have led Spowers's 1930s artwork to be categorized as "escapist or devoid of social comment," diminished as "a milder form of modernism" (355).

15 Selborne omits "the more conventional Bewick-style pictorial artists" from her vast study, but admits that "literal Bewick or symbolist Blakean elements are never far from the minds of most of those illustrators discussed who, consciously or unconsciously, are steeped in English pastoral and literary tradition." She continues, "Due largely to this inheritance and to the widespread interest in typography and printing, wood-engraved book illustration between the wars was essentially a British phenomenon." Selborne, *British Wood-Engraved Book Illustration*, 3.

16 Jaffé, *Women Engravers*, 45.

17 Leighton, *Wood Engraving and Woodcuts*, 94. Plock describes "self-professed highbrows" suspiciously monitoring the new public of readers "lest they debased cultural standards or, worse yet, encroached on [their] intellectual territories." Plock, "New Reading Public," 135.

18 Hamilton, *Wood Engraving and the Woodcut*, 113.

19 Hamilton, *Wood Engraving and the Woodcut*, 136.

20 Leighton told Gollancz in a letter that *Four Hedges* was not to be "a professional gardening book, but only a year in an ordinary garden." Quoted in Selborne, *British Wood-Engraved Book Illustration*, 379. For discussion of the period's trendsetting master gardener, Gertrude Jekyll, whose popular garden books began with *Wood and Garden* (1899), see Page and Smith, *Women, Literature, and the Arts*, "Introduction."

21 The slightly resentful description of Orwell is John Baxendale's, appearing in the introduction to his study of J. B. Priestley, who, like Leighton, is an important but understudied 1930s documentary writer, critically reimagined "as some kind of conservative ruralist." Baxendale, *Priestley's England*, 1.

22 Baxendale and Pawling, *Narrating the Thirties*, 45.

23 Glyn Salton-Cox describes Valentine Auckland's *Country Conditions*, brought out by the communist publisher Lawrence and Wishart (1936), as a more deeply committed socialist documentary of Depression-era rural life. He theorizes that a "certain

anxiety of influence" determined the similar styles and structures of the period's most famous documentary, *The Road to Wigan Pier,* and its "surprisingly queer progenitor." Salton-Cox, "Timely Interventions," 161.

24 Leighton, "The Convictions of a Writer-Artist," 74, lecture delivered at Coker College, 1949.

25 Harris, *Romantic Moderns,* 174.

26 Benjamin's "The Work of Art in the Age of Mechanical Reproduction" informs this as other arguments about the modernist possibilities of the arts of mechanical reproduction. See also Berger's critique of the values of auraed art in his mass-reproduced, verbal-visual, multimedia performance, *Ways of Seeing.*

27 For judiciously chosen, wisely introduced, and conveniently juxtaposed excerpts of F. R. Leavis's *Mass Civilization and Minority Culture* (1930) and Q. D. Leavis's *Fiction and the Reading Public* (1932), see Deane, *History in Our Hands.*

28 Harris, *Romantic Moderns,* 174. Where does reality end and dream begin? When accessed in February 2023, the Wikipedia entry for "Chalfont St Giles" included a photograph representing the same view and perspective as Leighton's 1931 wood engraving of the village center. As of this writing (May 2025), however, the image has been replaced by a close-up of the Norman church.

29 Readers may understand Boym's term "restorative nostalgia" as signaling this negative, bad, or regressive nostalgia. See Boym, *Future of Nostalgia,* xviii, 41–49.

30 A similar kind of thinking is implied by W. J. Keith's decision to begin each chapter in *The Rural Tradition* and *Regions of the Imagination* with unattributed, decontextualized Bewick vignettes.

31 Chase and Shaw, "Dimensions of Nostalgia," 2.

32 Lowenthal, "Nostalgia Tells It Like It Wasn't," 20; Chase and Shaw, "Dimensions of Nostalgia," 2.

33 Chase and Shaw, "Dimensions of Nostalgia," 2.

34 Chase, "This Is No Claptrap," 128.

35 Chase was in part responding to the Englishness debates of the 1980s launched by Wiener in *English Culture and the Decline of the Industrial Spirit, 1850–1980* (1981). Matless put these debates to rest in *Landscape and Englishness* (1998), redefining disciplinary priorities and approaches for twenty-first-century studies of rural history and geography. See, for example, Howkins, *Death of Rural England*; Burchardt, *Paradise Lost*; Wild, *Village England*; Brassley et al., *English Countryside.*

36 Chase, "This Is No Claptrap," 129.

37 Rural and visual culture studies of modern Britain come together most closely in
Harris, *Romantic Moderns*; Shirley, *Rural Modernity*; Elson and Shirley, *Creating the
Countryside*; Bluemel and McCluskey, *Rural Modernity*; Sillars, *Picturing England*;
Spalding, *Real and the Romantic*.

38 Sillars, publishing with Oxford University Press, aims for a trade market, his book
competing with Spalding's *The Real and the Romantic* in terms of price and number of
illustrations. Spalding follows Harris in choosing Thames and Hudson as a publisher
for her colorful, richly illustrated volume on interwar art. Although Spalding does not
treat women wood engravers, her study aims to bring "to the fore women, be they artists, collectors, editors or curators" (15), acknowledging the difference sex and gender
made for women artists "in a male-dominated art world" (12).

39 For a similar argument about multiplying nostalgias for the interwar and wartime
countryside and for the *literature* of the countryside, see Head, *Modernity and the
English Rural Novel.*

40 Sillars says that Leighton's illustrations for the 1929 reprint of Thomas Hardy's
Return of the Native succeed because they approach the "velvety depth" of an
eighteenth-century mezzotint, while the "image's stylistic control holds [the reader]
at a distance." Sillars, *Picturing England*, 153. While one might object that the
illustrations in this 1929 book are mucky, flat examples of Leighton's depth engraving,
the point is that elsewhere (for example, in his analysis of Edric Holmes's *London's
Countryside*, 1927), Sillars says that the artist's "distance" from his subject generates
bad or invented nostalgia through the same strategies that liberate Leighton into
the present.

41 Bowker, *Inside George Orwell*, 137. For analysis of relations between "Orwell's
landscape of sexual crisis," his fictional representations of "rural sex," and social
challenges to "the established patriarchy," see Wood, "George Orwell, Desire," 413. For
a memoir describing the violent turn Orwell's rural sexual ventures could take, see
Buddicom, *Eric and Us*. For an intelligent and sensitive assessment of this and other
accounts of Orwell's sexual aggression, see Taylor, *Orwell: The New Life.*

42 On the debate over Gollancz's likely advance to Orwell for his trip to the industrial
north, see Taylor, *Orwell: The Life*, 174–76. In the later work *Orwell: The New Life*,
Taylor writes simply that "an advance of £50 is thought to have changed hands" (233).

43 Bowker, *Inside George Orwell*, 180.

44 Orwell's biographers track his continuing conflicts with Gollancz, including the latter's refusal to consider *Homage to Catalonia* and his decline of *Animal Farm.* See Taylor, *Orwell: The New Life,* 327, 430–31.

45 The phrase is Orwell's from *Down and Out in Paris and London,* cited approvingly by Deane in *History in Our Hands,* which begins by citing Beatrix Campbell's early feminist critique of the "posh, lanky young man" Gollancz had commissioned to report on economic devastation in the north. Campbell, *Wigan Pier Revisited,* 1.

46 Taylor describes Orwell's "observant progress" north as "double-sided, awe and distaste for the dark, satanic landscapes mixed with sedulous nature notes." Taylor, *Orwell: The Life,* 171. For a more romantic view of Orwell's gardening and its meaning for his political reportage, see Solnit, *Orwell's Roses.*

"MY *WILD GOOSE CHASE*"

1 Uglow, *Nature's Engraver,* 59.

2 Donald, *Art of Thomas Bewick,* 113.

3 Donald, *Art of Thomas Bewick,* 105–6.

4 Donald, *Art of Thomas Bewick,* 106.

5 Donald, *Art of Thomas Bewick,* 106.

6 Donald, *Art of Thomas Bewick,* 196.

7 Tattersfield, "Peculiar Spirit and Fancy," 18.

FOUR JOAN HASSALL'S SALTIRE CHAPBOOKS

1 For biographical sources on Joan Hassall, see Chambers, "Books and Bookplates"; Chambers, "Hassall, Joan"; McLean, "Joan Hassall as Illustrator." See also Hassall, "Introduction."

2 Of the thirteen Saltire Chapbooks published, ten were designed by Hassall and feature her wood engravings.

3 Only Saltire Chapbook No. 1 lacks a colored cover border.

4 Addison, "Joan Hassall, Wood-Engraver."

5 For discussion of the "transitional books" of the eighteenth century that extended the forms and cultural values of chapbooks into the early nineteenth century, see O'Malley, *Making of the Modern Child,* 17–38. According to O'Malley, "Rational, moral, and more or less strictly didactic children's books coexisted with works combining

plebeian constructions and middle-class objectives, and with traditional chapbooks and fairy tales in the children's book market" (124).

6   Chambers, "Books and Bookplates," xxv–xxvi.

7   The Saltire Society Publications Committee's report of 1945–46 records: "We doubled our issue of Chapbooks this year, printing 4,000 instead of 2,000 and were amply justified by the results. The Marriage of Robin Redbreast and the Wren was immensely popular and had sold out a week before Christmas." Saltire Society, Publications Committee Minutes and Reports, Acc. 9393/936 n.d., circa 1944–49, NLS.

8   Bruce, *To Foster and Enrich.* For studies that honor Hassall as among the most dynamic of the twentieth century's wood engravers, see Addison, "Joan Hassall, Wood-Engraver"; Chambers, "Books and Bookplates"; McLean, "Joan Hassall as Illustrator." These studies combat interpretations such as Selborne's that describe Hassall as a producer of "parochial 'neo-picturesque' work." Selborne, *British Wood-Engraved Book Illustration,* 397.

9   This body was also sometimes referred to as the Saltire Society Publications Sub-Committee. The Saltire Society files held at the National Library of Scotland are inventoried, but the documents are not individually cataloged or numbered.

10 Marsh, "Patronage in Art To-Day," 78; Freedman, "Every Man His Own Lithographer," 104; Williams, "Art for the People," 115.

11 Hassall, "Introduction," ix.

12 Hassall, *Dearest Joana,* 62–63.

13 Hassall, *Dearest Joana,* 63.

14 Thomas, "Hassall, John"; McLean, "Joan Hassall as Illustrator," 10.

15 Thomas, "Hassall, John."

16 McLean, "Joan Hassall as Illustrator," 11.

17 Chambers, "Hassall, Joan."

18 McLean, "Joan Hassall as Illustrator," 12.

19 Chambers, "Books and Bookplates," xxii.

20 Bewick, *Memoir,* 63.

21 Biographers debate the exact dates of Hassall's stay in Scotland. McLean says she arrived in early 1941, while Chambers says she arrived in 1940. McLean, "Joan Hassall as Illustrator," 13; Chambers, "Books and Bookplates," xxv. Addison says that correspondence shows Hassall was back in London by 1945, although there is a letter cited in

Hassall's *Dearest Joana,* from 29 George Square, Edinburgh, to her brother Christopher that, according to editor Brian North Lee, was written in March 1946. The letter itself is undated. Addison, "Joan Hassall, Wood-Engraver"; Hassall, *Dearest Joana,* 1:134.

22 Joan Hassall to Ruari McLean, August 25, 1950, Joan Hassall Letters to Ruari McLean, Acc. 10732, 1950–1952, NLS.

23 McLean, "Joan Hassall as Illustrator," 14.

24 Joan Hassall to John Guest, undated, MS 4624 A/70, John Guest Collection, Special Collections, University of Reading.

25 Hassall to Guest, undated.

26 Joan Hassall to Ruari McLean, February 12, 1952, Joan Hassall Letters to Ruari McLean, Acc. 10732, 1950–1952, NLS.

27 McLean, "Joan Hassall as Illustrator," 15.

28 For information on Saltire Society networks, see Addison, "Joan Hassall, Wood-Engraver," in which Addison cites Smith, "Construction of Cultural Identity."

29 Most of the Saltire Society Publications Committee annual reports and minutes of the 1940s are stored at the National Library of Scotland in Edinburgh: Saltire Society, Publications Committee Minutes and Reports, Acc. 9393/936 n.d., circa 1944–49.

30 Minutes of 31 August [1943?], Saltire Society, Publications Committee Minutes and Reports, Acc. 9393/936 n.d., circa 1944–49, NLS.

31 Minutes of 25 September [1944?], Saltire Society, Publications Committee Minutes and Reports, Acc. 9393/936 n.d., circa 1944–49, NLS.

32 Minutes of 25 September [1944?].

33 Minutes of 17 May 1945, Saltire Society, Publications Committee Minutes and Reports, Acc. 9393/936 n.d., circa 1944–49, NLS.

34 Minutes of 17 May 1945.

35 Quoted in Bruce, *"To Foster and Enrich,"* 16.

36 Quoted in Bruce, *"To Foster and Enrich,"* 17.

37 Quoted in Bruce, *"To Foster and Enrich,"* 17.

38 Bruce, *"To Foster and Enrich,"* 15, 17. Hassall contributed her least characteristic, most modernist wood engravings to Eric Linklater's *"Sealskin Trousers" and Other Stories* (1947).

39 R.H. [Robert Hurd] to Sir Robert M'Vittie Grant, November 3, 1944, Saltire Society, Publications Committee General Correspondence 1941–1957, Acc. 9393/944, NLS.

40 R. H. to Grant, November 3, 1944.

41 Compare, for example, Sorensen's discussion of the "conflicting motives" of Virginia and Leonard Woolf's Hogarth Press in the early years, when it announced itself as publishing "at low prices" limited editions of works "which could not, because of their merits appeal to a very large public." Sorensen, *Modernist Experiments,* 195, 193.

42 *1944 Annual Report of Saltire Publications,* n.p., Saltire Society, Publications Committee General Correspondence 1941–1957, Acc. 9393/944, NLS.

43 *1944 Annual Report,* n.p.

44 Bruce, *"To Foster and Enrich,"* 24.

45 Bruce, *"To Foster and Enrich,"* 41.

46 Bruce, *"To Foster and Enrich,"* 41.

47 Bruce, *"To Foster and Enrich,"* 42. John Oliver was president of the society at the outbreak of the war and later honorary secretary. Bruce, *"To Foster and Enrich,"* 22.

48 The rise of women in book illustration, the arts, and the printing and publishing trades is directly attributable to the enlistment of able-bodied men in the armed services during World War II. One can measure the impact of war on women's local professional leadership by reading through the minutes of the Saltire Society Publications Committee. In terms of names mentioned, whether as officers of the society or as authors of books, women are much in evidence in the 1940s. In the postwar period, men dominate.

49 Whalley and Chester, *History of Children's Book Illustration,* 28.

50 Benson, *Printed Picture.*

51 McLean, "Joan Hassall as Wood-Engraver," 23, 22.

52 McLean, "Joan Hassall as Wood-Engraver," 23–24.

53 Leighton, *Wood-Engraving and Woodcuts,* 94.

54 Leighton, *Wood-Engraving and Woodcuts,* 94.

55 Leighton, *Wood-Engraving and Woodcuts,* 94. For an exploration of the meaning for this vast new public of the "everyday arts" of experimental modernism, see West, "'Within the Reach of All.'"

56 Leighton, *Wood-Engraving and Woodcuts,* 95.

57 Leighton, *Wood-Engraving and Woodcuts,* 94, 95.

58 Lambert, *Art in England.* See also Lewis, *Penguin Special.*

59 Marsh, "Patronage in Art To-Day," 79.

60 Freedman, "Every Man His Own Lithographer," 105.

61 Williams, "Art for the People," 115.

"I INWARDLY BID FAREWELL, TO THE WHINNEY WILDS"

1 During the Covid-19 pandemic, Cherryburn, like all other public monuments and museums, was shuttered. It reopened as a National Trust small property, open to the public two days a week and by appointment only.

2 Tattersfield, *Thomas Bewick: Complete Illustrative Work*, 1:125.

3 For consideration of the imperial contexts influencing Bewick's posthumous reputation, see Donald, *Art of Thomas Bewick*, 182–86.

4 Quoted in Benson, *Printed Picture*, 22.

5 Benson, *Printed Picture*, 22. The description "an artist of nature's own making" is quoted from Donald, *Art of Thomas Bewick*, 187, quoting Doubleday, "Life and Works" (1845).

6 Gubar urges us to resist the "colonization paradigm" of children's reading, which critically posits children as passive receptors of adults' texts, and to recognize instead "the tremendous power that adults and their texts have over young people, while still allowing for the possibility that children . . . can nevertheless navigate through this arena of competing currents in diverse and unexpected ways." Gubar, *Artful Dodgers*, 32–33.

FIVE PASTORALS AND PETTICOATS

1 In Pryor, *Virginia Woolf and the Raverats*, 110. See Bluemel, "'Definite, Burly, and Industrious.'"

2 Throughout this chapter, "pastoral" signifies the second, most general, of four uses of the word that Gifford enumerates in *Pastoral*: an "area of content" that "refers to any literature that describes the country as providing an implicit or explicit contrast to the urban. . . . A delight in the natural is assumed in describing these texts as pastorals" (2). Several of the motifs of classic pastoral, the "historic form" or "genre" of Gifford's first category in his pastoral taxonomy, are also relevant: not shepherds per se, but rather the "bucolic clown" ("Shakespeare's 'simples,'" "Thomas Hardy's 'heathfolk,'" or, we might add, Olga in Hart's *The Runaway*), who speaks complex truths in the language of a reader who, as a member of the court or metropolitan elite, is both motivation and destination of pastoral forms since Theocritus wrote his *Idylls* (7, 18, 16).

3 A confluence of diminishing metaphors has organized along similar binary paths histories of negative academic receptions of women's, children's, middlebrow, and

pastoral literatures. As feminist critics have long understood, preferred qualities associated with sexually compliant and conventionally gendered girls and women— weakness, prettiness, softness, dependence, and responsiveness—come, by a flip of a critical coin that transcends all dialectical logic, to represent exactly that which is despised in proximate places and discourses assigned to women: their houses, gardens, children, and writing. This history of sexist metaphorical thinking cautions us against any too-facile, too-righteous use of the word "pastoral" in the third, supposedly progressive, ecocritical tradition that Gifford defines: "'pastoral' as pejorative, implying that the pastoral vision is too simplified [like silly girls] and thus an idealization [like pretty women] of the reality of life in the country." Gifford, *Pastoral*, 2.

4 Leighton also published the children's picture book *The Musical Box* (1932), about restoration of a town, around the same time she was working on *The Wood That Came Back*.

5 Gifford, *Pastoral*, 11.

6 For comparison of criticism on modernist pastoral and rural modern literature, see Bluemel and McCluskey, *Rural Modernity in Britain*, "Introduction."

7 Empson, *Some Versions of Pastoral*, 170, 25.

8 Hubble, "Intermodern Assumption," 180.

9 Hubble, "Intermodern Assumption," 180. Empson had been revised within forty years by Williams's *Country and the City* (1973), Keith's *Rural Tradition* (1974), and Cavaliero's *Rural Tradition in the English Novel* (1977). See Gifford, *Pastoral*, 9–10, 72–75.

10 Hubble, "Intermodern Assumption," 180–81.

11 Empson, quoted in Hubble, "Intermodern Assumption," 180.

12 See Bluemel, "Introduction." For alternate approaches to and theories of pastoral modernism, see Esty, *Shrinking Island*; Light, *Forever England*; Humble, *Feminine Middlebrow Novel*; Head, *Modernity and the English Rural Novel*; Bluemel and McCluskey, *Rural Modernity in Britain*.

13 Harris, *Romantic Moderns*.

14 Marinelli, *Pastoral*, 12. For a concise summary of recent theories of pastoral's more or less escapist, conservative, or repugnant social and political effects, see Gifford, *Pastoral*, 10–13.

15 Gifford, *Pastoral*, 11, emphasis added.

16 Gubar finds evidence of Golden Age children's authors (often women) representing young people as coproducers of texts or, more accurately, "collaborators-after-the-fact."

Though unwieldy, this phrase helpfully deconstructs critical notions of separate adults' and children's literatures as it simultaneously deconstructs the binaries separating "innocent" Victorian children from experience and agency. Gubar, *Artful Dodgers*, 8.

17 Quoted in Gifford, *Pastoral*, 11.

18 Gifford, *Pastoral*, 22.

19 Boym, *Future of Nostalgia*.

20 The sexism implicit in such logic is evident in literary and art criticism that treats art deemed sentimental with distaste. For example, Donald describes "late eighteenth-century depictions of farming life, particularly those in popular prints intended for decorative applications" as "characterized by a prettifying sentimentality." She distinguishes such "confections" from Bewick's images, "which convey a refreshing authenticity." Donald, *Art of Thomas Bewick*, 125. Here Bewick's gender confirms the superiority of his authentic art, just as feminine terms like "decorative," "prettifying," and "confection" confirm the inferiority of sentimental art. Paradoxically, Donald preserves Bewick's art from a degrading sentimental taint while acknowledging that Bewick collected exactly the sentimental farming scenes that were (supposedly) sunk below his sights.

21 Jeffrey typifies this logic with his comment that "one way of laying hold on reality and of resisting the perils of a sophisticated environment was to walk back along what H. E. Bates called 'the summer road of my childhood.'" Jeffrey, *British Landscape*, 12.

22 Higonnet, *Pictures of Innocence*, 28; see 23–30. Like pastoral images, the image of the romantic child "replaces what we have lost, or what we fear to lose" (28–29).

23 Reynolds, *Children's Literature*, 16. Gubar argues that Golden Age authors like Carroll, Ruskin, and Barrie were skeptical critics who conceived of child characters and readers as "socially saturated beings," resisting the "Child of Nature paradigm." Gubar, *Artful Dodgers*, 4, 5.

24 Reynolds, *Children's Literature*, 15.

25 The Victorian cult of childhood is commonly seen as a cultural effect of social conditions that led to "appalling" rates of infant and childhood mortality. Reynolds, *Children's Literature*, 16. Even as late as 1913, infant mortality rates for England and Wales were 77 deaths under age one year per 1,000 live births for wealthier families, and 152 deaths per 1,000 for infants of unskilled laborers. Hendrick, *Children, Childhood*, 21.

26 Reynolds, *Children's Literature,* 15.

27 Reynolds, *Children's Literature,* 27. Sorby credits Roger Lancelyn Green with the first application of the Greco-Roman concept of a Golden Age to children's literature. Sorby, "Golden Age."

28 Reynolds, *Children's Literature,* 28.

29 Carpenter, *Secret Gardens.*

30 Iain Bain uses the words "minor classic" to describe Bewick's *Memoir.* Bain, "Introduction," ix. The minor/major designation means that Bewick demands reference in all histories of the relief print, yet he is not quite worthy of full scholarly endorsement.

31 Briggs, "Women Writers and Writing," 231.

32 Briggs, "Women Writers and Writing," 231. Compare these women's works to John Newbery's beloved mid-eighteenth-century classic, *Little Goody Two-Shoes.* Written by Newbery or a male contemporary, this "generic hybrid" is "not representative" of the majority of Newbery's children's titles, which "were more earnest and educational." Grenby, "Introduction," xxi, x. O'Malley argues that the literary antics of a Lear or a Carroll are "logical extension[s]" of earlier women writers' pedagogical texts "concealed in delightful packaging." O'Malley, *Making of the Modern Child,* 135.

33 Briggs, "Women Writers and Writing," 231.

34 Zipes, "Origins," 26. Zipes's groundbreaking studies of fairy tales are themselves legendary, from *Fairy Tales and the Art of Subversion* (1982) to *Buried Treasures* (2023) and beyond.

35 Zipes, "Origins," 27.

36 "Mere 'Formschneider,'" in Bliss's words. Bliss, *History of Wood-Engraving,* 197. By way of contrast, see Dalziel, *Brothers Dalziel*; Stevens, "Wood Engraving as Ghostwriting." See also Stevens's impressive *Wood Engravers' Self-Portrait.* Von Lintel describes how nineteenth-century, factory-produced wood engraved illustrations of art in publications of Louis Hachette in Paris, Sampson Low in London, and Charles Scribner in New York "sustained the elite field of art history and brought it into the realm of modern popular culture." Von Lintel, "Wood Engravings," 517.

37 Zipes, "Origins," 31.

38 Zipes, "Origins," 27.

39 Spalding, *Gwen Raverat,* 359. Raverat retained rights to her blocks for use in a possible later edition of the complete tales of Hans Christian Andersen. Selborne and Newman, *Gwen Raverat,* 59.

40 Selborne and Newman reproduce Raverat's "solid, well-built" *Witches* from 1924, suggesting "autobiographic" French origins for her 1935 Danish farmer's wife. Selborne and Newman, *Gwen Raverat,* 36–37.

41 For critical response to *The Bird Talisman's* color engravings, see, for example, Balston, *English Wood-Engraving,* 20; Smith, *Children's Illustrated Books,* 40; Whalley and Chester, *History of Children's Book Illustration,* 185; Selborne and Newman, *Gwen Raverat,* 58; Selborne, *British Wood-Engraved Book Illustration,* 207.

42 The book is a coproduction of its author-illustrator (Raverat), printer (Cambridge University Press's Brooke Crutchley), and designer (Faber and Faber's Richard de la Mare). See Selborne, *British Wood-Engraved Book Illustration,* 206–7.

43 The barely concealed sexual metaphors that define the course of the little princess throughout *The Bird Talisman*—her falls and flying—are exactly what ensure its impossible innocence as children's literature in Jacqueline Rose's terms. Rose, *Case of Peter Pan*; see also Higonnet, *Pictures of Innocence.*

44 *The Bird Talisman* is a classic Golden Age book not despite but because of its engagements with Orientalism. Kutzer's *Empire's Children,* Said's classic *Orientalism,* and Fowler's *Green Unpleasant Land* provide necessary critical contexts.

45 Decapitated queens and witches of folk legend and fairy tale are a single type in early second-wave feminist literary criticism. Powerful subaltern male characters like the enslaved and executed Baboof also belong in this feminist story.

46 The resistance to housing development amid the post–World War I campaign known as Homes Fit for Heroes had no relation to the limited "land fit for heroes" movement to improve housing in rural areas for agricultural laborers and domestic servants. See Howkins, *Death of Rural England,* 86–89; Burchardt, *Paradise Lost,* 89–92.

47 See Robins's autobiography, *Stranger Than Fiction.*

Bibliography

Addison, Rosemary. "Joan Hassall, Wood-Engraver." *Textualities* (2005), n.p. http://textualities.net.

Alderson, Brian. *Looking at Picture Books 1973: An Exhibition.* London: National Book League, 1973.

Alderson, Brian. *Sing a Song for Sixpence: The English Picture-Book Tradition and Randolph Caldecott.* Cambridge: Cambridge University Press, 1986.

Alderson, Brian, and Felix de Marez Oyens. *Be Merry and Wise: Origins of Children's Book Publishing in England, 1650–1850.* Newark, Del.: Oak Knoll Press, 2006.

Annan, Noel. *Our Age: English Intellectuals Between the World Wars.* New York: Random House, 1991.

Arizpe, Evelyn, and Morag Styles. *Children Reading Pictures: Interpreting Visual Texts.* London: Routledge, 2003.

Arnold, Dana. *Cultural Identities and the Aesthetics of Britishness.* Manchester: Manchester University Press, 2004.

Avery, Gillian, and Julia Briggs, eds. *Children and Their Books: A Celebration of the Work of Iona and Peter Opie.* Oxford: Clarendon Press, 1989.

Avery, Gillian, and Julia Briggs. "Introduction." In Avery and Briggs, *Children and Their Books,* 1–6.

Ayers, David. *English Literature of the 1920s.* Edinburgh: Edinburgh University Press, 1999.

Aymes, Sophie. *Modernist Mediascapes: Illustration, Print Culture, and the Matter of Books.* Oxford: Legenda, 2025.

Bailey, Christopher. "Rural Industries and the Image of the Countryside." In Brassley et al., *English Countryside Between the Wars,* 132–49.

Bain, Iain. "Introduction." In *A Memoir Written by Himself,* by Thomas Bewick. 1862; edited by Iain Bain, Oxford: Oxford University Press, 1975.

Baker, Niamh. *Happily Ever After: Women's Fiction in Postwar Britain, 1945–1960.* New York: St. Martin's Press, 1989.

Baldwin, Stanley. "England." In *"On England" and Other Addresses,* 1–9. London: Philip Allan, 1926.

Balston, Thomas. *English-Wood Engraving 1900–1950.* London: Art and Technics, 1950.

Balston, Thomas. *Wood-Engraving in Modern English Books.* Exhibition catalog. Cambridge: Cambridge University Press, 1949.

Baxendale, John. *Priestley's England: J. B. Priestley and English Culture.* Manchester: Manchester University Press, 2007.

Baxendale, John, and Christopher Pawling. *Narrating the Thirties: A Decade in the Making, 1930 to the Present.* New York: Palgrave Macmillan, 1996.

Beauman, Nicola. *A Very Great Profession: The Woman's Novel 1914–39.* London: Virago Press, 1983.

Beedham, R. J. *Wood Engraving.* Ditchling, East Sussex: Ditchling Press, 1920.

Behlmer, George, and Fred Leventhal, eds. *Singular Continuities: Tradition, Nostalgia, and Identity in Modern British Culture.* Stanford, Calif.: Stanford University Press, 2000.

Belloc, Hilaire. "Introduction." In *Woodcuts: Examples of the Work of Clare Leighton,* by Clare Leighton, vii–xii. London: Longmans, Green, 1930.

Benjamin, Walter. *The Arcades Project.* Translated by Howard Eiland and Kevin McLaughlin. Cambridge, Mass.: Harvard University Press, 1999.

Benjamin, Walter. "The Work of Art in the Age of Mechanical Reproduction." In *Illuminations,* 217–51. Edited by Hannah Arendt. Translated by Harry Zohn. New York: Schocken Books, 1968.

Benson, Richard. *The Printed Picture.* New York: Museum of Modern Art, 2008.

Benstock, Shari. "The Double Image of Modernism: Matisse's Etchings for 'Ulysses.'" *Contemporary Literature* 21, no. 3 (1980): 450–79.

Benstock, Shari. *Women of the Left Bank: Paris, 1900–1940.* Austin: University of Texas Press, 1987.

Benton, Megan L. "The Book as Art." In Eliot and Rose, *Companion to the History of the Book,* 493–507.

Berger, John. *Ways of Seeing.* London: British Broadcasting Corporation, 1972.

Bergonzi, Bernard. *Reading the Thirties: Texts and Contexts.* Pittsburgh: University of Pittsburgh Press, 1978.

Bergonzi, Bernard. *Wartime and Aftermath: English Literature and Its Background, 1939– 60.* Oxford: Oxford University Press, 1993.

Bewick, Thomas. "Preface to the Sixth Edition." In *A History of British Birds.* Vol. 1, *Land Birds.* 6th ed. Newcastle: Edw. Walker, 1826.

Bliss, Douglas Percy. *A History of Wood-Engraving.* London: J. M. Dent and Sons; New York: E. P. Dutton, 1928.

Bluemel, Kristin. "'Definite, Burly, and Industrious': Virginia Woolf and Gwen Darwin Raverat." In *Virginia Woolf and Her Female Contemporaries,* edited by Julie Vandivere and Megan Hicks, 22–28. Clemson, S.C.: Clemson University Press, 2016.

Bluemel, Kristin. "Illustrating *Mary Poppins*: Visual Culture and the Middlebrow." In Brown and Grover, *Middlebrow Literary Cultures,* 187–201.

Bluemel, Kristin, ed. *Intermodernism: Literary Culture in Mid-Twentieth-Century Britain.* Edinburgh: Edinburgh University Press, 2009.

Bluemel, Kristin. "Introduction: What Is Intermodernism?" In Bluemel, *Intermodernism,* 1–18.

Bluemel, Kristin. "Ordinary Places, Intermodern Genres: Documentary, Travel and Literature." In *British Literature in Transition, 1920–1940: Futility and Anarchy,* edited by Charles Ferrall and Dougal McNeill, 182–98. Cambridge: Cambridge University Press, 2018.

Bluemel, Kristin. "Windmills and Woodblocks: Agnes Miller Parker, Wood Engraving, and the Popular Press in Interwar Britain." In Bluemel and McCluskey, *Rural Modernity in Britain,* 84–102.

Bluemel, Kristin, and Michael McCluskey, eds. *Rural Modernity in Britain: A Critical Intervention.* Edinburgh: Edinburgh University Press, 2018.

Bonnett, Alastair. *The Geography of Nostalgia: Global and Local Perspectives on Modernity and Loss.* London: Routledge, 2016.

Bonnett, Alastair. *Left in the Past: Radicalism and the Politics of Nostalgia.* London: Routledge, 2010.

Bornstein, George. *Material Modernism: The Politics of the Page.* Cambridge: Cambridge University Press, 2001.

Bourdieu, Pierre. *Distinction: A Social Critique of the Judgement of Taste.* Translated by Richard Nice. Cambridge, Mass.: Harvard University Press, 1984.

Bowker, Gordon. *Inside George Orwell: A Biography.* New York: Palgrave Macmillan, 2003.

Boyes, Georgina. *The Imagined Village: Culture, Ideology and the English Folk Revival.* Manchester: Manchester University Press, 1993.

Boym, Svetlana. *The Future of Nostalgia.* New York: Basic Books, 2001.

Braby, Dorothea. *The Way of Wood Engraving.* London: The Studio Publications, 1953.

Bracco, Rosa Maria. *Merchants of Hope: British Middlebrow Writers and the First World War.* Oxford: Berg, 1995.

Branson, Noreen, and Margot Heinemann. *Britain in the Nineteen Thirties.* London: Weidenfeld & Nicolson, 1971.

Brassley, Paul. "British Farming Between the Wars." In Brassley et al., *English Countryside Between the Wars,* 187–99.

Brassley, Paul, Jeremy Burchardt, and Lynne Thompson, eds. *The English Countryside Between the Wars: Regeneration or Decline?* Woodbridge, Suffolk: Boydell Press, 2006.

Braydon, Gail, and Penny Summerfield. *Out of the Cage: Women's Experiences in Two World Wars.* London: Pandora Press, 1987.

Brett, Simon. *Engravers: A Handbook for the Nineties.* Cambridge: Silent Books, 1987.

Brett, Simon. *Wood Engraving: How to Do It.* New Castle, Del.: Oak Knoll Press, 1994; London: Herbert Press, 2018.

Briggs, Asa. *A Social History of England.* New York: Viking Press, 1983.

Briggs, Julia. "Women Writers and Writing for Children: From Sarah Fielding to E. Nesbit." In Avery and Briggs, *Children and Their Books,* 221–50.

Brittain, Vera. *Testament of Youth.* London: Gollancz, 1933.

Brontë, Charlotte. *Jane Eyre.* Edited by Beth Newman. New York: Bedford/St. Martin's, 1996.

Brooker, Peter, Andrzej Gasiorek, and Deborah Longworth, Andrew Thacker, eds. *Oxford Handbook of Modernisms.* Oxford: Oxford University Press, 2010.

Brown, Erica, and Mary Grover, eds. *Middlebrow Literary Cultures: The Battle of the Brows, 1920–1960.* New York: Palgrave Macmillan, 2012.

Bruce, George. *"To Foster and Enrich": The First Fifty Years of the Saltire Society.* Edinburgh: Saltire Society, 1986.

Bryant, Marsha. *Auden and Documentary in the 1930s.* Charlottesville: University Press of Virginia, 1997.

Buddicom, Jacintha. *Eric and Us.* Chichester: Finlay, 2006.

Burchardt, Jeremy. *Lifescapes: The Experience of Landscape in Britain, 1870–1960.* Cambridge: Cambridge University Press, 2023.

Burchardt, Jeremy. *Paradise Lost: Rural Idyll and Social Change Since 1800.* London: I. B. Tauris, 2002.

Burton, William. "The Decline and Fall of the Limited Editions Club." *American Book Collector* 1, no. 4 (1980): 3–7.

Calder, Angus. *The Myth of the Blitz.* London: Jonathan Cape, 1991.

Campbell, Beatrix. *Wigan Pier Revisited: Poverty and Politics in the 80s.* London: Virago Press, 1984.

Carpenter, Humphrey. *Secret Gardens: A Study of the Golden Age of Children's Literature.* Boston: Houghton Mifflin, 1985.

Carrington, Noel. *Popular Art in Britain.* London: Penguin Books, 1945.

Carrington, Noel, ed. *Puffin Picture Books.* Harmondsworth: Penguin Books, 1940–56.

Carrington, Noel. "Puffin Picture Books." In Rogerson, *Noel Carrington and His Puffin Picture Books.*

Carter, Alice A. "British Fantasy and Children's Book Illustration, 1650–1920." In Doyle et al., *History of Illustration,* 248–65.

Cavaliero, Glen. *The Rural Tradition in the English Novel, 1900–1939.* Totowa, N.J.: Rowman & Littlefield, 1977.

Cave, Roderick. *The Private Press.* 2nd ed. New York: R. R. Bowker, 1983.

Chambers, David. "Books and Bookplates." In *Joan Hassall: Engravings and Drawings,* edited by David Chambers, xxii–xxxvi. Pinner, Middlesex: Private Libraries Association, 1985.

Chambers, David. "Hassall, Joan (1906–1988), Artist and Wood-Engraver." In *Oxford Dictionary of National Biography.* Last modified September 23, 2004. https://www.oxforddnb.com.

Chandler, Katherine R. "Thoroughly Post-Victorian, Pre-Modern Beatrix." *Children's Literature Association Quarterly* 32, no. 4 (2007): 287–307.

Chase, Malcolm. "This Is No Claptrap: This Is Our Heritage." In Shaw and Chase, *Imagined Past,* 128–46.

Chase, Malcolm, and Christopher Shaw. "The Dimensions of Nostalgia." In Shaw and Chase, *Imagined Past,* 1–17.

Chatto, W. A., and John Jackson. *A Treatise on Wood Engraving, Historical and Practical.* 2nd ed. London: Chatto & Windus, 1861. https://www.gutenberg.org.

Clark, H. Nichols B. "Children's Book Illustration, 1920–2000." In Doyle et al., *History of Illustration,* 413–30.

Clark, Jon, Margot Heinemann, David Margolis, and Carol Snee, eds. *Culture and Crisis in Britain in the 1930s*. London: Lawrence and Wishart, 1979.

Clay, Catherine. *British Women Writers 1914–1945: Professional Work and Friendship*. Burlington, Vt.: Ashgate, 2006.

Cleverdon, Douglas. *The Engravings of Eric Gill*. London: Faber and Faber, 1934.

Collier, Patrick. *Modern Print Artefacts: Textual Materiality and Literary Value in British Print Culture, 1890–1930s*. Edinburgh: Edinburgh University Press, 2016.

Collini, Stefan. *The Nostalgic Imagination: History in English Criticism*. Oxford: Oxford University Press, 2019.

Colls, Robert, and Philip Dodd, eds. *Englishness: Politics and Culture 1880–1920*. London: Routledge & Kegan Paul, 1986.

Corbett, David Peters, Ysanne Holt, and Fiona Russell, eds. *The Geographies of Englishness: Landscape and the National Past, 1880–1940*. New Haven, Conn.: Yale University Press, 2002.

Corbett, David Peters, Ysanne Holt, and Fiona Russell. "Introduction." In Corbett et al., *Geographies of Englishness*, ix–xix.

Coutts, Gillie. *Gwen Raverat: Exhibition Held at New Hall, University of Cambridge*. Exhibition catalog. Cambridge: Fitzwilliam Museum, 1998.

Craig, Edward Gordon. *Woodcuts and Some Words*. London: J. M. Dent and Sons, 1924.

Crain, Patricia. *The Story of A: The Alphabetization of America from "The New England Primer" to "The Scarlet Letter."* Stanford, Calif.: Stanford University Press, 2000.

Cullen, Anthea. *Angel in the Studio: Women in the Arts and Crafts Movement, 1870–1914*. London: Astragal, 1979.

Cunningham, Valentine. *British Writers of the Thirties*. Oxford: Oxford University Press, 1988.

Dalby, Richard. *The Golden Age of Children's Book Illustration*. London: Michael O'Mara, 1991.

Dalziel, W. A. *The Brothers Dalziel: A Record of Work, 1840–1890*. London: Methuen, 1901; London: B. T. Batsford, 1976.

Darnton, Robert. "What Is the History of Books?" *Daedalus* 111, no. 3 (1982): 65–83. http://www.jstor.org/stable/20024803.

Darton, F. J. Harvey. *Children's Books in England: Five Centuries of Social Life*. Cambridge: Cambridge University Press, 1932.

Darton, F. J. Harvey. *Children's Books in England: Five Centuries of Social Life*. 3rd ed. Revised by Brian Alderson. Cambridge: Cambridge University Press, 1982.

Darton, F. J. Harvey. *English Fabric: A Study of Village Life.* London: George Newnes, 1935.

Daunt, Chris. *The Art and Craft of Wood Engraving.* Ramsbury, Wiltshire: Crowood Press, 2023.

Davies, Andrew. *Where Did the Forties Go?* London: Pluto Press, 1984.

Davis, Fred. *Yearning for Yesterday: A Sociology of Nostalgia.* New York: Free Press, 1979.

Davis, Thomas S. "Late Modernism: British Literature at Midcentury." *Literature Compass* 9, no. 4 (2012): 326–37.

Deane, Patrick, ed. *History in Our Hands: A Critical Anthology of Writings on Literature, Culture and Politics from the 1930s.* London: Leicester University Press, 1998.

de Certeau, Michel. *The Practice of Everyday Life.* Translated by Steven F. Rendall. Berkeley: University of California Press, 1984.

Delaney, Paul. *The Neo-Pagans: Friendship and Love in the Rupert Brooke Circle.* London: Hamish Hamilton, 1987.

Donald, Diana. *The Art of Thomas Bewick.* London: Reaktion Books, 2013.

Doyle, Susan, Jaleen Grove, and Whitney Sherman, eds. *History of Illustration.* New York: Bloomsbury, 2018.

Drucker, Johanna. *Figuring the Word: Essays on Books, Writing, and Visual Poetics.* New York: Granary Books, 1998.

Drucker, Johanna. *Graphesis: Visual Forms of Knowledge Production.* Cambridge, Mass.: Harvard University Press, 2014.

Drucker, Johanna. *Inventing the Alphabet: The Origins of Letters from Antiquity to the Present.* Chicago: University of Chicago Press, 2022.

Drucker, Johanna. *The Visible Word: Experimental Typography and Modern Art, 1909–1923.* Chicago: University of Chicago Press, 1994.

Dusinberre, Juliet. *Alice to the Lighthouse: Children's Books and Radical Experiments in Art.* 1987; London: Macmillan, 1999.

Edwards, Owen Dudley. *British Children's Fiction in the Second World War.* Edinburgh: Edinburgh University Press, 2007.

Edwards, Ruth Dudley. *Victor Gollancz: A Biography.* London: Gollancz, 1987.

Elegant Arts for Ladies. London: Ward and Lock, 1856.

Eliot, Simon, and Jonathan Rose, eds. *A Companion to the History of the Book.* Malden, Mass.: Blackwell, 2009.

Elson, Verity, and Rosemary Shirley. *Creating the Countryside: The Rural Idyll Past and Present.* London: Paul Holberton, 2017.

Empson, William. *Some Versions of Pastoral.* 1935; Harmondsworth: Penguin Books, 1995.

Esty, Jed. *A Shrinking Island: Modernism and National Culture in England.* Princeton, N.J.: Princeton University Press, 2004.

Falconer, Rachel. *The Crossover Novel: Contemporary Children's Fiction and Its Adult Readership.* London: Routledge, 2008.

Faulk, Barry J. "Modernist Urban Nostalgia and British Metropolitan Writing, 1908–1934." In *Modernism and Nostalgia: Bodies, Locations, Aesthetics,* edited by Tammy Clewell, 111–30. New York: Palgrave Macmillan, 2013.

Ferrall, Charles, and Anna Jackson. *Juvenile Literature and British Society 1850–1950: The Age of Adolescence.* London: Routledge, 2010.

Fletcher, Pamela, and Anne Helmreich, eds. *The Rise of the Modern Art Market in London, 1850–1939.* Manchester: Manchester University Press, 2011.

Flint, Kate. *The Woman Reader, 1837–1944.* Oxford: Clarendon Press, 1993.

Flower, Chloe. "The Exemplary Game: Going to War with H. G. Wells's Toy Soldiers." *Children's Literature* 51 (2023): 24–50.

Foss, Brian. *War Paint: Art, War, State and Identity in Britain, 1939–1945.* London: Yale University Press, 2007.

Fowler, Corinne. *Green Unpleasant Land: Creative Responses to Rural England's Colonial Connections.* Leeds: Peepal Tree Press, 2021.

Freedman, Barnett. "Every Man His Own Lithographer." In Lambert, *Art in England,* 104–9.

Friedman, Susan Stanford. "Definitional Excursions: The Meanings of Modern/ Modernity/Modernism." *Modernism/modernity* 8, no. 3 (2001): 493–513.

Friedman, Susan Stanford. *Planetary Modernisms: Provocations on Modernity Across Time.* New York: Columbia University Press, 2015.

Frow, John. *Cultural Studies and Cultural Value.* Oxford: Oxford University Press, 1995.

Fry, Roger. *Last Lectures.* Edited by Kenneth Clark. Cambridge: Cambridge University Press, 1939.

Fry, Roger. *Reflections on British Painting.* London: Faber and Faber, 1934.

Fry, Roger. *A Roger Fry Reader.* Edited by Christopher Reed. Chicago: University of Chicago Press, 1996.

Fry, Roger. *Vision and Design.* 1920; edited by J. G. Bullen, Mineola, N.Y.: Dover, 1998.

Furst, Herbert. *The Modern Woodcut.* London: John Lane, 1924.

Fussell, Paul. "Persistence of Pastoral." In *"Thank God for the Atom Bomb" and Other Essays,* 177–204. New York: Summit, 1988.

Fussell, Paul. *Wartime: Understanding and Behavior in the Second World War.* New York: Oxford University Press, 1989.

Gan, Wendy. *Women, Privacy and Modernity in Early Twentieth-Century British Writing.* London: Palgrave Macmillan, 2009.

Gans, Herbert J. *Popular Culture and High Culture: An Analysis and Evaluation of Taste.* 1974; rev. ed., New York: Basic Books, 1999.

Gardner-Medwin, David, ed. *Bewick Studies: Essays in Celebration of the 250th Anniversary of the Birth of Thomas Bewick, 1753–1828.* New Castle, Del.: Oak Knoll Press, 2003.

Gasiorek, Andrzej. *Post-War British Fiction: Realism and After.* London: Edward Arnold, 1995.

Gervais, David. *Literary Englands: Versions of "Englishness" in Modern Writing.* Cambridge: Cambridge University Press, 1993.

Gifford, Terry. *Pastoral.* 2nd ed. London: Routledge, 2019.

Gilbert, David, David Matless, and Brian Short, eds. *Geographies of British Modernity.* Oxford: Blackwell, 2003.

Gilbert, Sandra M., and Susan Gubar. *No Man's Land: The Place of the Woman Writer in the Twentieth Century.* 3 vols. New Haven, Conn.: Yale University Press, 1988–94.

Giles, Judy. *The Parlour and the Suburb: Domestic Identities, Class, Femininity and Modernity.* Basingstoke: Palgrave Macmillan, 2004.

Gitelman, Lisa. *Paper Knowledge: Toward a Media History of Documents.* Durham, N.C.: Duke University Press, 2014.

Gloversmith, Frank, ed. *Class, Culture, and Social Change: A New View of the 1930s.* Brighton: Harvester Press, 1980.

Goldman, Paul. *Looking at Prints, Drawings, and Watercolours: A Guide to Technical Terms.* Rev. ed. London: British Museum Press, 2006.

Goldman, Paul. *Victorian Illustrated Books 1850–1870: The Heyday of Wood-Engraving.* Boston: David R. Godine, 1994.

Goldthwaite, John. *The Natural History of Make-Believe.* Oxford: Oxford University Press, 1996.

Goodman, Sharon. "Words and Pictures: Introduction." In *Children's Literature: Approaches and Territories,* edited by Janet Maybin and Nicola J. Watson, 296–99. Basingstoke: Palgrave Macmillan, 2009.

Goodwin, Willard. "'A Very Pretty Picture M. Matisse but You Must Not Call It Joyce': The Making of the Limited Editions Club *Ulysses.*" *Joyce Studies Annual* 10 (1999): 85–103.

Graves, Robert, and Alan Hodge. *The Long Week End: A Social History of Great Britain, 1918–1939.* London: Faber and Faber, 1940.

Grenby, M. O. "Before Children's Literature: Children, Chapbooks and Popular Culture in Early Modern Britain." In *Popular Children's Literature in Britain,* edited by Julia Briggs, Dennis Butts, and M. O. Grenby, 25–46. London: Routledge, 2008.

Grenby, M. O. *The Child Reader, 1700–1840.* Cambridge: Cambridge University Press, 2011.

Grenby, M. O. "Introduction." In *"Little Goody Two-Shoes" and Other Stories,* by John Newbery, vii–xxxv. London: Palgrave Macmillan, 2013.

Grenby, Matthew, and Andrea Immel, eds. *The Cambridge Companion to Children's Literature.* Cambridge: Cambridge University Press, 2009.

Grossman, Carol Porter. *The History of the Limited Editions Club.* New Castle, Del.: Oak Knoll Press, 2017.

Gubar, Marah. *Artful Dodgers: Reconceiving the Golden Age of Children's Literature.* New York: Oxford University Press, 2009.

Halsey, Katie, and W. R. Owens, eds. *The History of Reading.* Vol. 2, *Evidence from the British Isles, c. 1750–1950.* New York: Palgrave Macmillan, 2011.

Hamer, Naomi, Perry Nodelman, and Mavis Reimer. *More Words About Pictures: Current Research on Picture Books and Visual/Verbal Texts for Young People.* New York: Routledge, 2017.

Hamilton, James. *Wood Engraving and the Woodcut in Britain c. 1890–1990.* London: Barrie and Jenkins, 1994.

Hammill, Faye. *Sophistication: A Literary and Cultural History.* Liverpool: Liverpool University Press, 2010.

Hammill, Faye. *Women, Celebrity, and Literary Culture Between the Wars.* Austin: University of Texas Press, 2007.

Hammill, Faye, and Mark Hussey. *Modernist Print Cultures.* London: Bloomsbury Academic, 2016.

Hammond, John L., and Barbara Hammond. *The Skilled Labourer.* 1919; edited by John Rule, London: Longman, 1979.

Hammond, John L., and Barbara Hammond. *The Town Labourer.* 1917; edited by John Lovell, London: Longman, 1978.

Hammond, John L., and Barbara Hammond. *The Village Labourer.* 1911; edited by G. E. Mingay, London: Longman, 1978.

Hammond, Mary. *Reading, Publishing and the Formation of Literary Taste in England, 1880–1914.* Burlington, Vt.: Ashgate, 2006.

Hapgood, Lynne. *Margins of Desire: The Suburbs in Fiction and Culture, 1880–1925.* Manchester: Manchester University Press, 2005.

Harris, Alexandra. *Romantic Moderns: English Writers, Artists, and the Imagination from Virginia Woolf to John Piper.* London: Thames and Hudson, 2010.

Harrison, Charles. *English Art and Modernism, 1900–1939.* 2nd ed. London: Yale University Press, 1994.

Head, Dominic. "H. E. Bates, Regionalism and Late Modernism: British Literature at Mid-Century." In *The Legacies of Modernism: Historicizing Postwar and Contemporary Fiction,* edited by David James, 40–52. Cambridge: Cambridge University Press, 2011.

Head, Dominic. *Modernity and the English Rural Novel.* Cambridge: Cambridge University Press, 2017.

Hendrick, Harry. *Children, Childhood and English Society, 1880–1990.* Cambridge: Cambridge University Press for the Economic History Society, 1997.

Hickman, Caroline Mesrobian. "Clare Leighton's Art and Craft: Exploring Her Rich Legacy Through the Pratt Collection." In *Quiet Spirit, Skillful Hand: The Graphic Work of Clare Leighton,* by Clare Leighton, edited by Jonathan Stuhlman, 7–16. Charlotte, N.C.: Mint Museum of Art, 2008.

Highmore, Ben. *Everyday Life and Cultural Theory: An Introduction.* London: Routledge, 2002.

Higonnet, Anne. *Pictures of Innocence: The History and Crisis of Ideal Childhood.* London: Thames and Hudson, 1998.

Hinds, Hillary. "Ordinary Disappointments: Femininity, Domesticity, and Nation in British Middlebrow Fiction, 1920–1944." *Modern Fiction Studies* 55, no. 2 (2009): 293–320.

Hodnett, Edward. *Five Centuries of English Book Illustration.* Aldershot: Scolar Press, 1988.

Holman, Valerie. "A Fruitful Symbiosis: Sculptors and Publishers in Britain Between the Wars." *The Space Between: Literature and Culture, 1914–1945* 7, no. 1 (2011): 109–23.

Holme, Geoffrey, ed. *British Book Illustration Yesterday and To-Day.* London: The Studio Publications, 1923.

Holmes, Edric. *London's Countryside.* London: Robert Scott, 1927.

Hopkins, Chris. *English Fiction in the 1930s.* London: Continuum, 2007.

Horne, Alan J. *Dictionary of 20th Century British Book Illustrators (1915–1985).* Woodbridge, Suffolk: Antique Collectors Club, 1990.

Howkins, Alun. "Death and Rebirth? English Rural Society, 1920–1940." In Brassley et al., *English Countryside Between the Wars,* 10–25.

Howkins, Alun. *The Death of Rural England: A Social History of the Countryside Since 1900.* New York: Routledge, 2003.

Howkins, Alun. "The Discovery of Rural England." In Colls and Dodd, *Englishness,* 62–88. London: Routledge & Kegan Paul, 1986.

Howkins, Alun. "Landowners and Farmers." In Howkins, *Death of Rural England,* 55–76.

Hubble, Nick. "The Intermodern Assumption of the Future: William Empson, Charles Madge and Mass-Observation." In Bluemel, *Intermodernism,* 171–88.

Humble, Nicola. *The Feminine Middlebrow Novel, 1920s–1950s: Class, Domesticity, Bohemianism.* Oxford: Oxford University Press, 2001.

Humble, Nicola. "The Reader of Popular Fiction." In *The Cambridge Companion to Popular Fiction,* edited by David Glover and Scott McCracken, 86–102. Cambridge: Cambridge University Press, 2012.

Hunt, Peter. *Criticism, Theory and Children's Literature.* Oxford: Basil Blackwell, 1991.

Hunt, Peter. *An Introduction to Children's Literature.* Oxford: Oxford University Press, 1994.

Hunt, Peter. *Understanding Children's Literature.* 2nd ed. London: Routledge, 1999.

Hussey, Christopher. *The Picturesque: Studies in a Point of View.* London: G. P. Putnam's Sons, 1927.

Hutton, Clarke. *15 Nursery Rhymes.* Harmondsworth: Penguin Puffin Picture Books, 1941.

Hutton, Clarke. *Punch and Judy.* Harmondsworth: Penguin Puffin Picture Books, 1942.

Illbruck, Helmut. *Nostalgia: Origins and Ends of an Unenlightened Disease.* Evanston, Ill.: Northwestern University Press, 2012.

Immel, Andrea. "Children's Books and Constructions of Childhood." In Grenby and Immel, *Cambridge Companion to Children's Literature,* 19–34.

Jaffé, Pat. "Introduction." In *The Wood Engravings of Clare Leighton,* by Clare Leighton, 7–22. Cambridge: Silent Books, 1992.

Jaffé, Patricia. *Women Engravers.* London: Virago Press, 1988.

James, David. "Localizing Late Modernism: Interwar Regionalism and the Genesis of the 'Micro-Novel.'" *Journal of Modern Literature* 32, no. 4 (2010): 43–64.

James, David, and Urmila Seshagiri. "Metamodernism: Narratives of Continuity and Revolution." *PMLA* 121, no. 1 (2014): 87–100.

Jameson, Fredric. *The Political Unconscious: Narrative as a Socially Symbolic Act.* 1981; London: Routledge, 2002.

Jameson, Fredric. *A Singular Modernity: Essay on the Ontology of the Present.* London: Verso, 2002.

Jeffrey, Ian. *The British Landscape, 1920–1950.* London: Thames and Hudson, 1984.

Jones, Owain. "Little Figures, Big Figures: Country Childhood Stories." In *Contested Countryside Cultures: Otherness, Marginalisation and Rurality,* edited by Paul Cloke and Jo Little, 158–79. London: Routledge, 1997.

Jones, Owain. "Naturally Not! Childhood, the Urban and Romanticism." *Human Ecology Review* 9, no. 2 (2002): 17–30.

Kalliney, Peter J. *Cities of Affluence and Anger: A Literary Geography of Modern Englishness.* Charlottesville: University of Virginia Press, 2006.

Keith, W. J. *Regions of the Imagination: The Development of British Rural Fiction.* Toronto: University of Toronto Press, 1988.

Keith, W. J. *The Rural Tradition: A Study of the Non-Fiction Prose Writers of the English Countryside.* Toronto: University of Toronto Press, 1974.

Kümmerling-Meibauer, Bettina, and Anja Müller. "Introduction: Canon Studies and Children's Literature." In *Canon Constitution and Canon Change in Children's Literature,* edited by Bettina Kümmerling-Maibauer and Anja Müller, 1–14. New York: Routledge, 2016.

Kutzer, M. Daphne. *Empire's Children: Empire and Imperialism in Classic British Children's Books.* London: Garland, 2000.

Laity, Cassandra. "Editor's Introduction: Towards Feminist Modernisms." *Feminist Modernist Studies* 1, nos. 1–2 (2018): 1–7.

Lambert, R. S., ed. *Art in England.* Harmondsworth: Penguin Books, 1938.

Leaper, Hana. *Sybil Andrews Linocuts: A Complete Catalogue.* London: Lund Humphries, 2015.

Leavis, F. R. *Mass Civilization and Minority Culture.* Cambridge: Minority Press, 1930.

Leavis, F. R., and Denys Thompson. 1933. *Culture and Environment.* London: Chatto & Windus, 1942.

Leavis, Q. D. *Fiction and the Reading Public.* London: Chatto & Windus, 1932.

Leighton, David. "Clare Leighton: Her Family Foundations." In *Quiet Spirit, Skillful Hand: The Graphic Work of Clare Leighton,* by Clare Leighton, edited by Jonathan Stuhlman, 3–5. Charlotte, N.C.: Mint Museum of Art, 2008.

Leighton, David. "Clare Leighton Remembered by Her Nephew." In *Clare Leighton: Wood Engravings and Drawings,* compiled by Anne Stevens and David Leighton, 13–15. Oxford: Ashmolean Museum, 1992.

Leighton, Marie Connor. *Boy of My Heart.* London: Hodder & Stoughton, 1916.

Lerer, Seth. *Children's Literature: A Reader's History from Aesop to Harry Potter.* Chicago: University of Chicago Press, 2008.

Lesnik-Oberstein, Karin. *Children's Literature: Criticism and the Fictional Child.* Oxford: Clarendon Press, 1994.

Lewis, Jeremy. *Penguin Special: The Story of Allen Lane, the Founder of Penguin Books and the Man Who Changed Publishing Forever.* London: Penguin Books, 2005.

Light, Alison. *Forever England: Femininity, Literature, and Conservatism Between the Wars.* New York: Routledge, 1991.

"Limited Editions Club." *Publishers' Weekly,* May 25, 1929.

Limited Editions Club. *Bibliography of the Fine Books Published by the Limited Editions Club, 1929–1985.* New York: Limited Editions Club, 1985.

Limited Editions Club. *Your Favorite Books, the Classics of World Literature: Illustrated by the Foremost Authors and Made into Volumes of Beauty by the Foremost Designers of Books.* New York: Limited Editions Club, 1929.

"The Limited Editions Club Is Organized." *Publishers' Weekly,* April 6, 1929.

Lowenthal, David. "Nostalgia Tells It Like It Wasn't." In Shaw and Chase, *Imagined Past,* 18–32.

Lowenthal, David. *The Past Is a Foreign Country.* Cambridge: Cambridge University Press, 1985.

Lowerson, John. "Battles for the Countryside." In Gloversmith, *Class, Culture, and Social Change,* 258–80.

Lubbock, Tom. "Defining the Vignette." In *Thomas Bewick, Tale-Pieces,* edited by Jonathan Watkins, 41–50. Birmingham: Ikon Gallery, 2009.

Lucas, John, ed. *The 1930s: A Challenge to Orthodoxy.* Brighton: Harvester Press, 1979.

Lundin, Anne. *Constructing the Canon of Children's Literature: Beyond Library Walls and Ivory Towers.* New York: Routledge, 2004.

MacCarthy, Fiona. *Anarchy and Beauty: William Morris and His Legacy 1860–1960.* New Haven, Conn.: Yale University Press, 2014.

Macdonald, Kate, ed. *The Masculine Middlebrow, 1880–1950: What Mr Miniver Read.* Basingstoke: Palgrave Macmillan, 2011.

MacKay, Marina, and Lyndsey Stonebridge, eds. *British Fiction After Modernism: The Novel at Mid-Century.* Basingstoke: Palgrave Macmillan, 2007.

Mackley, George. *"Shall We Join the Ladies?": Wood Engravings by Women Artists of the 20th Century.* Oxford: Studio One Gallery, 1979.

Mackley, George. *Wood-Engraving.* London: National Magazine, 1948.

Mandler, Peter. "Against 'Englishness': English Culture and the Limits to Rural Nostalgia, 1850–1940." *Transactions of the Royal Historical Society* 7 (1997): 155–75.

Mandler, Peter. *The English National Character: The History of an Idea from Edmund Burke to Tony Blair.* London: Yale University Press, 2006.

Mandler, Peter. *The Fall and Rise of the Stately Home.* London: Yale University Press, 1997.

Marcus, Laura. "'The Creative Treatment of Actuality': John Grierson, Documentary Cinema and 'Fact' in the 1930s." In Bluemel, *Intermodernism,* 189–207.

Marinelli, Peter V. *Pastoral.* London: Methuen, 1971.

Marsh, Edward. "Patronage in Art To-Day (b)." In Lambert, *Art in England,* 78–82.

Marwick, Arthur. *The Home Front: The British and the Second World War.* London: Thames and Hudson, 1976.

Marx, Enid. *A Book of Rigamaroles or Jingle Rhymes.* Harmondsworth: Penguin Puffin Picture Books, 1945.

Marx, Leo. *The Machine in the Garden: Technology and the Pastoral Ideal in America.* Oxford: Oxford University Press, 1964.

Mason, Anna, Jan Marsh, Jenny Lister, Rowan Bain, and Hanne Faurby. *May Morris: Arts and Crafts Designer.* New York: Thames and Hudson and the Victoria and Albert Museum, 2017.

Massey, Doreen. *For Space.* London: Sage, 2005.

Matless, David. *Landscape and Englishness.* 2nd ed. London: Reaktion Books, 2016.

McAleer, Joseph. *Popular Reading and Publishing in Britain 1914–1950.* Oxford: Clarendon Press, 1992.

McGann, Jerome J. *Black Riders: The Visible Language of Modernism.* Princeton, N.J.: Princeton University Press, 1993.

McGann, Jerome J. "Philology in a New Key." *Critical Inquiry* 39, no. 2 (2013): 327–46.

McGann, Jerome J. *The Textual Condition.* Princeton, N.J.: Princeton University Press, 1991.

McKibbin, Ross. *Classes and Cultures: England 1918–1951.* Oxford: Oxford University Press, 1998.

McKitterick, David. *A History of Cambridge University Press.* Vol. 3, *New Worlds for Learning, 1873–1972.* Cambridge: Cambridge University Press, 2004.

McLean, Ruari. "Joan Hassall as Illustrator." In *The Wood Engravings of Joan Hassall,* compiled by Ruari McLean, 7–21. 1960; New York: Schocken Books, 1981.

McLean, Ruari. "Joan Hassall as Wood-Engraver." In *The Wood Engravings of Joan Hassall,* compiled by Ruari McLean, 22–29. 1960; New York: Schocken Books, 1981.

McLean, Ruari. "A Summing Up." In *The Wood Engravings of Joan Hassall,* compiled by Ruari McLean, 30–32. 1960; New York: Schocken Books, 1981.

McNair, John R. "Chromolithography and Color Woodblock: Handmaidens to Nineteenth-Century Children's Literature." *Children's Literature Association Quarterly* 11, no. 4 (1986/87): 193–97.

Mellor, Leo. "The Documentary Impulse." In *A History of 1930s British Literature,* edited by Benjamin Kohlmann and Matthew Taunton, 257–70. Cambridge: Cambridge University Press, 2019.

Mellor, Leo. *Reading the Ruins: Modernism, Bombsites, and British Culture.* Cambridge: Cambridge University Press, 2011.

Mengham, Rod. *Literature of the 1930s: Border Country.* Edinburgh: Edinburgh University Press, 2012.

Mengham, Rod, and N. H. Reeve, eds. *The Fiction of the 1940s: Stories of Survival.* New York: Palgrave Macmillan, 2001.

The Middlebrow Network. Accessed April 21, 2025. https://middlebrownetwork.com.

Miele, Chris. *From William Morris: Building Conservation and the Arts and Crafts Cult of Authenticity, 1877–1939.* New Haven, Conn.: Yale University Press, 2005.

Miller, Kristine. *British Literature of the Blitz: Fighting the People's War.* New York: Palgrave Macmillan, 2009.

Minns, Raynes. *Bombers and Mash: The Domestic Front 1939–45.* London: Virago Press, 1980.

Mitchell, W. J. T. *Iconology: Image, Text, Ideology.* Chicago: University of Chicago Press, 1985.

Mitchell, W. J. T. *Picture Theory: Essays on Verbal and Visual Representation.* Chicago: University of Chicago Press, 1994.

Mitchison, Naomi. *Among You Taking Notes: Wartime Diaries 1939–1945.* Edited by Dorothy Sheridan. London: Gollancz, 1985.

Mitchison, Naomi. *You May Well Ask: A Memoir 1920–1940.* 1979; London: Flamingo, 1986.

Moebius, William. "Introduction to Picturebook Codes." *Word and Image* 2, no. 2 (1986): 141–58.

Montefiore, Janet. *Men and Women Writers of the 1930s: The Dangerous Flood of History.* London: Routledge, 1996.

Morison, Stanley. "First Principles of Typography" (1930). In *Books and Printing: A Treasury for Typophiles,* edited by Paul A. Bennett, 239–51. Cleveland: World, 1963.

Muggeridge, Malcolm. *The Thirties, 1930–1940, in Great Britain.* London: H. Hamilton, 1940.

Nesbitt, Jennifer Poulos. *Narrative Settlements: Geographies of British Women's Fiction Between the Wars*. Toronto: University of Toronto Press, 2005.

Neuberg, Victor E. *Chapbooks: A Guide to Reference Material on English, Scottish and American Chapbook Literature of the 18th and 19th Centuries*. 2nd ed. London: Woburn Press, 1972.

Neuberg, Victor E. *The Penny Chapbooks: A Study of Chapbooks for Young Readers over Two Centuries*. London: Oxford University Press, 1968.

Newby, Howard. *Country Life: A Social History of Rural England*. London: Weidenfeld & Nicolson, 1987.

Nikolajeva, Maria, and Carole Scott. *How Picturebooks Work*. New York: Garland, 2001.

Nodelman, Perry. *Words About Pictures: The Narrative Art of Children's Picture Books*. Athens: University of Georgia Press, 1988.

O'Malley, Andrew. *The Making of the Modern Child: Children's Literature and Childhood in the Late Eighteenth Century*. New York: Routledge, 2003.

op de Beeck, Nathalie. *Suspended Animation: Children's Picture Books and the Fairy Tale of Modernity*. Minneapolis: University of Minnesota Press, 2010.

Opie, Iona, and Peter Opie, ed. and comp. *The Puffin Book of Nursery Rhymes*. Illustrations by Pauline Baynes. London: Penguin Books, 1963.

Opie, Iona, and Peter Opie. *Three Centuries of Nursery Rhymes and Poetry for Children*. Exhibition catalog. New York: National Book League, 1973.

Opie, Iona, Robert Opie, and Brian Alderson. *The Treasures of Childhood: Books, Toys and Games from the Opie Collection*. New York: Arcade, 1989.

Orwell, George. *The Road to Wigan Pier*. 1937; New York: Harcourt, 1958.

Outka, Elizabeth. *Consuming Traditions: Modernity, Modernism, and the Commodified Authentic*. Oxford: Oxford University Press, 2009.

Page, Judith W., and Elise L. Smith. *Women, Literature, and the Arts of the Countryside in Early Twentieth-Century England*. Cambridge: Cambridge University Press, 2021.

Paley, Nicholas. "Experiments in Picture Book Design: Modern Artists Who Made Books for Children 1900–1985." *Children's Literature Association Quarterly* 16, no. 4 (1991): 264–69.

Parker, Rozsika, and Griselda Pollock, eds. *Framing Feminism: Art and the Women's Movement 1970–1985*. London: Pandora Press, 1987.

Parker, Rozsika, and Griselda Pollock. *Old Mistresses: Women, Art and Ideology*. London: Routledge & Kegan Paul, 1981; London: Bloomsbury Academic, 2021.

Patten, Brian, ed. *The Puffin Book of Twentieth-Century Children's Verse.* Illustrated by Michael Foreman. London: Penguin Books, 1991.

Paul, Lissa. "Enigma Variations: What Feminist Theory Knows About Children's Literature." *Signal* 54 (September 1987): 186–201.

Pearson, Joe. *Drawn Direct to the Plate: Noel Carrington and the Puffin Picture Books.* London: Penguin Collectors Society, 2010.

Peppin, Brigid, and Lucy Micklethwait. *Dictionary of British Book Illustrators: The Twentieth Century.* London: John Murray, 1983.

Peterson, William. *The Kelmscott Press: A History of William Morris's Typographical Adventure.* Berkeley: University of California Press, 1991.

Piette, Adam. *Imagination at War: British Fiction and Poetry, 1939–1945.* London: Papermac, 1995.

Plain, Gill. *Literature of the 1940s: War, Postwar and "Peace."* Edinburgh: Edinburgh University Press, 2013.

Plock, Vike Martina. "The New Reading Public: Modernism, Popular Literature and the Paperbacks." In *A History of 1930s British Literature,* edited by Benjamin Kohlmann and Matthew Taunton, 134–46. Cambridge: Cambridge University Press, 2019.

Pollock, Griselda. *Differencing the Canon: Feminist Desire and the Writing of Art's Histories.* London: Routledge, 1999.

Pollock, Griselda. "Modernity and the Spaces of Femininity." In Pollock, *Vision and Difference,* 70–127.

Pollock, Griselda. "Preface to the Bloomsbury Revelations Edition." In Parker and Pollock, *Old Mistresses,* xx–xxvi.

Pollock, Griselda. *Vision and Difference: Feminism, Femininity, and Histories of Art.* 1988; London: Routledge, 2003.

Priestley, J. B. *English Journey.* 1934; Chicago: University of Chicago Press, 1984.

Pryor, William, ed. *Virginia Woolf and the Raverats: A Different Sort of Friendship.* Bath: Clear Books, 2003.

Quinn, Peter. "'Their Strongest Pine': Thomas Bewick and Regional Identity in the Late Nineteenth Century." In Gardner-Medwin, *Bewick Studies,* 111–30.

Radway, Janice A. *A Feeling for Books: The Book of the Month Club, Literary Taste, and Middle-Class Desire.* Chapel Hill: University of North Carolina Press, 1997.

Radway, Janice A. *Reading the Romance: Women, Patriarchy, and Popular Literature.* Chapel Hill: University of North Carolina Press, 1984.

Randall, Bryony. *Modernism, Daily Time and Everyday Life.* Cambridge: Cambridge University Press, 2007.

Rayner, John. *Wood Engravings by Thomas Bewick.* London: Penguin Books, 1947.

Reeve, N. H. "The Girl on a Swing: Childhood and Writing in the 1940s." In MacKay and Stonebridge, *British Fiction After Modernism,* 88–98.

Rey, H. A. *"Mary Had a Little Lamb" and Other Nursery Songs.* Harmondsworth: Penguin Puffin Picture Books, 1951.

Reynolds, Kimberley. *Children's Literature: From the Fin de Siècle to the New Millennium.* 2nd ed. Tavistock, Devon: Northcote House / British Council, 2012.

Reynolds, Kimberley. *Left Out: The Forgotten Tradition of Radical Publishing for Children in Britain 1910–1949.* Oxford: Oxford University Press, 2016.

Reynolds, Kimberley. "Modernism." In *Keywords for Children's Literature,* edited by Philip Nel and Lissa Paul, 151–54. New York: New York University Press, 2011.

Reynolds, Kimberley. "Publishing Practices and the Practicalities of Publishing." In Reynolds and Tucker, *Children's Book Publishing,* 20–41.

Reynolds, Kimberley. *Radical Children's Literature: Future Visions and Aesthetic Transformations in Juvenile Fiction.* New York: Palgrave, 2007.

Reynolds, Kimberley, and Nicholas Tucker, eds. *Children's Book Publishing in Britain Since 1945.* Aldershot: Scolar Press, 1998.

Robins, Denise. *Stranger Than Fiction.* London: Hodder & Stoughton, 1965.

Rogerson, Ian. *Agnes Miller Parker: Wood-Engraver and Book Illustrator, 1895–1980.* Wakefield: The Fleece Press, 1990.

Rogerson, Ian. "Agnes Miller Parker: Wood Engraver and Illustrator." In *The Wood Engravings of Agnes Miller Parker,* edited and compiled by Ian Rogerson, 11–71. London: British Library; West New York, N.J.: Mark Batty, 2005.

Rogerson, Ian. "Creative Wood-Engraved Illustration in the Novels of Thomas Hardy." *Hardy Review* 17, no. 2 (2015): 59–88.

Rogerson, Ian, ed. *Noel Carrington and His Puffin Picture Books: An Exhibition Catalogue.* Manchester: Manchester Polytechnic Library, 1992.

Rollins, Carl Purington. "Limited Editions Club Again." *Saturday Review of Literature,* June 1, 1929.

Rooke, Noel. *Woodcuts and Wood Engravings: Being a Lecture Delivered to the Print Collectors' Club on January 20th, 1925, on the Origin and Character of the Present School of Engraving and Cutting.* London: Print Collectors' Club, 1926.

Rose, Jacqueline. *The Case of Peter Pan, or The Impossibility of Children's Fiction.* New York: Macmillan, 1984; Philadelphia: University of Pennsylvania Press, 1993.

Rose, Jonathan. *The Intellectual Life of the British Working Classes.* 3rd ed. New Haven, Conn.: Yale University Press, 2021.

Rosenbach, A. S. W. "Why America Buys England's Books." *Atlantic Monthly,* October 1927, 452–59.

Roylance, Dale Ronald. *Engraved on Wood: Prints and Illustrated Books by Clare Leighton.* New Haven, Conn.: Yale University Library, 1976.

Rubin, Joan Shelley. *The Making of Middlebrow Culture.* Chapel Hill: University of North Carolina Press, 1992.

Ruskin, John. "Appendix." In *The Art of England: Lectures Given in Oxford,* 167–84. New York: John Wiley, 1884.

Ruskin, John. "Fairy Land: Mrs. Allingham and Kate Greenaway." In *The Art of England: Lectures Given in Oxford,* 81–107. New York: John Wiley, 1884.

Ruskin, John. "The Technics of Wood Engraving." In *Ariadne Florentina: Six Lectures on Wood and Metal Engraving,* 58–84. New York: John Wiley, 1886.

Ruzicka, Rudolph. *Thomas Bewick Engraver.* New York: Typophiles, 1943.

Said, Edward. *Orientalism.* New York: Vintage, 1979.

Salaman, Malcolm C. *Modern Woodcuts and Lithographs by British and French Artists.* Edited by Geoffrey Holme. London: The Studio Publications, 1919.

Salaman, Malcolm C. *The New Woodcut.* London: The Studio Publications, 1930.

Salaman, Malcolm C. *The Woodcut of Today, at Home and Abroad.* London: The Studio Publications, 1927.

Salton-Cox, Glyn. "Timely Interventions: Queer Writing of the 1930s." In *The 1930s: A Decade of Modern British Fiction,* edited by Nick Hubble, Luke Seaber, and Elinor Taylor, 155–81. London: Bloomsbury Academic, 2021.

Samuel, Raphael. "The Middle Class Between the Wars: Part I." *New Socialist,* January/February 1983, 30–36.

Samuel, Raphael, ed. *Patriotism: The Making and Unmaking of British National Identity.* Vol. 3, *National Fictions.* London: Verso, 1989.

Samuel, Raphael. *Theatres of Memory.* Vol. 1, *Past and Present in Contemporary Culture.* 1994; London: Verso, 2012.

Samuel, Raphael. *Theatres of Memory.* Vol. 2, *Island Stories: Unravelling Britain.* Edited by Alison Light with Sally Alexander and Gareth Stedman Jones. London: Verso, 1998.

Sanders, Joe Sutliff. "Chaperoning Words: Meaning-Making in Comics and Picture Books." *Children's Literature* 41 (2013): 57–90.

Santesso, Aaron. *A Careful Longing: The Poetics and Problems of Nostalgia.* Newark: University of Delaware Press, 2006.

Scott, Bonnie Kime. *The Gender of Modernism: A Critical Anthology.* Bloomington: Indiana University Press, 1990.

Selborne, Joanna. *British Wood-Engraved Book Illustration 1904–1940: A Break with Tradition.* Oxford: Clarendon Press, 1998; New Castle, Del.: Oak Knoll Press, 2001.

Selborne, Joanna, and Lindsay Newman. *Gwen Raverat, Wood Engraver.* London: British Library; New Castle, Del.: Oak Knoll Press, 2003.

Seshagiri, Urmila. "Mind the Gap! Modernism and Feminist Praxis." *Modernism/ modernity Print Plus* 2, cycle 2 (August 7, 2017). https://doi.org/10.26597/mod.0022.

Shaw, Christopher, and Malcolm Chase, eds. *The Imagined Past: History and Nostalgia.* New York: Manchester University Press, 1989.

Shelden, Michael. *Friends of Promise: Cyril Connolly and the World of "Horizon."* London: Minerva, 1990.

Shirley, Rosemary. *Rural Modernity, Everyday Life and Visual Culture.* Burlington, Vt.: Ashgate, 2015.

Sillars, Stuart. *British Romantic Art of the Second World War.* London: Macmillan, 1991.

Sillars, Stuart. *Picturing England Between the Wars: Word and Image 1918–1940.* Oxford: Oxford University Press, 2021.

Sim, Lorraine. "The Linocuts of Ethel Spowers: A Vision Apart." *Modernist Cultures* 15, no. 3 (2020): 354–76.

Sinclair, Andrew. *War Like a Wasp: The Lost Decade of the Forties.* London: Hamish Hamilton, 1989.

Sitwell, Sacheverell. *Narrative Pictures: A Survey of English Genre and Its Painters.* London: Batsford, 1938.

Smith, Aileen. "The Construction of Cultural Identity in the Visual Arts in Scotland 1918–1945." PhD thesis, University of Aberdeen, 1998.

Smith, Janet Adam. *Children's Illustrated Books.* London: Collins, 1948.

Smith, Victoria Ford. *Between Generations: Collaborative Authorship in the Golden Age of Children's Literature.* Oxford, Miss.: University Press of Mississippi, 2017.

Solnit, Rebecca. *Orwell's Roses.* New York: Viking Press, 2021.

Sorby, Angela. "Golden Age." In *Keywords for Children's Literature,* edited by Philip Nel and Lissa Paul, 96–99. New York: New York University Press, 2011.

Sorensen, Jennifer J. *Modernist Experiments in Genre, Media, and Transatlantic Print Culture*. London: Routledge, 2017.

Spalding, Frances. *Gwen Raverat: Friends, Family and Affections*. London: Harvill Press, 2001.

Spalding, Frances. "'Not a Tear or a Prayer in It': Gwen Raverat's Illustrated Edition of *The Runaway*." In *Macmillan: A Publishing Tradition*, edited by Elizabeth James, 230–41. New York: Palgrave, 2002.

Spalding, Frances. *The Real and the Romantic: English Art Between Two World Wars*. London: Thames and Hudson, 2022.

Stansky, Peter, and William Abrahams. *London's Burning: Life, Death and Art in the Second World War*. London: Constable, 1994.

Starobinski, Jean. "The Idea of Nostalgia." *Diogenes* 54 (Summer 1966): 81–103.

Stevens, Anne. "Clare Leighton Wood Engraver." In Stevens and Leighton, *Clare Leighton*, 16–20. Oxford: Ashmolean Museum, 1992.

Stevens, Anne, and David Leighton, comps. *Clare Leighton: Wood Engravings and Drawings*. Oxford: Ashmolean Museum, 1992.

Stevens, Bethan. *The Wood Engravers' Self-Portrait: The Dalziel Archive and Victorian Illustration*. Manchester: Manchester University Press, 2022.

Stevens, Bethan. "Wood Engraving as Ghostwriting: The Dalziel Brothers, Losing One's Name, and Other Hazards of the Trade." *Textual Practice* 33, no. 4 (2017): 645–77.

Stevenson, Iain. *Book Makers: British Publishing in the Twentieth Century*. London: British Library, 2010.

Stewart, Susan. *On Longing: Narratives of the Miniature, the Gigantic, the Souvenir, the Collection*. Durham, N.C.: Duke University Press, 1993.

Stewart, Victoria. *Narratives of Memory: British Writing of the 1940s*. Basingstoke: Palgrave Macmillan, 2006.

Stone, Reynolds. "Raverat, Gwendolen Mary (1885–1957), Artist." In *Oxford Dictionary of National Biography*, revised by James Hamilton. Last modified September 25, 2014. https://www.oxforddnb.com.

Sturt, George. *The Wheelwright's Shop*. Cambridge: Cambridge University Press, 1923.

Styles, Morag. "'From the Best Poets'? How the Canon of Poetry for Children Is Constructed." In Styles, *From the Garden to the Street*, 186–96.

Styles, Morag. *From the Garden to the Street: An Introduction to 300 Years of Poetry for Children*. London: Cassell, 1998.

Sullivan, Melissa, and Sophie Blanch. "The Middlebrow—Within or Without Modernism." In "Middlebrow." Special issue, *Modernist Cultures* 6, no. 1 (May 2011): 1–17.

Sutcliffe, Peter. *The Oxford University Press: An Informal History.* Oxford: Clarendon Press, 1978.

Symons, Julian. *The Thirties: A Dream Revolved.* London: Cresset Press, 1960.

Tattersfield, Nigel. "A Peculiar Spirit and Fancy." In *Thomas Bewick, Tale-Pieces,* edited by Jonathan Watkins, 11–32. Birmingham: Ikon Gallery, 2009.

Tattersfield, Nigel. *Thomas Bewick: Graphic Worlds.* London: British Museum Press, 2014.

Tattersfield, Nigel. *Thomas Bewick: The Complete Illustrative Work.* 3 vols. London: British Library; New Castle, Del.: Oak Knoll Press, 2011.

Taylor, D. J. *Orwell: The Life.* New York: Henry Holt, 2003.

Taylor, D. J. *Orwell: The New Life.* New York: Pegasus Books, 2023.

Thomas, Bert. "Hassall, John (1868–1948)." In *Oxford Dictionary of National Biography,* revised by Ben Whitworth. Last modified May 27, 2010. https://www.oxforddnb.com.

Thomas, Keith. "Children in Early Modern England." In Avery and Briggs, *Children and Their Books,* 45–77.

Thomas, Zoë. *Women Art Workers and the Arts and Crafts Movement.* Manchester: Manchester University Press, 2020.

Thompson, Hilary. "Enclosure and Childhood in the Wood Engravings of Thomas and John Bewick." *Children's Literature* 24 (1996): 1–22.

Tickner, Lisa. *Modern Life and Modern Subjects: British Art in the Early Twentieth Century.* New Haven, Conn.: Yale University Press, 2000.

Tucker, Nicholas. "Setting the Scene." In Reynolds and Tucker, *Children's Book Publishing,* 1–19.

Uglow, Jenny. *Nature's Engraver: A Life of Thomas Bewick.* London: Faber and Faber, 2006.

Uglow, Jenny. *Sybil and Cyril: Cutting Through Time.* London: Faber and Faber, 2021; New York: Farrar, Straus and Giroux, 2022.

Upward, Edward. *In the Thirties.* 1962; London: Penguin Books, 1969.

Von Lintel, Amy M. "Wood Engravings, the 'Marvellous Spread of Illustrated Publications,' and the History of Art." *Modernism/modernity* 19, no. 3 (2012): 515–42.

Waldrep, Mary Carolyn, ed. *Women Illustrators of the Golden Age.* Mineola, N.Y.: Dover, 2010.

Weiss, Harry B. *A Book About Chapbooks: The People's Literature of Bygone Times.* Hatboro, Pa.: Folklore Associates, 1969.

West, Emma. "'Within the Reach of All': Bringing Art to the People in Interwar Britain." *Modernist Cultures* 15, no. 2 (2020): 225–52.

Westman, Karin E. "Children's Literature and Modernism: The Space Between." *Children's Literature Association Quarterly* 32, no. 4 (2007): 283–86.

Westman, Karin E. "'Forsaken Spots': At the Intersection of Children's Literature and Modern War." *Children's Literature Association Quarterly* 34, no. 3 (2009): 213–17.

Whalley, Joyce Irene, and Tessa Rose Chester. *A History of Children's Book Illustration.* London: John Murray and the Victoria and Albert Museum, 1998.

Wiener, Martin J. *English Culture and the Decline of the Industrial Spirit, 1850–1980.* Cambridge: Cambridge University Press, 1981.

Wiesner-Hanks, Merry E. "Why Do Old Mistresses Matter Today?" *Art Herstory,* April 21, 2019. https://artherstory.net/why-do-old-mistresses-matter-today.

Wild, Jonathan. *The Rise of the Office Clerk in Literary Culture, 1880–1939.* New York: Palgrave Macmillan, 2006.

Wild, Trevor. *Village England: A Social History of the Countryside.* London: I. B. Tauris, 2004.

Williams, Raymond. "The Bloomsbury Fraction." In *Contemporary Marxist Literary Criticism,* edited by Francis Mulhern, 125–45. London: Longman, 1992.

Williams, Raymond. *The Country and the City.* New York: Oxford University Press, 1973.

Williams, Raymond. *The Politics of Modernism: Against the New Conformists.* London: Verso, 1989.

Williams, Raymond. "Structures of Feeling." In *Marxism and Literature,* 128–35. Oxford: Oxford University Press, 1977.

Williams, W. E. "Art for the People." In Lambert, *Art in England,* 113–18.

Williamson, Henry. *Tarka the Otter.* London: G. P. Putnam's Sons, 1935.

Wong, Bang. "Negative Space." *Nature Methods* 8, no. 5 (January 2011). https://doi.org/10.1038/nmeth0111-5.

Wood, Jamie. "George Orwell, Desire, and Encounters with Rural Sex in Mid-Century England." *College Literature* 45, no. 3 (2018): 399–423.

Wood Engraving in Modern English Books: The Catalogue of an Exhibition. London: National Book League, 1949.

Woolf, Leonard. *Downhill All the Way: An Autobiography of the Years 1919–1939.* London: Hogarth Press, 1967.

Woolf, Virginia. *The Diary of Virginia Woolf.* Vol. 5, *1936–1941.* Edited by Anne Olivier Bell with Andrew McNeillie. London: Hogarth Press, 1984.

Woolf, Virginia. *A Room of One's Own.* 1929; New York: Harcourt Brace Jovanovich, 1957.

Wright, Patrick. *On Living in an Old Country: The National Past in Contemporary Britain.* Oxford: Oxford University Press, 2009.

Wullschläger, Jackie. *Inventing Wonderland: The Lives and Fantasies of Lewis Carroll, Edward Lear, J. M. Barrie, Kenneth Grahame, and A. A. Milne.* New York: Free Press, 1996.

Zimring, Rishona. "Ballet, Folk Dance, and the Cultural History of Interwar Modernism: The Ballet *Job.*" *Modernist Cultures* 9, no. 1 (2014): 99–114.

Zipes, Jack. *Buried Treasures: The Power of Political Fairy Tales.* Princeton, N.J.: Princeton University Press, 2023.

Zipes, Jack. *Fairy Tales and the Art of Subversion.* New York: Wildman Press, 1983.

Zipes, Jack. "Origins: Fairy Tales and Folk Tales." In *Children's Literature: Approaches and Territories,* edited by Janet Maybin and Nicola J. Watson, 26–39. Basingstoke: Palgrave Macmillan, 2009.

PRIMARY SOURCES

Selected Books Written and Illustrated by Thomas Bewick

Bewick, Thomas. *A General History of Quadrupeds.* Wood engravings by Thomas Bewick. Newcastle upon Tyne: S. Hodgson, R. Beilby, and T. Bewick, 1790.

Bewick, Thomas. *A History of British Birds.* Vol. 1, *Land Birds.* 1797; Newcastle: Edw. Walker, 1826.

Bewick, Thomas. *A History of British Birds.* Vol. 2, *Water Birds.* 1804; Newcastle: Edw. Walker, 1826.

Bewick, Thomas. *A Memoir Written by Himself.* 1862; edited by Iain Bain, Oxford: Oxford University Press, 1975.

The women wood engravers featured in this study all worked in different media, although they are famous for their wood engravings. Entries below for books that they illustrated with wood engravings include the phrase "Wood engravings by" the artist. Entries for books that the wood engravers illustrated using other means, such as pen-and-ink drawings, lithographs, linocuts, or scraperboard engravings, simply record "Illustrations by" the artist.

Selected Books Written or Illustrated by Joan Hassall

Austen, Jane. *Pride and Prejudice.* Wood engravings by Joan Hassall. London: Folio Society, 1957.

Austen, Jane. *Sense and Sensibility.* Wood engravings by Joan Hassall. London: Folio Society, 1958.

Austen, Jane. *Mansfield Park.* Wood engravings by Joan Hassall. London: Folio Society, 1959.

Austen, Jane. *Northanger Abbey.* Wood engravings by Joan Hassall. London: Folio Society, 1960.

Austen, Jane. *Persuasion.* Wood engravings by Joan Hassall. London: Folio Society, 1961.

Austen, Jane. *Emma.* Wood engravings by Joan Hassall. London: Folio Society, 1962.

Austen, Jane. *Shorter Works.* Wood engravings by Joan Hassall. London: Folio Society, 1963.

Bowen, Elizabeth. *Collected Edition of Elizabeth Bowen's Novels.* Wood engravings by Joan Hassall. 11 vols. London: Jonathan Cape, 1948–54.

Brett, Simon. *The Wood Engravings of Joan Hassall.* Cambridge: Silent Books, 1997.

Brett Young, Francis. *Portrait of a Village.* Wood engravings by Joan Hassall. London: Heinemann, 1937; New York: Reynal and Hitchcock, 1938.

Burns, Robert. *Poems.* Selected and with an introduction by Delancey Ferguson. Wood engravings by Joan Hassall. New York: Limited Editions Club; New York: Heritage Press, 1965.

Chambers, David, ed. *Joan Hassall: Engravings and Drawings.* Introductory memoir by Joan Hassall. Pinner, Middlesex: Private Libraries Association, 1985.

Church, Richard. *Calling for a Spade.* Illustrations by Joan Hassall. London: J. M. Dent and Sons, 1939.

Church, Richard. *Small Moments.* Wood engravings by Joan Hassall. London: Hutchinson, 1957.

Dunbar, William. *Seasonal Poems.* Saltire Chapbook No. 3. Wood engravings by Joan Hassall. Edinburgh: Saltire Society, 1944.

Four Scottish Poems of the Sixteenth Century. Saltire Chapbook No. 1. Wood engravings by Joan Hassall. Edinburgh: Saltire Society, 1943.

Gaskell, Elizabeth. *Cranford.* Wood engravings by Joan Hassall. London: George G. Harrap, 1940.

Gloriana's Glass: Queen Elizabeth I Reflected in Verses and Dedications Addressed to Her, Reports Concerning Her, and Her Own Words Written and Spoken. Compiled by Alan Glover. Wood engravings by Joan Hassall. London: Nonesuch Press, 1953.

Gooch, Bernard. *The Strange World of Nature.* Wood engravings by Joan Hassall. London: Lutterworth Press; New York: Thomas Y. Crowell, 1950.

Grisewood, Frederick. *Our Bill: Guide, Counsellor, Friend.* Illustrations by Joan Hassall. London: Harrap, 1939.

Hassall, Christopher. *Devil's Dyke.* Wood engravings by Joan Hassall. London: Heinemann, 1936.

Hassall, Christopher. *Penthesperon.* Wood engravings by Joan Hassall. London: Heinemann, 1938.

Hassall, Joan. *Wood Engraving: A Reader's Guide.* London: Cambridge University Press for the National Book League, 1949.

Hassall, Joan. *The Wood Engravings of Joan Hassall.* Compiled and introduced by Ruari McLean. 1960; New York: Schocken Books, 1981.

Hassall, Joan. "Introduction." In Chambers, *Joan Hassall,* vii–xii.

Hassall, Joan. *Dearest Sydney: Joan Hassall's Letters to Sydney Cockerell from Italy and France, April–May 1950.* Edited by Brian North Lee. Wakefield: Fleece Press, 1991.

Hassall, Joan. *Dearest Joana: A Selection of Joan Hassall's Lifetime Letters and Art.* Edited by Brian North Lee. Introduction by John Dreyfus. Wakefield: Fleece Press, 2000.

Lane, Margaret. *The Brontë Story: A Reconsideration of Mrs. Gaskell's "Life of Charlotte Brontë."* Illustrations by Joan Hassall. London: Heinemann, 1953.

Lane, Margaret. *Flora Thompson.* Illustrations by Joan Hassall. London: John Murray, 1976.

Lane, Margaret. *The Drug-Like Brontë Dream.* Illustrations by Joan Hassall. London: John Murray, 1980.

Linklater, Eric. *"Sealskin Trousers" and Other Stories.* Wood engravings by Joan Hassall. London: R. Hart-Davis, 1947.

Mackenzie, Agnes Mure, ed. *Scottish Pageant.* Wood engravings by Joan Hassall. 4 vols. Edinburgh: Oliver and Boyd for the Saltire Society, 1946–50.

Mally Lee and Three Folk Songs. Saltire Chapbook No. 2. Wood engravings by Joan Hassall. Edinburgh: Saltire Society, 1944.

The Marriage of Robin Redbreast and the Wren. Saltire Chapbook No. 4. Wood engravings by Joan Hassall. Edinburgh: Saltire Society, 1945.

Mayne, John. *The Siller Gun, or The Dumfries Trades.* Saltire Chapbook No. 13. Wood engravings by Joan Hassall. Edinburgh: Saltire Society, 1952.

Milne, A. A. *Books for Children: A Reader's Guide.* Wood engravings by Joan Hassall. London: Cambridge University Press for the National Book League, 1948.

Mitford, Mary Russell. *Our Village.* Introduction by Margaret Lane. Wood engravings by Joan Hassall. London: Harrap, 1947.

Morison, Stanley. *The Typographic Arts, Past, Present, and Future.* A lecture at College of Art, Edinburgh, February 17, 1944, with "ornaments" by Joan Hassall. Edinburgh: J. Thin, 1944.

Old Scottish Christmas Hymns. Saltire Chapbook No. 8. Wood engravings by Joan Hassall. Edinburgh: Saltire Society, 1947.

Oliver, John W., and J. C. Smith, eds. *A Scots Anthology.* Wood engravings by Joan Hassall. Edinburgh: Oliver and Boyd, 1949.

Opie, Iona, and Peter Opie, eds. and comps. *The Oxford Nursery Rhyme Book.* With additional illustrations by Joan Hassall. Oxford: Oxford University Press, 1955.

Pitter, Ruth. *Urania.* Wood engravings by Joan Hassall. London: Cresset Press, 1950.

Pitter, Ruth. *The Ermine, Poems 1942–1952.* Illustrations by Joan Hassall. London: Cresset Press, 1953.

Rashie Coat. Saltire Chapbook No. 12. Wood engravings by Joan Hassall. Edinburgh: Saltire Society, 1951.

Reid, J. M., ed. *The Fause Knicht and Other Fancies.* Saltire Chapbook No. 10. Wood engravings by Joan Hassall. Edinburgh: Saltire Society, 1950.

Scotland on Freedom. Saltire Chapbook No. 11. Wood engravings by Joan Hassall. Edinburgh: Saltire Society, n.d.

Scottish Children's Rhymes and Lullabies. Saltire Chapbook No. 9. Wood engravings by Joan Hassall. Edinburgh: Saltire Society, 1948.

Six Scottish Poems of the Nineteenth Century. Saltire Chapbook No. 7. Wood engravings by Joan Hassall. Edinburgh: Saltire Society, 1946.

Songs of the '45. Saltire Chapbook No. 5. Wood engravings by Joan Hassall. Edinburgh: Saltire Society, 1945.

Stevenson, Robert Louis. *A Child's Garden of Verses.* Wood engravings by Joan Hassall. Edinburgh: Hopetoun Press, 1947.

Strong, L. A. G. *Sixteen Portraits of People Whose Houses Have Been Preserved by the National Trust.* Illustrations by Joan Hassall. London: Naldrett Press for the National Trust, 1951.

Tennyson, Alfred Lord. *In Memoriam: Arthur H. Hallam.* Illustrations by Joan Hassall. London: Folio Society, 1949.

Trollope, Anthony. *Christmas Day at Kirkby Cottage.* Illustrations by Joan Hassall. London: Sampson Low, Marston, 1947.

Trollope, Anthony. *"The Parson's Daughter" and Other Stories.* Wood engravings by Joan Hassall. London: Folio Society, 1949.

Trollope, Anthony. *"Mary Gresley" and Other Stories.* Edited and with an introduction by John Hampden. Wood engravings by Joan Hassall. London: Folio Society, 1951.

Webb, Mary Gladys Meredith. *Fifty-One Poems.* Wood engravings by Joan Hassall. London: Jonathan Cape, 1946.

Weekley, Montague. *Thomas Bewick.* Wood engravings by Joan Hassall. Oxford: Oxford University Press, 1953.

Whitlock, Pamela, ed. and comp. *All Day Long: An Anthology of Poetry for Children.* Wood engravings by Joan Hassall. London: Oxford University Press, 1954.

Whuppity Stoorie. Saltire Chapbook No. 6. Wood engravings by Joan Hassall. Edinburgh: Saltire Society, 1946.

Young, Andrew. *Collected Poems.* Wood engravings by Joan Hassall. London: Cape, 1950.

Selected Books Written or Illustrated by Clare Leighton

Auslander, Joseph. *Letters to Women.* Wood engravings by Clare Leighton. New York: Harper & Brothers, 1929.

Benson, Stella. *"Christmas Formula" and Other Stories.* Wood engravings by Clare Leighton. Foreword by Geoffrey West. London: W. Jackson, 1932.

Brailsford, Mabel Richmond. *The Making of William Penn.* Wood engravings and other illustrations by Clare Leighton. London: Longmans, Green, 1930.

Brontë, Emily. *Wuthering Heights.* Wood engravings by Clare Leighton. New York: Random House, 1931.

Campbell, Marie. *Folks Do Get Born.* Illustrations by Clare Leighton. New York: Rinehart, 1946.

Campbell, Marie. *Tales from the Cloud Walking Country.* Illustrations by Clare Leighton. Bloomington: Indiana University Press, 1958.

Case, Josephine Young. *Freedom's Farm.* Wood engravings by Clare Leighton. Boston: Houghton Mifflin, 1946.

Clare Leighton: Wood Engraving. New York: Association of American Artists, 1983.

Damon, Bertha Clark. *Green Corners*. Illustrations by Clare Leighton. London: M. Joseph, 1947.

Farjeon, Eleanor. *Perkin the Pedlar*. Illustrations by Clare Leighton. London: Faber and Faber, 1932.

Fletcher, William Dolan. *Clare Leighton: An Exhibition; American Sheaves, English Seed Corn*. Wood engravings by Clare Leighton. Boston: Boston Public Library, 1978.

The Frank C. Brown Collection of North Carolina Folklore. General editor Newman Ivey White. Wood engravings by Clare Leighton. 7 vols. Durham, N.C.: Duke University Press, 1952–1964.

Hardy, Thomas. *The Return of the Native*. Wood engravings by Clare Leighton. New York: Harper, 1929.

Hardy, Thomas. *Under the Greenwood Tree; or, The Mellstock Quire; A Rural Painting of the Dutch School*. Wood engravings by Clare Leighton. London: Macmillan, 1940.

Holme, Constance. *The Trumpet in the Dust*. Wood engravings by Clare Leighton. London: Ivor Nicholson & Watson, 1934.

Leighton, Clare. *Woodcuts: Examples of the Work of Clare Leighton*. Introduction by Hilaire Belloc. London: Longmans, Green, 1930.

Leighton, Clare. *The Musical Box*. Illustrations by Clare Leighton. London: Gollancz; New York: Longmans, Green, 1932.

Leighton, Clare. *Wood-Engraving and Woodcuts*. How to Do It series. London: The Studio Publications, 1932.

Leighton, Clare. *The Farmer's Year: A Calendar of English Husbandry*. Written and engraved by Clare Leighton. London: Collins; New York: Longmans, Green, 1933.

Leighton, Clare. *The Wood That Came Back*. Illustrations by Clare Leighton. London: Ivor Nicholson & Watson, 1934.

Leighton, Clare. *Four Hedges: A Gardener's Chronicle*. Written and engraved by Clare Leighton. London: Gollancz; New York: Macmillan, 1935.

Leighton, Clare. *Wood Engraving of the 1930s*. Wood engravings compiled by Clare Leighton. London: The Studio Publications, 1936.

Leighton, Clare. *Country Matters*. Written and engraved by Clare Leighton. London: Gollancz; New York: Macmillan, 1937.

Leighton, Clare. *Sometime—Never*. Illustrations by Clare Leighton. London: Gollancz; New York: Macmillan, 1939.

Leighton, Clare. *Give Us This Day.* Illustrations by Clare Leighton. New York: Reynal and Hitchcock, 1943.

Leighton, Clare. *Southern Harvest.* Wood engravings by Clare Leighton. New York: Macmillan, 1942; London: Gollancz, 1943.

Leighton, Clare. *Tempestuous Petticoat: The Story of an Invincible Edwardian.* 1947; Chicago: Academy Chicago, 1984.

Leighton, Clare. *Where Land Meets Sea: The Tide Line of Cape Cod.* Wood engravings by Clare Leighton. New York: Rinehart, 1954.

Leighton, Clare. *Growing New Roots: An Essay with 14 Wood Engravings.* San Francisco: Book Club of California, 1976.

Leighton, Clare. *The Wood Engravings of Clare Leighton.* Selected and with an introduction by Pat Jaffé. Cambridge: Silent Books, 1992.

Leighton, Clare. *Quiet Spirit, Skillful Hand: The Graphic Work of Clare Leighton.* Edited by Jonathan Stuhlman. Charlotte, N.C.: Mint Museum of Art, 2008.

Leighton, Clare. "The Convictions of a Writer-Artist." In David Leighton, *Clare Leighton,* 73–75.

Leighton, Clare. "The Growth and Shaping of an Artist." In David Leighton, *Clare Leighton,* 5–33.

Leighton, David, comp. *Clare Leighton: The Growth and Shaping of an Artist-Writer.* Wood engravings by Clare Leighton. Pewsey, Wiltshire: Estate of Clare Leighton, 2009.

Parker, Elinor Milnor. *I Was Just Thinking: A Book of Essays.* Wood engravings by Clare Leighton. New York: Thomas Y. Crowell, 1959.

Plotz, Helen. *Imagination's Other Place: Poems of Science and Mathematics.* Wood engravings by Clare Leighton. New York: Thomas Y. Crowell, 1955.

Plotz, Helen. *Untune the Sky: Poems of Music and the Dance.* Wood engravings by Clare Leighton. New York: Thomas Y. Crowell, 1957.

Plotz, Helen. *The Singing and the Gold: Poems Translated from World Literature.* Wood engravings by Clare Leighton. New York: Thomas Y. Crowell, 1962.

Plotz, Helen, comp. *The Earth Is the Lord's: Poems of the Spirit.* Wood engravings by Clare Leighton. New York: Thomas Y. Crowell, 1965.

Roberts, Elizabeth Madox. *The Time of Man.* Wood engravings by Clare Leighton. New York: Viking Press, 1945.

Ross Williamson, Hugh. *The Flowering Hawthorn*. Wood engravings by Clare Leighton. New York: Hawthorn Books, 1962.

Stevens, Anne, and David Leighton, comps. *Clare Leighton: Wood Engravings and Drawings*. Oxford: Ashmolean Museum, 1992.

Thoreau, Henry David. *Cape Cod*. Wood engravings by Clare Leighton. New York: Thomas Y. Crowell, 1961.

Thoreau, Henry David. *Walden*. Introduction by Brooks Atkinson. Wood engravings by Clare Leighton. New York: Thomas Y. Crowell, 1961.

Thoreau, Henry David. *A Week on the Concord and Merrimack Rivers*. Wood engravings by Clare Leighton. New York: Thomas Y. Crowell, 1961.

Tomlinson, H. M. *The Sea and the Jungle*. Wood engravings by Clare Leighton. New York: Harper & Brothers, 1930.

Wilder, Thornton. *The Bridge of San Luis Rey*. Wood engravings by Clare Leighton. London: Longmans, Green, 1929.

Selected Books Illustrated by Agnes Miller Parker

Aesop's Fables. Translated by V. S. Vernon Jones. Introduction by Samuel Fanous. Wood engravings by Agnes Miller Parker. Oxford: Bodleian Library Publishing, 2020.

Bates, H. E. *"The House with the Apricot" and Two Other Tales*. Wood engravings by Agnes Miller Parker. London: Golden Cockerel, 1933.

Bates, H. E. *Through the Woods: The English Woodland—April to April*. Wood engravings by Agnes Miller Parker. London: Gollancz; New York: Macmillan, 1936.

Bates, H. E. *Down the River*. Wood engravings by Agnes Miller Parker. London: Gollancz; New York: Henry Holt, 1937.

Clarke, Hockley. *Country Commentary*. Wood engravings by Agnes Miller Parker. London: Allman and Son, 1940.

Davies, Rhys. *"Daisy Matthews" and Three Other Tales*. Wood engravings by Agnes Miller Parker. Waltham St. Lawrence, Berkshire: Golden Cockerel Press, 1932.

Edwards, Hugh. *Helen Between Cupids*. Introduction by James Agate. Wood engravings by Agnes Miller Parker. London: Jonathan Cape, 1935.

The Fables of Esope, Translated Out of Frensshe in to Englysshe by William Caxton. Wood engravings by Agnes Miller Parker. Newtown, Montgomeryshire: Gregynog Press, 1931.

Furst, Herbert Ernest Augustus. *Essays in Russet*. Wood engravings by Agnes Miller Parker. London: Frederick Muller, 1944.

Gray, Thomas. *Elegy Written in a Country Church-Yard*. Introduction by Sir Hugh Walpole. Wood engravings by Agnes Miller Parker. New York: Limited Editions Club, 1938; New York: Heritage Press, 1951.

Gray, Thomas. *Elegy Written in a Country Churchyard*. Introduction by Carol Rumens. Wood engravings by Agnes Miller Parker. Oxford: Bodleian Library Publishing, 2021.

Hardy, Thomas. *Far from the Madding Crowd*. Introduction by Robert Cantwell. Wood engravings by Agnes Miller Parker. New York: Limited Editions Club; New York: Heritage Press, 1958.

Hardy, Thomas. *The Return of the Native*. Wood engravings by Agnes Miller Parker. New York: Heritage Press, 1942.

Hardy, Thomas. *Tess of the D'Urbervilles: A Pure Woman*. Introduction by Robert Cantwell. Wood engravings by Agnes Miller Parker. New York: Limited Editions Club; New York: Heritage Press, 1956.

Hardy, Thomas. *The Mayor of Casterbridge*. Introduction by Frank Swinnerton. Wood engravings by Agnes Miller Parker. New York: Limited Editions Club; New York: Heritage Press, 1964.

Hardy, Thomas. *Jude the Obscure*. Introduction by John Bayley. Wood engravings by Agnes Miller Parker. New York: Limited Editions Club; New York: Heritage Press, 1969.

Housman, A. E. *The Shropshire Lad*. Wood engravings by Agnes Miller Parker. London: G. G. Harrop, 1940.

Jefferies, Richard. *"The Spring of the Year" and Other Nature Essays*. Edited and with an introduction by Samuel J. Looker. Wood engravings by Agnes Miller Parker. London: Lutterworth Press, 1946.

Jefferies, Richard. *The Life of the Fields*. Edited and with an introduction by Samuel J. Looker. Wood engravings by Agnes Miller Parker. London: Lutterworth Press, 1947.

Jefferies, Richard. *Field and Hedgerow, Being the Last Essays of Richard Jefferies*. Edited and with an introduction by Samuel J. Looker. Wood engravings by Agnes Miller Parker. London: Lutterworth Press, 1948.

Jefferies, Richard. *"The Old House at Coate" and Other Hitherto Unpublished Essays*. Edited and with an introduction by Samuel J. Looker. Wood engravings by Agnes Miller Parker. London: Lutterworth Press, 1948.

Jefferies, Richard. *The Open Air*. Edited and with an introduction by Samuel J. Looker. Wood engravings by Agnes Miller Parker. London: Lutterworth Press, 1948.

Le Corbeau, Adrien. *The Forest Giant*. Translated by J. H. Ross [T. E. Lawrence]. Wood engravings by Agnes Miller Parker. London: Jonathan Cape, 1935; New York: Doubleday, Doran, 1936.

Lewis, Eiluned. *Honey Pots and Brandy Bottles*. Wood engravings by Agnes Miller Parker. London: Country Life, 1954.

Marriott, Charles. *British Handicrafts*. Wood engravings by Agnes Miller Parker. London: Longmans, Green, for the British Counsel, 1943.

McCormick, Andrew. *The Gold Torque: A Story of Galloway in Early Christian Times*. Wood engravings by Agnes Miller Parker. Glasgow: William MacLellan, 1951.

Power, Rhoda D. *How It Happened: Myths and Folk-Tales*. Illustrations by Agnes Miller Parker. Cambridge: Cambridge University Press, 1930.

Powys, John Cowper. *Lucifer: A Poem*. Wood engravings by Agnes Miller Parker. London: Macdonald, 1956.

Roche, Aloysius. *Animals Under the Rainbow*. Wood engravings by Agnes Miller Parker. London: Hollis and Carter; New York: Sheed and Ward, 1952.

Rogerson, Ian, comp. *Agnes Miller Parker*. Exhibition catalog. Manchester: Manchester Polytechnic Library, 1983.

Rogerson, Ian. *The Agnes Miller Parker Collection in Manchester Polytechnic Library*. 2nd ed. Manchester: Manchester Polytechnic Library, 1989.

Rogerson, Ian. *Agnes Miller Parker: Wood-Engraver and Book Illustrator, 1895–1980*. Wakefield: Fleece Press, 1990.

Rogerson, Ian, ed. and comp. *The Wood Engravings of Agnes Miller Parker*. London: British Library; West New York, N.J.: Mark Batty, 2005.

Russell, Leonard, ed. *The Saturday Book, 1941–1942*. Wood engravings by Agnes Miller Parker. London: Hutchinson, 1941.

Russell, Leonard, ed. *The Saturday Book, 1943*. Wood engravings by Agnes Miller Parker. London: Hutchinson, 1942.

Sampson, John, comp. *XXI Welsh Gypsy Folk-Tales*. Wood engravings by Agnes Miller Parker. Newtown, Montgomeryshire: Gregynog Press, 1933.

Shakespeare, William. *Richard the Second: The Text of the First Folio, with Quarto Insertions*. Edited by Herbert Farjeon. Wood engravings by Agnes Miller Parker. New York: Limited Editions Club, 1940.

Shakespeare, William. *The Tragedies*. Introduction by George Rylands. Wood engravings by Agnes Miller Parker. New York: Heritage Press, 1958.

Shakespeare, William. *The Poems of William Shakespeare.* Edited and with an introduction by Peter Alexander. Wood engravings by Agnes Miller Parker. New York: Limited Editions Club, 1967; New York: Heritage Press, 1968.

Spenser, Edmund. *The Faerie Queene, Disposed into Twelve Bookes Fashioning XII Morall Vertues.* Introduction by John Hayward. Decorations drawn by John Austen. Wood engravings by Agnes Miller Parker. New York: Limited Editions Club; New York: Heritage Press, 1953.

Selected Books Written or Illustrated by Gwen Raverat

Andersen, Hans Christian. *Four Tales from Hans Andersen.* Translated and introduced by R. P. Keigwin. Wood engravings by Gwen Raverat. Cambridge: Cambridge University Press, 1935.

Brooke, Rupert. *The Collected Poems of Rupert Brooke.* Wood engravings by Gwen Raverat. London: Philip Lee Warner, 1919.

Cornford, Frances. *Spring Morning.* Wood engravings by Gwen Raverat. London: Poetry Bookshop, 1915.

Cornford, Frances. *Mountains and Molehills.* Wood engravings by Gwen Raverat. Cambridge: Cambridge University Press, 1934.

de la Mare, Walter. *Crossings: A Fairy Play.* Illustrations by Gwen Raverat. London: Faber and Faber, 1942.

Farjeon, Eleanor. *Over the Garden Wall.* Illustrations by Gwen Raverat. London: Faber and Faber, 1942.

Furst, Herbert, ed. *Gwendolen Raverat.* Wood engravings by Gwen Raverat. London: Little Art Rooms, 1920.

Goodge, Eleanor. *The Bird in the Tree.* Wood engravings by Gwen Raverat. London: Duckworth, 1940.

Grahame, Kenneth, ed. *The Cambridge Book of Poetry for Children.* Wood engravings by Gwen Raverat. Cambridge: Cambridge University Press, 1932; New York: G. P. Putnam's Sons, 1933.

Hart, Mrs. (Elizabeth Anna Hart). *The Runaway: A Victorian Story for the Young.* Wood engravings by Gwen Raverat. London: Macmillan, 1936; London: Persephone Books, 2002.

James, Norah C. *Cottage Angles.* Wood engravings by Gwen Raverat. London: J. M. Dent and Sons, 1935.

Memorial Exhibition of Woodcuts by Gwen Raverat. London: Thomas Agnew and Sons, 1959.

Modern Woodcutters: Fifty-Four Examples of the Most Characteristic Modern Work. Wood engravings by Gwen Raverat. London: H. Furst, 1921.

Newman, L. M., and D. A. Steel, *Gwen and Jacques Raverat: Paintings and Wood Engravings.* Exhibition catalog. Lancaster: University Library, 1989.

Pye, Virginia. *Red-Letter Holiday.* Illustrations by Gwen Raverat. London: Faber and Faber, 1940.

Raverat, Gwen. *Job.* Sets and costumes for Ralph Vaughan Williams's ballet. 1928; ballet first performed 1931.

Raverat, Gwen. *Period Piece: A Cambridge Childhood.* Illustrations by Gwen Raverat. London: Faber and Faber; New York: W. W. Norton, 1952.

Raverat, Gwen. *Gwen Raverat: Wood Engravings of Cambridge and Surroundings.* Edited by Rosemary Davidson. Cambridge: Broughton House Books, 2003.

Sterne, Laurence. *A Sentimental Journey Through France and Italy.* Wood engravings by Gwen Raverat. Harmondsworth: Penguin Books, 1938; London: Thomas Nelson and Sons, 1941.

Stone, Reynolds, comp. *The Wood Engravings of Gwen Raverat.* London: Faber and Faber, 1959; rev. ed. with postscript and additional selection by Simon Brett, Cambridge: Silent Books, 1989.

Street, A. G. *Farmer's Glory.* Wood engravings by Gwen Raverat. London: Faber and Faber, 1934.

Trollope, Anthony. *The Bedside Barsetshire.* Compiled by Lance O. Tingay. Illustrations by Gwen Raverat. London: Faber and Faber, 1949.

Uttley, Alison. *Mustard, Pepper and Salt.* Illustrations by Gwen Raverat. London: Faber and Faber, 1938.

Wedgwood, Henry Allen. *The Bird Talisman: An Eastern Tale.* Wood engravings by Gwen Raverat. London: Faber and Faber, 1939.

Yonge, Charlotte M. *Countess Kate.* Illustrations by Gwen Raverat. London: Faber and Faber, 1948; New York: Random House, 1960.

Archives and Museums Cited and Consulted

Agnes Miller Parker Archives, National Art Library, Victoria and Albert Museum, London

Agnes Miller Parker Archives, National Library of Scotland, Edinburgh

British Library, London

Cherryburn, National Trust

Joan Hassall Letters to Ruari McLean, National Library Scotland

Literary and Philosophical Society, Newcastle

Robinson Library Special Collections, Newcastle University, Newcastle

Saltire Society Archives, National Library of Scotland, Edinburgh

Thomas Bewick Archives, Natural History Society of Northumbria, Hancock Museum,
    Newcastle University, Newcastle

University of Reading Special Collections and Museum of English Rural Life, Reading

Index

KRISTIN BLUEMEL is professor of English and the Wayne D. McMurray and Helen Bennett Endowed Chair in the Humanities at Monmouth University. She is coeditor of *Rural Modernity in Britain: A Critical Intervention,* author of *George Orwell and the Radical Eccentrics: Intermodernism in Literary London,* and editor of *Intermodernism: Literary Culture in Mid-Twentieth-Century Britain.* Her research for *Enchanted Wood* was supported by a Leverhulme Visiting Professorship at Newcastle University, a Publication Grant of The Leonard A. Lauder Research Center for Modern Art and Monmouth University.